Reading and Writing Ourselves into Being

The Literacy of Certain Nineteenth-Century Young Women

A volume in
Language, Literacy, and Learning
Series Editors: Patricia Ruggiano Schmidt, *Le Moyne College*
Peter B. Mosenthal, *Syracuse University*

Reading and Writing Ourselves into Being

The Literacy of Certain Nineteenth-Century Young Women

by

Claire White Putala

For Donna Alvermann

Celebrating adolescent
literacy

Claire White Putala

7.8.06

INFORMATION AGE PUBLISHING

80 Mason Street • Greenwich, Connecticut 06830 • www.infoagepub.com

Library of Congress Cataloging-in-Publication Data

Putala, Claire White.
  Reading and writing ourselves into being : the literacy of certain
nineteenth-century young women / by Claire White Putala.
      p. cm. – (Language, literacy, and learning)
  Based on author's thesis (doctoral)–Syracuse University.
  Study of literacy based on a collection of correspondence, the Osborne
Family Papers, 1812-1968, located in the Special Collections Research
Center of Syracuse University.
  Includes bibliographical references.
  ISBN 1-59311-108-8 (pbk.) – ISBN 1-59311-109-6 (hardcover)
  1. American letters–History and criticism. 2. Young women–United
States–Correspondence–History and criticism. 3. Young women–Books
and reading–United States–History–19th century. 4. Literacy–United
States–History–19th century. 5. United States–Intellectual
life–19th century. 6. Young women–United States–Intellectual life.
7. Letter writing–History–19th century. 8. Young women–United
States–Language. 9. English language–United States. 10. English
language–19th century. 11. Osborne family–Archives. I. Title. II.
Series.
  PS417.P88 2004
  816'.309–dc22

                                                2004000412

Garrison Family Papers, Sophia Smith Collection, Smith College, Northampton, MA
[noted by *SSC*]; James D. Livingston, descendent and holder of literary rights to the
Wright family letters and papers in the Garrison Family Papers; and the Osborne Family
Papers, Syracuse University Library, Special Collections Research Center. Cover, photo-
graph, and letter document are from the Osborne Family Papers, Syracuse University,
Special Collections Research Center.

Printed in the United States of America

To my splendid sons,
Christopher and Theodore,
the
enduring memory of
Diane McDonnell Casey,
and
to honor
Peter Booth Mosenthal

CONTENTS

Appendices

ACKNOWLEDGMENTS

As I come to the end of this work, I feel a deep sense of gratitude to life as I reflect upon the many people over the years who have generously enabled me to accomplish, what Professor Joan N. Burstyn termed it from the start, my "life work." Coming from an Irish heritage, it is not my wont to think of myself as leading a particularly charmed life. Yet that is my sense of things as I come now to thank so many fine people, without whom this work could never have been completed. Their generosity over many years has made this finally happen.

My first acknowledgment must go to Joan N. Burstyn for providing such a wonderful assignment—"Go to the archives and do original research!"—and then for serving me so well in so many capacities for so long: on my dissertation committee; for encouraging the completion of this more recent version (no small task); for always being a supportive reader; and finally for her very generous and knowledgeable introduction, thank you so much.

I have also been fortunate in having had Pamela Michel over these long years as a wise and enabling reader. When I could go no further, she would take my current chapter and, with just a few marks on the text, bless it with a few supportive suggestions that always made the difference. When she declared a chapter done, I knew it was. For years, she did this, chapter after chapter, version after version. Wow. Mary Stanley's praiseful reading of a middle version has stood by me in the gritty times as a source of hope and encouragement, too. My thanks also go to Peter B. Mosenthal for taking on this project as dissertation chair when it was just still a sketch and a hope. I still owe much thanks for this act of faith and trust. And over the last few

Reading and Writing Ourselves into Being, pages ix–xi
Copyright © 2004 by Information Age Publishing

years, as an editor, I thank him for giving me the precious gifts of time and space.

Two special groups need to be thanked. My dissertation committee, in addition to Joan and Peter, also was blessed by Robert Bogdan—teacher-methodologist-supporter whose ways of thinking and doing research are embodied on every page of this study. Much thanks also goes to my defense readers, Don Leu and Jay Graves, who both had insightful suggestions that enabled a better document. Finally, it was an honor for me to have had John Briggs as the Chair because from him I had begun the long process of learning what it means to think like a historian.

My Learning Communities Group, begun and sustained all these years through the encouragement of Joan N. Burstyn, has been a continuous source of support and inspiration. It was and is always a wonder to see the play of ideas between and among all the women of this group, ideas that deepened my work and life. Being privileged in the early years of the group to witness the glories of idea-driven conversation between and among these exceptional women—Joan N. Burstyn, Diane M. Casey, Jane Hugo, and Mary Stanley, among others—provided me with a broader view for contemplating literacy and the world. I need especially to bear witness to Diane's continuous efforts toward helping me grow as a historian. Professor, historian, cultural and political critic, and eye-roller at the world's foibles, Diane's impact reverberates still. It is a sorrow that she is not here to read and critique this work that owes so much to her intelligence, knowledge, and integrity.

From the start of my graduate program I have been blessed by finding true friends who have made such a difference. Indefatigable Claudia Gentile from the start took this older student under her wing and continues to provide intellectual sparks. Anna Stave's hard-won, crystal-clear view of the academic scene continues to both instruct and amuse. In my early years at Oswego, Jane Partanen, who claims I was *her* mentor, was an exceedingly generous rudder and support and remains so. Finally, a deep and special thanks to Sharon Kane who is always and unstintingly there for me in more ways than I can ever count. Thank you.

Secretaries are undersung, yet without them there is no cohesive spririt and nothing gets done. Years ago, Lee Mento welcomed me warmly into Syracuse University's Reading and Language Arts family and Joan Simonetta made it possible, intelligently saving me from myself time and again. More recently at Oswego, Jan Ormsby and Stancy Smith have taken on these dual roles and I am very grateful.

I owe a great deal to Syracuse University, first for offering a culturally broad and rigorous education program staffed with first-rate, knowledgeable faculty for whom justice for all is their *raison d'etre*. Syracuse University is also well served by its able library staff and well-stocked shelves, without which this work could not have been visualized or accomplished. I am particularly grateful to the Special Collections Research Center on the sixth floor of the library where I spent wondrous hours reading and pondering the letters at the center of this work. It was thanks to the good offices of Carolyn Davis, with her broad and deep knowledge of the archival collections, that I was guided to precisely the right collection, the Osborne Family Papers. That has made all the difference to me. I also want to thank all the fine people past and present on the sixth floor, especially Terry Keenan, Mark Weimer, and Diana Cooter, for sharing their knowledge and expertise. Finally, I want to thank all the people at the circulation desk, run so well by Eileen Derycke, for all their unflagging good cheer and patience with me.

At SUNY Oswego, I was very fortunate to have been awarded two United University Professions professional grants and for these I want to declare a special thank you. One gave me the wherewithal to seek current studies and the other was a gift of time. I especially would like to thank Greg Auleta for his support and for all he does on behalf of the personnel of SUNY Oswego. For having recently been awarded tenure, I am also grateful.

To Shirley Brice Heath, whose telling question about writing instruction and 19th-century young women sparked this work, this is my belated thank you note, To her and all the scholars whose work undergirds this study and to all the above, not to mention my splendid sons, I am so grateful. You all have enabled me to make me feel, finally, lucky. Thank you.

POSTSCRIPT

As will be clear to the reader of this text, my debt to the insightful feminist theorizing of Patricia Francis Cholakian runs deep. Her death on September 27, 2003 is a grievous loss to her beloved family and friends as well as the world of scholarship. I will always owe her my thanks.

These I give, too, to both series editor Patty R. Schmidt for her support and to publisher George A. Johnson for his understanding and knowledge of text.

Thank you, all.

NOTES TO THE READER

NOTE ONE: GENEALOGY AND NAMES

This text is a study of literacy based upon a set of correspondence, the Osborne Family Papers, 1812–1968, housed in the Special Collections Research Center of Syracuse University. A collection of some 358 boxes, it is particularly well suited for a study on literacy. In addition to the voluminous public and private correspondence of prison reformer Thomas Mott Osborne (1859–1926), a vast and rich store of the family's literacy "works" have been carefully preserved. In addition to hundreds of letters, many between and among the women of the family, it also abounds with other literacy documents of interest such as ledgers, account books, travelogues, verse, diaries, and notes. Unusually and quite valuably, even scraps of children's writing have been preserved, making possible studies regarding emergent literacy practices of the times.

The documents themselves are in excellent condition and the finding aid, "The Osborne Family: An Inventory of Papers in Syracuse University Libraries," written in 1971 by John Janitz, has been a very helpful guide. A product of its times, the focus of the descriptions in the finding aid was on the lives and works of men. A joy of this work has been to uncover—having been directed to the possibility by Special Collections Research Center archivist Carolyn Davis—a rich correspondence by women, young and old, which has yielded this study on the intersection of gender and literacy.

While not all (or perhaps even most) of the correspondence has both the letter sent and its response(s), enough of these pairs exist to be useful (and to wish for more). Many of the letters are not primarily the product of

Reading and Writing Ourselves into Being, pages xiii–xviii
Copyright © 2004 by Information Age Publishing

a single writer or intended for a single reader. Moreover, other branches of the family's correspondence are in other archives, The Garrison Family Papers in the Sophia Smith Collection of Smith College and the Mott Manuscript Collection, Friends Historical Library, Swarthmore College.

For this text, which focuses on the time period from 1838 to 1862, approximately 300 letters, primarily of the Wright/Mott/Osborne women, were selected and copied for use. As a study set in the past, it has some of the characteristics of narrative, one of which is that it is peopled. To ease the reading of this manuscript, two steps have been taken, one is to provide a relatively concise genealogy of the correspondents.

The motivating force behind the correspondence came from the need of Anna Folger Coffin (1771–1844), born in Nantucket, to stay in touch with all her children. The two of her children who figure most prominently in this study are Lucretia Coffin Mott, Quaker minister, abolitionist, and women's rights advocate of Philadelphia, and Martha Coffin Wright of Auburn, New York, also a women's rights advocate These two sisters maintained a life-long devotion to each other and enjoyed, as well, a rich intellectual and political companionship. Two of their daughters, cousins Martha Mott Lord and Eliza Wright Osborne, formed early on a bond that expressed itself in a lifetime of correspondence and frequent visits. It is their letters to each other that are at the center of this study, which sees them through the early years of their marriages and child-bearing.

The genealogy below offers a guide for tracking the relationships that were, of course, taken for granted by the letter writers and yet are needed by the contemporary reader to make sense of the letters themselves. Following the genealogy is a brief description of the major correspondents as well as a list of most of the names (and initials) of the people who figure into the selections and quotations shared in this study.

At the center of this text is **Eliza Wright Osborne (EWO)** (1830–1911) who lived most of her life in Auburn, New York. A lifetime reader and praised for her fine letters, she was the daughter of feminist Martha Coffin Wright and Auburn lawyer David Wright. She married **David Munson Osborne (DMO)** who became financially comfortable with the establishment of a mowing and reaping machinery business. Living their lives in Auburn, New York, they had four children: Emily (Millie, Em, Emmy) who married Springfield banker Fred Harris; Florence (Floy) who died of typhoid fever at 20; Thomas Mott Osborne who became a famous prison reformer; and Helen who married James J. Storrow, a Boston banker.

Eliza's mother was **Martha Coffin (Pelham) Wright (MCW)** (1806–1875), feminist, organizer and member of the Woman's Rights Convention of 1848, former Quaker, married to David Wright, and mother of Eliza, Marianna, Tallman, Ellen, Willie, and Frank. Martha was a younger sister of **Lucretia Coffin Mott (LCM)** (1793–1880), noted abolitionist, Quaker min-

A CONCISE WRIGHT/MOTT/OSBORNE GENEALOGY

Thomas Coffin, Jr. (1766–1815)	m. 1.16.1790	Anna Folger (1771–1844)
Sarah Coffin (1790–1824)	Lucretia Coffin Mott (1793–1880)	Eliza Coffin Yarnall (1794–1870)
Thomas Mayhew (1798–1845)	Mary Coffin Temple (1803–1824)	Martha Coffin Wright (1806–1875)

James Mott (1788–1868)	m. 4.10.1811	Lucretia Coffin (1793–1880)
Anna Mott Hopper (1812–1874)	Thomas (I) (1814–1817)	Maria Mott Davis (1818–1897)
Thomas (II) (1823–1899)	Elizabeth (Lib) Mott Cavender (1825–1865)	Martha (Pattie) Mott Lord (1828–1916)

Martha Coffin (1806–1875)	m. 11.1824	Peter Pelham (1785–1826)

Marianna Pelham (1825–1872)	m. 7.28.1845	Thomas Mott (1823–1899)

Martha Coffin Pelham (1806–1875)	m. 11.18.1829	David Wright (1806–1897)
Eliza (1830–1911)	Mathew Tallman (1832–1854)	Ellen Garrison (1840–1931)
William (Willie) (1842–1902)	"Little Charlie" (1848–1849)	Francis (Frank) (1844–1903)

Eliza Wright (1830–1911)		m. 9.3.1851	David Munson Osborne (1822–1886)
Emily (Millie) (1853–1940)	Florence (Floy) (1856–1877)	Thomas Mott (1859–1926)	Helen (Nell) (1864–1944)

ister, feminist, organizer of the Woman's Rights Convention of 1848, and married to James Mott. Lucretia was the mother of Maria (Davis), Anna (Hopper), Elizabeth, called Lib (Cavender), Thomas, and **Pattie/Martha Mott Lord (MML)**. Pattie was both cousin and life-long friend of Eliza Wright Osborne. Called Pattie (to distinguish her from her Aunt Martha), she married George Lord in 1853 and had five daughters, four of whom survived childhood.

Marianna Pelham Mott (MPM) (1826–1872), witty and somewhat of a free spirit, she was the first child of Martha Coffin Pelham (Wright) and Peter Pelham. She was called "Sister" to mark her integrated status within the newly established family begun when Martha Coffin Pelham married David Wright in 1829. After a somewhat pained courtship, she and Thomas Mott, son of Lucretia and James, and thus her cousin, were given permission to marry. They had three children, Isabella, Emily, and Maria. **Ellen Wright Garrison (EWG)** (1840–1931) was also somewhat of a free spirit, more outspoken and livelier than her sister, Eliza. Ellen married William Lloyd Garrison, Jr., in 1864, had five children, and became a confidante of Susan B. Anthony.

Matthew Tallman Wright (MTW) (1832–1854) was the oldest of Eliza's brothers, and two years younger than she. He was often at odds with his father and spent long periods of time with the Motts in Philadelphia. He went to California to make his fortune but did return for Eliza's wedding in September 1851. He met an untimely death in San Francisco in 1854. The correspondence around the time of his death is sparse, as it is at the time of other family sorrows

In this text, for the marking of a letter citation, I have used their major initials, as noted above, to designate the writer and the recipient of the cited reference. The following is a list of most of those important to an understanding of the correspondence as it relates to this study. Those names found in the correspondence but not listed below will fall into three general categories: friends, cousins (the Wright/Mott/Osborne family kept in touch with their many Quaker relations, including the Earles, the Husseys, and the Needles), and persons prominent at the time. The names and identifying initials are:

WA   Warren Adams, suitor of Eliza Wright (Osborne); from King(s) Ferry, NY
NA   Nellie Adams, sister of Warren Adams, correspondent of EWO's.
CD   Carrie Dennis, life-long friend of EWO.
EMC   Elizabeth Mott Cavender, "Lib," daughter of LCM, wife to TC
TC   Thomas Cavender, husband of EMC
AFC   Anna Coffin, matriarch, mother of LCM and MCW as well as TC, ECY
TMC   Thomas Mayhew Coffin, son of AFC and TC; resident of Philadelphia
EWG   Ellen Wright Garrison, daughter of MCW; wife of WLG, Jr.
EOH   Emily Osborne Harris, daughter of EWO and DMO; wife of Fred Harris
IH   Isaac Hopper, young son of Anna Mott Hopper, daughter of LCM

GL	George W. Lord, husband of MML, father of four: Ellen, Mary, Anna, Lucretia
JL	Joseph (Joe) Lord, brother to George, friend of EWO and MML
MML	Martha Mott Lord, daughter of LCM; cousin/friend of EWO; wife of GL
JM	James Mott, husband to LCM, wool merchant, abolitionist
MPM	Marianna Pelham Mott, first daughter of MCP (MCW); wife of TM, children Isabella (Bel), Emily, and Maria (May)
TM	Thomas Mott, son of LCM and JM; husband of MPM
DMO	David Munson Osborne, husband of EWO; successful manufacturer
EWO	Eliza Wright Osborne, wife of DMO, mother of EOH, FO, TMO, HOS
FO	Florence Osborne, daughter of EWO and DMO; died at age 20 of typhoid fever
LP	Lottie Pearl, friend of EWO
HOS	Helen Osborne Storrow, daughter of EWO and DMO; wife of J.J. Storrow
KS	Kate Shotwell, school friend of EWO's
CW	Charles Wright, "Little Charley," son of MCW and DW; lived one year
DW	David Wright, lawyer, husband of MCW, father of EWO, MTW, EWG, WW, FW
FW	Francis (Frank) Wright, son of MCW and DW
MTW	Matthew Tallman Wright, son of MCW and DW; died in 1854 at age 22
WW	William (Willy) Wright, son of MCW and DW
BY	Benjamin Yarnall, husband to ECY, father to EY and RY
ECY	Elizabeth (Eliza) Coffin Yarnall, wife of BY, mother of EY and RY
RY	Rebecca Yarnall, daughter of ECY and BY; cousin and friend of EWO
EY	Ellis Yarnall, son of ECY and BY

NOTE TWO: TRANSCRIPTION PRINCIPLES

As much as possible, the selections from the letters have been kept as the correspondents wrote them, with only a minimal "regularization" being applied to them. The writers, particularly the younger ones, made very frequent use of the dash to signal many different things: the changing of topic, the ending of a sentence, the expression of emotion. Spacing was often used, as well, in the creation of meaning in the same manner, for the same reasons. Writing rules appear to have been more fluid than they have since become. Paragraphing was often not used and spelling was a little more relaxed as well. Because it is not my wont to "sic" them, I have let many of these variations from "proper" form stand. However, where meaning would be disrupted, I have put in ending punctuation in the place of the dashes and spaces. For clarity, a few commas have been strategically placed as well. Additionally, capitalization has been supplied where the spacing had made clear that a new sentence was commencing. Setting the gold standard for principles of thoughtful typographical transcriptions is Beverly Wilson Palmers's *Selected Letters of Lucretia Coffin Mott* (2002). Mine concur with hers; I want to thank her, too, for her splendid and useful footnotes. The work goes on.

FOREWORD

When David, my 13-year-old grandson, came to visit me in 2003, he spent hours on my computer "instant messaging" with his friends. One evening, I came up behind him and watched. The large screen was divided into several smaller ones, each with its ever-growing string of messages in computer shorthand. Back and forth, he and his friends in New York, Maine, and Wisconsin were conversing with each other instantly, in "real time." What a different world from the one Claire Putala describes in this book, where letters, written to family and friends at a distance, were sent by river and canal boats, horses and carriages, and the burgeoning railroads. Distance was not easily traversed; letters took days, sometimes weeks to reach their destination.

Claire Putala's skilled weaving together of scholarship from several disciplines has resulted in a tapestry that adds immeasurably to our understanding of the lives of educated families in mid-19th-century America. This is a book about literacy, what literacy means, how gender expectations limit or expand its influence, and from the examples of the letters written to and by Eliza Wright Osborne, how reading and writing influenced the lives of one family and their friends.

The letters analyzed in this book are special because they were written by young women whose mothers and aunts and their friends were well known for their public stance on behalf of women's rights. The daughters and nieces might have taken up the cause also, but Putala finds this was not so. In part, the times had changed; there was some backlash against the heady freedoms claimed by their mothers. In part, the families had matured; their status had improved, and the younger women saw their

Reading and Writing Ourselves into Being, pages xix–xx
Copyright © 2004 by Information Age Publishing
All rights of reproduction in any form reserved.

roles as more deeply involved with the cultural, rather than the political, life of their society. And, in part, the legacy that the older generation bequeathed was ambiguous. Not that the younger women were against "the cause"; only that it was not theirs to fight for with the insistence of their mothers and aunts. The ambiguity of the older generation's legacy went further; it lay in their insistence on behaviors expected of young women of the time. Eliza seems to have taken this insistence more seriously than others, such as her young sister Ellen. For instance, Eliza learned early on to be scrupulous in writing letters about the day-to-day events of her life, as her mother instructed her to do, a habit that led her, even later in life, to focus on the quotidian at the expense of concepts and ideas.

Claire Putala's reclamation of women's writing, among a group of women whose families were influential in their communities and who traveled and read widely, provides not only valuable insight into the social history of the period, but also a subtle analysis of the role of literacy in the lives of both women and men. Throughout her life, especially after her children grew up, Eliza Wright Osborne was a book collector. She meticulously recorded her purchases of books and her library was one that Putala draws attention to as an important cultural artifact.

Claire Putala is well versed in feminist textual analysis and the latest discourse on literacy, as well as being completely at home with the historical figures—Eliza Wright Osborne's family and friends—whose letters she so carefully lays before the reader. I can hardly do justice to the depth of Claire Putala's understanding of the authors of these letters. She has spent long afternoons with me talking about the Wright/Mott/Osborne families, how they visited one another in Philadelphia and Auburn, what books they were reading, and how they shared their opinions of the books in their letters, their family celebrations, and the difficulties Eliza faced when her husband traveled, leaving her at home with the children. Because of her firm grasp of literacy studies and feminist theory, Putala is able to throw new light on the unpublished literary work of these women and men. Many scholars try to weave together historical material with contemporary analyses; few do so with such elegance as Claire Putala does in this book.

—Joan N. Burstyn
Professor Emerita, Syracuse University

CHAPTER 1

BEGINNING TO CONTEXTUALIZE ELIZA WRIGHT OSBORNE IN HER LITERACY

What a composed, efficient
"one of a thousand" Eliza is.

(MCW to DW: 2.10.59)

In her last decade of life, Eliza Wright Osborne had the newly installed telephone poles in front of her South Street, Auburn, New York, residence chopped down for being too close to her property. Taken to court by the offending telephone company, she won the case, which then became a New York State precedent setter. With this single but egregious exception, whose meaning may well lie in her deeply rooted literateness and the changing technology of her times, the woman at the center of this study, Eliza Wright Osborne, led a relatively unnoted domestic existence. As befitting the daughter of feminist Martha Coffin Wright, she proudly provided in her fine home cultural space for the gathering of the by-then famous women of the suffrage movement, women who included Elizabeth Cady Stanton and Susan B. Anthony. And in her mid-70s, only five years before

Reading and Writing Ourselves into Being, pages 1–24
Copyright © 2004 by Information Age Publishing

her death, she traveled to Egypt, fulfilling a hope expressed during her school days.

A prolific letter writer of real distinction among her many correspondents, she was a worthy example of the old axiom that a "lady" was supposed to find her name in print only three times in her life—at her birth, for her wedding announcement, and upon her departure from earth. Yet, contemporary feminist research would have us consider if her "private" letter writing[1] might not be considered a form of publication (Patricia Francis Cholakian, personal communication, Summer 1991; Martha Nell Smith, 1992), a stubborn statement of worth, a stretching into the domain of the "public," as Catherine E. Kelly (1999) argues more recently.

Born into relatively comfortable professional family circumstances, Eliza Wright had a fortunate upbringing. She had two loving parents: her mother, intelligent feminist Martha Coffin Wright and her father, lawyer and writer, David Wright. Through the years, both parents often expressed their appreciation of and deep love for their daughter in correspondence preserved in the large Osborne Family Papers in Syracuse University's Special Collections Research Center.

From a very early age Eliza Wright was described as both intelligent and strong-minded, as signaled in letters written to her grandmother Anna Folger Coffin by her aunt, Lucretia Coffin Mott, noted abolitionist and Quaker minister (SSC; LCM to AFC: 8.3.35) as well as to Lucretia from her sister, Martha Coffin Wright (SSC; MCW to LCM: 5.19.41). From her middle years a dedicated and knowledgeable book collector, in her adolescent years Eliza Wright was often addressed as someone the other young women with whom she corresponded respected greatly as both a writer and reader. Indeed, one of her suitors, Warren Adams of King(s) Ferry, New York, conducted his (unsuccessful) courtship of her through letters that focused almost exclusively on literary texts (WA to EWO: 8.21.49, 12.22.50).

As a young writer, Eliza illustrated an important literacy thesis put forward by Shirley Brice Heath (1981) that young women of the 18th and 19th centuries helped to instruct one another to become better, more graceful correspondents. They "used their correspondence with each other for practice, instruction, and recommendations for further ways of improving the mechanics and style of their letters" (p. 32). Heath posits that it was due to this mutual support that "women excelled [in letter writing] not only because of the ["feminine"] qualities ascribed to them by critics, but because of their continual efforts to improve one another's writing" (p. 33). It was Eliza to whom the young women of her writing circle turned when they needed assistance in improving their letter writing. On December 4, 1848, young cousin Mary Woodall of Wilmington wrote to Eliza: "Please don't criticize to severly this my first attempt at writeing to you. can

I hope to hear from you soon?" It is interesting to speculate on Eliza's possible responses.

On her 21st birthday, September 3, 1851, Eliza Wright married David Munson Osborne, a hardware salesman who eventually became a successful and wealthy producer of farm machinery. When on sales trips around the country, selling first his hardware supplies and later his mowing and reaping machines, he wrote often to her with deep love and admiration, and retrospectives of him always speak of his devotion to his wife and four children.

The Auburn Citizen, the city's newspaper of record, in its almost full-page obituary notice of Eliza Wright Osborne the day following her death (which occurred on July 18, 1911), spoke of her as a "lover of books and a woman of wide reading." The unnamed author of the death notice must have interviewed her:

> Her home is filled with books and every chink and cranny contains a volume. In fact, a visitor would be mildly astonished, as was the writer, to see an old fireplace completely obliterated by conversion into a bookcase.... The nucleus for the present library was made many years ago when the house was rebuilt. At that time Mrs. Osborne purchased in London a very remarkable lot of books, and her selection, with subsequent additions, shows an extraordinary sense of literary values. There are few private libraries in this State that contain a finer selection. (*Auburn Citizen*, 7.19.11, p. 1)

Eliza Wright Osborne's many long book orders in the Osborne Family Papers to prominent booksellers attest to these observations and reveal a very informed book collector, who, from a feminist perspective, made many intriguing purchases. Not only did she construct a library that had the "expected" 19th-century standard works, American and British, but she reclaimed those texts of her youth and early womanhood that later years would come to ignore or even disdain—Miss Strickland's 12-volume *Queens of England* (1841–1848) and Miss Mitford's *Recollections of a Literary Life* (1852), as just two examples. Reaching back into her reading past—and the reading past of the community of readers of which she was a member—she systematically ordered and completed whole sets of these and other women authors, both American and European, who have only recently been resurrected as subjects of serious study.

Not only was Eliza Wright Osborne noted throughout her life for being an exemplary reader, she was also considered to be a fine writer. It is possible to trace over the span of her lifetime a writerly impulse, a conscious use of writing that she used to record her own and her family's experiences: a verse upon the subject of her first baby's nursery; journals; a travelogue of a train trip to the American West; a long and touching memorial address[2] reflecting upon the life of her mother, feminist Martha Coffin Wright. She also wrote incidental pieces—one in praise of her summer residence, Willow Point—and its visitors, her children and their friends.

Perhaps like the woman authors of the time as described by Nina Baym (1978), she was "profoundly Victorian [with] ... an oppressive sense of reality" (p. 18). The writings—the works—of Eliza Wright Osborne were always in the service of her family and friends. And if we can take an incident from the autobiography of Elizabeth Cady Stanton, *Eighty Years & More: Reminiscences, 1815–1897* (1898/1971) as any indicator, Eliza Wright Osborne was often intensely focused upon the domestic. Elizabeth Cady Stanton took Eliza, albeit humorously, to task for doing handwork on a "cotton wash rag" during a visit.

In a letter written on November 12, 1891, Elizabeth Cady Stanton responded to a remark by Eliza Wright Osborne to Elizabeth Smith Miller (daughter of abolitionist Gerrit Smith, cousin and friend of Cady Stanton and inventor of the Bloomer costume) that Eliza had found Mrs. Stanton "solemn" on that visiting day (p. 435):

> Looking forward to the scintillations of wit, the philosophical researches, the historical traditions, the scientific discoveries, the astronomical explorations, the mysteries of theosophy, palmistry, mental science, the revelations of the unknown world where angels and devils do congregate, looking forward to discussion of all these grand themes, in meeting the eldest daughter of David and Martha Wright, the niece of Lucretia Mott, the sister-in-law of William Lloyd Garrison, a queenly-looking woman five feet eight in height, and well proportioned, with glorious black eyes, rivaling even De Staël's in power and pathos, one can readily imagine the disappointment I experienced when such a woman pulled a cotton wash rag from her pocket and forthwith began to knit with bowed head. (1898/1971, pp. 436–437)

In what may have been the single time any of her many "works" were officially published, Eliza responded to Elizabeth Cady Stanton's letter in verse. The fifth of the seven verses reads:

> ...[A]s a daughter and a niece
> I pride myself on every piece
> Of handiwork created;
> While reveling in social chat
> Or listening to gossip flat
> My gain is unabated. (p. 437)

Now, the redoubtable Elizabeth Cady Stanton was not the only woman to take Eliza to task for not heeding talks with feminists. "Why in the world weren't you at a talk by Lucy Stone?" demanded Martha Coffin Wright uncharacteristically of her daughter in an undated letter of the mid-1850s.

Years later, in her several-page memorial to her mother, Eliza provided her own sad response:

> As the years went on Mother became more prominent in the Suffrage cause & always attended the convention, encouraging the faint hearted when all seemed so discouraging—trying to interest my thankless self more earnestly in the cause & to my lasting sorrow not succeeding so very well—I never went with her to the Washington Convention as she wanted so much I should & I let her go off all alone many a time when I should have gone with her. Family cares were always the excuse. (p. 12)

AN UNCOMFORTABLE QUESTION

To ask somewhat the same question Elizabeth Cady Stanton seemed to be circling and that Martha Coffin Wright posed rather more directly to her daughter: Why did not this young woman Eliza Wright Osborne—whose eyes rivaled De Staël's—hesitate to enter a more "public" arena that her obvious writerly bent *and* her intelligence, her energy, and her capacity for critique would have made possible? To pose such a question is not only most unfair to someone who cannot respond, but is also historically suspect. For better or worse, however, this is the unbidden thought that has over many years driven this inquiry.[3]

This most unfair question is one that is really posing the central question of women's past that Gerda Lerner (1993) thoroughly explores in *The Creation of Feminist Consciousness: From the Middle Ages to Eighteen-seventy*. Why have women collectively and individually had their intellectual talents "aborted and distorted ... for thousands of years?" (p. 10). As this has long been a critical question of the feminist research of the past 40-plus years, it is not out of line to ask the question and then to examine the social and cultural constraints of gender in this connection and their crucial intersection with literacy—the intersection of artifacts of texts with the processes and practices of reading and writing through their many manifestations.

Emily Dickinson: A Special Case

Born into "a society that prohibited women from entering the realm of "serious intellectual pursuits," as Cynthia Griffin Wolff writes of Emily Dickinson (1986, p. 179), it is possible, given other times and places and other circumstances, that Eliza—a keen reader, an aware writer, a well-informed book collector, a mother of a published (male) author—could have become the more public writer or speaker her talent with the word could have made possible.[4] This unfair speculation is one that, of course, has its reasons in desires for woman to fulfill her talents. *Not* speculation is that Emily Dickinson paid a fearsome price for her dedication to her own awesome writing talent. Wolff spells out these restrictions:

> Mid-nineteenth-century America offered women few opportunities to reap the full rewards of a "successful" life. They might have marriage and children. However, membership in the larger community was severely limited. They could not vote; under many circumstances, they could not even hold property in their own right. The arena allowed to a woman for the exercise of her talents was mostly defined by the domestic sphere. (p. 167)[5]

In describing the duties of the Victorian mother, a role Emily Dickinson elected to eschew but a role Eliza Wright Osborne sought eagerly and performed well, Wolff sheds light on the choice of Dickinson to remain single:

> In a way that her husband was not, a wife was accountable for every aspect of the lives of those in her house. She tended their sicknesses; she supervised their meals and clothing; she gave her children their earliest lessons in letters and numbers and religion. It is true that a mother might stir the cozy custards of the nursery; but when death visited the home, killing the resident grandparents or brothers and sisters with equal indifference, it was Mother who had to explain the universal impassivity of death and disease to her children. Women were assigned the responsibility for imposing day to day order on life's chaos—for sustaining a regulated life and emotional continuity. (p. 202, noting her use of the insights of groundbreaking feminist Nancy F. Cott [1977])

All these tasks fell to Eliza Wright Osborne and, from all accounts (including evidence from and of her own letters), she fulfilled all these obligations most worthily—and then some.

Literacy and "Individual Progress"

Thus, as we have just seen above and will throughout, Eliza Wright Osborne was literate, widely read, and a respected writer of letters; the daughter and niece of famous 19th-century feminists, her mother Martha Coffin Wright (1806–1874) and her aunt, abolitionist and Quaker minister Lucretia Coffin Mott (1793–1880). Yet not until her later years did she take up the feminist cause, and then her contributions were more social and cultural than political. There are, of course, any number of reasons and explanations for why humans do or don't do this or that, the reasons and explanations entering deep into personal and societal contexts and demands.

Still I wonder. The questions I wonder about—and that have driven this inquiry from its inception—concern the connections between literacy and gender. Why did Eliza Wright Osborne's literacy—her wide reading, her fine writing, and her knowledge of these tools (Ong, 1982)—not provide the vehicle for participatory engagement? What did literacy—for so long assumed to be the avenue of "individual progress" (Graff, 1987, p. 3)— have to do with her not taking up the women reformists' causes (at least during her mother's lifetime, for she did become in her later years a voter in school elections) of the mid-19th century? And why, like so many other talented women of the 19th century, did she not, as did her mother, take up her hand to write for an audience wider than her family and friends?

It is the Emily Dickinson scholarship that provides an intriguing avenue for pondering these questions of limitation and restriction regarding personal writing. Beginning in the late 1980s, sparked in part by the still exciting, now somewhat controversial, work of Sandra M. Gilbert and Susan Gubar, *The Madwoman in the Attic: The Woman Writer and the Nineteenth-Century Literary Imagination* (1979), Emily Dickinson's life and works became a site of celebration. A full complement of feminist researchers[6] rescued her from generations of male critics who promised that, although Emily Dickinson wrote a "good" poem now and then, in no way could she be considered a "major" poet. In her white dress, she was forever cloistered in her father's home, scribbling opaque verse that was dismissed as morbid and minor.

Martha Nell Smith (1992), building on and then extending the work on Emily Dickinson, asks her readers in *Rowing in Eden: Rereading Emily Dickinson*, to ponder an exciting possibility: What if we were to consider if Emily Dickinson, who engaged in a 30-year "literary relationship" with her next-door sister-in-law, Susan Dickinson, and who sewed together in fascicles some of her over 1,500 poems, did not in her own way engage in a form of publication? Such an idea opens fresh ways to ponder the "uncomfortable question" to which we shall return in our last chapter, "Endings."

Withdrawal into the Domestic

Of course, Eliza Wright Osborne and her friend, cousin, and life-long correspondent Martha Mott Lord (Pattie) were not the only women of the later Victorian decades not to become writers and reformists, though certainly some—even many—did. In her *Cradle of the Middle Class* (1981), Mary P. Ryan sums up her ground-breaking story of the activist women of the 1830s and 1840s from Oneida County, New York:

> In the end, the veterans of the reform era and their progeny would withdraw into the conjugal family, the better to nurture the values that had been cra-

> dled in association.... By mid-century ... the most exuberant, creative, evan-
> gelical phase of association had ended, and the responsibility for
> maintaining purity, sobriety, and docility had been largely absorbed by the
> private family. (p. 238)

Thus something larger than one woman's intentions and preferences were at work. The sum total of that "something"—which would document all the forces of constriction acting upon mid-19th-century young women—is beyond the scope of this study. Yet, through the many letters of the Wright/Mott/Osborne young women, it is possible to illustrate how such constrictions could have been encoded in the texts they read and enacted through the texts they themselves wrote. Such hints and guides to the phenomenon of constriction—along with its opposites of growth and transformation[7]—will be explored through the reading and writing of these young women and their community of family.

FAMILY LITERACY

Blessedly, the records of their lives (with thanks to the generous and keen foresight of the donation of the Osborne Family Papers as a whole by Eliza Wright Osborne's grandson, Lithgow Osborne)—letters, account books, school journals—are replete with specific references to their reading and are as well, of course, documents of their writings. These, in turn, serve to record the events of their lives. An entry in David Wright's account book for August 30, 1839, marks the date the Wrights moved to Auburn, New York, from Aurora in order that he could build a law practice. In an 1857 letter to his wife upon the death of his sister, Sarah, he is in a very reminiscent frame of mind and provides the origins of his choice of profession and wife:

> Entirely out of business. . , I commenced the study of law and soon became
> acquainted with a young widow [then Martha Coffin Pelham] with one of the
> dearest and sweetest little girls [Marianna Pelham] you ever saw, who lived at
> Aurora and how foolish I was to them then. (DW to MCW: 1.6.57)

Martha Coffin Pelham Wright: Widow and Teacher

The young widow was Martha Coffin Pelham, age 25 at her marriage to David Wright in 1829. Widowed at the age of 20 upon the death of Captain Peter Pelham in New Orleans on July 10, 1826, she had eloped with Pelham in November 1824. The "dearest and sweetest little girl" was Marianna Pelham (later Mott, for she would marry her first cousin, Thomas, the son of Lucretia Coffin Mott), born August 28, 1825. Martha was in Aurora, a handwriting teacher, sharing with her mother, Anna Folger Coffin, the duties of running a Quaker school by which they supported themselves. Established by Susan Marriott, its head teacher was Rebecca Bunker, educated in France and a niece of Anna Folger Coffin (Bacon, 1980, p. 46).

By 1840, and now in Auburn where David Wright was establishing his law practice, the family of Martha and David consisted of Marianna (called "Sister"), age 15; Eliza, age 10; and Matthew Tallman, age 8. Over the next eight years, Martha would bear four more children: Ellen in 1840; William (Willie and sometimes Willy) in 1842; Francis (Frank) in 1844; and "Little Charlie" in 1848. Born four months after the Seneca Falls Woman's Rights Convention of 1848, he was to die only a year later. Matthew Tallman was destined to die early as well, the victim of a shipping accident in San Francisco Bay in 1854 (Bacon, 1980, p. 155). Ellen was to enjoy a fine marriage with William Lloyd Garrison, Jr., and both Willie and Frank became farming entrepreneurs in Florida.

David Wright: Lawyer and Subscriber

Throughout his life, David Wright recorded his expenditures and some of his business activities in handmade, hand-sewn notebooks approximately 2-1/2 by 3-1/2 inches, small enough to be tucked into one of his pockets. These little books, written from both ends, give record to a pattern of literacy and provide a barebones outline of significant family events. As lists, they provide a means for coming to understand Eliza Wright Osborne as reader and writer.

Her father's account books give evidence of a broad and rich base of print that entered the family in a flow, enfused and embedded in all domestic activities (Leichter, 1984). They give evidence, too, that this family thought of themselves as part of a cosmopolitan network (to use literacy concepts outlined by Hannah Fingeret [1983]) rather than belonging simply to their local, "hometown" one. (Occasional comments by Martha Coffin Wright over the years do indicate a keen appreciation of this distinction!) David Wright recorded almost yearly purchases for a subscription to the *Liberator*, William Lloyd Garrison's abolitionist newspaper. In the year 1845, he also recorded a purchase of the [*National*] *Anti-Slavery Standard* (for $4.00). In the 1840s, he subscribed to the *Albany Argus* as well as the *Albany Evening Journal*.

In addition to the *Liberator* as an instance of purchase of a periodical with circulation in several states, David Wright subscribed to the *New York Evening Post* (1845, 1846) and, at least for one year, to the *New England Review* (1846). And upon their publishing inception, he also was a regular purchaser of both *Harper's* and *The Atlantic Monthly*, the former commencing publication in 1851, the latter in 1857. Rather than subscribing, however, he bought these periodicals monthly for 25 cents apiece. In 1858, he spent $5.00 for a binder for his issues of *The Atlantic Monthly*. Regular subscription purchases to the *Cultivator* also appear.

For local publications, he recorded subscribing to the Free Soil, Cayuga County *Daily Tocsin* (Storke, 1879, p. 52), the *Cayuga Patriot*, the *Genesee Farmer*, and the *Auburn Journal*. The publisher of the latter, Richard Oliphant, also put out the *Auburn Daily Advertiser*, the city's daily "newspaper of record" (p. 52), which the family received and read. An almost regular monthly entry appears over these years for newspaper postage and, on December 3, 1855, there is this entry: "Pd for Daily Advertiser to Jan 1/55, $7.50."

Local Newspapers and Bookstores

The front pages of the *Auburn Daily Advertiser*, begun in September 1846, were (and are) a primer of 19th-century local literacy. Its front pages were full of bookstore advertisements and the issues of its first weeks of publication recorded the presence of four bookstores in town: City Bookstore, J. C. Derby & Co., H. & J.C. Ivison, and R.G. & P.S. Wynkoop. By comparison, the four pages of the *Seneca County Courier*, a weekly for Seneca Falls, of July 21, 1848, contained only two advertisements for books; these to be found in only one bookstore. Not only did the bookstores of Auburn advertise daily, they often had multiple ads, sometimes featuring only a single book. J. C. Derby, for example, offered on September 15, 1846, *The Cow and the Dairy*—"A book for every one who keeps a cow, a Treatise ... by John S. Skinner." Two days later, City Bookstore offered *Natural History Illustrated*, a monthly purchase that "should be in every home" (*Advertiser*, September 17, 1846).

More commonly, the bookstores advertised their book offerings either by designated group, or they provided long lists of separate titles. On this same day, Wynkoop's told its readers they had "JUST REC'D a new supply of Homeopathic Books." One column over was a 7-inch-long advertisement, headed "VALUABLE SCHOOL BOOKS." An Ivison advertisement, it provided a list of the standard 19th-century school texts: Sander's Series of Reading Books, Day & Thompson's *Higher Arithmetic*, Hitchcock's *Geology*, and Porter's *Rhetorical Reader*, among the many listed and offered for sale that September 1846. Derby & Co. also carried school books, of course, but, on September 22, chose to call attention to the "large supply of new and valuable SABBATH SCHOOL BOOKS."

The advertisements of single listings of books, such as those of Derby's and Wynkoop's of September 22, 1846, are a preview of some of the texts that will figure into an understanding of the patterns of reading, both specifically and generically, of the young Wright/Mott/Osborne women. Wynkoop was pushing *The Essays of Elia* by Charles Lamb, while Derby suggested M. Thier's *History of the French Revolution*. Both bookstores offered their customers varied travel books and biographies as well.

On September 23, 1846, the Wynkoops paid specific attention to their female customers, suggesting the "very popular *Two Lives, or to Seem and to Be*, by Maria McIntosh" and "Miss Beecher's *Receipt Book*, new supply." Indeed, many of the advertisements in the newspaper were specifically directed toward women. City Bookstore, which must have carried a diversified line of goods, on October 10, 1846, had an advertisement that read: "TO THE LADIES—Purse and Bag trimmings" and Ivison told the "Ladies, we have just received a new kind of PERFORATED PAPER, ahead of any thing of the kind ever brought to this market."[8]

In another foreshadowing, both Wynkoop's and Ivison's, on this October day, suggested G.P.R. James's latest novel, *Heidelberg, a Romance*. The works of this author, whose wordy historical novels are said by some to be the inspiration of the writing contest that asks contestants to begin their entries with "It was a dark and stormy night . . .," are, as set out in a letter of October 25, 1850, an object of contempt to Eliza Wright. As a 62-year-old woman, however, she was kept "mezmerized" by James's *Old Oak Chest*, according to an 1890 letter from her son to one of his sisters.

Auburn, New York: A Center of Publishing

David Wright's entries into his account books recorded purchases at the Derby as well as the Ivison bookstores. He recorded, as well, the payment for bookstore bills at both stores. Auburn was an important center of publishing during the 1840s and 1850s and at least one of the bookstores that David Wright patronized was active in the printing business.

According to Elliot G. Storke's *History of Cayuga County* (1879), Derby, Miller & Co. was the largest publishing house in New York State from 1848 until its liquidation in 1857. Alden & Markham (later Alden, Beardsley & Co.) was the other book publishing company in Auburn between 1852 and 1856. Storke estimates that "hundreds of thousands of standard and miscellaneous books issued" from these two publishing houses (p. 50). The manager of the Ivison bookstore, Mr. Henry Ivison, left Auburn in 1846, and his "name now stands at the head of the largest and most honorable publishing house in this country—Ivison, Blakeman, Taylor & Co., New York" (p. 214).

In his invaluable *A Short-Title List of Books . . . Printed in Auburn, New York* (1936), prolific and noted bibliographer Douglas McMurtrie[9] states:

It will be observed that, for its geographical location and for the time period here covered, there was an astonishing degree of printing activity in Auburn. Analytic study of Auburn imprints will throw much light on the cultural history of the community. (p. 4)

In *A Fictive People: Antebellum Economic Development and the American Reading Public* (1993), Ronald J. Zboray connects literacy with the coming of the railroad in the 1830s and 1840s:

Along the route, local development proceeded apace as new town names leaped into prominence and opened to publishers untried markets. The quick rise and fall of Auburn, New York, as a publishing center ... hearkens back to this stage [of railroad development]. (p. 65)

The local histories of Auburn all highlight this early and ongoing relationship to the printed word as well as its role first in print's local dissemination and then in a more national diffusion. According to Storke, Auburn had its first library as early as 1810 (1879, p. 212) and Joel H. Monroe, in his *Historical Records of a Hundred and Twenty Years* (1913), notes the origins of Auburn's first bookstore by Auburn banker James S. Seymour:

Through Mr. Seymour's initiative and money investment the first book store was established in Auburn about 1830. This bookstore, with its value and demonstrated influence in the community, led to the establishment of the Seymour Library more than 45 years later. (p. 149)

Monroe notes too the significance of the link between the paper companies and book publishers: "The local book publishers, Derby & Co. and Alden, Beardsley & Co. were practically consuming the product of the mill" (1913, p. 159), a plant that had began in 1827 and changed owners several times.

The center of what is now Auburn is located on the same site as the Cayuga village of Osco "on the bank of the Owasco outlet.... This village comprised a little huddle of bark huts, which was the biding place of a small band of the Cayuga tribe" (Monroe, 1913, p. 7). The first settlement by whites took place in 1793, attracted by

the swift flowing Owasco outlet with its many falls, cascades and the possibilities in water power [that] appealed to the matured business instinct of Col. John Leonard Hardenbergh when he chose the lower land along the stream for the building of his village and town. (p. 11)

By 1795 "crude and imperfect" (Monroe, 1913, p. 21) roads, largely configuring their present arrangement, were being constructed. Taverns, stores, and a settlement school soon followed. In 1805 "the name of the Village was changed from Hardenbergh Corners to that of Auburn, thus giving the place greater dignity and a stronger claim to the county seat"—which was granted in June of that year (Monroe, 1913, p. 71). Incorporated as a village in 1815, Auburn was chartered as a city in March 1848.

"The mail," according to Monroe (1913), "was brought to the community once a week, usually by a postman on horseback. In 1804 the mails arrived twice a week and, by the year 1808, the Genesee Turnpike, the main east to west road, "was the scene of a daily stage line" (p. 30). Several mills lined the Owasco outlet and there were many hotels for "travelers and prospective settlers" (p. 30). By 1810 it was "something of an industrial center" with five saw mills, four grist mills, three distilleries, two carding mills, two fulling mills, one linseed oil mill, and a triphammer forge. Along the outlet there were six dams" (p. 75). By 1815, the year Auburn was incorporated, "there were well up towards 40 business institutions" (p. 110) and the population "was about one thousand" (p. 110). By 1838 the population was "not more than 5000" (p. 120), 7000 by 1845, and 9000 by 1850.

In addition to the vigorous publishing industry, Auburn was also the home of former Governor and Secretary of State William Seward (whose wife, Frances, was a visiting acquaintance of Martha Coffin Wright and their children played together) as well as the prominent Auburn Theological Seminary. With abundant train service, the famous of the day, including Jenny Lind in 1851 (Monroe, p. 64) and Louis Kossuth in 1852 (p. 90), made their pilgrimages. It was not a place excluded from the currents of the time and its cultural opportunities.

Parents as Writers

Not only did Eliza Wright Osborne live in this town turned city that was a vital center of publishing, she had parents who were published authors, one more often formally published than the other, but still from both her parents she could draw upon examples of genuine authorship. Martha Coffin Wright "read some satirical articles she had published in the daily papers answering the diatribes on woman's sphere" (Rossi, 1973, p. 415) at the Seneca Falls Woman's Rights Convention of 1848 and, in some accounts, she is given much credit for the drafting of the Convention's now famous "Declaration of Sentiments." Additionally, she wrote occasional reviews for political and abolitionist publications such as the *Liberator.*[10] Within the family, as noted in the correspondence, she is said to have been an occasional writer of poetry and verse and was called upon to read them. Eliza Wright Osborne credited her mother with writing a book for one of the younger children in the family. Lastly, Martha Coffin Wright, as the chair of her share of woman's rights conventions, was no stranger at writing the speeches she needed to deliver as convention chair. She is not in the list of local authors as noted by Storke (1879, p. 55).

Martha's husband, David Wright, is on Elliot Storke's list. He was a writer of a formally published work, a many-editioned text providing legal information: *Executor's, Administrators and Guardian's Guide*. It contains a summary of the laws of New York State and was first copyrighted in 1844. The book was published by J. C. Derby & Co., later Derby & Miller. Many entries in his account books record the printing and copyright activities involved in the publishing and sale of his book.

From her father, Eliza also had the example of someone who, even if he did read novels, very rarely bought them. His only two listed novel purchases (in the account books in the Osborne Family Papers) were *Uncle Tom's Cabin* and an 1843 Bulwer novel, *The Last of the Barons*, which received a favorable review "because of the entire absence of that pandering to corrupt or vitiated tastes" of his other novels, as noted by Nina Baym in her *Novels, Reviews, and Reviewers* (1984, p. 178). Otherwise, David Wright's purchases were of the nonfictional variety: biographies, travel books, and law books.

During the early years of David Wright's law practice, his account book records show that he built his law library book by book. Yearly, he purchased Sipion's *Laws*. As he became more affluent, his book purchases became more varied in subject matter but still centered on "serious" travel books and biographies. He frequently purchased books when on trips or on the road as a circuit lawyer. Often these books appear to have been gifts for nieces and nephews. In a final category of his purchases (and especially prominent in the 1840s and 1850s) were textbooks for his children: a Geography for Eliza in August 1838; a School Book for Tallman (MTW) on July 3, 1840, and a year later a Geography for him; seven years after that, a Geography for Ellen (EWG); and a final example, a Speller for Willie (WPW) on October 4, 1848.

Educating Eliza

Clearly, Eliza Wright was born into a family that placed a high value on literacy and education. Martha Coffin Wright, both as a former teacher and a feminist, appreciated the importance of education. David Wright, too, who had studied law and written a law text, knew well its value and had struggled to attain it (DW to MCW: 1.6.57). Along with her brothers and sisters, Eliza "had," to use Mary Kelley's felicitous phrase, "been welcomed into the world of reading by [her] parents" (1996, p. 409). "Moreover, she found that world expanded and [her] habits of reading reinforced during the years [she] attended an academy or seminary" (p. 409). Eliza attended both, but still gender differentials can be seen operating within the family regarding the matter of education. Both of Eliza's brothers, Willie and Frank, attended Harvard while neither Eliza nor her sisters Marianna and Ellen ever attended institutions of higher learning. Throughout the correspondence, however, concern for the education of the young women can be traced.

An important institution in Auburn, attended by Eliza in the early 1840s, was the Auburn Female Seminary, which opened in 1837, a year before the Wrights moved to Auburn. According to Auburn historian Joel H. Monroe, "The Seminary enjoyed a considerable degree of prosperity. Its pupils came not only from the best families of the village and county, but from many different states" (1913, p. 37). Writing in *Auburn, 200 Years* (1993), Martha J. Shosa states that the curriculum included Latin and Greek. However, Monroe provided a different course outline: "The courses of study, including both music and art, were of sufficient scope to insure a very fair measure of education, together with culture and finish in the fine arts" (p. 37).

As the building of the Seminary burned in 1849, its records have unfortunately been lost. However, evidence in the letters suggests it is more likely that the curriculum was in accord with Monroe's outline (Putala, 1988). It is educational historian Carl F. Kaestle's judgment that women's

> work of socialization [in schools] was a very different process from that of men's and the definition of woman's proper roles was a central element in the ideology of the antebellum generation [that] had a profound impact on education. (1983, p. 84)

Zboray, in his study of literacy in the antebellum period that has as its main thesis the cultural fragmentation of the period, makes much of the need for "the reader to engage essentially in a process of self-construction" (1993, p. 110) as the older institutions no longer were able to function amidst all the changes of industrialization. The task of the reader and thus, of course, of the reader's family "was to create personal educational strategies with which to confront the antebellum institutions involved in literacy" (p. 110).

Illustrating this fragmentation, perhaps, is the remainder of Eliza's education. In addition to her years at the Auburn Female Seminary, she spent as well one year, 1846–47, at Mansion Square, a boarding school in Poughkeepsie, New York. Although she seemed to have worked hard and done well at Mansion Square, developing friends with whom she continued to correspond, she decided against spending a second year there. Upon her return home, she continued her French in private lessons and took dancing lessons as well. Although she had once expressed an interest in hydrotherapy (perhaps when such a school almost opened in Auburn), her year at Mansion Square ended her formal education.

After that, her wide reading, innumerable lectures, sermons, and conversations of the famous people who came to her parents' and her famous aunt's home became her education. Mary Kelley (1984) stresses the importance of the education that occurred within families: "The more informal education provided in the home ... continued to be important, particularly in more privileged families" (p. 62). But citing author Catharine Maria Sedgwick's own words, Kelley makes note of the fragmentary nature of her education (pp. 62–63). More recently and consistent with this study, Kelley has highlighted the role of reading itself in the life of Sedgwick as indeed "'constitut[ing]' her education" (1996, p. 407).

Following the Family Traditions of Literacy

After her marriage, Eliza Wright Osborne, like her father (and her mother), kept careful accounting of her expenditures.[11] The record of these accounts (as preserved in the Osborne Family Papers) began the year after her marriage to David Munson Osborne in September 1851. In her 1852 listing of daily expenses, Eliza purchased a copy of *Jane Eyre* at the end of January, perhaps to begin building her own library. On Valentine's Day, she bought the novel *Nathalie* by Miss Kavanagh. In April she bought her own copy of *Uncle Tom's Cabin* as well as Miss Mitford's *Recollections*, the former for $1.50, the latter for $1.00. In July, this bride of nine months purchased on successive days, first Miss Beecher's *Cookbook* and, on the next, Miss Beecher's *Domestic Economy*. Each was purchased for 88 cents. This same year Eliza Wright Osborne also listed two other literacy expenses: $3.00 for *Harper's* (now in its second year of publication)[12] and $5.00 for the *Daily Times*.

Her 1853 listings show that she, like her father, purchased her *Harper's* month by month at 25 cents a copy. One of her letters to her husband expressed irritation with herself for having left her copy in traveling in New York City, suggesting its importance to her. In February and March, Eliza listed four book purchases, one of which, on March 11, was Charlotte Brontë's *Villette*, a powerful story of an "independent" woman. The other three books she recorded purchasing are works of nonfiction. On February 26, Eliza made note that she bought for $1.00 "Dr. Nic[h]ol's Book." On March 8 for $2.50, she purchased "Dr. Trall's Book," and 10 days later, a week after purchasing *Villette*, she spent 25 cents for "Water Cure Book." Both Russell Thatcher Trall and Thomas Low Nichols were dedicated proselytizers for hydrotherapy, and the latter was a proponent of sexual pleasure for women, the author of *Esoteric Anthropology*, an early and explicit "marriage manual."[13] In 1853 the bookstores in which Eliza made some of these purchases were Alden Beardsley & Co. and Osborn, Barker, & Baldwin. The names may have changed, but Auburn, New York, was still a place where the very latest in books and periodicals could be purchased.

In addition to this record from account books by Eliza Wright Osborne and her parents, the many letters in the Osborne Family Papers provide not just specific titles and authors that members of the family read—and the focus herein is on the literacy of the young women—but also commentary upon such reading. Like the lists of the account books, their remarks and comments about the books and periodicals they were reading help us further understand the meaning(s) the young women made and took from their texts and even perhaps the effects of such reading.

Like the lists, too, the reading of the young women, as noted in their letters, lends itself to a preliminary outline of significant reading patterns. As we have seen above, the reading that can be verified included local as well as more cosmopolitan newspapers; the important periodicals of the times, *Harper's*, *The Atlantic Monthly*; and those texts important both in "standard" 19th-century reconstructions (e.g., Hart, 1965) as well as in the more recent resurrections of the forgotten titles written and read by so many women of the 19th century (Baym, 1978; Harris, 1990; Tompkins, 1985).

Certainly, some of their reading had a male authorship, and those readings can be categorized into five varieties: Dickens (the moment he was in print either in his continuing chapters in periodicals or in book form); canonized authors such as Carlyle; medical and water cure authors who were protofeminists; the male sentimentalists (who were *not* feminists of any kind); and authors important in the extended family's liberal causes, such as Frederick Douglass, Charles Kingsley, Charles Reade, and Eugene Sue. But what appears most striking is how much of the reading that they mentioned, listed, responded to, and/or "discussed" consisted of books by and about women. With the exception of Dickens, the books they shared and commented on the most as young women were novels such as Maria McIntosh's *Charms and Countercharms* and biographies by and about women such as Miss Strickland's *Queens of England*. Moreover, not only was their reading heavily weighted toward women authors, they appeared to have a great deal of interest in women authors.

Zboray (1993), however, cautions against a view of 19th-century reading that would differentiate between the title selections of women and men, arguing against what he sees as the assumption of a separate women's sphere, which would dictate "an ordered distinction between the reading of men and women" (p. 158). Rather, holding "the view of antebellum cultural fragmentation," Zboray sees that "reading patterns reflected the unpredictability, rampant interdisciplinarity, and sometimes utter confusion of a boundless culture" (p. 158).

In his analysis of New York Society Library charge records, Zboray found the charging patterns of the texts themselves were not strictly gendered:

> Men and women charged out on the average almost the same proportion of biography, belles lettres, and novels; though women charged slightly more novels and men more travel, the positions reversed in the second three year sample. Only in history ... would men maintain a small lead in the two periods. So, in proportion of books charged, the reading patterns of men and women differed little. (1993, p. 163)

He does, however, note some "gender shadings" in the kind of novels chosen between the sexes, with women reading the more sentimental ones, and with males tending toward adventure novels such as those by James Fenimore Cooper (p. 164).

Their "Literate" Knowledge

Not surprisingly, for such wide, varied readers as well as frequent correspondents, and living in families where literacy was such a prominent and significant facet of everyday life, the young women of this study—Eliza and her cousins and friends, particularly Pattie (MML)—possessed a great deal of sophisticated knowledge regarding texts, authors, and authorship as well as the conventions of the 19th-century publishing world.

They knew books could be continuations of each other (MML to EWO: 5.17.45); they knew about the physical attributes of the book as artifact, as when Pattie wrote to Eliza that another cousin had received "the complete works of N. P. Willis handsomely bound" (5.9.48); obviously, they knew, too, who this then-prominent writer/editor was. And they knew books came in different editions—Pattie wanted the "new edition of Miss Strickland's *Queens of England* (MML to EWO: 9.8.48). These few examples illustrate their working knowledge of some of the more technical aspects of the burgeoning book publishing trade of the mid-19th century (Baym, 1984; Coultrap-McQuin, 1990; Kelley, 1984; Zboray, 1988, 1993).

They also appeared to have understandings regarding the use of different reading strategies for different kinds of readings. Like the good 19th-century readers that they were, they understood that a good reader is "supposed" to read for a moral. Upon offering a moral reading of a Dickens Christmas tale, Pattie finished her long explication with "my mind is too common for anything more" (MML to EWO: 2.5.49). On another occasion, Pattie made a distinction between the plot of a text and its moral: "I think [*Alton Locke*] is very good—not as a novel, the plot is nothing but the sentiments therein expressed are of the right kind" (MML to EWO: 12.22.50). They understood, too, that the act of reading required actual differing styles depending on the material, as revealed in a letter written on October 25, 1850, by Eliza to an unnamed male friend:

> Elly [Eliza's sister Ellen] was reading over for the hundre[d]th time your note to her, the other evening (she reads it regularly every evening before retiring on the same plan as a chapter in the Bible, I suppose) when Willy said, "I shouldn't be so *darned* proud of a letter"—her only objection to it, is that 'tis not so long as mine. (EWO to DMO?: 10.25.50)

Ten-year-old sister Ellen can be seen here as understanding that some texts required careful reading and that length of letters had some connection to worth of relationship!

Much of the young women's knowledge of reading was linked to considerations of gender and suggests their real awareness of the knowledge that aspects of reading were gendered. On more than one occasion, they took on the critics of the day to disagree regarding the gender identity of an author. On December 8, 1848, Pattie took to task the prominent editor and writer N. P. Willis who "thinks *Alton Locke* is by the author of *Jane Eyre*—but it seems to me very different—& I should think was written by one of the sterner sex" Pattie was not wrong. *Alton Locke* was authored by one of the sterner sex, Charles Kingsley. Ten years later Eliza's sister, Ellen, away at Eagleswood School in New Jersey, wrote to her: "Let's see … aren't you glad the *Drummer's Daughter* isn't by Mr. [Thomas Wentworth] Higginson[11] & that *Physical Courage* is? Have you written to Cheesey yet?" (10.28.58). "Cheesey" was Miss Chesbro (Caroline Cheesebrough), the author of the *Drummer's Daughter* and known to the family.

Thus, in addition to being "good" 19th-century readers in their knowledge of the prominent writers and editors of their day, they also possessed knowledge of the publishing industry itself as it mattered to the serious reader. In addition, they possessed reading strategies to help them with the ways of reading their texts, distinguishing between plot and moral and knowing how to "read" to articulate that moral. Clearly, too, they knew that a reader should not necessarily read a letter in the same manner as the Bible.

Moreover, they were able to perceive that gender matters when it comes to authorship—and by extension to the reading of a text. They were very much gendered readers and had some very clear notions about what the differences between the genders were supposed to be as well as how this set of expectations could play itself out in texts. Susan K. Harris (1990), in her introduction to *19th-Century American Women's Novels: Interpretive Strategies*, spoke to both these crucial issues—reading strategies and the genderedness of 19th-century reading:

Although analysis of the mechanics of reading behavior is a peculiarly twenti-eth-century concern, nineteenth-century writers and readers, surrounded as they were by militant definitions of the differences between male and female intelligence, nature, and experience, would have accepted the idea that men and women read, as well as wrote, differently. If they had not, they would not have placed such emphasis on reading suited to each sex. Intuitively aware of these cognitive predispositions, writers could, consciously or not, structure their works so that male and female readers could extract different meanings from them. (p. 23)

As we have seen above, while some researchers such as Ronald J. Zboray would take exception to Harris's view on the gendered nature of reading activities, the data generously provided by the Wright/Mott/Osborne young women in the Osborne Family Papers concur more with Harris's study. Zboray, however, may have provided a way out of this impasse by sug-gesting that the question may not be a simple one as "the same literature can be interpreted from different gendered perspectives" (1993, p. 169).

Before moving on to these and other issues, attention needs to be given to some of the antecedents of the Wright/Mott/Osborne literacy mural.

A More Distant History

This backdrop to the rich and varied literacy heritage of Eliza Wright Osborne had a more distant history that can be traced in the Osborne's family archives to some of its roots in 18th-century Nantucket. Someone so wanted to read the ship's log of Thomas Coffin, father of Martha Coffin Wright and Lucretia Coffin Mott, that they borrowed and never returned it. Almost a hundred years later, its loss was still being lamented. In her memorial address to her mother, written some time after Martha Coffin Wright's unexpected death in January 1875,[15] Eliza wrote of her grandfa-ther, Thomas Coffin (1766–1815): He was "always a sailor but courteous and refined.... He was an interesting writer & narrator. His log book was loaned about among his friends and finally disappeared." It was not only from her parents that Eliza had an inheritance of broad and multiple liter-acy possibilities.

Regarding the reading of texts, particularly fictional ones, the Wright/Mott/Osborne family also had a history. A long-standing family ambiva-lence toward novel and story reading can be detected, not unusual, of course, in a family of Quakers. In a very early letter in the Osborne Family Papers, written by Lucretia to her mother Anna Folger Coffin),[16] Lucretia commented on the reading of two young female children in the family, her sister Martha's eldest daughter, Marianna, and a Nantucket branch cousin. "I hope Martha," she wrote to her mother Anna Coffin, "won't let [10-year-old] Mary Anna[17] pour over *Arabian Nights* too much. Ellis [an older cousin] asked if it was well for her to read it at this early age or much in it at any age" (LCM to AFC: 8.3.35). Young Phebe Earle's reading patterns came under discussion, too: "They say [she]'s so fond of her book & so little of work that they have had to limit her to 3 hrs a day."

That Martha would have *Arabian Nights* as part of her oldest daughter's reading, considering its rather racy reputation, is suggestive of a life-long complex and ambivalent relation to story. She held the form in some suspicion and she shared this view with her daughters. It is very unlikely that Lucretia Coffin Mott, who was not at all shy about sharing her belief system, would not also have conveyed to *her* daughters that novel reading was not the best use of their time, as her comments regarding little Phebe suggest.

Otelia Cromwell (1958), in her biography of Lucretia Coffin Mott, traces some of this family ambivalence toward story. Cromwell characterizes much of Lucretia's reading as "intensive" (p. 28), a literacy label given to an older pattern of reading in which readers would ponder through rereading only a few selected texts such as the Bible. In contrast is reading marked as being in an "extensive" mode, having many volumes at one's disposal that are presumed to be more perused than studied. Assumed by some literacy historians to be a less worthy manner of reading, this presumed "less deep kind of reading" has often been used to refer pejoratively to women's reading, particularly their reading of novels.

Martha Coffin Wright, describing her sister Lucretia's health after a serious illness to her family in Auburn, conveyed to them that Aunt Lucretia was on the mend: "She was up in bed reading William Penn!" This was not everyone's idea of sick bed material! Lucretia could be persuaded to read particular novels—*Uncle Tom's Cabin*, for example, but, in general, she tended to frown upon the form. In contrast, Cromwell confirms that Martha did take a more relaxed view of novel reading and "reveled in the novels of Scott and Dickens" but, according to Cromwell, conceded that her sister Lucretia was on higher ground: "My sister's intellect being of so much higher order she could take to profound literature 'as a cat laps milk' and she falls into the very common error of judging other people's minds by her own" (1958, p. 28), wrote Martha.[18]

A more recent biographer of Lucretia Coffin Mott, Margaret Hope Bacon (1980), connected Martha's relative permissiveness regarding novel reading to her forced abandonment of her Quaker practice:

Martha, having lost her membership as a result of her marriage to Peter Pelham [in 1824 but widowed in 1826] was through with the Society of Friends. In addition to studying art she began to read novels and to wear gay colors. Soon she was keeping company with a dashing lawyer, David Wright, just now setting up his practice in the Auburn area. (p. 46)

While no cause-and-effect relation between novel reading and marrying a "dashing" lawyer is made (nor should be), taking pleasure in the reading of novels does appear to be somewhat at variance with Martha's Quaker heritage.

FORESHADOWINGS

These ambivalences play themselves out in the next generation of women readers, as we will see in some detail. Yet, too, the reading selections and patterns of this newer generation followed those that have been uncovered by the feminist researchers of the last decade. Making distinctions is important in knowledge making. To know that it is "better" to read a novel of piety, that such is preferred to the reading that one is actually doing—and to enjoy it—is to begin to build a knowledge and preference base. To be able to share such inchoate beliefs with friends and cousins of the same age who, after all, would share generational understandings, is to begin to be able to build a knowledge base for understanding the next novel read as well as the next and the next. In so doing, these young women were in the process of differentiating themselves from the generation(s) that preceded them.

While this process of differentiation may have occurred, at the same time, these young women readers were building on the rich literacy practices of those who had gone before them. Now, their broad and rich record of full participation in the literature and literacy offerings of the time was not without its ambivalences and contradictions, reflecting perhaps generational tensions as well as tensions over gender patterns and inequalities. The ambivalences and contradictions may reflect, as well, the complexities inherent in reading practices and processes. Unlike their forebears, these young women had access to a broad range of texts and authors made possible by advances in both printing and circulation of materials. The very availability and variety of printed matter and its permeation through their lives, homes, and writing made possible a wide and deep knowledge about literacy and 19th-century culture. Some of these ramifications are explored below.

To write about Eliza Wright (Osborne), as young girl and young woman, and the intersection of gender and literacy within the meaning of her life, is to foreshadow her mid- and later life activities as a book collector. Intriguing is that so many of the books she bought—from Estes & Lauriat in Boston or Sotheran in London—are those very titles, no longer part of everyday "literate" currency, she and her reading companions took so seriously in the mid-19th century. While not really part of the following, Eliza's reclaiming of the books she shared with her friends and relatives—mother, father, sisters, brother, aunts, cousins, and in-laws—necessarily adds to the need to take more seriously many texts no longer part of our mainstream American heritage.

And taking the reader seriously is at the heart of reader-response theory wherein, as set forth succinctly by Stanley Fish: "The reader's activities are at the center of attention, where they are regarded as not leading to meaning, but as *having* meaning" (1980, p. 172). The meaning that the above reading had in the lives of the Wright/Mott/Osborne women is a story that speaks to their gendered 19th-century status and what sense they were able to make of that within their literacy community.

It is a story that tells of survival—of making and taking materials that privileged one's existence and extended it as far as possible. Even in thinking of their own really vast writing production as a form of publication, thinking of these young women and their mothers and aunts and cousins as creating a text of and from their own lives (Martha Nell Smith, 1992), it is still a story that tells, too, of horizons that were not limitless. And for all that, it is a story that in Susan K. Harris's (1990) felicitous words "celebrates female genius" (p. 23).

ONWARD

The heart of this study is an in-depth look at the intersection of the reading and writing processes and practices of the young Wright/Mott/Osborne women with their mid-19th-century gendered condition. Chapter 2, "Wherein the Problem is Set," is a discussion centering upon an understanding of literacy as an agent of liberation as well as a force of constriction. Chapter 3, "Reading the Writing of 'The Particular': A Methodology," addresses issues regarding this study's methodology. Following upon these discussions are two chapters on reading, reflecting its duality: "On Their Own: Women Reading (Mostly) Women," and "*Not* on Their Own: Mothers and Men Prescribe Their Reading." The importance and ramifications of intersections of gender and literacy continue to reveal themselves in Chapter 6, "Writing Well: In Search of 'The Particular,'" and then is highlighted more specifically in Chapter 7, "'Fixed Very Nicely, Indeed!: A Focus on Gender.'" Conclusions to these matters are the subject of the last chapter, "Endings."

NOTES

1.   This is the source of this study of literacy along with the correspondence of other members of this extended family.
2.   Box 236, Osborne Family Papers.

3. This thought is not unconnected to my own experiences as a woman coming of age in the 1950s.

4. Thinking of her letter writing—and the mutual correspondence of which it was a part—as a form of publication, as Martha Nell Smith (1992) lays claim for Emily Dickinson, may be a way out of this impasse. More current scholarship that gives larger ground to women's activities and literacy's benefits is yet another avenue, as we will see in later chapters.

5. More current Dickinson scholarship reviewed and extended by Elizabeth A. Petrino (1998) suggests a more complex relationship between Dickinson's recognition of the limits upon the 19th-century woman and her spectacular creative achievement.

6. Barker (1987), Dobson (1989), Howe (1985), Petrino (1998), Smith (1992).

7. What Harvey J. Graff (1987) calls "the literacy myth" and Mary Kelley (1996), along with Ronald J. and Mary Saracino Zboray (1999), call "self-fashioning," citing the work of Renaissance scholar Stephen Greenblatt.

8. A critical theorist would find evidence here of both the construction and production of woman as purchaser, one flattered to be considered on the frontiers of the new!

9. The full title reads: *A Short-Title List of Book, Pamphlets, and Broadsides Printed in Auburn, New York, 1810–1850.* Anyone concerned with the printing and/or reading of texts in Auburn is fortunate also in having available Karl S. Kabelac's similarly invaluable *Book Publishing in Auburn, New York, 1851–1876, An Introduction and an Imprints Bibliography* (1969).

10. As currently being documented by Sherry H. Penney and James D. Livingston, a great-great grandson of Martha Coffin Wright, in their forthcoming biography of Martha Coffin Wright from the University of Massachusetts Press, *A Very Dangerous Woman: Martha Wright and Women's Rights.*

11. Boxes 285 and 291, Osborne Family Papers.

12. Over the years, *Harper's* magazine reinvented and renamed itself several times.

13. *Shameless: The Visionary Life of Mary Gove Nichols* (2002), by Jean L. Silver-Isenstadt, provides a sound recounting of the book's reception history as well as a valuable dual biography of the Nichols and the water cure movement.

14. Writer, Unitarian minister, leader of a black Civil War regiment, and a man who famously didn't encourage Emily Dickinson to write for publication (but redressed the wrong posthumously) (Wolff, 1986, *passim*).

15. Box 236, Osborne Family Papers.

16. And typed by someone, possibly Eliza's son, Thomas Mott Osborne.

17. Family names, as we have seen, often have more than one spelling.

18. The source of the quotation is the Garrison Family Papers (*SSC*), but Cromwell provided few dated references.

CHAPTER 2

WHEREIN THE PROBLEM IS SET

We know we are without a text, and must discover one.

Carolyn G. Heilbrun (1988)

"Eliza, I am trying to keep a journal or rather a diary this year and I wish you were here to help me," wrote 15-year-old Rebecca Yarnall of Philadelphia in a January 1845 letter to her same-age, Auburn, New York, cousin Eliza Wright (later, Osborne). Clearly illustrating a thesis of ethnographer of literacy Shirley Brice Heath (1981) that young women of the 19th century became proficient and artful letter writers through mutual instruction and supportive practice, this brief quotation is from one letter of many in the large Osborne Family Papers.[1] Even in its brevity, it suggests that, for these two young cousins and correspondents of the mid-19th century (and their aunts and mothers, fathers, uncles, brothers, and husbands without whom their stories cannot be told), writing was a shared cultural practice—one of sufficient importance to warrant calling upon one another for assistance in such endeavors.

Some four years later, another of their cousins, Pattie (Martha Mott, later, Lord), wrote to Eliza regarding literacy practices: "Eliza: Don't read novels just because the year is up" (MML to EWO: 9.21.49). The meaning of this cryptic statement regarding reading, embedded as it is in both this

---

Reading and Writing Ourselves into Being, pages 25–50
Copyright © 2004 by Information Age Publishing

25

long-standing correspondence between and among cousins/peers/friends as well as in a multitude of mid-19th-century contexts, is both suggestive and elusive. Within it, we can read the age-old censoriousness regarding young women's reading, and we can also detect their internalization of that deep cultural criticism.

From the imperative, we can assume not only a bond of community between these two young women; we can also surmise that this was not their first conversation about reading and books. Moreover, we can imagine that such conversations were part of the bonds that held them together. We might also infer from our own taken-for-granted belief in the power of texts that Pattie was encouraging both her cousin Eliza and herself to continue their reading of novels, such benefits not spelled out for us but well understood between these two frequent, life-long correspondents. Their bonds of trust and true friendship, forged through years of loyal letter writing and shared reading, provide, in a rich matrix of shared everyday understandings, the material for this study. Their correspondence, as we will see in a variety of germane contexts, gives full evidence of the intertwining nature of gender and literacy.

THE "WHY" QUESTION

Not all that long ago we could have asked ourselves what we really knew (or why we should care) about mid-19th-century young women's literacy—understood for now as both the ability to garner meaning from their reading and the capacity to communicate with others through the printed word—except that they wrote letters and were criticized for reading the novels of that "da__ed mob of scribbling women"? Notwithstanding Hawthorne's too often quoted complaint to his editor,[2] we would have agreed with Jill Ker Conway, regarding "the relationship between literacy and economic mobility [for women] in the nineteenth century," when she stated in 1982: "Those who study the history of women's education have yet to ... raise questions about the meaning of literacy to nineteenth-century women" (p. 84). What we have known about the literacy practices of 19th-century women has come largely from the work of male historians of literacy who informed us that the letter writing of women was merely "functional" or "pretty" and that women—the young and the old—read too many "light" novels.

More recently, Catherine Hobbs (1995), in her introduction to *Nineteenth-Century Women Learn to Write*, "which interweaves thick feminist social history with theoretical perspectives garnered from such diverse fields as linguistics and folklore, feminist literary theory, and African-American and Native American studies" (p. xi), states: "Stories of women's learning to write and the effects of women's literacy have often been collapsed into men's" (p. 4).

As Hobbs (1995) notes, past studies have defined literacy by the activities of males and, thus, the literacy practices of women have been devalued and hidden in all the many ways that women's stories have always been hidden, as traced so well in Gerda Lerners's *The Creation of Feminist Consciousness* (1993). In this well-documented lament, Lerner has forcefully articulated, through a century-by-century travelogue, woman's erasure on the one hand and her continuous struggle to gain education for the development of mind and autonomy. Her key point—that women throughout history were deprived of the knowledge of their own knowledge-making to their extreme detriment—resonates in any study of women's literacy. Cathy N. Davidson's *Revolution and the Word: The Rise of the Novel in America* (1986) underscores the value of education for women as she shares how few women novelists of the early Republic did not stress to their female readers the importance of acquiring as much education as they possibly could.

The New Cultural Historians

Thanks to groundbreaking interdisciplinary studies such as Davidson's, our views of what might constitute literacy practices worth caring about have undergone significant changes over the past several years. These changes—as any others in the social order of things—have come from many directions, many under the umbrella of the new cultural history as shared by Lynn Hunt (1989) in her eponymous text. Reading and writing practices are central for many of the theorists selected by Hunt to explicate and illustrate the interdisciplinary development of the new cultural history. Frequently cited in both the introduction and throughout the essays are historical ethnographers Natalie Zemon Davis and Robert Darnton, both indebted to the work of anthropologist/interpretationist, "thick descriptionist" Clifford Geertz[3] (Hunt, 1989). Davis's (1975) "reading" of the literacy and rituals of the 17th-century French peasant have had an immense impact, while Darnton shows throughout the essays in his *The Great Cat Massacre* (1985) that reading *is* his methodology.

More recently, Helen M. Buss (1996), a scholar of women's private writings and herself a "thick descriptionist," notes that Geertz's "thick description" is a rereading "in such a way as to reveal through the analysis of tiny particulars the behavioral codes, logics and motive forces controlling a whole society" (p. 86, citing Veeser's *The New Historicism* [1989]). Certainly, too, at the heart of Michel Foucault's postmodern critique are the very discursive practices of reading and writing that undergird the political landscape (Hunt, 1989, p. 7). The broad revisionism of literacy itself is central to both historian of literacy Harvey J. Graff (1987) and historian of the book (cited by Hunt, 1989) Roger Chartier (1994). Finally, Davidson's (1986) similarly revisionist, theoretical work on the early American novel and its readers makes clear how deeply the notion of value is implicated within all literacy practices, inseparable from its historical context.

For their studies, these scholar-revisionists draw upon the literacy practices and documents, often fugitive, of populations not previously thought of as sources of historical information. These theorists, particularly Graff, have helped to correct views of literacy that hold this phenomenon to be an unalloyed good, a cause sufficient unto itself, a way of thinking Graff (1987) labels "the literacy myth."

Drawing in revisionist spirit from the work of these theorists, as well as generating their own bank of knowledge and insights, have been feminist researchers whose decades of gender work over a wide spectrum of disciplines have not only made it unnecessary to defend a study of the writings of young women (as was true when this study was first envisioned) but has also helped ensure that future historians of literacy will not overlook the reading and writing practices of young women.

A Changing Model

Literacy theorists within the field of education, too, are building upon the historical work and insights of these gifted revisionists with even sharper criticisms of what Brian V. Street (1995) and others have labeled the older "autonomous" model of literacy, against which both Graff and Davidson developed key arguments and understandings. This model "isolates literacy as an independent variable and then claims to be able to study its consequences" (p. 29). Rather, Street stresses "the socially embedded nature" (p. 89) of literacy practices, and (along with literacy theorists like Brandt, 1995; Brodkey, 1996; Daniell, 1999; Minter, Gere, & Keller-Cohen, 1995) Street underscores the nature of literacy as always culturally embedded.

Furthermore, like the new cultural theorists such as Hunt and Chartier and the historical ethnographers Darnton and Davis, inherent in the work of all these more recent theorists is the understanding that literacy practices are inherently and deeply riveted in political practices and structures. Daniell, in her broadly based review article of 1999, "Narratives of Literacy: Connecting Composition to Culture," cites Street's (1984) critique of the great divide theory that privileges written over oral modes "to assert that literacy is never autonomous, never separate, never innocent, but always embedded in and embodying the practices, beliefs, and values of a culture, always therefore ideological" (p. 398). Daniell credits J. Elsbeth Stuckey's outspoken, passionate text, *The Violence of Literacy* (1991) as having

> stripped many people of their last vestiges of naive and romantic belief in literacy as an open door to the middle class. In the society around us we could see that restricting access to literacy is an effective way to deprive particular groups of power. (p. 399)

Power Relations: "Technologies of Gender"

The connection, thus, of the range of literacy practices to political structures and processes, that is, power relations, has become abundantly clear. Michel Foucault's (1976) postmodern understandings regarding the role of discursive practices as sites of political ideology have proven particularly useful for many feminists and, in line with the insights of the literacy theorists above, have altered our perceptions regarding what counts as reading and writing practices worthy of study. Of special interest to this study of literacy and gender is the analytic work of feminist film theorist Teresa de Lauretis (1984, 1987). Using Foucault's concept of technologies of power (especially as explicated in his *The History of Sexuality, Volume 1,* 1976), de Lauretis illustrates the mechanics of power through which women are inculcated into their unequal status through reading and writing practices. These "technologies of gender," according to de Lauretis (1987), are pervasive, as well as subtle, and operate through literacy and other cultural practices.[4]

Following upon these approaches and insights have come continuing and sometimes even more radical discussions of women's literacy practices. These feminist and literacy scholars—Buss (1996), Cholakian (1991, 2000), Hansen (1994), Hobbs (1995), Kelley (1996), Kelly (1999), Kitch (1993), Motz (1996), Petrino (1998), M. N. Smith (1992), and Zboray and Zboray (1999)—have come from a variety of historical and literary perspectives and disciplines.

Building on the exciting wave of feminist scholarship of the 1970s, extending the more theoretical and argumentative waves of the 1980s into the 1990s (which included such powerful scholars of reading and writing as Baym, 1978, 1984; Harris, 1990; Radway, 1984; and Sicherman, 1989), these more recent scholars/historians have, through their own deeply contextualized literacy studies (in interaction with the broader forces above), shown why it can be immensely valuable to care about the reading and writing practices of the 19th-century young woman.

It Was Not Always Thus:
A Midwife's Tale: The Case of Martha Ballard

Several significant historical studies of literacy written by male research-ers at the end of the 1980s and into the early 1990s—Brown (1989), Gilmore (1989), Graff (1987), Zboray (1993)—have done much to advance our understandings of 19th-century literacy, with Graff's magiste-rial history, *The Legacies of Literacy: Continuities and Contradictions in Western Culture and Society*, shifting the conceptual ground of literacy with his understandings across centuries based not simply on elite uses of literacy. Indeed, his work has made possible many of the above, more current stud-ies. The primary emphasis of these research undertakings, including Graff's, while more "democratic" than many past approaches to literacy, remains on the literacy products and processes of males, with the reading and writing experiences of women largely subsumed into those of men. These studies tell us little about women's literacy practices beyond their novel reading and letter writing.

Zboray (1993), however, does incorporate these practices into his over-all understandings of shifting literacy patterns of mid-19th-century Amer-ica. His somewhat bleak reading of the transformative nature of literacy is posited against the backdrop of his appreciation of agrarian life in opposi-tion to his perception of the atomization forced upon 19th-century Ameri-cans by increasing industrialization:

> Within communities and families among categories of gender and age, in institutions and association, and even within the self, antebellum develop-ment forced a wide variety of new relationships between the printed word, the reader, and the world. (p. 68)

Richard D. Brown in his *Knowledge is Power: The Diffusion of Information in Early America* (1989) states that women's uses of their literacy were in the service of entertainment. More egregiously, in his use of the 1785 to 1812 diary of Maine midwife Martha Ballard for his chapter on women's literacy, Brown does not read her original diary but rather depends on previously published extracts. With her diary, he is trying to illustrate that wives of this era used their literacy in a broader, more community-based way than their daughters. While admitting that Martha Ballard "was cognizant of society beyond her own domestic sphere" (p. 182), he nonetheless goes on to say that she "seldom use[d] her literacy to supply emotional reinforcement, genteel lessons, or social insight" (p. 183).

More importantly for Brown, whose book is on the diffusion of knowl-edge, "the information Martha Ballard acquired and conveyed dealt mostly with persons, not business, political, or religious affairs, and made her something of a community resource for gossip in the growing but still thinly populated, comparatively isolated Maine interior" (1989, p. 183). Even though the focus here is on the literacy activities of a woman of vital importance to her community, the gratuitous pejorative belies the content. It is "gossip" when women are the conduits of information but is "news" when conveyed by men. Business, politics, and religion are usually conducted by "persons," that is, not women.

In *A Midwife's Tale: The Life of Martha Ballard, Based on her Diary, 1785–1812*, a Bancroft winner, Laurel Thatcher Ulrich (1991) has written a stunning, historically contextualized reading of this country woman's diary that forever gives the lie to an approach to a history of literacy that either ignores or trivializes women's literacy productions, one that tries to dismiss them with labels of "entertainment" or "gossip." From a full reading of this terse, late 18th-century diary full of misspellings, the same one from which Brown finds only a nexus of "gossip," Ulrich has reconstructed not only the complex life and interrelationships of the Ballard family—from which the reader can garner a great deal of knowledge regarding rural Maine life—but also, through the diary entries of Martha Ballard, she presents a well-developed account of the health care system of the era: "The trivia that so annoyed earlier readers provide a consistent, daily record of the operation of a female-managed economy" (p. 33). Moreover, Ulrich has delineated a portrait of Martha Ballard, both through the midwife's own words and her own reading of those words, that has rescued from the archives an expert, feisty, undaunted woman who was an integral part of the health system of her time, with a remarkable record of successful births in the 816 deliveries she performed from 1785 to 1812.

Between these two approaches to women's literacy productions—one that provides only minimal and/or critical coverage and the other (exemplified by Ulrich) that respectfully accords to these same writings a significant role in the social fabric as a whole—lie avenues for thinking about literacy and its meanings in the lives of 19th-century young women. Several current studies (Hansen, 1994; Hobbs, 1995; Kelley, 1996; Kelly, 1999; Kitch, 1993; Motz, 1996; M. N. Smith, 1992; Zboray & Zboray, 1999) exemplify how the latter approach broadens and deepens literacy's meanings. Additionally, thanks to these feminist revisionists of literacy, it is no longer necessary to have to justify such work. The energies are now for continuation of the preservation of "feminist consciousness," that it not be lost yet again, as Gerda Lerner (1993) pleads so eloquently.

LITERACY: MYTH AND CONTEXTS

Before engaging more specifically with these more current studies in coming to understand the meanings and import of the literacy practices of the young Wright/Mott/Osborne women, it is essential to discuss a crucial aspect of literacy that still, according to Harvey J. Graff in his *The Legacies of Literacy*[5] (1987), haunts and challenges all discussions of literacy. It is his central thesis, explicated and illustrated across ancient to modern historical contexts, that literacy is not simply a beneficent gift that enabled the modernization of the West, but must be seen to operate within specific contexts much more complexly. For Graff, the phenomenon of literacy is as much a modernizing force as a conservative one, as much a force for liberation as a source for constriction.

Keith Walters, in his opening paragraph to "Language, Logic, and Literacy" in *The Right to Literacy* (1990), underscores Graff's point:

> The reputed consequences and promised blessings of literacy are legion. For society at large, increased literacy means at least a chicken in every pot, lower levels of unemployment, improved competitiveness for our nation in the world's markets, and greater participation of citizens in the democratic process. (p. 173)

Graff's conceptual work in the history of literacy has helped to shape the understandings of Walters and the entire field of the history of literacy. At the heart of his work, and helping to explain the meaning of Walter's irony, is a conception of literacy that rests on its social and historic paradoxes. Graff's conceptual framework for understanding literacy centers around the necessity to see both literacy's continuities and its contradictions. These, for him, lie at the very heart of literacy.

Graff's approach "is a corrective to the long-standing interpretation that slights the roles of continuities and traditions, the legacies of literacy" (1987, p. 8). He states that to "focus on continuities does not require neglecting changes or discontinuities.... [Rather] it is useful to employ the language of continuity and its implications when describing circumstances in which development and change tend to be more gradual than rapid" (p. 8). A focus on continuities corrects what Graff calls "the myths of literacy."

Such myths, Graff explains, are embedded in most discussions of literacy and are responsible for some of literacy's perceived contradictions. The "literacy myth" holds that "literacy is not only important and useful, but also an unambiguously positive thing, associated closely with the vital necessities of 'modern,' 'developed,' persons and societies" (1987, p. 382).

Too often, Graff writes, discussions of literacy make too-easy assumptions about the power of literacy:

> Literacy is said to correlate with economic growth and industrialization, wealth and production, political stability and participatory democracy, urbanization, consumption, and contraception. Such claims are not well documented; nor are their relationships well specified or conceptualized. Any meaning that they retain has substance and credibility only in precisely defined contexts. (p. 382)

For Graff, "literacy is best seen as a *dependent* factor, a result itself, and more an interactive, conditioning, and shaping instrument than a determining one" (p. 383), "'an enabling rather than a causal factor'" (Graff, quoting K. Gough, p. 2).

Graff (1987) believes most discussions of literacy "are surprisingly facile [and] founder because they slight efforts to formulate consistent and realistic definitions of literacy, have little appreciation of the conceptual complications that the subject presents, and ignore the vital role of sociohistorical context" (p. 3). Thus, according to him, three tasks are essential in any discussion of literacy:

> a consistent definition that serves comparatively over time and across space; stress[ing] that [literacy] is above all a technology ... for communications and for decoding and reproducing written or printed materials ... [and] alone is not an "agent of change"; [and] ... understanding literacy requires a further, large step into precise, historically specific materials and cultural contexts. (pp. 3–4)

While for Graff the first two of these three tasks are important, "the main effort [is] reconstructing the contexts of reading and writing" (p. 4).

Graff outlines seven points that, when reconstructed, provide the material for answering questions regarding literacy in ways that will not (hopefully) be wrongfully influenced by the literacy myth. His list for "reconstructing the contexts of reading and writing"—both past and present—appears both straightforward and complete:

> how, when, where, why, and to whom the literacy was transmitted; the meanings that were assigned to it; the uses to which it was put; the demands placed on literate abilities; the degrees to which they were met; the changing extent of social restrictedness in the distribution and diffusion of literacy; and the real and symbolic differences that emanated from the social condition of literacy among the population. (1987, p. 4)

For Graff, "answers to these questions," which he both uses and tests throughout his book, "are not easy to construct; nevertheless, an awareness of their overriding importance is only beginning to appear in some research and discussion" (1987, p. 5). He continues: "The meaning and contribution of literacy, therefore, cannot be *presumed*; they must themselves be a distinct focus of research and criticism" (p. 5).

It is not, of course, my wish or intention to slight Graff's impressive achievements and insights into the paradoxes and complexities of literacy. However, the omission of the concept of gender from this list for understanding literacy across time reinforces his admonition regarding "the meaning and contribution of literacy": they must indeed be "a distinct focus of research and criticism." The creation of an additional "context," one to explore the intersection of gender and literacy, is thus crucial—the crux for coming to new understandings regarding both critical areas of knowledge.

Knowledge and Power

Important to understanding the literacy myth, especially in its intersection with gender, are issues and aspects of power and knowledge; literacy rates and value; and the connection of literacy rates and power. The nexus of power with its location is of course the issue. Always central to feminist understandings and gender studies, power—making choices, having autonomy, the ability to earn and own and vote, having and making knowledge—is crucial. As Patricia Francis Cholakian clearly states: "A woman desires the power that will elevate her to the status of subject" (1991, p. 3). We will see in Chapter 7, "'Fixed Very Nicely Indeed!': A Focus on Gender," how this desire finds its expression in the very content of the young women's letters.

Especially egregious, as we saw above, in excluding women in his overall conceptualization of literacy that he understands as a vehicle of power is Richard D. Brown (1989) in his study of the social consequences of knowledge through information gathering. His book chronicles how men of all socioeconomic classes used information to advance themselves in the new Republic. He sees the growth and development of printing in the Republic from the 18th into the 19th centuries as offering opportunity for the individual "to discover his or her own coherent culture from within the galaxy of religious sects, political parties, and reform societies that were thriving" (p. 296). This stood in contrast to the "common, coherent Christian culture" of earlier times, in which elite white men had a lock on information through their monetary advantages, which allowed them the luxury of wide print information sources.

While Brown acknowledges that women in the mid-nineteenth century could, even though "gender was an important boundary," read widely, women still were limited regarding literacy:

> The most important factors limiting [women's literacy] choices, however, were not social prescriptions, but the actual circumstances of their lives.... [T]hey did not enjoy much leisure time. Where they did have options, the choices they made reveal that the information they sought related to their own lives; so they seldom regarded their exclusion from large categories of "male" information as troublesome. (1989, p. 283)

Brown here seems not to see that "social prescriptions" may have had some connection with the "actual circumstances" of women's lives. Perhaps inadvertently, he illustrates how literacy (and writing about literacy) can produce and reproduce restrictions and inequalities. Through his assumption that what men do with literacy *is* literacy, his presentation replicates stereotypic understandings of 19th-century literacy and gender by keeping women's experiences relatively invisible. How he knows that women did not regard their exclusion from males sources of information—and thus power—to be a problem, he does not explain.

If knowledge is power, as both Brown (1989) and the literacy myth would have it, were the young "literate" women above—Eliza Wright Osborne, Martha (Pattie) Mott Lord, and Rebecca Yarnall—troubled by "their exclusion from large categories of 'male' information"? Were they excluded? Did they have access to any avenues of political, economic, and cultural power? Did access to literacy lead to access to avenues of power?

By continuing to devote the same kind of time to women's literacy practices as Brown and others have devoted to men's, it may well be possible to come to appreciate how women might have felt or been influenced (or how literacy might have been affected, as Hobbs notes) by such vital exclusions. Furthermore, if "the meaning and contribution of literacy ... cannot be *presumed* ... [but] must themselves be a distinct focus of research and criticism" (Graff, 1987, p. 5), feminist researchers must continue to push harder on literacy's gendered aspects. And they have. Before addressing issues of exclusion and access to culture, it is important to have shared understandings of definitional issues and issues of literacy rates and how these reveal societal values. Literacy and value are inseparable concepts.

Literacy and Women: Definitions, Rates, and Values

Defining literacy is, of course, somewhat of a national pasttime, more often contentious than illuminating, and always reflecting the bias of the definer. Graff opens his 1987 history, *The Legacies of Literacy*, with several key quotations from a range of reputable scholars to show the word's multiple uses and understandings. His plea is for a consistent definition across times and contexts that will help discussions of literacy and literacy practices, not confound them. While Graff stresses the need for a stable definition of literacy to hold across time and space, his definition requires a focus on the "*primary levels of reading and writing*" (p. 3, original emphasis). Such a requirement, while certainly a necessary aspect of many discussions of literacy, could stand as an impediment to other discussions.

Central to the work of many current theorists of literacy are postmodern understandings that question the received truths and binary oppositions[6] of the 18th and 19th centuries. Davidson, Graff, and Street view literacy not as an autonomous set of skills to be defined once and for all but rather as a complex fluidity that can only be understood within a specific, historic context. Central, too, to feminist research from its awakenings in the 1960s and 1970s is a deep suspicion of what Jean-Francois Lyotard (1984) calls the "grand narrative." It has now burrowed into our consciousness to question sweeping generalizations that proclaim transcendent truths.

Rather, there is what Myra Jehlen (1981) in a much referenced article has called the Archimedean dilemma. Somewhat like Archimedes who never found a place from which to use his lever, so "feminists questioning the presumptive order of both nature and history—and thus proposing to remove the ground under their feet—would appear to need an alternative base" (p. 576). Taking the womanist 19th-century novel as her base for discussion, Jehlen finds only "points of contradiction . . . where we can see the whole structure of our world most clearly implies the immanent relativity of all perception and knowledge" (pp. 600–601). On the verge of this "shaping something like a new epistemology" (p. 601), she concludes her article. Profoundly affected by this broad shifting toward a postmodern perspective, literacy studies are now more inclusive, seeking, through what Lyotard calls "little narratives" (1984, p. 60; see also Daniell, 1999), truths, not truth! Implicated deeply in the discourses of power relations, literacy can no longer be labeled as the "high and low" (Miller, 1998), "the oral and the literate" (Street, 1995), but rather needs to be viewed as context-dependent, rooted in culture, and freighted with the political, to be explored, not defined, *in situ.*

Many literacy theorists had, on the cusp of the postmodern and perhaps leading the way, reached consensus regarding literacy as irreducibly social, embedded within language. As early as 1981 for Sylvia Scribner and Michael Cole in their very important work, literacy took its meanings only within particular contexts. For qualitative researcher Robert C. Bogdan (1982), "literacy—the practice of it, the study of it, how we think about it, what we do with it, how it is taught, and its creation—is social through and through" (p. 4). As a social construction it is interactional; is a characteristic that says as much about the definers as those being labeled; is self-defined by individuals through their interactions with others; is political; is situational, having "particular meaning in particular contexts"; and finally, has a moral meaning (Bogdan, pp. 9–12).

Rates: Numbers and Meanings

Literacy discussions have often begun with considerations of literacy rates. From the 1840 census, we know, according to Graff (1987), that "a strikingly low national level of illiteracy (9 percent) was reported" (p. 342). The illiteracy rates for New York and Pennsylvania were even lower, 4 and 5 percent, respectively. The 1850 census, where male and female literacy rates were tallied separately, shows for the Middle Atlantic states a disparity of three percentage points between that of males and females and a somewhat lower disparity in the 1860 census. Catherine Hobbs (1995), in her review of the literacy data,[7] states that "even the most helpful studies ... do not treat gender as a central factor in literacy" (p. 11).

Cathy N. Davidson (1986), in her study of novels and reading communities of the early Republic, which does *not* slight the literacy experiences of women, points to how little we really know (and by extension, how little we are saying) when we use just rates and numbers in discussions of literacy:

> Literacy is not simply the ability to decode letters upon a page, the ability to sign a name instead of making a mark. Literacy is a value. In a democracy especially, literacy becomes almost a matter of principle, a test of the moral fiber of a nation.... In Benjamin Nelson's phrase, literacy is "the social basis of cultural belief and value systems." It is not simply a "rate," a "measurement," but a vital aspect of culture, inseparable from its educational systems and values, its larger goals and aspirations, its meaning and definition of itself. To say that women's literacy was only 50 percent or even 75 percent of that of men's is to say something about the principles upon which a new nation was based. (pp. 58–59)

Linda K. Kerber (1980), too, writing about literacy in the early Republic, notes the moral and social significance of any differences that exist in literacy rates between men and women as well as the difference between speaking of literacy as merely the ability to sign one's name or as a critical tool of assessment:

> These disparities in literacy [between men and women] from the basic ability to sign one's name and to read simple prose to the sophisticated ability to read difficult or theoretical prose ... have enormous implications for the history of the relations between the sexes. (p. 193)

For Davidson as for Bogdan as for Kerber, for Hobbs, and as for Graff, *passim*, literacy discussions, even those of seemingly "neutral" topics such as rate, have moral dimensions and implications.

Beyond Rates to the Role of the Literacy Myth

By the first few decades of the 19th century, in the name of Republican motherhood (Cott, 1977; Kerber, 1980), educational opportunities for women had improved, as more or less reflected in their literacy rates. But such rates by themselves do not reveal much about literacy as a practice, a technology for use in relation to the cultural, economic, political world. Nor do rates tell us what meaning literacy had in their lives, a point Catherine Hobbs (1995) highlights in her introduction to *Nineteenth-Century Women Learn to Write*:

> The history of women's struggle for literacy, especially advanced practices of literacy that assume text production, has only begun to be written.... Our knowledge would be enriched if we understood the value of literacy to women's lives and how they felt about their reading and writing. (pp. 1–2)

It is interesting to note that Hobbs, in her edited volume focusing on 19th-century women's writing, although well aware of the ideological aspects of literacy practices, still uses language that suggests that the hopes embedded in the literacy myth still abide. In other words, what has been termed the literacy myth still seems to be an inescapable aspect of literacy discussions in spite of all the postmodern revisionism embedded in most recent literacy studies. Davidson contrasts "formal education [which] almost necessarily institutionalizes social hierarchies" (1986, p. 65), with "the vital movement throughout the new nation of self education" (p. 65): For Davidson, "True literateness ... ideally entails increased autonomy. With access to the world of books, the reader can choose among different authorities and take them according to the reader's evaluation of their worth" (p 69). She questions whether this ideal is ever fully met in a capitalist society, but still leaves open the possibility. This doubled-natured aspect of literacy is the mark of its Graffian "complexities and contradictions."

Writing before the publication of Graff's *The Legacies of Literacy* (1987), Carl F. Kaestle (1985) wrote:

> The uses of literacy have not been the subject of much historical study, but obviously they are various. Princeton historian Lawrence Stone once remarked that if you teach a man to read the Bible, he may also read pornography or seditious literature; put another way, if you teach a woman to read so that she may know her place, she may learn that she deserves yours. (p. 34)

Kaestle follows this remark with an understanding akin to Graff's: "These are the Janus faces of literacy" (p. 34). Hobbs (1995), too, comments on this aspect of literacy using the metaphor of the "'double-edged sword' [which] acknowledges that literacy can be used for social control yet suggests that it also has the tendency to become private and idiosyncratic, veering off in unexpected and unsettling directions" (p. 10).

By invoking Janus, the Latin deity with two faces, Kaestle appears to share Graff's understandings of literacy as replete with contradictions and complexities. Have literate women taken men's place? Did (indeed, do) equal literacy rates ensure the same measure of equality? According to Graff, literacy has not even in "the present with virtually universal literacy produced a truly egalitarian society." In fact, in contradiction to perceived wisdom, it has seemed to have "served to exacerbate inequalities" (1987, pp. 383–384). Yet the myth holds that literacy is a tool, the possession of which will confer equality of power. If literacy rates for women had increased from the 18th to the 19th century to the point where they were essentially the "equal" of men's, was there an accompanying increase in their political opportunities? Did their increased literacy grant women equality of power in their communities? Access to political power?

Rates and Equality of Power

Regarding this central issue of women and power through literacy, Catherine Hobbs (1995) asks rhetorically: "Have women who gained equal literacy shared equally in these rewards or have they been taken in by 'the myth' of literacy?" (p. 2). She highlights ways the literacy myth might have acted upon women's writings in the 19th century and then, like most of us, finds it impossible not to fall for it:

> Throughout the century, women's texts ... reflect the aspiration that achieving literacy would bring economic gain, social status, freedom, or suffrage, and would surely construct a more ethical society. These hopes, part of an ideology of literacy, endure in some form today, yet the history of women's achievement in literacy and its meaning and consequences for us are not fully understood. (p. 2)

This question that Hobbs asks regarding literacy's role as an avenue to equality of reward is one that has often been posed by feminist historians who have long noted, of course, that equality was not the condition of most women. In her biography of Catharine Beecher, Kathryn Kish Sklar (1976) wrote:

> Along with an absolute loss of economic status, and a relative loss of political status [that accompanied the transfer of economic production from the home to the factory], women ... experienced an absolute loss of personal autonomy during the middle decades of the nineteenth century. (p. 194)

Sklar goes on to cite Carroll Smith-Rosenberg's (1972) observation that, during this same period, "rigid dependency roles for women ... enclosed them in a circle of paralyzed potentiality" (p. 195). In their work on the social construction of families, Mary P. Ryan (1981) and Stephanie Coontz (1988) paint the same picture of this enclosure of mid-19th-century women into the home, although some more recent studies (Hansen, 1994; Kelly, 1999; Motz, 1996) paint a picture of more active involvement in societal affairs, making larger claims regarding women's activities and their impact in the "public" sphere.

Commenting on the enclosure of women, Joan B. Landes (1988), in her text *Women and the Public Sphere in the Age of the French Revolution*, raises an interesting paradox: that the rise of urban cultural institutions that "were all distinctive products of a swelling verbal and written culture" (p. 39) did not "seem to have resulted in a situation of gender equality. To the contrary, . . . forces that would eventually limit women's access to public speech and power were already under way" (p. 41). Landes connects literacy and power in a way antithetical to the literacy myth: "The new print culture was a major factor contributing to the constitution of a way of life that featured the restricted family domain and focused attention on the interior landscape of the privatized individual subject" (p. 61). Even Richard D. Brown (1989), although his *Knowledge is Power* is focused on the personal literacy experiences of men, makes the same observation about the American literacy picture of the 1850s: "Gender roles circumscribed the cultural enfranchisement of women that female literacy and the general encouragement of women's reading and voluntary associations fostered" (p. 193).

Thus, there is a paradox here: the middle-class women who appeared to be withdrawing into the home were, according to literacy rates and other evidence, more able readers and writers than those of previous generations. Indeed, the increased ability to read, as well as the increased leisure of these middle-class women, helped to fuel the publishing industry of the mid-19th century (Baym, 1978, 1984; Coultrap-McQuin, 1990; Douglas, 1977; Kaestle, 1985; Kelley, 1984), although Zboray (1993, p. 191) cautions against simplistic reading of the data that do not take into account the diversity of texts available to readers. Yet, according to Ryan and others, the increased literacy rates did not appear to encourage wider public engagement for many if not most women, as the literacy myth might suggest would occur. More recent feminist scholarship, however, makes stronger claims regarding literacy's role in enlarging women's engagement with a wider world, again with Zboray noting the regional nature of literacy rates (p. 134).

DIFFERING VIEWS

More Celebratory Claims Akin to the "Literacy Myth"

In line with the new cultural history that "wander[s] through the archives" (to use Robert Darnton's words [1985, p. 4]), these more recent studies, which have women's literacy practices as their focus, use women's private writings in attempting to see how literacy operates within specific historic contexts for those whose works and lives have not previously been privileged. Interestingly, many of these studies of (mostly) 19th-century women are united in seeing literacy more in its liberatory than constraining mode.

Mary Kelley (1996), for example, in a well-argued, richly documented article, "Reading Women/Women Reading: The Making of Learned Women in Antebellum America," reconstructs from archival "tracings,"[8] the reader-responses of several late 18th- to mid-19th-century women. The reading of these mostly high-born, white women is seen by Kelley as personally transformative for them, a vehicle through which "they constructed an alternative possibility" (p. 403), "self-fashioning"[9] themselves into learned women.

Ronald J. and Mary Saracino Zboray (1999) also make use of the concept of self-fashioning in their "'Month of Mondays': Women's Reading Diaries and the Everyday Transcendental." For the Zborays:

> [Women's] reading materials not only transported women into the public arena of politics, philosophy, social issues, and cultural production, but the public world of letters addressed, and ultimately transformed those private, domestic spaces as well. (p. 7)

In his earlier full study of print and reading in the antebellum period, Zboray (1993) argues that for the antebellum woman—and man—the act of reading became a necessary process of self-construction as the older relationships of work, transportation, family, and so on, were under extreme pressure. Only through their reading could Americans gain a "mastery over an increasingly uncertain social environment" (p. 130).

Like Mary Kelley and the Zborays, Catherine E. Kelly (1999), in her study also of women of predominantly high-born status, *In the New England Fashion: Reshaping Women's Lives in the Nineteenth Century,* sees literacy—both reading and writing practices—as unequivocally empowering:

> In both its public and private forms writing allowed women to articulate their experiences just as it allowed them to articulate the meaning of those experiences. But it also allowed them to define themselves as thinkers whose conscious and unconscious decisions about subject matter and language testify

> to their intellectual engagement with the world around them. Letters and
> diaries, friendship books and commonplace books, schoolgirl essays and
> published poetry marked women as writers, as readers, as participants in a
> community of letters. (p. 7)

For Kelly, her archival "sources offer an intellectual history of people who
were not intellectuals in any canonical sense" (p. 7). It is her contention
and the subject of her significant, carefully documented study that "provincial women constructed urban change and rural continuity" (p. 7).

Similarly positing a celebratory view of women's literacy practices, Marilyn Ferris Motz, in "The Private Alibi: Literacy and Community in the Diaries of Two Nineteenth-Century Women,"[10] asks two important questions:
"How did literate people negotiate the relationship between what they
read and what they experienced?" and "How did they bridge the gulf
between public and private, individual and communal, universal and particular, global and local, political and personal?" (1996, p. 189). Arguing
against a view of woman as "bound by the limits of the domestic sphere" (p.
189), she explores the literacy practices of two women—one from the same
generation as the young women of this study and one from the succeeding
generation—"who were not passive consumers of culture or inheritors of
ideas but were critics and commentators" (p. 191) and even "agents of
change in their communities" (p. 202).

Motz (1996) writes: "Far from being isolated and provincial, these
women used that most private form, the diary, to establish themselves as citizens of the world" (p. 191). And "through their reading, the two women
were introduced to new ideas [and thus] the potential existed for them to
apply these ideas to their own lives and their own communities" (p. 202).
Motz concedes, however, that both women of her study were "expected to
hide their erudition from their associates" (p. 194). She concludes her
essay on a positive note: "In accepting and embracing the marginality of
their status, they were able to transcend the boundaries of their communities" (p. 206).

Thus, from their archival material of women's writing and their offerings regarding their own reading of these writings, these creative and careful scholars have presented their cases for literacy's transformative powers
as well as its (presumed) power to connect women with the public sphere.
It is important, however, not to assume that for *all* 19th-century women,
even taking into account only the high-born, reading and writing practices
serve as equivalent experiences. Not all contexts have been nor are currently created equal!

More Cautionary Views

Earlier researchers such as Ann Douglas (1977) and Felicity A. Nussbaum (1988, 1989) took a markedly darker view of women's reading and writing practices, arguing that such practices could be viewed—and they make convincing cases, too[11]—as practices that actually reproduced societal inequalities. Jane P. Tompkins (1985) and Susan K. Harris (1990) using historic contexts, and Janice A. Radway (1984) within a contemporaneous setting, all make significant observations and arguments regarding women's literacy practices and the power of those practices for the betterment of the readers' and writers' lives, but their claims are rooted in an understanding of women's social and political enclosure. For these researchers, the women of their study used the very material of their boundedness to enrich their lives and provide for the longed-for activity of mind.

Thus, we can see two stances, the first marked by the celebratory (Kelley, 1996; Kelly, 1999; Motz, 1996; Zboray & Zboray, 1999), which often makes quite large claims akin to the "literacy myth," relative to how women were able to negotiate their unequal status through their literacy practices to gain ground in the wider world. The second stance (Douglas, 1977; Harris, 1990; Nussbaum, 1988, 1989; Tompkins, 1985) clearly recognizes (and celebrates in its own ways) how women were able, through their own reading and writing practices, to enrich and enlarge their daily lives. Yet, these researchers are still cognizant of the impact and influence of the political and social strictures of the times. That feminist analysts might wend their way between these two stances serves to affirm one of Graff's central points: Throughout history, complexity and contradiction have been literacy's handmaidens. Only through detailed attention to specific Graffian historical contexts can we make claims. Even then, we must be careful: Women are not, to use Sandra Harding's words, "unitary" but rather are "multiple, heterogeneous, and contradictory or [even!] incoherent" (1993, p. 65). Thus, where some researchers see liberatory aspects to the literacy practices of the women they study, others may legitimately see more restrictive patterns for the role(s) played by literacy in the lives of the women of their own historically situated study.

CONTEXTING READING AND WRITING

Clearly, for the past 30 years, feminist researchers, whether making larger or smaller claims relative to the "literacy myth," have stressed the utter importance of women's literacy practices as part of their centuries-old struggle to gain autonomy, to have power over their existence, to be subjects—not objects.

Embedded in many of the novels written to be read by women, as noted above, was encouragement of women's literacy through acquiring education. According to Nina Baym (1978):

> Almost all the heroines of this fiction were devoted to books and hungry for formal education. The woman authors saw cultivation of the mind as the great key to freedom, the means by which women, learning to think about their situation, could learn how to master it. Like Benjamin Franklin before them and Malcolm X after them, they saw literacy as the foundation of liberation. (p. 31)

Cathy N. Davidson (1986), too, notes of the earlier fiction of her study, its insistence on the educational import of women's reading. The very novels that women read, according to her, encouraged women to better themselves through education. Moreover, writing was part of this education: "The female reader was also assured [in the early American novel] that writing—and writing well—was a virtue; an unblemished prose style was as proper to a would-be heroine as a spotless reputation or a winsome smile" (p. 73).

In her key article on 19th-century writing instruction previously cited, Shirley Brice Heath (1981) posited that the young women of the period, limited in their educational opportunities, helped one another become better letter writers. Davidson (1986), drawing on Heath's work, quotes from British Sunday School leader and moralist Hannah More, who wrote in 1799:

> "Copy well!" Hannah More admonished her readers.... She observed: "Ladies, though they have never been taught a rule of syntax, yet, by a quick facility in profiting from the best books and the best company, hardly ever violate one; and ... often exhibit an elegant and perspicuous arrangement of style, without having studied any of the laws of composition." (p. 74)

Davidson shares, too, a quotation from a 1797 letter in which one Margaret Smith, writing to a younger sister, suggests her sister write often to improve her writing skills and "'constantly read ... elegant writing'" (1986, p. 74). By copying selections from their reading, intense practice in writing itself, and by wide reading of "elegant writing," young women could learn how to become better writers.

Recapping Reading and the Literacy Myth

Barbara Finkelstein, in her 1979 essay, "Reading, Writing, and the Acquisition of Identity in the United States: 1790–1860," makes the assumption that literacy in and of itelf can be liberatory, at least for high-born women of the 19th century (though her arguments are much more subtle and complex for the urban poor and for slaves and former slaves). She writes: "For students who learned to read and write in schools, the process of acquiring literacy was not as unequivocally liberating as it was for the very rich [while not rich, the young women of the Wright/Mott/Osborne correspondence were "high born"] and the very lowly" (p. 132). But her description of how literacy was "unequivocally liberating" for women of the upper classes raises questions:

> For the progeny of the high-born, the acquisition of literacy involved them in an exclusive domestic and social circle, in which was reflected and advanced a distinctive sort of social presence. For this group, the acquisition of literacy and the manipulation of words and ideas proceeded simultaneously. As they learned to read and write, they were required to cultivate the capacity to retrieve the written word, and to place it in the service of social and political persuasion and subjective imagination. (p. 132)

Up to this point, Finklestein does not make any distinctions regarding possible differential treatment between males and females, but when she does, she calls attention to a problem:

> Required to practice the arts of criticizing, arguing, persuading, and exhorting, in close proximity to their parents, high-born male children were learning how to acquire influence, and to keep it. High-born female children were learning the delights of escape into literature. (p. 132)

"Learning the delights of escape into literature" and "learning how to acquire influence and keep it ... through the manipulation of ideas ... and the arts of criticizing, arguing, persuading, and exhorting" do not possess equal weight. Intertwined with the literacy myth are claims regarding literacy's cognitive benefits (e.g., Scribner & Cole, 1981). Certainly "criticizing, arguing, persuading, and exhorting" would tend to do more for stretching intellect than "escaping into literature." Also citing Hannah More is Sidonie Smith (1992) in her article "Resisting the Gaze of Embodiment":

> [Women] seem not to possess in equal measure the faculty of comparing, combining, analyzing, and separating ... ideas; that deep and patient thinking which goes to the bottom of a subject; nor that power of arrangement which knows how to link a thousand connected ideas in one dependent train, without losing sight of the original idea. (p. 82)

Is it possible that reading for women—what they did with it and through it; how they were taught it; the messages they derived from it—could be reproducing gender inequalities by foreclosing avenues of power through focusing women's attention on "escape" rather than on what are considered "higher" levels of cognitive processing—analyzing, comparing, synthesizing? The importance of studying these sources of influences upon young women and girls, both from relatives and teachers as well as from their own reading, has been suggested by Joan N. Burstyn (1985) and, in fact "is crucial for historians if they are to understand the impact of ideology on the individual" (p. 61).

Because sources of reading can be so influential in the construction and understanding of the self—otherwise, the moral exponents of the day would not have had to warn against novel reading—it has been important for this study of young women's literacy to trace and contextualize the reading materials noted by the Wright/Mott/Osborne young women. The reading that they record has been traced to information sources for publication data and genre type and then explicated upon, drawing from many of the feminist sources above as well as others compatible with a social-constructivist perspective. While Burstyn (1985) warns of the difficulty of detecting the influence of didactic literature upon young girls, she also suggests the importance of undertaking such a search. And Carl F. Kaestle (1983), too, warns that it is one thing to note the directives inherent in didactic literature and another to know if people followed its decrees.

Recapping Writing and the Literacy Myth

Just as in reading, so in writing: Relative to the literacy myth, huge claims have often been made for what writing can do for people. Its role in the rise of civilization and modernization has long been noted (e.g., Goody, 1987; Graff, 1987). At a more personal level, Jacqueline Jones Royster (1990), writes: "Knowledge is indeed power. In our day and time, literacy is indeed power. It allows us ... to write ourselves into being" (p. 107). She writes convincingly regarding the role of literacy abilities, noting, for example, that while Sojourner Truth "was not literate enough to read 'such small stuff as letters,' ... she was able to see what was there and not there, to grapple with complex situations, and to emerge as a rational and capable thinker" (p. 107). Royster[12] names black women as "interpreters and articulators of experiences" of their people. They "looked at the world, saw what was there and not there, were articulate about their visions of reality, and worked tirelessly to get things done that they thought would bring their ideals to life" (p. 108). She highlights the role of writing in the lives of these women:

> They used their writing to appreciate the people and the world around them,
> to discover personal identity by race and gender, to define and label relation-

ships, to address sociocultural issues, to respond to power and to offer solutions to pressing problems. (p. 108)

More recently, Marilyn Ferris Motz (1996), too, finds in the "private" writings of the two 19th-century women of her study avenues of critique in which these women used their diaries "to create themselves on paper, establishing themselves as citizens of the world" (p. 191). Yet, even as Motz makes these large claims, she also reveals how these women—in ways that also echo through the lives and letters of the Wright/Mott/Osborne women— "were constrained by the limitations placed on them by societal expectations . . . and by the [narrow] range of activities open to them" (p. 190).

Catherine E. Kelly (1999) also makes large claims regarding writing— that it allowed them "to articulate their experiences just as it allowed them to articulate the meaning of those experiences" (p. 7). She goes even further, suggesting that their writing in letters and diaries "also allowed them to define themselves as thinkers whose conscious and unconscious decisions about subject matter and language testify to their intellectual engagement with the world around them" (p. 7).

Interestingly, Pam Gilbert and Sandra Taylor (1991), the authors of *Fashioning the Feminine*, did not detect writing's liberatory possibilities in the young women of their study. Rather, in illustrating a piece by a 10-year-old girl that was "drawn rather obviously from a predictable generic formula" (p. 118), they observed how the "girl writer is trapped within traditional generic frames [with] . . . no speaking position of authority available to her, no alternative discourses which offer her other [i.e., nonformulaic] ways of constructing gendered subjects." Moreover, they continue, "she does not yet know how to write 'as a woman'—or at least a woman constructed and positioned by discourses other than romantic ideology" (p. 119). Woman's writing has, of course, traditionally been devalued. In a phrase that prefigures an important theme of our Chapter 6, "Writing Well: In Search of the 'Particular'," one of the school-age writers mentioned by Gilbert and Taylor spoke of her decision to write "as a man" (p. 120). The question of what constitutes "woman's writing" is a key issue in this study of the Wright/Mott/Osborne young women.

REGARDING GENDER AND WRITING

At the core of this study of the letter writing of the Wright/Mott/Osborne young women, and the knowledge regarding literacy that it can yield, is the concept of gender. In her book-length, eponymous study of a piece of writing, "The Tidy House," by a small group of working-class little girls, Carolyn Kay Steedman (1977) avers: "Every instinct possessed by those who grew up in the culture that produced 'The Tidy House,' insists that it must have been written by little girls and that it could never have been written by little boys" (p. 135). With this statement, she signals the crucial impact of gender in both the writing of a text as well as in any subsequent analysis of that text.

In this study, as we read the letters written by the Wright/Mott/Osborne young women, we will examine the impact of gender, to see, as did Steedman, whether the letters could only have been penned by women. Will "every instinct …insist that [these letters] must have been written by [women] and that [they] could never have been written by [men]?" To argue that the Wright/Mott/Osborne letters may be unmistakable productions of women is not necessarily to take Helen Heineman's (1983) "essentializing" view of letter writing: "Letters had always been more a female form than a male form of expression" (p. 64). Such a broad statement that seeks to explain differences in letter writing by the accident of the biology of sex needs to be questioned. It is interesting to note in this connection that at least three men of the family consciously tried to write a letter in the same form that the women wrote everyday. Is it possible to mark writing as by one gender or another? More theoretical than Steedman and drawing upon the work of Hélène Cixous (Cixous & Clément, 1986)—who boldly states there *is* such a thing as woman's writing—is the work of Patricia Francis Cholakian (1991). In her analysis of the *Heptaméron* of Marguerite de Navarre, she suggests that it is "women's desire to be defined as 'subjects'" that shapes woman's writing (p. 3).

PURPOSES

Woman's experience within any historic period is hardly a mirror of man's. Neither is her connection to literacy. To be able to see how—or if—the literacy myth plays itself out, along with Graff's conceptions of its continuities and contradictions, it is important to have a more detailed look at a "precise and specific historic context" that takes seriously women's reading as well as their actual writing productions. Carroll Smith-Rosenberg (1975/1985) testifies to her own historiographic milestone: "I ceased to look in men's writing for the truth of women's experience" (p. 72). It is, thus, important to understand gender within a particular context, of what it means culturally in a given setting at a given time to be of one sex rather than the other. This difference, according to feminists, is a crucial one, without a deep understanding of which the substance and meaning of women's lives—as well as gendered phenomena such as literacy—cannot be understood.

The entire Osborne Family Papers provide a rich opportunity for a study of 19th-century woman's writing, the encoding of her own literacy. The

bulk of the carefully preserved collection of over 350 boxes contains primarily the wide-ranging correspondence of prison reformer Thomas Mott
Osborne (1859–1923), the son of Eliza Wright Osborne and David Munson
Osborne. It also includes the correspondence of Eliza Wright Osborne's
lawyer-father, David Wright, as well as that of her industrialist husband. The
Osborne Family Papers also include, although relatively little noted in the
finding aid, hundreds of letters to and from the women of the family. What
makes this collection a powerful tool for literacy analysis is that the materials in it range from the 1820s to the 1950s. Moreover, somewhere deep in
the family consciousness was an impulse to preserve not only their own correspondence (a relatively obvious form to save), but to keep, as well, many
notes, scraps of children's writings, account books, school advertisements,
and invitations. The materials offer both breadth and depth for a study of
young women's literacy.

Therefore, the purpose of this study is to look at this crucial intersection of literacy and gender in the lives of these mid-19th-century young
women, especially as this intersection relates to issues of power and gender construction (and constriction), first by seeing what meaning literacy
had in their lives, and second, by developing a context of understandings
(as will be explicated in the next chapter, "Reading the Writing of 'The
Particular': A Methodology") around the body of the correspondence
from which the opening elusive, suggestive, and "literate" reading and
writing selections came.

Because literacy is a significant vehicle of socialization (Berger & Luckmann, 1966; Finklestein, 1979; Gilbert & Taylor, 1991), understanding literacy's role and meaning in these young women's lives can provide a
means to see how they perceived themselves through their reading and
writing as well as how they may have been influenced by the discourses of
their day that maintained the doctrine of separate spheres. It is at these
critical but elusive junctures that literacy's meaning, as tending toward the
liberatory or restrictive, can be observed. The goal is to speculate about literacy and women's lives in the mid-19th century; to see in this context
"what literacy can and cannot do for people" (Graff, 1987). Finally, it will
be important to see not only what and/or if literacy enables, but also if the
acts and practices of literacy may actually dis-enable the very capable young
women literacy practitioners of the Wright/Mott/Osborne family.

In line with studies that are now doing just what he called for, Harvey J.
Graff (1987) advises that for understanding literacy "the main effort [is]
reconstructing the contexts of reading and writing" (p. 4). He says that the
step "into precise, historically specific materials and cultural contexts" (p.
4) is a large one. Before entering into the materials and cultural contexts
that help make up the reading and writing processes and practices of the
young Wright/Mott/Osborne women, a methodological discussion is nec-

essary in order to locate this study within the new cultural history and other meaning-based approaches; highlight this study's interdisciplinary nature; discuss what makes a relevant context; connect gender and "technologies of literacy"; and finally, outline the procedures followed in entering the world of the Wright/Mott/Osborne young (and not so young) women.

We then step into their times and their reading and their writing to ask with Catherine Hobbs (1995, p. 3) not only "How did literacy affect women?" but also "How did women affect literacy?"

NOTES

1. Housed in the Special Collections Research Center at Syracuse University and the main archival source of the letters and documents of this study.

2. "Hawthorne to William D. Ticknor, January 1855, quoted in Ticknor (1913, pp. 141–142)." This reference is owed to Mary Kelley, 1984, p. 345, fn. 2, with thanks.

3. This is not surprising as they have both taught with Geertz at Princeton.

4. And will be taken up again in Chapter 7, "'Fixed Very Nicely Indeed!': A Focus on Gender."

5. Subtitled *Continuities and Contradictions in Western Culture and Society.*

6. And which, as Linda Brodkey (1996) avers, always imply a negative evaluation.

7. For which she uses Lee Soltow and Edward Stevens's careful work of 1981, *The Rise of Literacy and the Common School in the United States, a Socioeconomic Analysis to 1870.*

8. A term and approach Kelley credits to Roger Chartier (Hunt, 1989).

9. A concept attributed to Renaissance scholar Stephen Greenblatt (1980).

10. An intriguing and very useful concept, The Private Alibi, as set forth by Motz, was any cover women could use to hide their own intellectual needs or pursuits, for example, using local political concerns to divert attention away from their national or even international interests (p. 204).

11. As will be seen in Chapters 4, 6, and 7.

12. Making use of Joseph Williams's definition of critical thinking just as I made good use (unconsciously) of Roysters' "to write ourselves into being" (p. 107) for my title.

CHAPTER 3

READING THE WRITING OF "THE PARTICULAR": A METHODOLOGY

I ceased to look for the meanings of women's lives in men's writing.

Carroll Smith-Rosenberg (1975/1985)

"Tell us your topics, your calls, your domestic arrangements, we want to know everything," wrote Lucretia Coffin Mott to a family member (Bacon, 1980, p. 156) in the mid-19th century. This directive of abolitionist, Quaker minister, feminist, mother to Pattie Mott (Lord) and aunt to both Eliza Wright (Osborne) and Rebecca Yarnall of our introductory chapters, echoed through the years and became integral to the family's understanding of itself. Written for the most part by the women of the family, young and old, the letters' role in providing women of the 19th century with deep bonds of comfort and support was articulated by Carroll Smith-Rosenberg (1975/1985) almost 30 years ago and verified over and over in the Wright/Mott/Osborne correspondence.

Letter upon letter, year after year, Lucretia Coffin Mott's command was granted. The young women of the family were instructed in the genre and supported one another in learning, perfecting, and practicing the family form just as Shirley Brice Heath has suggested (1981). What was both

Reading and Writing Ourselves into Being, pages 51–81

prized and praised in the letters was "the particular"—that singular detail that both informed and delighted. A favorite and frequently used family word, each and every "particular," the everyday detail, was sought eagerly, and even demanded, becoming both directions for writing and an organizing text principle.

As their frequent and long letters to each other touched on the tangibles of so many aspects of their daily experiences, a study of such particulars offers a view into meanings of these young women's lives, as these meanings are inscribed—explicitly as well as implicitly—in their letters. Too, of course, the role of literacy as both carrier and subject of these meanings can be illuminated, as they were both avid readers and frequent letter writers. Through such study, it is possible to probe deeply into the lives and meanings of these young women for, inevitably encoded in their letters, is an avenue into their mid-19th-century world that can be decoded in the present.

The purpose of this chapter is three-fold. The first is to set forth the methodological implications for any feminist study of the existence and use of women's private documents as signaled in Carroll Smith-Rosenberg's powerful epigraph and developed so well since then by caring, knowing researchers such as Buss (1996), Hampsten (1982), Kelley (1996), Kitch (1993), Motz (1996), M. N. Smith (1992), Ulrich (1990), and Zboray and Zboray (1999).

A second purpose is to celebrate the interdisciplinary nature of such an undertaking and the often messy procedural means by which we come to understood these young women's literacy productions and practices. From these means, feminist modes of reading are highlighted. Concomitant issues of gender and power and gender and culture are addressed as well.

Third, the nature and selection of contexts of understanding are undertaken to appreciate the embedded meanings and effects their literacy practices might have had on these young women. Finally, a review of the procedures of this study are outlined. We then move on to the four chapters that focus on the selected specific contexts, melding research and data for an understanding of the meanings of the "particulars."

LITERACY: CARRIER OF MEANINGS, VEHICLE FOR QUESTIONS

Literacy as cultural phenomenon—the very political processes and practices of reading and writing as well as their multiple and specific contexts—is backdrop, content, and carrier of meanings not only for its own study but for the study of its meaning(s) in a particular time and place. Hence, historian of literacy Harvey J. Graff (1987) often refers to its contradictions and complexities. For this study that has gender at its center, literacy may be thought as value and tool; vehicle and medium; a benefit but yet, too, a constraint, a delimiter, not necessarily as liberatory as the literacy myth as explicated in Chapter 2, "Wherein the Problem is Set," would have it. As feminist researchers have made abundantly clear over the past three decades, literacy practices—reading and writing—are instruments for the development of a gendered subjectivity. For women especially, the practices encoded in and via literacy may be seen to be instruments for limitations (Cholakian, 1991, 2000; Foucault, 1976; de Lauretis, 1987), although some more recent studies (Kelley, 1996; Kelly, 1999; Motz, 1996) highlight more liberating aspects of women's literacy proficiency and practices. These studies, too, are a larger frame of reference regarding "the spheres" within which women were allowed to operate.

As wide and frequent readers as well as frequent and proficient letter writers, the young, mid-19th-century women of this study—Eliza Wright (Osborne), Pattie Mott (Lord), Rebecca Yarnall—were very much immersed in, as well as participants of, the cultural activities of their times. They read the discourses of the day—textbooks, newspapers, journal articles. Most of these, of course, were freighted with the many moral strictures and guidelines that prescribed the "proper" behavior of young women of the time. Yet, the young women were also reading with appreciation (and critique) the much frowned-upon "romances" that feminist readers/theorists such as Susan K. Harris (1990) and Jane P. Tompkins (1985) have found to encode messages of liberation and survival.

At the same time that they were absorbing these conflicting messages through their reading practices, these young women were active creators of a cultural form of their own, a sustained correspondence that was both a source of intense satisfaction as well as the site of genuine labor. Not only a personal venture between one another, their letters were also a semi-public form, read aloud as the centerpiece of family gatherings both large and small (Bacon, 1980). Such cultural performances were very important for the nurturing of the families' sense of community, allowing for the maintenance and continuity of extended family networks as well as emotional sustenance (Smith-Rosenberg, 1975/1985).

What effect did the discourses of control of the culture at large—textbooks, sermons, the lectures of the day, etiquette books, gift books, letter-writing books, and even flower books (Petrino, 1998)—have upon these young Wright/Mott/Osborne women? How much room was there for them within these constructs that sought to create and maintain the mid-19th-century ideology of gender?

While there was contemporary debate about the content of the ideology (Helsinger, Sheets, & Veeder, 1983), the stretch was not infinite. As active users, creators, and absorbers of the print and symbolic orders, were these young women able to make/take room for themselves to construct a gendered self with expectations wider than that thought "proper" for the young women of the era as the literacy myth would have it? Or did they consider themselves citizens of the world, operating beyond the "separate spheres," as Hansen (1994), Kelley (1996), Kelly (1999), and Motz (1996) have recently suggested? Very much aware of the literacy history of their forebears and themselves schooled in the literacy practices of the family as set forth in Chapter 1, we can certainly assume that the Wright/Mott/ Osborne women were conscious of the significance of their reading and writing practices for the good of their entire family community. But did they consider themselves as having cultural power through these practices?

Such guiding questions, along with their uses, have been drawn from feminist historical studies such as Joan N. Burstyn's (1985) "Sources of Influence: Women as Teachers of Girls" and Ann Douglas's (1977) *The Feminization of American Culture* as well as feminist studies more specifically addressed to reading and writing issues. These latter studies are compatible with both the meaning-based methodology of symbolic interactionism (Bogdan, 1982; Taylor & Bogdan, 1984) as well as studies of the new cultural history (see Chapter 2), which have the reading of the documents of the previously "unheard" at their core. Such theorists include Buss (1996), Cholakian (1991), Davidson (1986), Hunt (1990), Landes (1988), Kelley (1996), Motz (1996), and M. N. Smith (1992).

The value of such questioning as a methodology is set forth well by Cholakian (1991) at the conclusion of her invaluable text, *Rape and Writing in the* Heptaméron *of Marguerite de Navarre.* She asks:

> Is it possible ... to articulate a theory or methodology for identifying feminine writing? I believe that it is, if the feminist scholar is willing to adopt an attitude rather than a set of rules. It is not possible to paste twentieth-century ideology on an older text or force it into a preconceived mold. It is better to begin with an open-ended set of questions. How does the writer portray women? How does the writer portray men? What ideas or themes does she dwell on? What does she leave out? What does she say about her own writing, her purposes, her difficulties? (p. 220)

Although specific to narrative texts, these "listening" questions (Michel, 1994) posed by Cholakian have proven invaluable for pushing upon the meanings embedded in the Wright/Mott/Osborne documents, for discerning their (and literacy's) gendered meanings in their letters. Furthermore, these questions suggest an outline for the emergence of a feminist mode for reading/understanding the unpublished documents created by the young women of our study, long a central preoccupation of feminist researchers.[1] To hear the meanings requires a special kind of listening, a special kind of reading.

DISCOVERING WOMEN'S WRITING(S)

The explosion of studies by and about women that occurred during the 1960s and 1970s was made possible and encouraged by the vast uncovering of private as well as published but forgotten writings of women that had been back-shelved in libraries, disparaged by literary critics, and forgotten in attics. Publishing hundreds of social, political, and personal documents of historical worth, Toni Cade Bambara (1970), Nancy F. Cott (1972), Gerda Lerner (1972, 1977), and Alice Rossi (1973) offered accessible sources for coming to know that women had a history and had helped to form "history." Andrea Hinding's (1979) still invaluable, prodigious listing of archival sources reinforced the message of the value of women's private documents.

In her preface to *Literary Women* (1976), an indexical offering of women's (mostly white) literary history, Ellen Moers ironically stated as her intention "to be useful to those whose principal work in life is making up the theories about and even prescribing directives for the female sex" (p. vi). But without bibliographic access to the range, substance, and chronology of literary writing by women and their indebtedness to one other, later work on the effect of these texts on women[2] would simply not have been possible.

"If ever there was a time which teaches that one must know the history of women to understand the history of literature it is now," wrote Moers (1976, p. xiii). Only a year later, Elaine Showalter's *A Literature of Their Own* (1977) showcased the continuities and links among and between British women novelists, "minor," and not so minor, to write another, yet differing history of the woman writer. All these reference works revealed the sheer amount of extant women's texts, literary and personal, thus forever giving the lie to histories and studies that would overlook the vast abundance of the writings of half the population.

Both implicitly and explicitly, these archaeologists of women's documentary and literary history understood that "business as usual" would not work. Showalter's "gynocritics" (1981), Cott's interdisciplinary approach to doing history (1977), Gilbert and Gubar's (1979) study of the anxiety of the woman writer[3]—all signaled how crucial new methodological approaches were. The works of women—personal, public, literary— needed modes of questioning, listening, and reading appropriate to the work and historical setting. Like innovative buildings, these new modes often needed to be devised on site to fit the individual works and their historical contexts.

It was Carroll Smith-Rosenberg (1975/1985) who heralds the need for these new approaches to understanding the meaning within women's documents. Her key enunciation: "I ceased to look for the meanings of women's lives in men's writings" still rings as a methodological epiphany. New cultural historian Lynn Hunt (1989) both celebrated and explicated Smith-Rosenberg's approach:

> The work of Carroll Smith-Rosenberg ... is exemplary of the ways in which women's or gender history can advance the history of culture as a style of investigation and writing. In [her] essays collected in the volume *Disorderly Conduct*, [she] brings to bear both anthropological and literary analysis. (p. 18)

Smith-Rosenberg calls attention to her use of literary analysis "using the dialectic between language as social mirror and language as social agent [for] my analysis" (1975/1985, p. 45). Cholakian (1991), too, stresses the interdisciplinary nature of the undertaking: Hearing the meanings of those who made no wars and ran no countries requires an eclectic and interdisciplinary methodology. So too this study. An amalgam of symbolic interactionism, anthropology, ethnography, literary analysis, historical documentation, and feminist critique, this literacy study is grounded in (a not particularly radical) postmodern understanding of the world. All these approaches are required to help us gain insights into the meanings in the letters and to address some of the many questions suggested by Cholakian (1991) and Burstyn (1985).

Reading as Feminist Methodology

The reading—the understanding—of women's private writings presents several challenges that feminist studies (such as the collected studies within *Inscribing the Daily: Critical Essays on Women's Diaries* [1996], edited by Suzanne L. Bunkers and Cynthia A. Huff) have helped to codify. Helen M. Buss (in "A Feminist Revision of New Historicism to Give Fuller Readings of Women's Private Writing" [1996], for example) lists among her theoretical needs "a reader-response theory that is grounded in a feminist ethic" (p. 88).

Placing herself within the new historicism that uses a more materialist vocabulary than the new cultural history but that shares the latter's goal of "breathing new life into formerly ignored texts" (1996, p. 86), Buss, like the New Cultural Historians, invokes Geertz's commitment to

> "thick description" in which an event or anecdote is "re-read ... in such a way as to reveal through the analysis of tiny particulars the behavioral codes, logics and motive forces controlling a whole society." (p. 86, citing Veeser, p. xi)

Buss notes her own intellectual training in the "close reading" techniques of the New Critics but finds them not helpful for the reading of archival documents (p. 86). These practices left me bereft of an adequate critical practice [whereas] "thick description" allows me to use my training to a different purpose, not to identify the markers of a literary consciousness, but to read the trace of a human person constructing her identity in her historical, social, cultural, and gendered place. (1996, p. 86)

Summarizing her methodology, Buss cites Elizabeth Hampsten's thoughtful *Read This Only to Yourself: The Private Writings of Mid-Western Women, 1880–1910* (1982). Buss writes of my

need for an interdisciplinary reading strategy [i.e, Geertz's "thick description"] and a refreshed critical vocabulary, my need for a poststructuralist reading strategy informed by a consciousness of the social power of language. (p. 88)

Buss (1996) shares how Hampsten's approach, attentive listening to the letter writings of the mid-western women of her study, "has taught me about new strategies of close reading with her advice on the 'inventive patience' needed in examining women's accounts" (p. 89). Indeed, Hampsten's work provides the ground for this study, too, suggesting as she does the "difference" (Cholakian, 1991) of women's writing and thus the requirement of a feminist mode of reading.

Buss, as do most students of women's private documents, calls attention to the issue of power:

When reading personal documents, an informed consciousness of the power systems that are operational [in a particular time and place] is essential. However, reading strategies that take into account language's double nature are also necessary. (1996, p. 99)

Buss stresses "language's ability to maximize some condition" to underline its value and languages' "ability to suppress and absent other conditions" (p. 99) as crucial for coming to understand women's private documents.

In her study, Hampsten (1982) marks one of the crucial differences between men's and women's private writings with the word "commodious." It is easier to enter into and "understand" what men are writing about because, so frequently, their writings are located within contexts that are already known to the reader—the lumber business, mining (and in the case of the Wright/Mott/Osborne correspondence, lawyering and manufacturing). On the other hand, an understanding of women's private writings is centered within a network of family relationships. Unless the family is well known publicly or known to the reader, much of what is being written about can be unclear because it involves an unknown network of kin and friends. To be successful in unraveling this network, the reader must first center herself within the relationships to be able to make sense of the writings.

For example, one of the first letters I encountered in the Osborne Family Papers was in a folder marked 1833. Although the finding aid of the collection had full and clear genealogical information, I was unable to make sense of the material in the letter because such understanding depended upon a recognition of patterns of kinship—wives and husbands; children and in-laws. As I proceeded through the correspondence, I came to see that the letter had been written in 1853, not 1833. With that knowledge, I was then able to unravel the pattern of relations to better understand the meanings within this letter.

A key point Hampsten (1982) makes throughout her study is the difficulty of entering into and understanding these private writings. Where the writings of men are based on what she calls the "principle of derring-do" (p. xi) and have, for the reader, a more readily understood public experience,

> the private writings of women ask of us ... a special inventive patience. We must interpret what is not written as well as what is.... "Nothing happened" asks that we wonder what, in the context of a particular woman's stream of days, she means by "something happening." (p. 4)

A thought Hampsten often repeats regarding the text she is sharing (and a thought I too have often and continue to have in this study) is her statement, "I would like to know more" (p. 13).

Over and over, in the writings of the women of her study, Hampsten (1982) detects a sense of self-effacement:

> What I have been looking for are passages that tell me what it is the writers have on their minds, and the quest has been difficult. So much of the writing gives the appearance of information ... without leaving a residue of something said. (p. 17)

Hampsten's plea "I want to know what it was like" (p. 17) speaks to this work, too. In fact, Hampsten's insights provide a way of pushing upon the content and modes for thinking about how the young Wright/Mott/Osborne women revealed the gendered nature of their lives through their writing.

These modes of feminist reading become our methodological tools, to be explicated in more detail throughout this chapter and connected to the many meaning-based approaches used. To hear the meanings requires that special kind of listening as well as an eclectic methodology. As Buss highlights the goal so well: It is to "breathe new life into formerly ignored texts" to allow us "to speak with the dead" (1996, p. 86).[4]

Ethnography as Reading

Robert Darnton, historian of the book and a cultural historian of 18th-century France, is frequently cited by Lynn Hunt in *The New History* (1989) for his interdisciplinary approaches. A scholar with a deft touch, Darnton is both ethnographer and methodologist of the archives. Of his work in *The Great Cat Massacre: And Other Episodes in French Cultural History* (1985), he says: "It is history in the ethnographic grain [that] attempts to show not merely what people thought but how they thought—how they construed their world, invested it with meaning, and infused it with emotion" (p. 3). Similarly, to feminist researchers working with the documents of those whose voices have not been heard (Hunt also cites the work of Carroll Smith-Rosenberg), Darnton "listens" through documents to printers (who indeed did kill their master's cats), overly inquisitive police inspectors, and Rousseau's readers to come to "make contact with [the] vanished humanity" (p. 263) of the time period.

In his ethnographic probings, Darnton highlights the role of reading and writing as both vehicle and medium for "actors" making sense of their world. In his introductory essay to *The Great Cat Massacre*, he explains that "the ethnographic historian studies the way ordinary people make sense of the world" (1985, p. 3). Darnton admits to wandering through the archives in search of interesting documents by which to "read" people and their times. Reading *is* his methodology:

> The notion of reading runs through all the chapters, for one can read a ritual or a city just as one can read a folktale or a philosophic text. The mode of exegesis may vary, but in each case one reads for meaning—the meaning inscribed by contemporaries in whatever survives of their vision of the world. (p. 5)

Lynn Hunt, in her introductory essay to *The New Cultural History* (1989), also notes the links between Clifford Geertz as "the most visible anthropologist in cultural historical work" (p. 12) and Darnton who, she says,

> clearly stated the advantages of Geertzian interpretive strategies. Cultural history, [Darnton] announced, is "history in the ethnographic grain.... The anthropological mode of history ... begins from the premise that individual expression takes place within a general idiom." As such, it is an interpretive science: its aim is to read "for meaning—the meaning inscribed by contemporaries." (p. 12, citing Darnton, 1985, pp. 4–6)

According to Darnton, "most people tend to think that cultural history concerns high culture, culture with a capital C [but] the history of culture in the lower case goes back as far as Burckhardt" (p. 3).

Despite this clarification by Darnton, the term "culture" (probably now with a capital *C*), and for now meaning symbolic activity,[5] has until relatively recently been viewed as a masculine construct. Indeed, Joan B. Landes (1988) in *Women and the Public Sphere in the Age of the French Revolution*, states, "Some feminists have proposed that the entire symbolic order (of language, of culture) is a masculine construct" (p. 202). For Landes, a "reconceptualization [of] the problematic relationship of women to the modern public sphere" (p. 2) is, for this reason, necessary. Problematizing the relationship of gender and culture, Landes asks: What is "the relationship between culture, discourse, and gender relations?" (p. 203). This is, obviously, a large question. But perhaps a history in the ethnographic vein, one that reads the personal documents of young women who record the cultural activities of their lives, can suggest ways of thinking about the question. The need, according to methodologists Acker, Barry, and Esseveld (1991), "is to provide women with understandings of how their everyday worlds, their trials and troubles, were and are generated by the larger social structure" (p. 135). How are we to understand this problematic in the lives of young 19th-century women?

The Problematic of Women and Culture

As suggested above by Robert Darnton, ethnography has the explication of "culture" at its center but, as he notes, "culture in the lower case goes back as far as Burckhardt" (1985, p. 3). Women's relation to the cultural, of which literacy is both vehicle and component, is, of course, an important issue.[6] Women of the 19th century wrote letters, read books, attended the opera, played musical instruments, went to plays and concerts and lyceum lectures, spoke French, and collected art. Are these "cultural activities" or merely the expression of a "petit" culture, not quite the real thing, not quite "high" culture, culture with a capital C (which it would be if men were performing the same activities)?

The young Wright/Mott/Osborne women, as we have seen, were both wide readers and frequent letter writers. At the same time that they were absorbing the messages of the culture, these young women were active creators of a personal yet cultural form: letters. They were also participants in the cultural activities of their day and not only as readers and writers; for instance, they went to plays, museums, and the opera; saw the Panorama of the Mississippi[7] and a Model of Paris; heard Jenny Lind sing; enjoyed the music of Olé Bull and the Hutchinson Family Singers.[8] Their correspondence was not only a personal venture, it was also a semi-public form—within the family community—read aloud at family gatherings both large and small. Whether this is culture in the large or small sense is a matter of interpretation. We saw in Chapter 2 the tendency of many of the male historians of literacy to assume the small c in their somewhat limited presentations of women's literacy practices. (This is a question to which I turn in the last chapter, "Endings.")

Yet, the importance of the concept of culture and its connection to the personal is suggested by anthropologist Marilyn Strathern (Moore, 1988) whose

> work reminds us that gender constructs are linked to concepts of self, personhood and autonomy. Any analysis of such concepts necessarily involves some consideration of choice, strategy, moral worth and social value as they relate to actions of individual social actors. These are the areas of social analysis where the connections between the symbolic or cultural aspects of social life and the social and economic conditions under which life is lived can be most clearly recognized and investigated. (p. 41)

Moore concludes this discussion of Strathern's work by noting that it is at the juncture of the symbolic and the actual that the study of gender makes its contributions to anthropology.

The authors of the three-volumed text, *The Woman Question: Society and Literature in Britain and America, 1837–1883* (Helsinger, Sheets, & Veeder, 1983), ask: "What really were the culture's attitudes toward men and women?" (p. vi). They say the question is not as easy to answer as it once was because:

> Close study of public opinion between 1837 and 1883 suggests that the traditional model of "a" Victorian attitude—patriarchal domination, expressed publicly as "woman worship"—is inadequate. The predominant form of Victorian writing about women is not pronouncement but debate. Moreover, the arguments in this debate were both more complex and fluid than the model of a single dominant cultural myth would indicate. For Victorians of "the articulate classes," the Woman Question, as they themselves called it, really was a question. (p. xi)

Helsinger, Sheets, and Veeder (1983) make clear, however, that they are not suggesting "that public perception was always at odds with private practice and belief" (p. xiv) but, rather, they want to reveal that the ideology was not a monolith and that there was debate and even contradiction. As they note, even Elizabeth Cady Stanton (p. xi) could vocalize "the conflicting cultural myths about women in the same speech." Thus, there were "not positions but a set of competing, though not mutually exclusive, myths or models for women's place in society" (p. xiv).

If we are not dealing with a monolith but rather with a fluid, ongoing, topical, unsettled debate, is this debate revealed in the letters? Are the ongoing tensions and contradictions regarding "the woman question" revealed? What assumptions and beliefs about gender did the women (and their fathers, husbands, and sons) of the letters hold? What characteristics of gendered roles can be noted as the correspondents wrote to each other? What were those unspoken assumptions about what constituted being a man and being a woman? Were these views compatible? Did they contain complexities, ambiguities, or contradictions? It is in trying to understand the meaning that gender had in their lives and then connecting such understandings to their cultural productions and activities, and connecting these in turn to present-day feminist explications of reading and writing (components and medium of culture) that this study is concerned.

THEORISTS OF AND ON POWER

Embedded in all issues of literacy and certainly central to feminism and gender studies thereof is the issue of power and its concomitant control. For understanding the ways in which systems of control, or discourses (modes of literate genres), work in the process of the engendering of females, many feminist theorists have drawn upon the work(s) of Michael Foucault in developing their own understandings regarding the meaning gender has in the lives of women. Sociologist Carol Warren opens her 1988 text, *Gender Issues in Field Research,* by outlining the importance of the concept of gender:

> Being a man or a woman is at the core of our social lives and of our inner selves. Gender and age ... are among the basic categories of the social fabric; the elaboration of them into the division of labor forms the bedrock of culture in history. Living within a society ... presupposes a gendered interaction, a gendered conversation, and a gendered interpretation. Just as all knowledge—even language itself—is political, reflecting power relations (Foucault, 1976 [*The History of Sexuality, Vol. I]*), all knowledge is gendered. (p. 10)

Film critic and feminist theorist Teresa de Lauretis's (1987) explication of gender uses more radical language to describe the crucial role gender plays in a woman's life. However, she, too, finds it useful

> to think of gender along the lines of Michael Foucault's theory of sexuality as a "technology of sex" and proposes that gender, too, both as representation and self-representation, is the product of various social technologies, such as cinema, and of institutionalized discourses, and critical practices, as well as practices of everyday life. (p. 2)

Later in her essay, de Lauretis expands upon this account. These technologies

> involved the elaborations of discourses (classification, measurements, evalua-
> tion, etc.) about four objects of knowledge: the sexualization of children and
> of the female body, the control of procreation, and the psychiatrization of
> anomalous sexual behavior as perversion. These discourses, which were
> implemented through pedagogy, medicine, demography, and economics,
> were anchored or supported by the state and became especially focused on
> the family; they served to disseminate and to "implant," in Foucault's sugges-
> tive term, those figures and modes of knowledge into each individual, family,
> and institution. (p. 12)

In her much-cited, methodologic text *Critical Practice* (1980), Catherine
Belsey draws more from Derrida (1976) and Lacan (1977) than Foucault.
However, her words echo those of de Lauretis:

> Women as a group in our society are both produced and inhibited by contra-
> dictory discourses. Very broadly, we participate both in the liberal-humanist
> discourse of freedom, self-determination and rationality and at the same
> time in the specifically feminine discourse offered by society of submission,
> relative inadequacy and irrational intuition. The attempt to locate a single
> and coherent subject-position within these contradictory discourses, and in
> consequence to find a non-contradictory pattern of behaviour, can create
> intolerable pressures. (pp. 65–66)

Belsey states that one of these patterns is exemplified by the woman who
becomes sick, who takes to bed or couch as a form of resistance. This pattern of behavior, of course, represents one of the stereotypes of the Victorian woman.

For Joan A. Scott (1986), in her frequently cited essay, "Gender: A Useful Category of Historical Analysis," the construction of

> gender involves four interrelated elements: first, culturally available symbols;
> ... second, normative concepts [which] ... are expressed in religious, educa-
> tional, scientific, legal, and political doctrines and typically take the form of a
> fixed binary opposition;....[third], the kinship system; and the fourth aspect
> of gender is subjective identity. (pp. 1067–1068)

By this last category, Scott refers to the psychological makeup of a person
but, for the same reason that she rejects the Lacanian theories of language,
she also rejects the idea of a gendered identity being based on the universal claims of Freud—for example, the castration complex—because

> if gender identity is based only and universally on fear of castration the point
> of historical inquiry is denied. [Rather,] historians need ... to examine the
> ways in which gendered identities are substantively constructed and relate

their findings to a range of activities, social organizations, and historically specific cultural representations. (p. 1068)

For Scott, the best models for such deeply contexted studies are biographies such as that of Catharine Beecher by Kathryn Kish Sklar (1976). No doubt the recent and rich biographies of Harriet Beecher Stowe (Hedrick, 1994) and of Lydia Maria Child (Karcher, 1994), deeply rooted as they are in their 19th-century culture and events, would also meet with her approval.

Felicity A. Nussbaum's writings on Hester Thrale (1988, 1989), a daily and insightful chronicler of both Samuel Johnson and her own family, speaks well to this study. In an article discussing the family writings of 18th-century Hester Thrale, that takes seriously the idea that women are culturally constructed through contradictory discourses (building upon the work of Foucault), Nussbaum stresses the importance of placing such accounts in their specific historical context. She states:

"Woman" can be read as a historically and culturally produced category situated within material conditions that vary at historical moments and in regional locations. Within these parameters, we may then identify certain regimes of truth, of discourse, and of subjectivity available to women. (1988, p. 148)

Nussbaum continues by pointing out that, of course, a "woman's room" is none too large: "Eighteenth-century women, as a gendered category, had little access to philosophic discourse, to equal wages, or to equality under the law... " (p. 148), all of which were avenues, of course, available to men.

It is Nussbaum's (1988) contention that the "everyday" writings of women are sites of revelation regarding gendered inequalities:

This experience [of being gendered in and by these discourses], as variously depicted in [women's] autobiographical texts, both participates in and contests existing categories of woman. Thus, women's commonplaces—the places where meanings about gender meet and struggle for dominance—are not universal categories but may serve various and contradictory ideological purposes in the writing of gendered subjectivity. (p. 149)

Furthermore, Nussbaum continues:

It is in these spaces between the cultural constructions of the female and the articulation of individual selves and their lived experience, between cultural assignments of gender and the individual's translation of them into text, that a discussion of women's autobiographical writing can be helpful. (p. 149)

If it is in "the spaces in the commonplaces where the meanings meet," then, within these spaces, what are the meanings that arise when these women write so often and over so many years?

In their writings, in the production of their own letters, did the women of the Wright/Mott/Osborne axis reveal any of these "intolerable pressures" noted by Belsey (1980, pp. 65–66)? Can we see if they were submissive or felt inadequate or displayed irrational intuition? What was their relation to the larger society wherein liberal discourse was located? How did what they read (and wrote) of the technologies of gender—textbooks, politeness manuals, the advice genre—affect them (de Lauretis, 1987)? How did their use of language mark them as female? How did they feel about being a member of the female sex? How much freedom of thought and action did they have, given the strong voices of control that operated in mid-19th-century America?

COMING TO CONTEXTS

Conjoining Context and Meaning

While not part of the new cultural history, symbolic interactionism (a qualitative methodological approach within the social sciences that conjoins meaning and context) provides the underpinnings for this study. Taylor and Bogdan (1984), citing Herbert Blumer, state:

> Symbolic interactionism rests on three basic premises. The first is that people act toward things, including other people, on the basis of the meanings these things have for them.... Blumer's second premise is that meanings are social products that arise during interaction.... The third ... is that social actors attach meanings to situations, others, things, and themselves through a process of interpretation. (p. 9)

For Blumer (Taylor & Bogdan, 1984, quoting Blumer, 1969), this process of interpretation

> has two distinct steps. First, the actor indicates to himself [sic] the things toward which he is acting; he has to point out to himself the things that have meaning. Second, by virtue of this process of communicating with himself, interpretation becomes a matter of handling meanings. The actor selects, suspends, regroups, and transforms the meanings in the light of the situation in which he is placed and the direction of his action. (p. 10)

Meaning for Blumer is not "out there," it is constructed.

The linkages between history and the social sciences are noted by practitioners from both fields of study. Says ethnographer and linguist Shirley Brice Heath (1978), "Social historians share emphases, methods, and data with sociologists" (p. 84). Historian Linda Gordon (1986) concurs:

The incorporation of the subjectivity of the object of study is a theme that has been raised by sociologists, anthropologists, and historians for decades, men as well as women. It is a method that I recognize in my own work; I listen very hard to my subjects, and operate on the assumption that their own self-inter-pretation is likely as good as mine. (p. 29)

Though she does not place herself within a symbolic interactionist framework (and clearly her work as cited here is prior to the formulations of the new cultural history), Nancy F. Cott (1977), in her milestone *The Bonds of Womanhood: "Women's Sphere" in New England, 1780–1835*, does bring together intellectual and social history. She states that she uses women's personal documents "because no other historical source is likely to disclose women's consciousness" (p. 17). Because Cott also wanted to "establish the cultural milieu in which women found themselves," she also needed to draw upon the "organizational writings and prescriptive litera-ture" (p. 10) that helped establish the "emphatic sentence of domesticity" (p. 8) upon 19th-century women. Her explication of her methodology is suggestive of the importance of context in determining meaning. The goal of Cott's book was to "provide an interpretive framework for a thorough social history which has yet to be written" (p. 16) by working back and forth between the texts of women's lives; the texts that surrounded them, and their experiences. Her

purposes demand doubling back and forth between evidence and interpreta-tion, between circumstance and ideology, between experience and con-sciousness, and repeatedly reviewing the same chronology with reference to different topics in order to establish overlapping patterns which should rein-force and help explain one another. (p. 18)

This "method" may not appear to be particularly "scientific"; but it has parallels with Glaser and Strauss's (1967) explication of the constant-com-parative method of qualitative research and has within it, as well, the means of triangulation (Taylor & Bogdan, 1984, pp. 68–70). As noted above, Robert Darnton (1985), in his conclusion to *The Great Cat Massacre*, admits to the same methodological approach:

I can only testify to the importance of working back and forth between texts and contexts. That may not be much of a methodology, but it has advantages. It does not flatten out the idiosyncratic element in history, and it allows for consideration of the common ground of experience. (p. 262)

Darnton, thus, connects the new cultural history with the work of earlier anthropologists and ethnographers: "It is history in the ethnographic grain [that] attempts to show not merely what people thought but how they thought—how they construed their world, invested it with meaning, and infused it with emotion" (p. 3).

Connecting to Contexts

The purpose of this study is to look at the crucial intersection of literacy and gender in the lives of the mid-19th century, young Wright/Mott/ Osborne women, especially as this intersection relates to issues of power and gender construction (and constriction). Using their own documents, and using knowledge sources from a variety of disciplines to build contexts of understanding, the search is for, as so well put by Felicity A. Nussbaum, "the places where meanings meet and struggle for dominance" (1988, p. 149).

Because literacy is a significant vehicle of socialization (Berger & Luckmann, 1966; Finkelstein, 1979; de Lauretis, 1987), understanding literacy's role and meaning in these young women's lives can provide a means to see how they perceived themselves through their reading and writing. It can help us see, as well, how they may have been influenced by the discourses of their day that maintained the doctrine of separate spheres, limiting young women's expectations for themselves.

It is at these critical but elusive junctures that literacy's meaning as tending toward the liberatory or restrictive can be observed. The goal is to speculate about literacy and women's lives in the mid-19th century—to see in this context "what literacy can and cannot do for people" (Graff, 1987).

Their words in themselves, however, while both powerful and plenty, are not enough. To understand what meaning literacy had in the lives of these communicating, communicative women, and to understand the meaning of their lives as revealed by the content of their letters to each other from the distance of over 150 years, it is important that a context of understanding be built around this correspondence. Two book-length models, both on early literacy experiences, consistent with the approaches of the theorists above, paved the way.

The Deeply Contexted "Tidy House"

The Tidy House: Little Girls Writing, by Carolyn Kay Steedman (1982), is a deeply contextualized study of "a four-part collaborative story of just over 2,000 words" written by three (later, four) working-class 8-year-old British girls "during one week of July 1976" (p. 41). This outstanding but little-known, book-length study by a teacher-writer embeds the girls' dialogic story, "The Tidy House," in a multiple of historical and theoretical contexts that assist in making sense of their story. "The Tidy House," is focused on "romantic love, marriage and sexual relations, the desire of mothers for children and their resentment of them, and the means by which those children are brought up to inhabit a social world" (p. 1).

Steedman's text is a critique of the sentimental view of education that tells teachers "that intelligence is largely innate and that education can do little more than keep children moving in their alloted ranks" (1982, pp. 4–5). Steedman states that she "examined the [children's] text for evidence of the huge mythologies of love and sex that inform our culture and of the way in which working-class girls become working-class women" (p. 12). In developing ways of understanding this socialization process, Steedman draws upon diverse, informational contexts that include the work of Henry Mayhew in his interviews of working-class girls in the London of the 1880s; the century-long history of journal writings of little girls' writings; writing theory; and theories that connect gender and language.

Although denying in her introduction that the reader would find much in the book regarding education, Steedman explores various aspects of what Peter B. Mosenthal (1984) calls "the romantic ideology" of education, and she stresses the importance of taking seriously "the *matter*" of children's writing. Furthermore, she connects the "sustained and passionate attacks on [the] destruction of young children's lives such as *Death at an Early Age* [Kozol, 1967] and *The Way Things Spozed To Be* [Herndon, 1968]" with her critique of the social class structure in Great Britain (1982, p. 3). Through her development of well-chosen, relevant contexts, Steedman shows how all these crucial issues are implicit elements in the story written by these little working-class girls.

The Making of a Reader

Similarly to Carolyn Steedman, Marilyn Cochran-Smith (1984) embeds her study of storybook reading in a private Philadelphia nursery school within multiple informational contexts. In her introduction, she writes that her text is based on "two constructs that help to provide both a conceptual organization framework for reading and interpreting the findings of this study: (a) the notion of print as contextualized and decontextualized; (b) the notion of multiple layers of context" (p. 3). Her text provides a "peel[ing] away [of] the layers of context into which story telling is embedded" (p. 37). Her chosen contexts, "allowing [her] to reach the center of her ring which is story telling" (p. 7), are four:

(a) the literacy attitudes, values, and practices of the adult community; (b) the general nursery-school atmosphere and environment; (c) the network of literacy events that surround and support story reading; and (d) the immediate physical and verbal environment in which story reading occurs. (p. 37)

Cochran-Smith develops all these contexts in rich detail, each in its own chapter, and then concludes with a thorough, well-informed discussion of the use of book knowledge by the children ("life to text") and the knowledge ("text to life") that flowed from story reading to become part of who they were. The list of what these children gained as knowledge opens her last chapter and represents a wide repertory of understandings regarding literacy's practices, purposes, and benefits.

In the final chapter of *The Making of A Reader,* Cochran-Smith (1984) presents the rationale for her methodology:

> The way of looking at early literacy that underlies this work is ethnographic in its perspective. That is, it is based on the belief that the meaning of all human behavior, including print-related behaviors and habits, is embedded within social and cultural contexts. (p. 254)

More Recent Studies

Several more current studies focused upon literacy practices that likewise embed their ethnographic studies in appropriate contextual understandings. Two of these focus specifically on the interaction of gender and literacy. *She Say, He Say: Urban Girls Write Their Lives* by Brett Elizabeth Blake (1997), for example, makes use of both the public and private situational contexts within which the young women of her study used their

> writing to seriously attend to the implications and consequences of their life experiences. They also used writing to challenge and resist other's voices and to become active in wanting to change social conditions. (p. 125)

In *Just Girls: Hidden Literacies and Life in Junior High* (1997), Margaret Finders highlights the literacy practices of the junior high women in her study as political activities. Contextualizing her study in language—both the "appropriate" language of the classroom as well as the "literate under-life" (p. 129) that also flourished within the school domain—she found that only in the latter context "were these girls provided any opportunity for more freedom, independence, or responsibility" (p. 129).

All these deeply contextualized studies illustrate the value of heeding a multiple of specific contexts before making claims regarding literacy's benefits and effects. When gender is taken up as a context along with others as appropriate to the setting of the study, its role in interactions with literacy events can be seen to be an operative factor for understandings.

Context(s): But Which Contexts?

Thus, from varying perspectives and disciplines, Blake (1997), Cochran-Smith (1984), Darnton (1985), Finders (1997), Graff (1987), de Lauretis (1987), Nussbaum (1988), and Steedman (1982) all cite the crucial importance of context for understanding either or both literacy and gendered subjectivities.

From early anthropologists such as Malinowski (as explicated by Halliday & Hasan, 1985) to ethnographers such as Robert Darnton (1985) and Marilyn Cochran-Smith (1984), an important part of their own explications of that which they were studying was the development of circles of understanding, or contexts. In gender studies, too, where essentializing (positing claims of maleness or femaleness based on biology) is not the goal, the need to develop contexts specific to the time and place of the study is stressed, and such context development is also taken for granted by the historians admired by Joan A. Scott (1986).

Fortunately, the extensive feminist scholarship of the past 30 years provides both the context and the contexts. While it is not possible to elaborate upon everything we would like to know, I think it is possible that the present study, in providing relevant research and insight from feminist sources in conjunction with content analysis of the Wright/Mott/Osborne letters, we will see women's literacy in the 19th century as a complex social phenomenon embedded within the historical or cultural currents of the times. The gendered aspects of literacy as process and practice, ignored in the recent past by the male historians of literacy as we saw in Chapter 2, are brought into closer focus. Its contributions can then become part of the ongoing envisionment of literacy that is more inclusive in outlook.

Recent explorations over several broad areas of knowledge—broad speculations about the nature of literacy from a revisionist perspective, gender theorizing, reader-response theory, current reading and writing theory including emergent literacy work, methodological probings via the new cultural history—are critical contexts for coming to understand the literacy productions of the young Wright/Mott/Osborne women. The need is to explicate the gendered meanings of the often elusive and cryptic "particulars" within their letters.

The Centrality of Context

Robert Darnton (1985) sees meaning not as "out there" but rather as constructed by actors. If meaning varies from context to context, then any particular group or individual to be understood must be seen in and against that context. In their introduction to *Interpreting Women's Lives* (1989), the Personal Narratives Group explicates the importance of context:

> Acknowledging the centrality and complexity of context reveals the range of experiences and expectations within which women live, and provides a vital perspective from which to interpret women's ways of navigating the weave of relationships and structures which constitute their worlds. (p. 19)

Thus, the Personal Narratives Group suggests why a multidisciplinary approach makes sense and why any single approach would be limiting—a point stressed by Helen M. Buss in her recent feminist essay on the reading of women's private writings (Bunkers & Huff, 1996), which also emphasizes the need for "an informed consciousness of . . . power systems that are operational" (p. 99) within any specific setting.

The Personal Narrative Group's (1989) definition of context likewise stresses the importance of searching for meaning within the actors' frame of reference: "The word context literally means to weave together, to twine, to connect. This interrelatedness creates the web of meaning within which humans act. The individual is joined to the world through social groups, structural relations, and identities" (p. 19). They caution against a reductive approach:

> Context is not a script. Rather, it is a dynamic process through which the individual simultaneously shapes and is shaped by her environment. . . . Furthermore, addressing context involves understanding the meaning of life in its narrators frame of reference, and making sense of that life from the different and necessarily comparative frame of reference of the interpreter. (p. 19)

Halliday and Hasan (1985), in *Language, Context, and Text: Aspects of Language in a Social-Semiotic Perspective,* trace the idea of context in their work to anthropologist Bronislaw Malinowski, who

> with some apologies, in an article written in 1923 ["The Problem of Meaning in Primitive Languages" (printed in Ogden and Richard's *The Meaning of Meaning* (1923)], coined the phrase "Context of Situation". . . . By Context of Situation he meant the environment of the text. . . . But he also saw that it was necessary to give more than the immediate environment. He saw that in any adequate description, it was necessary to provide information not only about what was happening at the time but also about the total cultural background, because involved in any kind of linguistic interaction, in any kind of conversational exchange, were not only the immediate sights and sounds surrounding the event but also the whole cultural history behind the participants, and behind the kind of practices that they were engaging in, determining their significance for the culture, whether practical or ritual. All these played a part in the interpretation of the meaning. So Malinowski introduced the two

notions that he called the Context of Situation and the Context of Culture; and both of these, he considered, were necessary for the adequate understanding of the text. (p. 7)

While Brian V. Street (1995) cautions against Malinowski's "context of situation" as implying a static functionalist approach (1995, p. 165), in effect, the above historians, ethnographers, anthropologists, and feminists, in stressing the importance of context building in understanding social practices, do so with the flexibility urged by Street: "Recent approaches within anthropology have emphasized the dynamic nature of social processes and the broader structure of power relations" (p. 165).

For this study, with Street's cautions in mind, building a context can be seen as two-layered, paralleling the two categories of context: context of situation and context of culture. The first layer will roughly follow Graff's (1987) list for building the specifics for any given literacy context. His list can be seen to consist of three differing entities: those specifics that are straightforward and descriptive; those that require an understanding of the meaning literacy events had in the lives of its participants; and those that require interpretation between the historic time period and present-day understandings of literacy. Thus, his straightforward list is not quite so straight (and, as we saw in Chapter 2, omits considerations of gender). But it does show the importance of a description of actual literacy practices – "context of situation"—before a wider context—"a context of culture"— can be built around them to reach the broader goals of understanding and interpretation.

The second layer of context (roughly corresponding to Malinowski's [Halliday & Hasan, 1985] idea of context of culture) consists of bringing together present-day (largely, but not exclusively, feminist) understandings of and questions about reading and writing. Such understandings should help enlarge our understandings of the meanings encoded in the correspondence—"in the commonplaces," to use Felicity A. Nussbaum's (1988) felicitous phrase—regarding gender construction, effects of the discourses of the day; and relevant issues regarding literacy and power.

As Nussbaum avers (to repeat) as an article of faith:

It is in the spaces between the cultural constructions of the female and the articulation of individual selves and their lived experience, between cultural assignments and the individuals' translation of them into text, that a discussion of women's autobiographical writing can be helpful. (1988, p. 149)

Thus, a study that looks at women's shared letter writing and what they read should be able to detect and provide clues to some of the above considerations. To "the commonplaces" to find the meanings.

PROCEDURES

This study represents a long-standing project. To provide a list of "procedures" is somewhat, though not intentionally, misleading. While a list conveys the steps of the project, at some point the discrete steps of this project evolved into an operation of going "back and forth" (Cott, 1977; Darnton, 1985)—between text and context, between letters and data analysis, between letters and account books, between girls and women, women and men, letters and feminist texts, data analysis and feminist theories. This "betweening" turned into more complex layering, which, in turn, became concentric circles and feedback loops. Thus, rather than the more straightforward, deductive procedures of "science," a continual process of triangulation—"the combination of methods or sources of data in a single study" (Taylor & Bogdan, 1984) in conjunction with "the constant comparative" strategy whereby "the researcher simultaneously codes and analyzes data in order to develop concepts" (p. 126)—was the order of the day (years, actually!). However, analysis and memories must be presented in linear fashion.

This project had its origin in the archives as part of a class requirement for the course "Women in Higher Education" with Joan N. Burstyn.[9] The assignment was to work with original documents. A reading of a significant article on the history of writing instruction suggested a search for verification of a literacy thesis, proposed by linguist and ethnographer Shirley Brice Heath (1981), that young women of the 19th-century helped one another to perfect their writing. Upon finding explicit textual evidence in the Osborne Family Papers (to which I was guided by the good offices of Carolyn Davis, manuscript librarian) that indeed the young Wright/Mott/Osborne women *did* seek writing instruction from one another, I drew upon the work of Carroll Smith-Rosenberg (1975/1985) to suggest the importance of letter writing both as a literacy practice and as a vehicle of community support in the lives of these young women. For that first study of 1987, "Women Writing Letters to Women: Is Learning to Write Involved," 58 letters were used.

The Context of Situation

Thus, prior to the construction of this document, I wrote other studies using the Osborne Family Papers (but with a smaller selection of archival materials and covering a shorter time span), one exploring gender, one education, and the next, issues of literacy and power. The paper on gender, "No Great Expectations" (Putala, 1988), was written for a course on qualitative research. In the writing of that paper, a coding system for analyzing the documents was developed, one that is still useful.[10]

First Round of Coding

The preliminary content analysis of the letters of the young women focused primarily on those written between 1840 and 1850—that is, the letters of the young women in the early years of their young womanhood before marriage and children. Because so much of what was written dealt with the tangibles of their everyday experiences, many of these categories could be labeled in a straightforward way: flowers, visiting, opera, book title, as examples. The coding of the data into these relatively concrete categories revealed a world dominated by specific gender activities and tasks. What this content analysis clearly revealed was that the content of their lives—as revealed in the content of their letters—revolved around the future roles of keeper of the evening sanctuary, homemaker, and mother as set forth by Carl F. Kaestle (1983).

In trying to put together the meaning of these concrete, very obviously gendered categories, I "heard" something that was noticeably not present in the letters of these young women. Listening to the silence, as Hampsten (1982) outlines above, though I hadn't yet read her, I tried to detect what was not there. I wrote:

> Strikingly absent in all the many words that were penned between and among these young women that foreshadow their eventual roles are any expectations for themselves, either as developing anything resembling a career or showing any interest in a world wider than their doorsteps or gardens. (Putala, 1988, p. 6)

Of the social concerns that dominated the lives of their feminist, abolitionist mothers, very little could be observed. Understandable, of course, within its 19th-century context with its doctrines of "separate spheres" within which the "cult of true womanhood" flourished, nevertheless, questions remained, especially one: What, then, was the meaning of their literateness?

Second Round of Coding

Broadening the study with literacy questions derived mostly from the work of Harvey J. Graff (1987), which questioned easy assumptions of literacy as an exclusively liberatory force, I widened my search within the Osborne Family Papers and kept gathering letters and combing the noncorrespondence boxes of the collection for literacy documentation. The same methods of coding were applied to the letters and materials. While some categories needed to be added as the lives of the young women changed somewhat as they matured, the coding system stood the test of time, but could not yield all that was necessary.

Coding Their Reading. One of the original coding categories pertained to the reading of the young women. Indeed, it was the abundance of the reading references made by the young women, as well as other members of the family, that suggested that the correspondence would make a fitting literacy study. In a rereading of the letters, these very plentiful reading references were taken down in their entirety, first in text form and then on file cards. Book, journal, and newspaper titles as well as the readers' comments regarding their reading activities and practices were noted in full. Information regarding specific titles of their reading was gleaned from noncorrespondence material such as account books, ledgers, and day books and was noted as well. David Wright's account books as well as a daily record of household expenditures kept by Eliza Wright Osborne were particularly helpful.

After all the reading references were recorded in chronological order as text, this same material, as individual items, was placed onto file cards in order to detect common categories and themes. Several significant ones emerged—the young women's knowledge regarding the literacy scene of their times; reading as a vital avenue for assuaging loneliness; reading as a vehicle for community communication; the reading of women authors, as examples.

Coding Their Writing. Because the original paper from which all this work has stemmed revolved around young women instructing each other in their writing, some of the specific categories and themes had already suggested themselves—the use of journals for writing; the praise good letter writing elicited; the hunger for letters as a way to ease loneliness, as examples. On a rereading, these categories, and others as well, emerged and were also noted on file cards. It was observed that the letter writers spent a fair measure of space and time addressing issues directly related to writing, as well as the act of writing, with many concerns expressed over ink and pens. Issues related to audience and organization were often directly expressed by the writers, and it was also observed how often the writers spoke of their writing in terms of conversation. This researcher further recorded the deeper functions the letters actually served and documented, as well as the knowledge the young women possessed of writing rules and conventions. Actual issues relative to language, such as their use of graceful prose as well as their use of language to describe their genderedness, were also documented. Finally, the actual means for sending the letters—both via travelers and the postal system—and the complex rounds to family members (along with the privacy issues that thus arose) were also noted and placed on file cards for sorting. Again, significant themes arose from these categories.

Coding of Gender. The third category in this second round of coding involved gender issues. This category turned out to be much less straightforward than the material related to actual reading and writing issues. In some sense, the entire correspondence of the women is one long gender reference, as so much of the content directly related to their very gendered existence.

As these young women became young wives and mothers, the content of the letters became more difficult to characterize by any simple content analysis; moreover, the categories themselves became more complex with a simple concrete label not really covering the content. For example, when the health of children became involved, they had to be very precise regarding what is illness and what is health. Gendered relationships also, of course, became more complex. Thus, a decision was made to find the substantive quotes about gender—using their own words—in addition to the continuing coding of the obvious and many very concrete manifestations of gender that made up their letters.

Much thought was given as to what counted as a gender reference. As their mothers became more willing to address—even in these rather public letters—more complex and sensitive issues and activities, that question became very important. For example, in writing to Eliza, Martha Coffin Wright told her now-married daughter of a relative who had just given birth to twins. Her command to her daughter was, "Look out!" This imperative encodes several significant gender issues: sexual activity, sexual desire, birth control, frankness between women regarding sexual matters, and knowledge regarding all these issues, part of which knowledge acquisition is not unrelated to literacy issues.

This cautionary regarding twins can be seen as a category of story as well as one I had already labeled as "mother discourse." A form of writing "talk," "mother discourse" was a directive from mother to daughter, with the goal apparently having been to get across a moral message, preferably one that would be acted on. But somehow, the imperative herein to "Look out!" is not quite of the same order as "Write prettily" to your uncle, an earlier corrective from mother to daughter. It may not even have been an imperative but rather was a wise and philosophical remark intended to invoke a mutual, gendered understanding of the haplessness of gendered existence. Or perhaps it was Martha's way of saying—in code—"Sex is fun!" Then again, it might have been her way of saying in code, "Ain't it awful." As this brief "reading" shows, understanding the gendered messages encoded both in the letters and the life stories of these women became more complex, and could not be exhausted by any single method of coding or theory of reading.

This dilemma of the difficulty of doing a solely straightforward content analysis was addressed in two ways. First, I resorted to very broad coding with an obvious "g" for gender being used to mark such utterances and sometimes even whole passages. Second, after a second or third reading, the most salient of these was placed—in whole or in part—on a 3 x 5-inch file card under the same very broad category for further sorting in a search for more subtle themes. From this sorting emerged such categories as "boredom," "cautionary story," and "male discourse." From these themes, the gender chapter was, in part, based.

The Context of Culture

Having, in some senses, fulfilled the "context of situation"—noting and coding "the environment of the text" (Halliday & Hasen, 1985, p. 7)—the near-at-hand and relatively concrete and thus with a (sense of a) relatively secure grasp of daily specificities as they related to literacy, the next task was to develop the "context of culture"—the cultural significance of these practices and specificities.

As the reading texts were most directly (and easily) related to the culture of the time, this area became an important focus. First, I separated out the easily separated, the reading references themselves. A list was made of the titles and the authors (often only one or the other was provided by the readers). The next task was to locate the reference. Nina Baym's (1978) work was invaluable here as was *The National Union Catalogue*. More currently, World Cat as a database on SUNY Oswego's Penfield Library's website has been helpful. Other bibliographic tools, such as the reference works by Hart (1965), Spiller (1963), and Wright (1965, 1969), were also invaluable as were the back-page book advertisements of 19th-century texts. Having assembled (and now listed) what was relatively concrete, the next moves were not quite as neat and relatively delimited.

Interpretation

What could all those particulars mean? How did gender, reading, and writing come together? How could the silences be heard? How could the questions of Burstyn and Cholakian be addressed? Indeed, how could my own? Obviously needing to go beyond content analysis to analyze what was off the page, what next to do?

Linda Flower (1989) makes an important point in her article "Cognition, Context, and Theory Building" in suggesting that one of the dilemmas of qualitative research is that seldom do we show how we get our results. She goes on to say that not only may it be difficult to show how we get our "results," and that we can know "our interpretive acts cannot be 'right' in any final sense ... unfortunately ... they can be wrong in some important ways" (p. 304). She goes on to list ways our acts of interpretation can be wrong: "They can fail to fit or account for the experience at hand; they can fail to do justice to the data, to the process, or to the people we are trying to understand" (p. 304). Not wishing to give up on "observation-based theory building" (p. 309), she says the best we can do is "to listen to that data—to construct meaning—in a systematic way" (p. 305).

Fully granting all these difficulties, the charge herein was to develop a context of understanding around these letters. From my own reading in a variety of areas, given the deeply gendered nature of the letters, it appeared to me that the best place to search for "answers" to the meaning of the women's data was within the significant and powerful feminist research of the past 20 years. The various theorists cited throughout this study offered insights and explanations that appeared to provide the understandings that, to me, illuminated the words and lives of the young Wright/Mott/Osborne women.

Searching for Ground

Tania Modleski (1986) notes Teresa de Lauretis's use of Charles Peirce's concept of "ground" to designate

> precisely that place from which it is possible to theorize, construct, modify, and make conscious female experience. Far from being a simple concept, 'ground' for de Lauretis's work is a precise theoretical concept that allows for communication to occur between sender and addressee, writer and reader, and is thus a relational term. (p. 135)

De Lauretis (1987) herself outlines Charles Peirce's theory of semiotics and discusses that leap between data and interpretation. But the issue is, "How do you know when that ground is relatively solid?" It appeared to me that what I was about—to use this comforting concept of ground—was a double (or triple) grounding: finding the grounds of their beliefs about gender; grounding their reading in theoretical work that has gone toward an understanding of gendered 19th-century texts; connecting their reading to their grounded gender beliefs; moving from these grounded beliefs and associations to both their letter writing and the experiences they reveal in their writing, possible because so much of their day-to-day experience was the very ground of their texts.

While this may not have pulled into a fully cohesive "master" theory of reading, writing, and gender, it does, I hope, expand our understandings of literacy's possibilities and problematics, as well as help make gender a visible category of analysis in future studies of literacy.

It should be noted that the writing process itself is probably one of the answers as to how we derive what feels like the ground of our interpretations of what makes sense (at least to us, as writers). The drafting, cutting and pasting, reworking, rereading for sense making, responding to various readers clarifies the thinking. And then more moving back and forth between and among the various theorists in varying fields: "Well, this really doesn't illuminate this section or point; or, oh, what a fine fit. I see now what that category or theme might mean in the experience of their lives."

Going Back and Forth—"Not Much of a Methodology"

While I "unpacked" the meanings within the young women's data "through narrative, explication, and argument" (Himley, 1988), I also did a great deal of "going back and forth," Darnton's (1985) methodology for "history in the ethnographic vein" (p. 1). I went back and forth between the particulars of the young women and literacy theories; back and forth between the data and feminist theories; back and forth between feminist reading and writing theories; back and forth between letters and coding systems; back and forth among the coding systems.

Thus, what I did stands in contrast to the definitive procedures described by Pamela Michel in her remarkable *A Child's View of Reading: Understandings for Teachers and Parents* (1994)—data collection with clearly separated procedures of participant observation, interviews and document analysis; clearly defined steps of theoretical sampling; well-defined data analysis of filing-coding categories and color-coding subcategories with "the goal being to identify formally themes and make hypotheses" (Bogdan & Biklen, 1982), thus providing "the necessary framework from which to better understand children's perceptions of reading" (p. 21). This study may resemble more the unknotting of a skein of yarn than exhibit the precision of scientific inquiry—but grounded it is.

LIMITATIONS: A KNOTTY PROBLEM— MY ONGOING DILEMMA

In her own methodology section, Pamela Michel (1994) stresses the importance of examining her own "role in a given setting" (p. 22). Having examined my own personal history as a woman of a certain age with its own history of "no great expectations," I believe that the extra time I have taken with this study has been the result of the fear that I could bring my own biases to the setting—and no doubt I have! For one thing—it's hardly a unique personal history; rather, it is the central dogma of the feminist project—women (and other nondominant groups) are not able to extend their experiences in ways that allow development of their talents. Now certainly males are often crippled by socioeconomic factors from developing their full intellectual and artistic potential as well. But by being given the opportunity to be "out there," they at least have the potential for discovering (or having others discover) their talents—latent or manifest.

It was only when I was relatively convinced that my own biases were not center-stage and that I probably could see what I was seeing in their lives and productions, that I was ready to sit down and write. I did look for counterarguments regarding the seeming limitations on these young women by going to the Auburn YMCA for the early records of an organization to which Eliza belonged, the Women's Industrial and Educational Union, for evidence of possible social concerns. Later, wandering in the archives, I did find that Eliza Wright Osborne—"with [her] glorious black eyes, rivaling even De Staël's in power and pathos" (to quote again Elizabeth Cady Stanton, 1898/1971)—indeed did come to find scope for her intelligence and talents as a book collector, certainly a cultural activity with the capital C!

TO CONCLUDE BEFORE MOVING FORWARD

I have tried throughout to be faithful to the work and works of the Wright/Mott/Osborne women, especially with Eliza Wright Osborne: in having kept the correspondence going; in having kept it to such high standards; in providing the solicitous, caring, and intelligent reader all the other correspondents counted on as both reader and listener. With all this I want to keep faith and to celebrate: "My mission has been (and continues to be) to showcase as much of your work and words as I possibly can— for your letters encode much more than I can tell and no doubt even much more than I can detect—and you do it so often with such real art and intelligence that I appreciate the mission I have been fortunate enough to be able to pursue."[11]

Second, I have tried to let the categories within the particulars emerge. Although I am in some ways the definer of these categories, I have tried to be conduit not determiner. "For you, the writers, set the major ones—from your own particulars and from your own intense writing and reading."

Third, I have tried to keep faith with feminist research—in all its richness, contradictions, and ambiguities. Although I have only scratched the surface, I have tried in this study to reveal that women's literacy as a field of study is very complex and needs to become incorporated into the substance of the field. Additionally, I have tried to show for our times the importance of the reader's and the writer's contexts, as well as the complexities of literacy processes.

Of all these matters, I have fallen short of the mark. But if their words and meanings can live outside the folders of the Osborne Family Papers and we can see more clearly literacy's role in the production and reproduction of gender, I will be more than satisfied. Five more chapters follow. Two will address the specific contexts of the reading of the young women through two different lenses. Following these two chapters will be a chapter devoted to their writing, and then a chapter that addresses issues specific to gender as these issues arise in their documents. The last chapter, "Endings," gathers together the threads and themes related to the major issue of the literacy myth, and its role in gender construction. Is proficient literacy, for the young Wright/Mott/Osborne women, a liberating vehicle or a force that tended to constrict and constrain them as they lived their lives?

NOTES

1. In Chapter Two we have already witnessed such a mode of reading in Laurel Thatcher Ulrich's *A Midwife's Tale: the Life of Martha Ballard, Based on her Diary, 1785–1812* (1990).

2. Harris, 1990; Radway, 1984; Sicherman, 1989; and Tompkins, 1985.

3. To cite just a few of influential feminists texts that broke forth in the early 1970s.

4. Citing Stephen Greenblatt, quoted in Veeser (1989).

5. Mary Kelley, in her study of the literary domestics, *Private Woman, Public Stage: Literary Domesticity in 19th-Century America* (1984), particularly in Chapter 8, offers ways of thinking about how women novelists of the time period struggled with the concept of culture.

6. See Kathleen D. McCarthy's *Women's Culture: American Philanthropy and Art: 1830–1930* (1991) for a very fine rendition of the struggles endured by even very wealthy, well-connected women within the cultural institutions of the late 19th century.

7. Most likely they saw John Banvard's in motion "'three mile picture'" (Avery, 1999).

8. Lawrence W. Levine in *Highbrow, Lowbrow: The Emergence of Cultural Hierarchy in America* (1988) is very instructive on the intermingling of lower- and uppercase culture in the mid-19th century, where of these and similar 19th-century activities, understandings of "culture" had not yet quite split into the "high and the low."

9. For which and to whom I am forever grateful.

10. See Appendix C.

11. "To speak with the dead" (Greenblatt, cited by Buss [1996, p. 87]) for just a moment.

CHAPTER 4

ON THEIR OWN: WOMEN READING (MOSTLY) WOMEN

A bewitching novel Nathalie resembling Jane Eyre
was the means of paving a hole in my day.

(MPM to EWO: 2.9-11.55 [or 52])

In the middle of November 1846, 17-year-old Eliza Wright (EWO) asked of her Philadelphia cousin and friend, Pattie Mott (MML), "What are you reading nowadays?" Maintaining the dialogue regarding texts, if some 4 months later, Pattie asked Eliza: "Have you read *The Battle of Life*?"[1] Seldom in the many, many letters between these young women was the topic of reading—the sharing of titles, the varied roles reading played in their lives, the effects of their reading—not a category of their shared discourse.

As we will see over the next two chapters, which specifically address the reading practices, both liberatory and constraining, of these young women, their correspondence bears testimony not only to the power of the written word, but it also bears witness to the sway their chosen texts had over them. Throughout the letters they wrote to one another, the act of reading both as understood by them collaboratively (and now as teased apart via the scholarship of our own times) was almost always a category of discussion, clearly a vital matter in their lives.

Reading and Writing Ourselves into Being, pages 83–114

TO THE SCHOLARSHIP

What do women read? Why do women read? What do they take from their reading? Over the ages, these, of course, have been questions that have concerned those who have chosen to worry about the effects of women's thoughts and behavior on others. Women, after all, were (still are) the carriers and caretakers for both the present and future generations (Cott, 1977; Kerber, 1980; Kuhn, 1947).

Over the last several years, these same questions regarding women's reading have been the subject of varied and intense speculation by feminists but with an altogether different set of purposes. Impelled to understand both the secondary status of women and their contributions and recognizing, as well, the importance of reading as an aspect of gender construction, feminist researchers of many persuasions and disciplines have probed and delineated, speculated upon and pondered the many aspects of reading and reading practices—both historical and contemporary—in a search for the "effects" of reading in all its multiplicity upon woman's construction of self and her impact on the larger world.

Among those who have studied the questions from a historical perspective have been Baym (1978), Davidson (1986), Harris (1990), Kelley (1984, 1996), Kelly (1999), Motz (1996), Sicherman (1989), Tompkins (1985), and Zboray and Zboray (1999). Among those approaching the questions from the perspective of the more contemporary reader of relevance to this work have been Fetterley (1978) and Radway (1984).

This abundance of study focused on women's reading practices does not speak with one voice, reflecting as it does the varied theoretical orientations within feminism as well as the variety of subject matters that reflect the authors' specific discipline(s). However, all of these studies are concerned with the act of reading as a historical and/or political practice that intersects with women's lives and thought in ways that may be liberatory or constraining, or both.

A Privileging of the Reader

It was Cathy N. Davidson's much-praised, multilayered *The Revolution and the Word: The Rise of the Novel in America* (1986), a study of the early American novel and its readers, that opened critical vistas for thinking about the ways texts, specifically novels, could act on their readers' consciousness. Grounded in postmodern literary and reader-response theories, Davidson opens the "lost" texts of early America to argue against a view of the country's past determined by interpretations from one point of view only. Rather, she privileges the nonprivileged reader—the lower classes, both female and male—to find in their readings, as well as in the texts they loved to read, messages of suppressed equality consonant with the hopes and ambitions of the country as a whole. She argues "that the novel inspired education by stressing the sentimental and social value of literacy" (p. 14). Moreover, "novels allowed for a means of entry into a larger literary and intellectual world and a means of access to social and political events from which many readers (particularly women) would have been otherwise largely excluded" (p. 8). For women, "during the first decades of the ninteenth century," Davidson writes, "a cult of 'true womanhood' all but smothered the cry for female equality, a cry faintly but subversively heard in [the] sentimental novels" (p. 135) of the time. Creatively using the scant reader-response material available for this time period such as fly-leaf inscriptions, Davidson found passionate responses to these early novels. How these novels acted to change people's perspectives is, of course, impossible to say, but passionate responses mean, at the least, that responsive chords were being tapped in readers.

In her introductory chapters, Davidson explores the reasons that clergy and critics were worried about the effects of novels on women: "Fiction ... necessarily ruled out the very intermediation that the preacher was professionally prepared to provide" (p. 43). Ministers feared they would lose control over women's thoughts. Novel reading in the Republic, as Davidson points out, could not be controlled easily. But women did read novels! Indeed, by the mid-19th century, the growth of female readership had produced an important and profitable industry (Baym, 1978; Coultrap-McQuin, 1990; Kelley, 1984). Zboray (1993), however, cautions that it may well have been the other way around (p. 135).

Privileging Their Texts

Just as Davidson unearthed the texts of the early American reader, feminist scholars over the previous two decades had been bringing to light the long-buried, ignored, and often disparaged texts—especially novels—that women read in the mid-19th century. Helen Waite Papashivly (1956), in *All the Happy Endings*, was one of the first to map out this territory in a manner that took even somewhat seriously such demeaned and neglected works. Still valuable because of its historical role in calling attention to these almost lost works[2] as well as for its insights regarding how these texts might have mattered to their readers, nevertheless, her book has been critiqued by both Kelley (1984) and Harris (1990).

According to Harris (1990), Papashvily's interest was as much in commenting on the mores of the 1950s as it was with understanding women's reading of 19th-century fiction. Moreover, Harris makes clear that Papashvily's attitude toward her woman readers was, at best, ironic and, at worst, quite critical (p. 6). Mary Kelley goes even further in saying that, according to Papashvily, the novels "encouraged [in their women readers] a pattern of feminine behavior, so quietly ruthless, so subtly vicious that by comparison the ladies of Seneca appear angels of innocence" (p. 345).

Ann Douglas (1977), writing some 20 years after Papashivly in her much contested *The Feminization of American Culture*, saw in these same novels written by and for women a falling off from Puritan culture. As analyzed by one of *her* critics, Nina Baym, Douglas saw "women as partners with a demoralized clergy in the sentimentalization (a word she uses synonymously with feminization) and degradation of the old style Calvinist world view, and takes them seriously to task" (Baym, 1978, p. 310).

It was this negative stance toward 19th-century woman readers—and writers—that earned Douglas years of criticism from feminists. But more recently, her critical stance has become rehabilitated for having carved out—in a postmodern prefiguration—this territory as worthy of critical attention and as ground for serious cultural (re)evaluation. Susan K. Harris (1990), in her *19th-Century American Women's Novels: Interpretive Strategies*, though she takes a very different view of the texts women read in the mid-19th century and their impact, praises Douglas for her recognition of the importance of the transactive relationship between the reader and her text.

Douglas is clear in her critique of the female reader: "The supreme product of feminine fashion, the chief emblem of the emerging female consumer, was not found in the ladies' clothing, but rather, odd as it may initially sound, in her reading and writing" (1977, p. 61). Douglas does not put the full blame on women, but looks to the source of their desires with a definite Marxist slant:

> The feminine proclivity for novels, the young miss's resort to the pen and the confidante, a standard theme for jest in eighteenth- and nineteenth-century fiction, had a serious side. A Marxist might argue persuasively that American girls were socialized to immerse themselves in novels and letters in order to make their powerlessness in a masculine and anti-humanist society more certain and less painful. (p. 61)

Douglas becomes even more damning: "The stories they read and wrote were themselves courses in the shopping mentality, exercises in euphemism essential to the system of flattery which served as the rationale for the American women's economic position" (1977, p. 62). Not the only literary critic to be concerned about issues of power related to the reading of the mid-19th-century young woman, Douglas speculates about the possible benefits to women of such collusion: "In the patriarchal middle-class culture of mid-nineteenth-century America, the females were apparently being granted special status more as a substitute for power than an acknowledgment of it" (p. 61). Damning the novels, their authors, and their readers, Douglas summarizes these texts: "This literature seems today both ludicrous and painful in the evidence it offers of the enormous need of its authors and readers for uncritical confirmation of themselves and instantaneous satisfaction of their appetites" (p. 63). Most feminist scholars care to disagree.

Celebrating the Woman Reader—And Her Texts

Other researchers—Baym (1978), Harris (1990), Kelley (1984), Tompkins (1985)—have found in these same novels more complex, more humane, more "liberatory" messages of understanding. Nina Baym's 1978 text, *Woman's Fiction: A Guide to Novels by and about Women in America, 1820–1870*, remains an invaluable reference to the novels of the time. In sharp contrast to Douglas, Baym celebrates the woman author, her reader, and the novels they loved to write and read. While conceding it is not a radical literature (though some feminist scholars disagree), Baym seeks to understand the call and mission of the novel from the perspective of the reader herself; unlike Douglas, who is on a mission of critique of that same reader.

Baym (1978) outlines the tale the novels relate:

> The many novels all tell, with variations, a single tale. In essence, it is the story of a young girl who is deprived of the supports she had rightly or wrongly depended on to sustain her throughout life and is faced with the necessity of winning her own way in the world. (p. 13)

While Baym concedes that the authors of these novels knew that it was their obligation to produce stories that were certainly "entertainment" (1978, p. 16), she also makes clear that "entertainment is not a simple concept since there are such divergences in what different groups find entertaining" (p. 16). And, in any case, these authors, according to Baym, had a mission: "They meant their readers to take away something from their reading that would help them in their lives" (pp. 16–17). Baym next, in calling attention to the didactic function, makes a move that underlines the potential seriousness and complexity of the concept of entertainment:

> Instruction is not at cross-purposes with entertainment in this fiction, nor is entertainment the sweet coating on a didactic pill. The lesson itself is an entertainment in that the heroine's triumph over so much adversity and so many obstacles is profoundly pleasurable to those readers who identify with her. (p. 17)

Baym next describes the structure these texts generally follow:

> The authors' solutions [to the problems facing the heroine] are different
> from case to case and somewhat less simple than the dilemma, but all involve
> the heroine's accepting herself as female while rejecting the equation of
> female with permanent child. Thus, while commiserating with the heroine in
> difficulties not of her own making, the stories hold her entirely responsible
> for overcoming them. (p. 17)

In contrast to Ann Douglas's stance toward the 19th-century woman reader,
Baym's respect for her readers is evident, a pattern that still resonates.

Jane P. Tompkins (1985), a reader-response theorist and author of *Sensational Designs: The Cultural Work of American Fiction: 1790–1860*, takes as one
of her fundamental assumptions that women in the 19th century suffered
from a lack of political and property rights. She calls women's reading of
the 19th-century sentimental novel "a strategy of survival" (p. 169), calling
attention to the bind of both the woman author and the woman reader.
She writes:

> The ethic of sentimental fiction, unlike that of writers like Melville, Emerson,
> and Thoreau, was an ethic of submission. But the relation of sentimental
> authors to their subservient condition and to the dominant beliefs about the
> nature and function of women was more complicated than Tocqueville supposed (p. 161)

—or Ann Douglas!

Tompkins (1985) outlines the problems women faced that this domestic
fiction set about solving: issues of power (specifically, lack of), limitation to
the home, and the pain and rage such limitations aroused. She says of the
first and overriding issue: "It is no exaggeration to say that domestic fiction
is preoccupied, even obsessed with the nature of power" (p. 160). In this,
she concurs with Douglas that power is indeed the issue. Tompkins next
shows how this issue worked its way through the novels:

> The two questions these female novelists never fail to ask are: what is power
> and where is it located?... [They] could not assume a stance of open rebel-
> lion ... for they lacked the material means of escape or opposition. They had
> to stay put and submit. And so the domestic novelists made that necessity the
> basis on which to build a power structure of their own. Instead of rejecting
> the culture's value system outright, they appropriated it for their own use ...
> [in ways] that allowed them both to fulfill and transcend their appointed
> roles. (pp. 160–161)

Tompkins highlights the central issue for both the women authors of these
novels as well as that of the devoted reader of the texts:

Since they could neither own property, nor vote, nor speak at a public meeting if both sexes were present, women had to have a way of defining themselves which gave them power and status nevertheless, in their own eyes and in the eyes of the world. That is the problem sentimental fiction addresses. (p. 161)

Tompkins argues that these novels celebrate the detail of the everyday as the answer to the required submission of the self necessary to their perceived situation of political powerlessness. The novels illustrate how "piety and industry ... can set you free ... [by providing] a way of thinking about [your] work that redeemed the particularities of daily existence" (p. 168). By offering, thereby, a way for women to save the whole world by taking excellent care of their small corner of it and thereby "learning to conquer her own passions" (p. 172), such novels offer a "strategy for survival."

Susan K. Harris (1990), in her study of "textual structure and reading behaviors" (p. 13), asks the question of her own reader: "How do we make sense of a book?" (p. 2). To help her own readers become better readers of the mid-19th-century domestic novel, she describes the codes embedded in these books that the authors were able to take for granted that their 19th-century readers would understand: "the Protestant code of piety; the privileging of sentiment; and the privileging of the female experience" (pp. 78–79).

Offering a differing reading of these novels than Baym (1978) or Tompkins (1985), Harris (1990) finds "a far more radical vision of female possibilities embedded in the texts" (p. 13). Calling them "ideologically subversive," she sees them as "embed[ding] radical possibilities within their thematic and rhetorical frameworks" and says that "these deviations were accessible to contemporary readers" who were "capable of configuring ... the texts differently than the cover story indicated" (p. 13). According to her, 19th-century women readers "could recognize the need for multiple reading strategies" (p. 18). She goes further and states that these "women's novels function as a means of testing women's possibilities for alternative modes of being" (p. 19), and embedded in these books are adventures—"verbal, structural, and thematic" (p. 20).

These books, while conventional in beginning and end, she continues, have "middle portions [which] establish an area of female independence, competence, emotional complexity, and intellectual acumen that sets the stage ... for other women to 'read' a far different message than the one the novels overtly profess" (p. 21). The cover plot, she says, for the woman's novels is that "women need men for protection" (p. 20). But the radical underplot is "that women can learn how to achieve physical, emotional, and financial independence" (p. 21).

Nina Baym (1978) argues against this view of the novels consisting of cover story and hidden message:

Although I do not doubt that these women had as many conflicts, conscious or unconscious, as human beings generally do, I do not find their fiction beset by contradictions, defenses, or duplicities. As I have argued, this was not a profoundly radical fiction by any means, neither on the surface or in its depths; but such progressive ideas as it had are clearly there and constituted its major intention. (p. 311)

Celebratory Regarding Reading

Whether considered a vehicle for radical messages of independence, a means of solace and survival, a source of strength by celebrating the detail of the everyday, a source of verbal adventure for the most part these scholars from the 1980s and 1990s (Nina Baym, Susan K. Harris, Jane P. Tompkins) tended to see the novels of the women readers of their studies not as avenues for politicization, but as vehicles for validating women's experiences and value to themselves and their network of kin and friend.

Taking a stronger view of literacy's potential for change and politicization, a view that has implicit in it a definition of literacy as a tool for advantage, a tool for use in a wider social world than the sphere of the home, several current theorists tend to make much larger claims for reading's transformative benefits, consistent with Cathy N. Davidson's claims for the role of the early American novel and akin to the literacy myth as set forth by Harvey J. Graff (1987).

The key message within Ronald J. and Mary Saracino Zboray's thoughtful "'Month of Mondays': Women's Reading Diaries and the Everyday Transcendental" is implicit in its title. Throughout their study of reading diaries, they highlight "the vibrant role of literacy in transcending the everyday" (1999, p. 1), clearly taking a view that differs from Jane P. Tompkins, whereby the reading of novels that sacramentalize the everyday become a "strategy of survival." The Zborays write: "Calling upon personal papers to understand women's literary imagination is not new" (p. 2). Many authors (and they cite several identified above), have used personal writings "in order to comprehend the ways women's reading subverted gendered prescriptions, were instrumental to self-fashioning, or otherwise helped them transgress the boundaries of their sphere" (p. 2). Comparing the reading diary offerings of men and women, for the Zborays, the men's responses to their reading—or lack thereof—suggested that, for men, reading was not integrated into their lives. For the women of their study the opposite was true:

Their writing in diaries described reading in two interrelated ways: they wrote about allying domestic chores with reading or they wrote about literature as a way to transcend the mundane into the world of more public or universal concerns. Either way, the reading diary for women was devoted to enhancing intellectual, imaginative activity, while remaining firmly rooted in everyday routines. (p. 4)

Using Marilyn Ferris Motz's concept of the private alibi (1994)—wherein women use the domestic as a cover for thoughts and activities the 19th-century would "normally" accord to males—the Zborays show how "many women who kept reading diaries … commented upon intellectual issues as part of [their] reception of reading matter" (p. 5). These intellectual issues, according to the Zborays, could take the shape of a hunger for ideas. Indeed one of their diarists, Harriet Low, vowed "at the beginning of her 1829 journal, to write every day and put some ideas or extracts of what I have been reading in the course of the day.… It will serve to impress it [reading] upon my mind" (p. 2).

Another of the diarists of their study, Martha Barrett, wrote in 1855:

The thought of wanting so much intellectually and physically almost unnerves [me], and yet why should it, how many have had to do more than I have to, and have succeeded. I want to study but have neither the time or the means. [M]any people would laugh at the idea of wanting to study at my age, but the older I grow the more I feel my intellectual needs. (p. 6)

For African-American Charlotte Forten, the intellectual issues took the shape of a lifelong critique of slavery and oppression. As an example, the Zborays quote from one of her journal entries: "[I]ndignant about the arrest of Anthony Burns as a fugitive slave [she] quoted William Cowper's 'The Task'" (p. 6), a critique of slavery.

Mary Kelley also makes much of the "transformative potential" of woman's reading through "self-fashioning." Viewing literacy from the perspective of the reader rather than that of the author as she did in *Private Women, Public Stage: Literary Domesticity in the 19th Century* (1984), Kelley, in her 1996 article "Reading Women/Women Reading: The Making of Learned Women in Antebellum America," challenges the idea of "female reading as passive consumption of textually determined meanings" (p. 405). Instead, she finds that the women of her study showed

a remarkable engagement with reading. Reading women embraced books, literally and figuratively—companions on voyages of discovery, they relished the play of ideas, delighted in unexpected insights, and meditated upon newly found knowledge to spark flights of fancy, relieve solitude, provoke laughter and furnish refuge. Consistently books served as the ground on which woman readers built a dense and diversified mental life.… Perhaps most important, reading women made books a site for experiments in personal transformation. (pp. 402–403)

It is Kelley's contention that, through their reading, the women were transforming themselves, thereby creating a new ideal—"that of the learned woman" (1996, p. 403). She takes on the perceived ideology of the time to challenge the notion of the passive female reader. Rather, she finds that the women of her study "exercised an agency that historians and literary critics ... have disregarded" (p. 405). She argues that her reconstruction of the reading world of the women of her study "challenges the ... familiar idea of female behavior as reflecting an ideology of domesticity that sharply limited impulses toward self-determination" (p. 405).

Marilyn Ferris Motz, in "The Private Alibi: Literacy and Community in the Diaries of Two Nineteenth-Century American Women," likewise makes large claims for the role of reading in women's lives. The two women of her study

> [Lucy] Keeler, as a published author, and [Harriet] Johnson, as a school-teacher, were engaged in occupations directly involving literacy. While both women apparently were poorly paid and neither occupation seems to have been among the most highly respected in the communities, their jobs probably afforded Keeler and Johnson the acknowledged, although devalued, privilege of following intellectual issues. (p. 195)

Both of these women, according to Motz "created themselves as actors moving in circles that were simultaneously local, national, and universal" (p. 201). Furthermore, their reading provided them "with options to the attitudes and mores of the local community"; helped them enter "vicariously into a community of literacy and ideas that provided them with ways to approach their own lives"; and "positioned [them] to act as agents of change in their communities" (p. 202).

Thus, differences of opinions exist in the import and effect of women's reading of the womanist texts of the 19th century. The theorists above ponder readings' use as a strategy of survival (Harris, 1990; Tompkins, 1985); as a vehicle "for the construction of individual consciousness" (Motz, 1996); as an "instrument for self-fashioning" (Kelley, 1996); and as a vehicle for "transgressing the boundaries of their sphere" (Zboray & Zboray, p. 2, 1999)

Of the texts themselves and their possible influence—regardless of whether they are taken to be seductive manuals for learning how to become the shopping paragon so vital to the success of capitalism; manuals of strategies for ensuring emotional survival; guides for self-development in the event of economic or social catastrophe; or handbooks of general subversion against the political order—the key is that woman *is* often the privileged subject, as Cathy N. Davidson articulates so well:

> Only in fiction would the average early woman reader encounter a version of her world existing for her own sake, and, more important, only in the senti-

mental novel would her reading about this world be itself validated. As an added bonus, in not a few of these novels, women readers encountered women characters whose opinions mattered. (p. 123)

TO THEIR ACTUAL READING

Holding these possibly conflicting, disparate roles of literacy in abeyance for now, let's turn to the "traces" the young (and not so young) Wright/ Mott/Osborne women left in their writings. These young women were devoted readers of many of those very texts—novels and nonfiction—that the feminist researchers above are devoted to arguing about. What is most striking in looking at their reading references embedded in the correspondence, especially through the 1840s and 1850s when the young women were in their formative years, is how many of the books they mentioned in their letters and recommended to one another were the very books rescued from their oblivion by the above feminist researchers. The novels that they read were frequently by, for, and about women and had, as their central theme, the development of the young girl into the woman who can, albeit within a relatively constricted environment, lead a life true to her psyche and talents. Confirming the "highly eclectic" patterns of reading of the New York Society patrons of Zboray's study (1993, p. 169) as well as the women of Mary Kelley's study who "read widely" (1996, p. 404), we see, too, how the young Wright/Mott/Osborne women also read nonfictional texts, many of which centered on women and their lives.

Certainly not all the resurrected titles and authors are mentioned in the correspondence, and there are a few titles that had wide readership at mid-century that are missing from this reconstruction of their reading.[3] Indeed, Susan K. Harris makes the point that often these titles are scarcely mentioned in correspondence or diaries, their readers knowing full well the general evaluation of these texts. We must be very grateful for the amount of data recorded by these readers. In sum, their patterns of reading along with many specific titles follow many theorists' reconstructions of mid-19th-century women's reading.

While devoted readers of these novels, the young Wright/Mott/ Osborne women were, at the same time, full participants in the general current of mid-19th-century reading—as members of their class and their mothers' political and social bent. They didn't read "just" these novels, as the male historians of literacy would have it. They read Dickens as soon as his texts were off the boat; they read the canonical authors of the day—Carlyle, Lamb, Ruskin; and they read the male sentimentalists as well. Moreover, they were devoted newspaper readers, sharing and sending issues to one another, and they also were regular readers of the important periodicals of the times such as *Harper's* and *The Atlantic.* Of course, too, although it is not a focus of this study, they had their own school textbooks that were filled with selections from the "best" authors of the day, male and female.

PURPOSES

The purposes of this chapter are three-fold. The first is to begin to delineate the outline and patterns of their actual reading; the second is to begin to reveal from the evidence in the letters of the young Wright/Mott/Osborne women their responses to these texts and the place they held in their lives. And the third is to begin to place these varied and often vivid responses within the context of the feminist research above. The overall goal, reserved for the "Endings" chapter, is to have these understandings provide the context within which to comprehend what reading might have meant to the Wright/Mott/Osborne women and how it intersected with their gendered lives as 19th-century women as either a liberatory or constraining force, or both. Finally, it has always been my hope to bring these understandings to an inchoate history of literacy that takes the reading experiences of women as seriously as the reading experiences of men, joining and adding to all the scholarship cited herein.

Their Wide Reading: Women Reading (Mostly) Women

As we saw in the opening of this chapter, on November 16, 1846, Eliza Wright asked of her cousin Pattie, "What are you reading nowadays?" before volunteering her own recent reading. This question that Eliza asked of her cousin Pattie can often be "heard" in the correspondence of these young women because so often they describe or mention the titles of their most recent reading in their replies to their letters from Eliza. Her inquiries must be made frequently as to what her correspondents of the moment are reading because often letters to her begin with an inquiry regarding her own reading, such as the one from Pattie, her most faithful correspondent: "Yes, I have read [Dickens's] "The Haunted Man" (MML to EWO: 2.5.49). A year and a few months later a friend, Lottie Pearl, wrote to Eliza: "You wished to know what I was reading" (LP to EWO: 5.5.50).

The correspondence from 1845 to 1850 in the Osborne Family Papers consists more of letters to Eliza Wright than from her. The person addressed—by cousins, sister, and would-be boyfriends—was one who is very interested in books as well as knowledgeable about them. A cousin by marriage made a point of sending her poetry from a newspaper he was editing (TC to EWO: 11.10.45; TC to EWO: 11.23. 45), and Eliza herself often sent books and newspapers to her cousins and friends, sometimes in lieu of letters, writing important information in the margins of the paper (*SSC*, EWO to MCW: 4.3.46). During these 5 years, before any of the friends and cousins became engaged or married, their letters to one another revealed that they were knowledgeable readers and critics eager to be kept aware of the others' reading and, eager, too, to share their own reading. In Nina Baym's words, they were participants in "a broad-ranging and widely circulated discourse about the novel" (1984, p. 270) that was taking place in mid-19th-century America.

In May 1845, Rebecca Yarnall wrote from Philadelphia to her cousin Eliza Wright (Osborne) in Auburn. The closing few lines of the letter are all about reading:

> Because you write me a good long letter by Tom Mott, I will send you Sowing & Reaping & Alice Franklin which is a continuation of the first. I think you will like them & they are the only ones that I have that you have not read I believe. I mean all the interesting ones. Good bye. Yours Truly, Your cousin, Becka (RY to EWO: 5.17.45)

Encoded in this closing of Rebecca's letter was a great deal of information regarding both the reading of these particular young women, and the reading of 19th-century young women as reconstructed by the above feminist researchers. In these few lines, Rebecca Yarnall showed her cousin Eliza to be very much a reader and a careful evaluator of what she had read. It suggested that both of them were current in their reading as well as knowledgeable regarding publishing conventions. They knew that titles of books could both stand alone and be connected serially, that books were published within a time frame. Moreover, by not having to state the author of these texts, Rebecca revealed the amount of shared knowledge the cousins possessed regarding this particular author, the British author and Quaker Mary Howitt (whose works were sometimes credited to her husband).

A certain loyalty to the author seemed to be indicated as well, as does a certain skepticism regarding the interest level of all Mary Howitt's texts, which were more "pious" than much of their reading. The lines also revealed that an important task of the books they read and shared was to be "interesting." And, of course, the book titles they mentioned were by a woman. Probably more didactic than some of their reading or than the novels the feminists cite, one reviewer of a Mary Howitt novel noted "that the 'incidental reflections are excellent in their tendency'" (Baym, 1984, p. 123).

These few lines also reveal an overriding feature of both the correspondence as a whole and the separated-out offerings on reading: these young women belonged to a community of writers sharing the details of their lives, and they belonged to a community of readership that was both local and cosmopolitan. That is, they shared titles and authors with one other as cousins and friends, *and* these readings are very much in accord with all the reconstructions of female 19th-century reading. For this particular family there may be a weight toward authors and texts of a Quaker and abolitionist bent, but their reading still looks like the hypothesized version of what the more fortunate, 19th-century young woman was most probably reading.

The next excerpt selected from the correspondence (which could have used a little editing by its writer) is from a letter written on May 11, 1847, by Rebecca's (and Eliza's) cousin, Pattie, and is addressed to Eliza:

> Read a book about Tom Thumb who is exhibiting himself here at the present—Have read To Seem and To Be. Have you read Crock of Gold—saw it at the museum last week. (MML to EWO: 5.11.47)

This brief excerpt, too, reveals a great deal about their reading. It shows how important reading is to them and how important is the sharing of that practice—along with its titles—within this community of women relatives and writers. It also reveals the interconnectedness of reading within the context of the cultural performances and activities of the day. Often in the correspondence, this connection of reading with cultural events was highlighted. Frequently, going to a play—whether by the famous Dickens or by the now-forgotten Edward Fitzball[1] as is the case here with "Crock of Gold" (the book from which the play was taken)—either encouraged the reading of that book or the reading of the book had prompted attendance at the play. Whether Pattie went to see Tom Thumb this month of May in 1847 we don't know, but we do know she read this book, and we can assume that the Philadelphia newspaper read by the Motts, the *Public Ledger*, would have had both advertisements and news articles about this exhibition.

To Seem and To Be, the subtitle Pattie used for *Two Lives* by Maria McIntosh, was published in 1846 and was, according to Nina Baym (1978),

> the first of the new wave of woman's best sellers. It uses a pair of contrasting heroines [as did many of these novels]; with one it pursues the theme of the dangers of dependency, with the other it shows the dangers of independence. (pp. 91–92)

While this description might indicate that the moral of the story might have something to do with the despairing thought—not new to us—that women can't win, Baym says that the plot's twists and turns indicate dependency, which has for so long been presented to women as good strategy for their weakness, is in fact bad policy. Independence, when it means following principle instead of fashion and when it does not degenerate into inflexibility, is more than its own reward. (p. 93)

Perhaps someday among the collections not yet tapped, Pattie's or Eliza's response to this novel will be unearthed. Until then, we can only assume the possible effect of such a story within a setting of limited opportunities—political, economic, educational, and cultural.

The next excerpt is also from Pattie and addressed to Eliza. In it she wrote that she had read the sequel of *To Seem and To Be*. Lonely, her opening sentences to Eliza on September 8, 1848, was packed with reading references:

> While Mother was away last week, I felt more lonely than ever you did—two days were spent at Coulter's but the evenings were mostly alone. I longed for you to be here—you have no idea how stupid it was—nobody in town—My last resort was novels—Sir Theodore Broughton and Charms & Countercharms were all I read. The first is pretty good but don't read it though—the other is much better than To Seem and To Be—it is very interesting. I want father to give me Miss Strickland's new edition of the Queens of England but we are so "darned" poor that I don't expect to have it. Last Sunday Mr. Furness preached against persons spending all their time in making money. How few were happy with it and a lot of very pretty ideas that one likes to hear. But I confess that he did not convince me that money didn't add to happiness. (MML to EWO: 9. 8. 48)

The book Pattie suggested that her cousin Eliza *not* bother to read is by G. P. R. James, the British author of historical novels who is one of the inspirations of the writing contest that has would-be authors begin their contest entry with "It is a dark and stormy night." An 1842 reviewer of one of his books wrote:

> There may be those who can throw aside the veil which hides the human heart, trace the windings of its tortuous, self-returning labyrinths, coolly watch the fierce conflict between the passions that inhabit them, and then, returning to this "upper light" spread before us a faithful map of their wanderings, and a graphic picture of their struggles; but if such there be, Mr. James is not one of them. (quoted by Baym, 1984, p. 95)

As Pattie Mott knew, *Charms and Countercharms* (1848) was a sequel to *To Seem and To Be* (or *Two Lives*, 1846), which went through eight editions and sold 100,000 copies (Baym, 1978, p. 87). The novel "is an ambitious, unconventional treatment of the theme of destructive feminine dependency [that] introduces two heroines" (p. 93), one of whom needs to learn the lesson that "piety and independence are closely allied, because the woman who depends on God does not need to depend on men" (p. 95). Placing some of the blame for her plight on woman's education, the narrator of the story says:

> Woman was not intended solely as an embellishment to the life of man.... However they may have been neglected or even repressed by her education, she has aspirations as high, desires as vast as he, and powers fitting her at least to follow his lead, and sympathize with his noblest efforts. (quoted by Baym, 1978, p. 94)

Needless to say, the heroine learned the lesson and made a good marriage for herself. The effect on woman readers of such messages through these authorial reflections and plot lines we cannot know, but that so much of the reading of the 19th-century young woman was exactly of such stories, we can assume that these stories had resonance and gave pleasure.

A year later a friend wrote to Eliza:

> You wished to know what I was reading. I have had no regular course during the winter mostly miscellania. I have just finished Mrs. Ellis's "Hearts and Homes" and liked it very much. I think it would interest you. (Lottie Pearl to EWO: 5. 5. 50)

The "miscellania" Lottie Pearl would have read in the winter of 1849 or 1850 could have been a periodical, such as "The Ladies' Repository" or "Godey's Lady's Book" (Baym, 1984, pp. 16–17), or perhaps a more religiously oriented compendium such as *The Casket*. Such books were a staple of women's reading in the 19th century and often contained excerpts of novels or short stories by woman authors. Nina Baym (1984) cites reviewers' comments on Mrs. Sarah Ellis. One in 1851 called her "'[a]n excellent domestic writer'" (p. 203) while an earlier one, in 1843, wrote: "'Mrs. Ellis belongs to the class of utilitarian novelists, which are, we are happy to say, gaining ground'" (p. 215). A writer of more didactic novels than Maria McIntosh, authors like Sarah Ellis[5] coexisted with those who offered more feminist messages. From the rather cloying prose of Lottie Pearl's letters to Eliza Wright, it is not surprising that this was the kind of novel she would enjoy.

To backtrack slightly, one of the books Pattie cited and that she had put on her wish list was Miss Strickland's *Queen's of England*. Not a novel, although written by an author of historical romances (Baym, 1984), it represents another important genre (one that appeared with relative frequency in the letters), books of nonfiction written by women and that often have women as their subject. While sometimes noted in the critical literature (Flint, 1993; Grever, 1989), this genre has not yet been accorded as much critical attention as the novels of the mid-19th century. Yet, in their privileging of woman as subject, often as historical reclamations of their lives, this form served some of the same functions of the above novels.

The next instance of this genre goes in the other direction—from Philadelphia to Auburn, as Pattie wrote to Eliza:

> I am going to get Miss Martineau's Eastern Travels. Have you seen it? It is highly spoken of. Stephen's Monk I have not read. I should like to very much. If I am left alone next summer it will be a nice time to read. My French takes up considerable time & dissipation considerable more. (MML to EWO: 2.5.49)

The author of the book on Pattie's wish list, *Eastern Travels*, was Harriet Martineau. Often a visitor in her mother's home, Martineau (1802–1876), was British, an abolitionist, a social critic, novelist, writer, and feminist whose 1837 *Society in America* was "sharply critical of the treatment accorded women" (Gurko, 1974, p. 271). Pattie had obviously heard (or read) positive responses to Miss Martineau's writings.

Thus, to summarize, much of the reading that these young women were doing and sharing with one another—both as titles they hoped the other would read but also as a vehicle for keeping their community of communication alive—were those very novels resurrected from their oblivion by the feminist literary researchers Baym (1978, 1984), Davidson (1986), Douglas (1977), Harris (1990), Kelley (1984), and Tompkins (1985). Whether these novels served as guidebooks to consumerism, taught strategies for survival, and/or provided models for finding the "right" man, is not, of course, quite clear yet. But what is clear and will be clearer still was the power of these texts to move the emotions (Baym, 1984, pp. 272–274).

Their Reading of Male Authors—Dickens: A Special Case

Quite clearly, woman authors—both writers of fiction and nonfiction—figured prominently in the reading practices of these young Wright/Mott/Osborne women. This is not to say, however, that they didn't also read—and interact positively with—novels authored by males. One male author, in particular, held their allegiance throughout the correspondence, and that, of course, was Charles Dickens. The allusions to his books are not only almost a complete publishing list of his titles, but the references in the letters often corresponded to the precise date of American publication, either as book or serial presentation.

These titles mentioned include several of his Christmas stories as well as the novels. "Have you read The Battle of Life [?]" asked Pattie of Eliza on

March 23, 1847 (MML to EWO: 3.23.47). "I do not like it as well as his other Christmas Stories but it is very interesting." They had read, as well, *Dombey & Son, David Copperfield,* and *Bleak House* and, as we shall see, the characters in these novels were an important vehicle for communication for the women. In 1856, Eliza's sister, Ellen Wright (later, Garrison), age 16 and away at school, went so far as to say, in relation to a play being presented at her school, Eagleswood:[6] "Would that I were Dickens—what excellent scope" (EWG to EWO: 11.10.56).

Dickens was not the only male author to elicit positive response. There was a positive reference to the works of Scott, with one of the cousins receiving the *Poetical Works* for a present as well as one to a work by Alexandre Dumas. Pattie's reference to Dumas doesn't name the title, but does contain high praise: "That fancy dress does not require short skirts—get the book and read it—it is by Dumas and a first rate novel" (MML to EWO: 11.21.5). Certainly, not all the referents are clear but the command is!

Two other male authors that evoked a more or less positive response were Charles Kingsley, writer of *Alton Locke,* and Eugene Sue, author of *The Mysteries of Paris.* Both writers were viewed favorably within the extended family because of the social critique embedded within their novels. However, while Pattie liked the former novel, it is clear that Eliza didn't, regardless of its appropriate critique. Pattie asked her, in response to what must have been a sentiment expressed in Eliza's last letter to her, on December 22, 1850: "Why don't you like Alton Locke? I think it is very good—not as a novel, the plot is nothing but the sentiments therein expressed are of the right kind" (MML to EWO: 12.22.50). Eugene Sue's *The Mysteries of Paris,* which kept Pattie company over 150 years ago, had a reputation at the time for being a risqué book, its "political correctness" only a cover for its presumed more racy content.

Other male authors didn't fare as well. As we have seen, the historical novels of G. P. R. James did not seem to evoke the favorable responses of the novels of Maria McIntosh. Indeed, in 1850, Eliza referred to James's novels as "forlorn." (Eliza, as she was so often, was on the mark, as almost any random opening of that novel, *Sir Theodore Broughton,* will illustrate: "Decay is in every thing, and as certainly follows complete development as old age follows manhood" [p. 99], to provide just one example.) Thus, while books by and about women held the attention and loyalty of these young women, they did not ignore those written by the sterner sex.

Later Reading—with Jane Eyre, A *Very* Special Case

As the young Wright/Mott/Osborne women became engaged and then married, their interest in and attention to novels appeared not to have diminished. They continued both to share their readings and to use them as a vehicle for communicating their thoughts and feelings.

In a letter written over a two-week period, Martha Mott (Lord) wrote to her cousin Eliza Wright Osborne, now married and expecting her first child:

> Thursday March 3.... I am glad for you to have an opportunity to hear Thackeray. I think you will like him—how much time you have to read—a great advantage which communities have not—the paper you speak of we never see—We only take the Tribune & Evening Post—both very good—I think your Father takes the latter—read "Mr. Whitehead's W[M?]ill"—it is smart & amusing. Bleak House don't interest me as much as Copperfield or Dombey— I always forget it till it appears in the papers—I was quite interested last evening looking over "Daisy Burns"—by Miss Kavanagh. I went up to Mrs. Lords to tea & while at table an invitation came from Mrs. Slade to George to wait on her to the Opera—I was glad for him to go & not caring to spend the evening there without him, I cut some in a hurry & in the same manner he cut around to Slade's—found Anna Brown here—she & Edward soon became engrossed in chess—Tom was in New York—& Marianna & I had an "enjoyment time" novel reading. We have operatic tickets for Friday & Saturday—Norma & Loumary ___ [?] it is the first opera troupe we have had this winter—and now only for 4 nights. Anna Brown is going with her brother Edward—Walter is out West—Mother has been on a large prison spree to New York—but she will enlarge upon so I need not. (MML & MPM to EWO: 2.14–3.3.53)

This excerpt reveals the dual parameters of their cultural *milieu*, that which had as its site the public spaces of 19th-century Philadelphia—attendance (or lack of) at lectures by famous authors, casual attendance at the opera, knowledge of the specifics of these offerings, including the current literary fare. In a two-page addition to this letter (harbored for a couple of weeks), Marianna wrote: "We enjoyed very much the reading of Mother's nice letter yesterday. The wit we all appreciated & shouted at" (MPM to EWO: 3.3.53). This additional excerpt, in combination with the above, provides a window into the cultural activities within the family spaces—the playing of chess and the reading of newspapers, novels, and their own letters.

Of the many book titles listed in this letter excerpt, Dickens was, of course, well represented but lesser-known titles such as *Mr. Whitehead's M[W]ill*—which is "smart and amusing"—had their place as well. But the title that held the keenest interest for the "older," young women readers here was Julia Kavanagh's *Daisy Burns*. It was, most probably, one of the novels with which Pattie and Marianna had "an enjoyment time" reading. And most likely it was the pleasure that novel-reading provided them that explains the rather idiosyncratic use of "enjoyment time" here. As with most of the women, Pattie was no slouch with individual vocabulary choices. She seemed, here, to want to mark off the time she and her cousin/sister-in-law had spent that evening in a special way that would be heeded by her knowledgeable reader, Eliza. An 1855 reviewer of one of Miss Kavanagh's novels, perhaps *Daisy Burns*, wrote that "'her minute painting gives a reality to her fictions, which makes them more interesting than those of most other novelists'" (Baym, 1984, p. 155). From this review excerpt and the title we can see that *Daisy Burns* was one of the many novels privileging the lives of women.

The next three excerpts of note from the Osborne Family Papers concerning the later reading of these young women contain references to both the book title and the character, *Jane Eyre*. Published in 1847, the book has long been a keystone of critical attention by feminist researchers. Praised and damned for its depiction of "rebellious feminism" (Gilbert & Gubar, 1979, p. 338), *Jane Eyre*, novel and character, tapped a raw gender nerve on both sides of the Atlantic and was an important referent for the gendered understandings of the Wright/Mott/Osborne women.

Many references from the Osborne Family Papers show that both the book and the character are genuine touchstones for these women's beliefs about gender. Moreover, their references to Jane, as they thought of her, pointed to the importance of literary characters in their psychic lives.

On February 9, 1855, Marianna Pelham Mott wrote to her sister, Eliza, now pregnant with her second child: "Yesterday I intended to devote to you—but a bewitching novel—Nathalie—resembling Jane Eyre—was the means of paving a large area in that warm place" (MPM to EWO: 2.9–11.55). Here, Marianna appeared to be calling attention to the novel itself. In her comparison, we can infer how exciting *Jane Eyre* as a novel must have been to her. We can see, too, how novel reading—at least the reading of novels that bewitch—could be the occasion for putting aside necessary tasks. Although a task sometimes spoken of as somewhat of a burden, letter writing was often a labor of love. One wonders how large an area a novel could pave when the task was less appealing! And we know from this excerpt that knowledge about *Jane Eyre*, the novel, could be taken for granted.

Another reference to Jane Eyre, in this case, the character, appeared in a letter written on June 7, 1854. Martha Mott Lord, married now for a year, wrote to her cousin and friend, Eliza Wright Osborne, regarding her reading of some books given to her by a male cousin, Ellis Yarnall, brother of Rebecca.

> George [her husband] has been missing since 10 o'clock. He promised to return to dinner & now it is nearly 4 & I've nearly strained my eyes out looking for a white horse—It's real lonesome, Elizy, not to have her here. Won't she come again? I never did know such pison long days. It is positively dis-

gusting. I read, sew, walk, sweep & dust, look out the window, examine the garden. I have an hour or so that I don't know what on airth to do. Them books of Ellis'—is overpowering—"Lingard" causes severe pain in the eyelids. De Quincey is very entertaining—but Agatha's Husband is not at all to my fancy.... It makes women such a poor little dependent fool—not a bit like Jane. You remember Kate spoke highly of it. (MML to EWO: 6.5.54)

Somewhat of a contradiction existed here between Pattie's critical attitude toward women who appeared fools because they were dependent— and her description of her day—trouble filling up the hours, pursuing activities that for the most part appear to be limited (at this time she was living in a small, rented summer place), and "straining" her eyes looking for her husband to return home, and on a white horse! The books by male authors presented by cousin Ellis have a mixed reception from Pattie: literati De Quincey was readable but Lingard, quite possibly the sermons of John Lingard, clearly was not. It was Miss Mulock's *Agatha's Husband* that elicited the most personal response from the reader. Clearly, the character in this romance compared unfavorably to Jane (Jane Eyre) in Pattie's eyes, and Pattie was quite clear as to where that difference rested.

The last reference from the Osborne Family Papers to be cited here referring to Jane Eyre, character and/or book title, was in a letter written in 1859. From Martha Coffin Wright to her daughter Eliza, it related some remarks made by a young man about whom Martha and other family members seemed to have had reservations:

John Plumly[7] called on Sunday; he and his mother called for Ellen, the evening before to go to a Concert. He told us that the audience was a very intelligent one, there was not a snob there—I asked him how he ascertained that fact—and cousin Mary pinned him up so to definitions that he was rather scared, and wanted Ellen to sit farther off from her, but she didn't.... He thought somebody was exactly like Jane Eyre—Mary asked him who he meant—Jane Eyre was but an imaginary personage—"Still," I said, "our knowledge of 'Charlotte Brontë' made her real to us"—John said, she was as real to us as Jack Falstaff or _____,' or 'Jack Frost' said Mary [Earle]. (MCW to EWO: 3.8.59)

While there are certainly some ambiguities of reference in this excerpt, what is clear here is that, for Martha Coffin Wright and by extension, her daughters and nieces (but not for Mary Earle, an older cousin), Jane Eyre was "real" to them. By that, it seems as if they took the character of this novel to be a personage about whom they could talk, as they "spoke" about their relatives or acquaintances, moralizing, sharing, supporting, a character to whom they could relate their own experiences and use as a vehicle for communication.

Character(s)

Just as the character, Jane Eyre, and the characters of Dickens's novels were very real to the Wright/Mott/Osborne women, so Barbara Sicherman (1989), in an article on the reading of the well-placed, 19th-century Hamilton family women,[8] points to the importance of the characters these passionate readers found in the books they had read: "The Hamiltons' world was peopled with fictional characters. It was not just that as readers they were 'admitted into the company and present at the conversation'" (p. 81, quoting Davidson [1986] quoting Benjamin Franklin). No! "The fictional company was very real to them" (p. 81).

The Wright/Mott/Osborne family members made many uses of Charles Dickens's characters, often in matters of deportment. In 1847, Pattie wrote to Eliza about the current Dickens tale: "Poor little Paul's death was so sorrowful" and she made a prediction: "Mr. Dombey, I think, will take Walter into the firm & he will marry Florence—Mary has an invitation to spend next winter with J. Hallowell. I'm used up now.... Goodbye" (MML to EWO: 3.23.47). In addition to using his characters for morality checks and promises for future mutual reading, the characters in Dickens were also used by the women as a vehicle to personify praise:

> We thought Mother [MCW] very brilliant today. Of course it is more comfortable to be a Mrs. Nickleby than a Minerva—and much more agreeable to most of humanity—To think of Mother [MCW] ever complaining when she confesses to 0 [zero] pleasures in life—Lucky mortal that she is—many would feel satisfied with less—All those intellectual treats I will leave for Mother Mott [LCM] to dwell upon with suitable gusto. (MML & MPM to EWO: 2.9–11.52)

Interestingly, Marianna ended this sentence in the letter with a putdown, characteristic of her as well as of some of the other women: "[A]lso all moral disquisitions and abstruse questions involving an exercise of the brain detrimental to the growth of hair." Where could she have learned women need to ration their brain power for the sake of their appearance?

This quotation especially illustrates Sicherman's (1989) point regarding the Hamiltons: "Books provided a way of ordering, and understanding, their lives [by] providing a common language and a medium of intellectual and social exchange that helped the women define themselves" (p. 80). One of the ways fiction did that for them was to give them a "symbolic code and shorthand for experience.... When [they] were geographically distant, a literary allusion captured experience in relatively few words" (p. 80). Sicherman provides an example in which one of the young women was able to describe a rector as "a delicious mixture of Trollope and Mrs. Oliphant and Miss Yonge and expect to be understood perfectly" (p. 80).

Just so, the Wright/Mott/Osborne women could say Jane Eyre was real to them and describe their longtime dressmaker, Miss Soule, as being like a character from Harriet Beecher Stowe's *The Minister's Wooing*, thus illustrating how in Sicherman's words, "the fictional company was very real to them" (p. 210). According to her, it was not surprising that "there was a reciprocal relation—a continuum—between fiction and life" (and again she cites Davidson, pp. 112–135). Sicherman calls this fluidity between the boundaries of life and novels "the fictionalizing of their lives" (p. 81). Such fictionalizing, she surmises, could have provided models for behavior or family projects or fantasy.

Susan K. Harris (1990), in her introductory chapter to *19th-Century American Women's Novels: Interpretive Strategies*, confirms this when she writes that, while the material recording what it is that 19th-century women actually read is not as full as we would like, she does note: "Among this community of readers, however, there are several consistent patterns of response indicating that women readers, consciously or not, were drawn to independent, heroic, and even deviant female characters" (p. 24). Harris goes on to state: "One consistent pattern among women who recorded their reading is an intense interest in biographies of heroic women" (p. 24). Not only were the characters in the novels that they read part of their everyday understandings and part of the currencies of their conversations—especially independent (some have and would say "sexually rebellious") characters like Jane Eyre. And these young women also read and responded favorably to biographies of independent women (Agnes Strickland's *Queens of England* and the travel works of Harriet Martineau). For Mary Kelley (1996), this linkage between reader and character is very powerful. She sees the women of her study as constructing alternative possibilities through their identification and emulation of "learned women" such as Madame de Staël and Hannah More:

> These women were perceived as agents of their own fate. Reading them and then fashioning oneself upon them validated a female self who made herself heard in the discourses that shaped her society. (1996, p. 417)

The question of character(s) is not only a matter of concern to feminist researchers but is also, of course, tied up with that crucial 19th-century issue of morality. For Zboray (1993), the matter of character is much tied up with his thesis that the antebellum population was hard pressed by all the industrial changes and much in need of buffers and safe havens (p. 189):

> The women's sphere blurs into the theme of character that runs though antebellum literature. "Character"—an expression of the socially-mediated interaction of roles with formal expectations—refers to a conscious construction of selfhood to master the new exigencies of industrial capitalism. (p. 169)[9]

As someone who had been buffeted by the economic strains of the times, the matter of "character," in perhaps both these senses, was important to Martha Coffin Wright. During her winter of 1850–51 visit to Philadelphia, she had left her daughter Eliza, age 20, with the domestic responsibilities of the residence in Auburn. Eliza had just become engaged and so perhaps her social life was a bit more active than usual. Her cousin Pattie (Martha Mott [Lord]), whose mother, Lucretia Coffin Mott, was Martha's sister, and with whom Martha was staying, wrote to Eliza: "Your whist parties are more flourishing than the reading society—How does it happen that you waltz so much. What has become of your scruples?" (MML to EWO: 1.26.51).

Pattie was writing here in the hyperbolic mode that the young women sometimes used with one another and that reflected their understanding of their place in society and the messages aimed at them. It was not at all likely that Eliza had lost her moral bearings, as her cousin and confidante, Pattie, was well aware. But, Mother Martha was ever-vigilant and viewed Eliza's activities in a different light than did Pattie. In a letter to Eliza on February 10, 1851, after describing a trial of importance related to the Fugitive Slave Act, a visit to cousin Lib's [EMC] where Martha and other family members "wrote haphazard verses," which she had saved to show Eliza, and giving Eliza a message to relay to her brother Tallman, Martha Coffin Wright extended to her daughter this advice:

> Don't spend too much time playing whist—cards were doubtless introduced at parties in consequence of the predominance of stupid people who could not talk & did not know how to amuse themselves by studying character. I wouldn't be one of them. How many hours a day do your housekeeping & visiting duties allow you to practice [the piano]? Don't forget to tell me whether you have the peices[10] I mentioned, & whether you want me to bring them— Anna has been playing the Daughter of the Regiment beautifully this morning. Louisa did not know any of your tunes. I wanted to hear them. Has Ellen sewed on her patchwork any? (MCW to EWO: 2.10.51)

Showing here strong beliefs and strong—and intellectually elitest—language, Martha allowed Eliza the choice of what kind of person she could choose to be—a "stupid," card-playing one, or one capable of good talk and the study of character. It was likely that the point was well taken by Eliza.

Mother/daughter interchanges were not the only sites of discussion of the issue of character in the mid-19th century. The importance of character and characters has been a theme not only in the books we have seen that the women had been reading, but also in their interactions and uses of the books and characters that meant so much to them, such as *Jane Eyre*. One of the points Nina Baym (1978) stressed regarding the plot of the midcentury novel was how it consistently showed the importance of the heroine accepting herself as female—not as a child-like female but rather one able to stand on her own two feet.

Reading as Transport

Many of the novels read and commented on by the Wright/Mott/Osborne women can be characterized as belonging to what Jane P. Tompkins (1985) has called "the literature of feeling" (p. 215), which stands in contrast to the novels of piety so much recommended by the early and even mid-19th-century moralists such as Hannah More, Mrs. Sigourney, and Eliza Rotch Farrar. The literature of feeling, according to Tompkins, "is designed to give the reader certain kinds of emotional experience rather than to mold character or guide behavior, and is aimed at the psychic life of individuals rather than at collective standards of judgment on public issues" (p. 215). She notes that the characteristic of this literature is that it "had been the means of producing transport" (p. 215).

Clearly and often, the Wright/Mott/Osborne women used in their correspondence the vocabulary of transport to describe the effects of their reading. "Charmed," "dazzled," and "bewitched" are words sprinkled through their letters over the years as ways of telling *their* reader how they were affected by the books they were reading. "Anna Hopper [is reading a Dickens novel and] is quite charmed with it" (MML to EWO: 2.5.49). Marianna Pelham Mott declared to Eliza that she had been going to write earlier "but a bewitching novel—Nathalie resembling Jane Eyre was the means of paving a hole in my day (2.11.52 or 1855)." Even Martha Coffin Wright, with all her "inherited" Quaker unease regarding novels, could speak of being "tantalized" by a story. "I got Blackwood yesterday—a very tantalizing chapter leaving off just at that point where you wish it had begun. I will send it by Munson" (SSC; MCW to EWO: 9.7.55 [just days after Martha's return from being chair of a Woman's Rights Convention in Saratoga, New York]).

Even their readings of family letters had the capability of engendering these keen emotional responses: "Sister's [MPM] addition to Aunt L[ucretia]'s sheets was most truly appreciated, the reading of which left us in a state of intense weakness and general satisfaction" (EWG to EWO: 10.27.58). It would appear that these women were not passive readers and were appreciative when their novels could transport them out of the everyday—and are disappointed when they don't. They comment accordingly: "I wasn't quite carried away though it is very well written" (SSC; EWO to MCW: 2.12.59).

The Wright/Mott/Osborne women, especially the young ones, like other mid-Victorians, wanted their reading to be "interesting" (Baym, 1984). The word recurred over and over as they described their reading to one another. Pattie wrote to Eliza on November 16, 1849, "I am reading Greece of the Greeks. It is quite interesting—Pa got a bushel of walnuts the other day." While this word "interest" or "interesting" may have become a pallid word for us,[11] Nina Baym (1984) reveals what an important word it was to the 19th-century reader:

> However they might elaborate on this idea, all reviewers acknowledged that the basis of the novel-reading experience was interest, which might vary in intensity but could never be entirely foregone and which, at its greatest, could be so exciting as to be painful.... The heart of the experience of reading novels, the *North American* asserted as early as April 1828, lies in "the interest, the natural, irrepressible interest, which the passions of men [sic] will always take in lively descriptions of passion, the absorbing heed which their affections will render, while the world stands, to writings which address and excite them." (pp. 53–54)

With just a change in the pronoun, we can see that in their use of the word "interesting" the Wright/Mott/Osborne women would be describing the often powerful emotions their reading could evoke.

Running through the letters was another association with reading and emotions and one as powerful as the wishes to be "bewitched," "dazzled," and "interested." Nina Baym (1978) claims that the Victorians tended to view the self as profoundly social, and certainly one of the powerful determinations of Carroll Smith-Rosenberg's (1975/1985) influential understandings concerned the power of community, made possible through correspondence, within the lives of mid-19th century women. Illustrated, too, by Mary Kelley in the women of her study, this aspect of reading's benefits is seen by her as a conscious choice of these women readers who "made reading a collective practice. Sharing books both literally and figuratively, they recommended volumes, exchanged ideas, and celebrated the pleasures of reading" (1996, p. 420).

Corroboration of this account of women's emotional lives is contained within many of the reading references of the Wright/Mott/Osborne women, which made a connection between the act of reading and a marked discomfort with being—or even feeling—alone. The discomfort obviously tapped into deep feeling and was a constant in the letters from adolescence through their adulthood. As we have seen, on September 8, 1848, Pattie (Martha Mott) wrote to Eliza about a lonely time she had been having: "My last resort was novels." Some five years later, as a young married woman, Pattie echoed the same thought to Eliza and took the same cure for her lonesomeness. "It's real lonesome, Elizy, not to have her here. Won't she come again? I never did know such pison long days...." (MML to EWO: 6.5.54). As we have seen she does eventually turn to books that lonesome afternoon, *Agatha's Husband* among them, just as she had when she had written to Eliza in 1848.

In September 1846, Rebecca Yarnall wrote to cousin Eliza after a visit in Auburn:

> When I left you early in the morning we arrived at the cars, just as the cars came in from Rochester and you may be sure it felt rather lonesome to be there without you. I finished that book you lent me before I got to Albany and I was very glad to have it. (RY to EWO: 9.11.46)[12]

And once more: "If I am left alone next summer it will be a nice time to read. My French takes up considerable time and dissipation considerable more" (MML to EWO: 2.5.49).

From the evidence above, the reading of both books and letters was often in this family a community activity and, in fact, many of their activities guaranteed social connections—visiting, actual family gatherings, and letter writing. Perhaps picking up a book was yet another means of assuaging loneliness by keeping them in touch with the sense of community. They knew they would be sharing the experience in their next letter. They would be able to tell about (write) the actual reading of the book during a time when they were lonely, and they would also be able to share the book's contents and characters as well as their reactions to it. Thus, reading as a substitute for the company they were missing was not just a negative experience, but was one they could turn into a positive, vital experience.

Reading could also quite specifically provide solace. After seeing her husband off on an 1859 business trip, Eliza wrote: "Feeling not very smiley around the mouth, but teary round the lashes—so to console me I stopped into Hewson's book store and borrowed Mansfield Park" (SSC; EWO to MCW: 2.12.59). Even maturity seemed not to have been an antidote to loneliness! In this same letter to her mother Eliza revealed yet another connection with reading: reading as a way to get through time when alone. "I read Shirley to pass away the time" (SSC; EWO to MCW: 2.12.59). The practice, at least in conjunction with this book by Brontë, more than served its purpose: "I found it quite as entertaining as at the first reading" (SSC; EWO to MCW: 2.12.59). This same use of reading had also helped Pattie as she was waiting that long day for her husband to return home. Reading appeared to be a real companion in need—especially when the men were away! On May 28, 1853, Pattie wrote, "George is generally away all the morning—I amuse myself fixing our room—reading, writing & sewing."

These strong feelings attached to the practice of reading hint at what the women may have been seeking when they turned to books, and they provide, as well, a window for thinking about what their reading meant to them and how it intersected with their gendered understandings and life

activities. While it is always a treacherous undertaking to apply more contemporary models upon another era's thinking, Janice A. Radway's 1984
model of the female romance reader has a great deal to offer.

A MODEL OF THE FEMALE READER

Janice A. Radway's (1984) first-rate, original qualitative study of readers who
patronized a Smithton, Long Island, book store specializing in romances,
Reading the Romance, still provides what has been called, by Cathy N. Davidson, "the best model of [the female] reader, to date" (1986, p. 5). Seeking to
understand the meaning these romances had to their readers, in contrast to
the critical commentary of, among others, Ann Douglas,[13] Radway interviewed both the patrons and the bookstore owner, Dot. Instead of dismissing
the women's responses as unimportant, as many studies of mass culture have
done, Radway analyzed their comments, their life conditions, and the novels
themselves in terms of plot and language in order to help understand the
role of these readings in women's lives and thoughts.

Radway's analyses and conclusions provide a highway for understanding
the meaning reading now and in the past offered to the girl and woman
reader. She posits a reader who is emotionally needy, living in a world so
narrow that the vocabulary and historical information found in romances
becomes a voyage of learning and discovery. For them, the romance provides escape in two ways. The first is a literal form of escape whereby "it
ministers to them while they temporarily escape having to minister to their
family" (1984, p. 92). It is not, Radway explains, escape from children or
husband *per se*. "Rather, what reading takes them away from, they believe, is
the psychologically demanding and emotionally draining task of attending
to the physical and affective needs of their families, a task that is solely and
peculiarly theirs" (p. 92).

The second form of escape is more figurative. In what Radway characterizes as the "good romance," readers are able to "escape figuratively into a
fairy tale where a heroine's similar needs are adequately met" (1984, p.
93). In this way, the women are able to "vicariously attend to their own
requirements as independent individuals who require emotional sustenance..." (p. 93). One of the main requirements of the romance for the
Smithton bookstore reader is "restoring a depleted sense of self" (p. 213)
or, as Radway writes earlier in her text, the romance appears to be a "search
for emotional gratification" (p. 93). The romance readers of Smithton, as
1970s and 1980s suburban women, lived isolated lives with a "lack of insti-
tutional support" (p. 96). Radway suggests that "through romance reading
the Smithton women are providing themselves with another kind of female
community capable of rendering the so desperately needed affective sup-

port" (p. 96). She contends further that this community of support is not a local one but is "rather . . . a huge, ill-defined network composed of readers on the one hand and authors on the other" (p. 97). As we have seen, the Wright/Mott/Osborne women had a community already in place, using reading—their own actual reading and then their sharing of that reading with others—to keep community alive and well.

But, according to Radway, the chief reason why the individual woman "turns to romances [is] because they provide her with the opportunity to experience pleasure and happiness" (1984, p. 159), a "gift she gives to herself" (p. 91). Like the Wright/Mott/Osborne women, and so, perhaps, showing how reading fulfilled similar needs, the romance readers of Radway's study have many positive words for what reading meant to them: "replenish," "restore," "a kind of tranquilizer or restorative agent," and "beneficial" (p. 62).

In-depth interviewing is not, of course, possible for the Wright/Mott/ Osborne women, but I think what we have seen in their own words regarding their reading suggests there may be sufficient parallels between Radway's findings regarding the role of romances in the lives of her subjects to make some offerings regarding the role of reading in the lives of the women of this study. With all the evidence we have, it does not feel like a leap to say that reading for them was a form of nourishment that supplied, from their own explicit testimony, emotional gratification as well as often a means for assuaging loneliness.

And Radway (1984), too, like the researchers above,[14] speaks to the importance in women's lives of the characters in the novels they read: "The characters and events of romance fiction populate the woman's consciousness even as she withdraws from the familiar social scene of her daily ministrations" (p. 92). What can it mean to have the characters in novels as familiar personages in one's head? It's a *lingua franca*, a touchstone for personal understandings; company to assuage loneliness; a peopled haven for escape. While, of course, we can only speculate, there is ample evidence from both the words of the Wright/Mott/Osborne women—and from the researchers who corroborate so much of their words—that reading was a powerful activity and a source and vehicle for what mattered to them.

Radway, quoting one of her readers, Kit, found that yes, she reads for escape but:

> "At least you learn something when you're reading books." Romance reading is "better" than other forms of escape in Kit's mind because, in addition to the enjoyment the activity gives her, it also provides her with information she would otherwise miss. (1984, p. 108)

In this sense, it earns the label of "compensatory" from Radway, meaning that it "fills a woman's mental world with the varied details of simulated travel and permits her to converse imaginatively with adults and [further helps her] feel that education has not ceased for her" (p. 113).

In thinking about reading as an activity that can encourage patterns of thoughts and activities that encourage growth and development, Radway's analysis of what she calls "the bad novels" is interesting in connection with Pattie's reaction to *Agatha's Husband*. She bemoaned how "it makes women such a poor little dependent fool—not a bit like Jane," Jane Eyre, of course, but all the while acting in a nonindependent way, simply marking time—"I read, sew, walk, sweep & dust, look out the window, examine the garden"—until her husband made his way home. According to Radway, quoting the analysis of Dot, the romance bookseller and observer:

> It is the bad romances ["characterized by a weak or gullible heroine"] that most often start the women thinking.... In reading some of those "namby-pamby books about the women who let the man dominate them," Dot explained, the readers "are thinking 'they're nerds.'" And they begin to reevaluate. "Am I acting like that?" They begin to say to themselves, she added, "Hey, wait a minute—my old man kinda tends to do this." And then, "because women are capable of learning from what they read," they begin "to express what they want and sometimes refuse to be ordered around any longer." (p. 102)

Now, whether Pattie changed as a result of recognizing her dislike of passive, dependent women or even if she recognized the connection is, of course, impossible to say with any kind of certainty. What is interesting, thanks to Radway's model, are such possibilities. Less free to come and go in her marriage to George Lord, than Eliza was in her marriage to David Munson Osborne, Pattie had more reason to question.

CONCLUDING—FOR NOW

In this chapter, I have presented—using both chronological and thematic organization—the reading of the Wright/Mott/Osborne women, especially the younger ones, as it intersected with their gender (and I am hard put to find in the correspondence of these young women any aspect of their reading that does *not* intersect in some manner with the fact of their gender). Furthermore, I have shared aspects of their reading practices that would fit in the "liberatory" column, where literacy can be viewed as a "good"! In the next chapter some darker aspects of their literacy experiences will be on view.

For now, here, briefly, are possibilities for what their reading, particularly of novels, appeared to have been doing for them. It appeared to have helped them, in many ways, build a community sense of themselves; it gave them characters in common for everyday references; it appeared to have provided solace and emotional nurturance as well as grist for their minds; and, lastly, it privileged their way of being in the world in what may have been a compensatory way.

By letting Martha Coffin Wright have the last words in this chapter, we will allow the power of the novel in the lives of these women to shine through this former Quaker's words. In a letter to her daughter, Eliza, dated November 6, 1858, Martha was commenting on a writer (unnamed). According to her, this writer had

> some of the characteristics of Miss Chesbro's writings—she never carried out any plan—I am extremely glad for that young lady to get her old lover back but somehow I fancied a different ending. It seemed so much like that other heroine we read of—"What no soap? And so he died and she married the barber, and the gunpowder ran out of his boots." (MCW to EWO: 11.6.58)

It would appear that, here, Martha Coffin Wright was making fun of the formula of the 19th-century romance novel, but doesn't it also appear as if she were as caught up in them as were her daughters and nieces? Obviously not exhibiting too high a regard for the particular text she was comparing to the genre as a whole, still wasn't she reflecting the power of story, if not for its own sake, perhaps for the sake of sharing with her daughters and nieces? Whether this sharing was the sharing of pleasure, the sharing of ideas, the sharing of story, or the use of story as vehicle for moral lessons was not laid out for us explicitly—but all of these possibilities are there to infer—especially in light of all the feminist research that has found similar patterns among middle- and upper-class white antebellum women. For the sake of community, they read and their reading kept the community together.

NOTES

1. A Christmas story by Dickens noted in a letter: MML to EWO: 3.23.47.
2. Which other researchers (Kelley, 1984; Moers, 1976; Showalter, 1977) took up.
3. I would give a deal for these readers to provide a response to Warner's popular *The Wide, Wide World.*
4. Adapted from the novel by M. F. Tupper.
5. Whom Gilbert and Gubar (1979) call "Victorian England's foremost preceptress of female morals and manners" (p. 24).

6. A coeducational school in New Jersey run by Theodore Weld to which many abolitionists and/or Quakers sent their children. Ellen's brothers, Willie and Frank, also attended the school.

7. In all likelihood the son of Benjamin Rush Plumly, "Edward M. Davis' right hand man in his store" (Palmer, 2002, pp. 181–182) with Davis a son-in-law of the Motts.

8. Which included the future, well-known writer of Greece and Rome, Edith Hamilton.

9. Zboray provides a marvelous example from Lydia Maria Child's own reading whereby she "slipped into the role of [a] male hero" (p. 169).

10. A family spelling pattern that also extended to the word "niece."

11. One of the "rules" of writing one of my high school English teachers stressed so often that I can still remember was: "There is nothing interesting about the word 'interesting!'"

12. Seldom in this correspondence do travelers embark on their trip without reading material. See Zboray (1993, pp. 72–75) for an interactive account of railroad travel and reading.

13. Who wonders how women could stand to see themselves "as some men would like to see them: illogical, innocent, magnetized by male sexuality and brutality" (quoted by Radway, 1984, p. 4).

14. Baym, 1978; Harris, 1990; Kelley, 1996; Sicherman, 1989/1992; and Zboray, 1993.

CHAPTER 5

NOT ON THEIR OWN: MOTHERS AND MEN PRESCRIBE THEIR READING

Cousin to cousin: "I don't like pious novels."

(MML to EWO: 3.23.47)

Mother to daughter: "You must be guarded in your conduct.
Avoid reading—such books are exciting."

(MCW to EWG: 7.29.55)

In the last chapter, we saw reading as a meaningful and intense experience for the young women of the Wright/Mott/Osborne family as well as a
powerful medium for communication. Like the Hamiltons of Barbara
Sicherman's (1989) study, "Sense and Sensibility: A Case Study of Women's
Reading in Late Victorian America," the young women of this study "peopled their lives with fictional characters" from the novels they read (p. 84).
The Wright/Mott/Osborne women seemed to take particular delight in
that "angry feminist" Jane Eyre, but they also responded to the characters
of Dickens's novels.

They used reading when they were lonely and what they found in their
reading, they characterized with powerful words: "charmed," "dazzled,"

Reading and Writing Ourselves into Being, pages 115–141
Copyright © 2004 by Information Age Publishing
All rights of reproduction in any form reserved.

and "bewitched." From the evidence, the choice of these reading selections, which appeared to have brought so much satisfaction, was left to them. It appears, too, that they were able, in spite of the somewhat anti-novel prejudice both from within the family consistent with its Quaker heritage, and from without, to make of their reading what they would, free to take the messages encoded in their reading for their own uses. As we have seen, these messages, such as those of the Brontë novels, tended toward a genuine appreciation of woman's dilemmas and were coupled with a pleading for her rights (Gordon, 1994).

SURROUNDED BY A SEA OF MORALIZING

In their reading, these young women were also surrounded by the relentlessly moralizing, 19th-century discourses that depicted them in need of instruction in piety, behavior, and etiquette, all in the service of "the cult of true womanhood." Even the novels analyzed by feminist researchers Nina Baym (1978) and Susan K. Harris (1990) as providing models for attaining independence, still have, as part of their 19th-century origins, a language steeped in impossibly high and unrealistic standards of behavior.

On almost any page of these novels can be found an example. Let's take one from *Charms and Counter-Charms.*

> A true affection for Evelyn had more than once been touched into life in [his] heart ... by what were the real excellencies of her nature—its transparent ingenuousness—its delicate purity—its devotedness. (McIntosh, 1848, p. 305)

The slightly melodramatic situations presented in the novels, along with the accompanying flowery language, provided the "cover story," which allowed the young woman reader to feel free to read the novel in the first place. However, those messages that contradicted the ones of independence and self-development, which both Baym and Harris have uncovered, were still pervasive throughout their reading and not only in their novels.

Their schoolbooks, too, were packed with selections that drove home the Victorian messages of the day regarding the need for women to sacrifice themselves and to have impeccable character. In her well-documented study of the 19th-century textbook *Guardians of Tradition*, Ruth Miller Elson (1964) wrote:

> The ideal woman of nineteenth-century American schoolbooks has no interests or ambitions of her own. Her every desire, her every action is bent to serve her husband and children. She is a model of self-abnegation; her only role in life, her only fulfillment comes in helping the male fulfill his

ambition.... She is modest, meek, and silent. Women, like violets, are "Born to dignify retreat,/ Unknown to flourish, and unseen be great." (p. 303)

As signified by her use of the quotations from these texts, Elson underscores that, within these texts, the "restrictions on female behavior are carefully delineated" (p. 304) as is the depiction of her proper place—within the home: "'Within the circle of her own family and dependents lies her sphere of action.' And she can console herself by realizing that moral rectitude is greater than mental achievements" (p. 307). Clearly such a statement could not be conducive to the 19th-century ideal of self-cultivation except in the service of others, although both the Zborays (1999) and Mary Kelley (1996) stress the role of reading in women's self-fashioning, or construction of the self.

COMPENSATION AND/OR COMBATIVENESS

Cathy N. Davidson's (1986) thesis regarding the early American novel, particularly as it relates to young women, concerns their refusal to be constructed by such conservative voices and forces. According to her, the novel is, by its very nature, anti-authority "signify[ing] a new relationship of audience to authority (the reader may *choose* which books to cherish) and different possibilities for political action and social change" (p. 73). In this regard two salient excerpts leap from the Wright/Mott/Osborne reading references, both from Pattie (Martha Mott [Lord]) and both to Eliza Wright (Osborne):

> I have been reading Amy Herbert & I don't like it, did you ever read it? It is edited by a Reverend Somebody. I don't like pious novels. Sunday. This is the only day that I can find time to write, I'm such a gadder—out every day and almost every evening. (MML to EWO: 3.23.47)

Pattie, in her reference to *Amy Herbert*, a novel by Elizabeth Missing Sewell,[1] very clearly stated her dislike of "pious novels." In her reference to "Rev. Somebody," she was exhibiting her knowledge about text and text conventions, as already noted in Chapter 1. She seemed also to be exhibiting the kind of resistance to being constructed by authority that Davidson posited for the novel readers of the early Republic. This stance of Pattie's toward the moralizing aspect of novels, which she expected her cousin Eliza to take under consideration, if not agree with, indicated that these young women (like the readers of Davidson's study) were not totally at the mercy of texts that would try to reconcile them or keep them reconciled to a position of domestic confinement in which "mental achievements" were actively discouraged.

In her analysis of woman romance readers, Janice A. Radway (1984) shows what sense the women made of their reading. Concluding her text, she writes that the romance readers of her study saw "the act of reading as combative and compensatory" (p. 211). In the last chapter, we saw how Radway saw reading as a compensatory act for her readers because it allowed them to be able to focus on the self within a space of their own choosing. She states that her readers, in a larger sense, also saw their reading as a combative act because "it enables them to refuse the other-directed social role prescribed for them by their position within the institution of marriage. In picking up a book ... they refuse temporarily their family's otherwise constant demand they attend to the wants of others" (p. 211). By reading romances, they got "out from under." Such reading allowed them to refuse their social roles—at least for a while.

In a wonderfully long commentary, full of self-deprecating irony, Pattie wrote on February 5, 1849, to her friend Eliza of a Dickens Christmas story:

> Yes, I have read "The Haunted Man." I don't like it as well as the other Christmas stories. The Tetterby's are complete—but that savage boy is awful and Mr. Smidgeon is very tiresome. Anna Hopper [a sister] thinks there is a moral in it too deep for common minds. She is charmed with it. I can see when all misfortunes are forgotten the heart becomes hardened and the happy moments lose their charms—it is therefore necessary to unite the good and evil to enjoy life—and my mind is too common for anything more. (MML to EWO: 2.5.49)

While frowning upon novel reading, 19th-century moralists, of course, considered it more acceptable if such books were read for the lessons and morals embedded within them. This was clearly a well-understood reading practice for Pattie, one she was undertaking in this part of her letter to Eliza. While perhaps not being "combative" in exactly the same sense as Radway's (1984) contemporary readers (as set forth in the previous chapter), it does appear that Pattie was exhibiting a kind of "refusal." Surrounded by moral messages, in the textbooks she had to read and here in the story being read, presumably for enjoyment, Pattie expressed here a certain combativeness, a making fun of the moral, and a making fun of the making of a moral. In effect, she seemed to be saying; "Hey, I can do this. You insist I make a moral of what I read. Fine; here it is." At the same time, her slightly mocking words and tone suggested the kind of refusal suggested by Davidson. She will make of her reading what she will, thank you.

Of course, something compensatory may be occurring as well. Perhaps Pattie was using Dickens's tale to "do" the same sort of literary criticism (Baym, 1984) found in almost any mid-19th-century newspaper and periodical. Such literary practice would provide both her and her reader—here Eliza—with intellectual fodder. Her long commentary and intellectual stance—though she mocked both—may have served to keep active not just a community of spirit but also a community of mind. Pattie, and by extension, the other young women of this study, appeared to have some defenses against "pious" novels and stories with morals that could serve to work against their own interests.

The Canonical: No Woman Authors Need Apply

During 1849 and 1850, Warren Adams, a young man from King(s) Ferry, New York, exchanged letters and books with Eliza Wright (Osborne). Indeed, Cousin Pattie thought he could be the winner in the Eliza-courtship sweepstakes. At least part of this courtship appears to have been conducted through the exchange of books, both via the mails in actuality and through book talks in their letters. In this epistolary vehicle of courtship, Warren Adams first mentioned he was returning two books to her, two books that Eliza must have felt were worthy of being shared. The first was "your volume of Miss Edgeworth's Works." Maria Edgeworth, whose "moral tales were the childhood reading of the first generation of American women authors," (Baym, 1978, p. 29) was a writer who belonged more to Eliza's mother's generation than her own and was essentially a conservative voice.

Noting Edgeworth's titles on the 1840 and 1841 inventories of a New York City bookstore, Ronald J. Zboray (1993) calls attention to the "transatlantic nature of the book trade" and states that Edgeworth (as well as other novelists on the inventories) was "one of the high Victorian novelists [whose texts] embody the spirit of the age as traditionally defined" (140). His study of reading patterns found in library charges of the New York Society Library of midcentury, where Edgworth's titles figured, reveals that her works were checked out more by men than women, in line with his thesis that such evidence "points away from the idea of strictly separated intellectual spheres for men and women" (p. 167).

The second of the books suggested by Warren Adams in this letter was *Aurifodina, or Adventures in the Gold Region* (1849) by George Washington Peck. Of these two books, Warren promised: "When we meet I will give you my opinion of them" (WA to EWO: 8.1.49). Along with these books "I also send," he continued, "the 3rd & 4th volumes of 'Noctes.' I have never admired the 4th volume as much as the others—still it contains 'full many a gem of purest ray serene,' and I should part with it with regret." The "Noctes" were *Noctes Ambrosianae*, a collection of the editorial contributions of John Wilson (who went by the pen name of Christopher North [1785–1854]), to *Blackwood's Magazine*, "the very stronghold of Tory conservativism in literature" (Woods, Watt, & Anderson, 1941, Vol. I, p. 18).

Three weeks later Warren wrote to Eliza that he had:

> sent you a box of books. . . . With this you will receive another. In the index to [Daniel] Webster's Speeches you will find my favorite articles marked and I know of no finer specimens of pure English or true eloquence. I would call your attention to the 'Argument on the Trial of John Knapp.' The gifted orator unravels the deep mystery in which that tragedy is involved with so much beauty and power that I am never tired of reading it. 'Jeffrey's Essays' have been a rich treat to me for the last few days. I have always been interested in reading Reviews of works with which I am familiar—and if (as I take for granted) our tastes are similar in this respect, I am persuaded you will be delighted with this volume. In the note which accompanied the other packages I neglected to thank you for marking the Noctes. (WA to EWO: 8.21.49)

Clearly, Warren Adams's reading list for Eliza outlined above, shared through rather pretentious language and sentiments, was a primer of 19th-century conservatism from both sides of the Atlantic. Francis Jeffrey (1773–1850) was the editor of the "very conservative" *Edinburgh Review* (Woods et al., 1941, p. 18) and "perhaps the best known critic of his day" (p. 197) against whom Walter Scott published the *Quarterly Review.* And the *Noctes,* above, were likewise written by a conservative.

Eliza Wright's social and intellectual heritage, upon which her beliefs would have been based, were in opposition to those voiced by the writers Warren suggested she should read. And yet he "takes it for granted" that she shared his conservative (it would appear) views. In light of the extended family's well-known abolitionist stance, Warren Adams's choice of the speeches of Daniel Webster, whose support of the South's position on slavery was common knowledge, appears particularly obtuse.

The next letter from Warren in the Osborne Family Papers was written on December 22, 1849. Opening with a poem by Burns, he continued to try to elevate Eliza's reading taste and moral judgments. As promised, he told her what he thought about the writings of Maria Edgeworth, comparing them unfavorably to the works of Dickens and Scott. He asked Eliza, too, to compare them. If only she would, he seemed to be trying to tell her, she would see the error of her ways (WA to EWO: 12.22.49). In this letter, Warren made mention of "your kind parting note ... your forever & forever farewell" at their last meeting. A gap exists in the correspondence at this point, most likely because of the death of Martha Coffin and David Wright's last child, year old "little Charley."[2] This December 22, 1849, letter was the next to last of Warren's in the Papers for many years.

On October 25, 1850, Eliza wrote to an unnamed male and once again male authors figured prominently. The recipient of the letter could have been Warren Adams but more likely, given the farewell noted above, it was from the man to whom she became engaged just 2 months later, David Munson Osborne.[3]

In the kind of prose that had already won her plaudits from her correspondents, which praise would continue throughout her life, Eliza wrote:

> the weather continues beautiful & another young lady & myself are trying to get up a reading society—it would give us great pleasure if you would join us—I think you would find it rather more interesting than sitting up half the night earning dust [?]—What shall we read first? [Thomas Carlyle's] Sartor Resartus, [Charles Lamb's] Essays of Elia. Anything in fact you recommend, we shall no doubt find interesting—We think of commencing with Stephen's Travels in Europe. I have read them but there are a good many who have not and I do not think there are many persons here that care about reading anything but G.P.R. James' forlorn novels, in fact they have hardly three ideas to boast of. However, they can dance and "carry-on"—so I've no doubt we shall have quite a nice time, if we can really get it up, which I somewhat despair of—we ought to be out drumming up recruits, this splendid weather, but I have hurt my foot in some way. (EWO to DMO?:10.25.50)

What marked this reading list that Eliza suggested for the hoped-for reading society was its obvious difference from the reading fare most often read, shared, and commented on by the young women. The focus of the Reading Society was obviously to be on canonical male authors, Carlyle and Lamb, those privileged as significant and important in the mid-19th century (and, of course, into and through our times as well). In *Sartor Resartus*, Carlyle developed his persona of the professional writer (male assumed), contrasting the "high" cultural critic/writer from the "hack," to his own advantage (Corbett, 1992, pp. 42–55).

Several of Lamb's *Essays of Elia* illustrate Elaine Showalter's concept of woman's "long apprenticeship in negative capability" (quoted in Fetterley, 1978, p. xxi) where "man" is the object of study and whereby "women are estranged from their own experience" (p. xxi). For example, Lamb's essay, "The Two Races of Men" begins: "The human species, according to the best theory I can form of it, is composed of two distinct races, the men who borrow and the men who lend" (1823/1885, p. 28). Lest the point be lost, the last nine words cited here are italicized. Though the "Letters of that princely woman, the thrice noble Margaret Newcastle" (p. 32) rate a favorable mention, the topic of the essay is centered on men lending books to men. The next essay in the collection, "New-Year's Eve," commences: "Every man hath two birthdays: two days at least, in every year, which set him upon revolving the lapse of time, as it affects his mortal duration" (p. 33).

Clearly, Eliza was versed in and comfortable enough with the content of this canonical literature to have it as the basis for an evening's conversation with "the sterner sex." What seems obvious, too, is that the woman authors these young women loved to read—at least among themselves—were not represented by even one title on this reading list. It is speculation, but one guess would be that these knowledgeable, young women readers were quite clear regarding society's evaluation of their beloved, woman-authored novels.

Mother Discourse: Martha Coffin Wright Sets Some Limits

Someday, somewhere will be found Eliza's evaluation of the first (and perhaps last) evening of the Reading Society, which she really did manage to "get up," hurt foot notwithstanding. Two responses exist in the correspondence and one is only a mention by Pattie. The other is a thunderous one (relative to the rest of her letters to Eliza) from her mother. On January 22, 1851, Martha Coffin Wright wrote from Philadelphia to her daughter, Eliza, who obviously had much of the responsibility for the care of the Auburn household while her mother was away. It would have included her father, her sister Ellen (age 11), and her brothers, Willie (age 9), Frank (age 7), and possibly her oldest brother Tallman (age 17 or 18). Martha began slowly:

> On Sunday I went to Cherry St[reet] & heard a good sermon from *our pastor* (Mrs. Mott) on the necessity for charity to complete the Christian character. I was very glad that I went....The reading society has lasted quite as long as I thought it would. I should have much preferred that you had not made the attempt. You did not say what you read on that meteoric evening. I told you it did not have the elements of success. Now that you have the responsibilities of a house-keeper, you must guard against mistakes that will keep you out so late as 3 a.m.—In your next, I hope you will enter rather more minutely into your everyday experiences. Are you making progress in your music? Have the children gone regularly to school since the next Monday after I left? (MCW to EWO: 1.22.51)

After this sharp rebuke, in which Martha Coffin Wright uncharacteristically used her vaunted irony against her daughter, came tender inquiries regarding Eliza's homemaker hands, roughened by work, as she substituted for her visiting mother:

> We have delightful mild weather here—Are you freezing?—By the weather telegraph in the Tribune I saw that you had it very cold last Saturday—are your hands, poor thing, as rough as mine were before I left home? Mine have got so nice & smooth—Did you play for Aunt Sarah & her niece? (MCW to EWO: 1.22.51)

Why would a mother, herself one of the writers of the revolutionary 1848 Declaration of Sentiments, have come down so hard on her 20-year-old daughter, Eliza, whom, it is clear from other evidence, she otherwise trusted very much, as this daughter attempted to begin a Reading Society in a town Martha herself often found intellectually wanting?

A thoughtful master's thesis of 1974 suggests some ways of thinking about this puzzling, even paradoxical, response. Anne L. Hoblitzelle's study, "The Ambivalent Message: Sex-role Training in Mid-19th Century United States as Reflected in the Correspondence of Martha Coffin Wright to Ellen Wright Garrison," explores Martha Coffin Wright's advice to her daughter, Ellen. The youngest of Martha's three daughters, Ellen was born in 1840, 10 years after Eliza, and the first of the four children Martha was to bear during the 1840s. From the correspondence used by Hoblitzelle[1] and that of this study, Ellen would appear to have been more of a management challenge to her mother than Eliza, the rebuke regarding the Reading Society notwithstanding.

What strikes Hoblitzelle, who wrote in 1974 without the benefit of contemporary feminist theory, is how Martha Coffin Wright had limited Ellen's horizons to the domestic, never suggesting that she could prepare herself for a future vocation. Instead, Martha sent "the inescapable message ... that marriage would be the important thing in Ellen's life and it would be in marriage that she would need to exercise all her carefully developed capabilities" (p. 33).

Hoblitzelle finds the explanation for the paradox of Martha holding up to Ellen the strong role model of feminists such as Lucy Stone on the one hand and on the other of writing letters full of both housewifely suggestions and advice on seeking and finding an appropriate mate, in Martha's own personal history. Within a family structure of strong and supportive women in which Martha was always cared for, even after her two marriages, perhaps, Hoblitzelle suggests, she suffered "a foreshortening of vision" (1974, p. 17). She "lived in a private family culture that sustained its women so well that they were virtually the equals of the men in their families" (p. 18). Perhaps, she continues, this setting helped to preclude the drive that motivated both her entrepreneurial mother, Anna Folger Coffin, and her older sister, Lucretia Coffin Mott, who was both a social activist as well as a Quaker minister. She speculates:

> Whatever the reason, Martha Wright's letters to her daughter Ellen Wright Garrison contained the ambivalent message that women must work for and aspire to more than they had previously been allowed in 19th century society, while at the same time developing those traits and talents that would foster strong families through their service to their children and husbands. Her sex-role training was a curious juxtaposition of 18th century rationalist and

19th century social concept of female self-sacrifice as the source of "true happiness" for women, their families, and America. (p. 18)

Another possible source of Martha's ambivalence, although Hoblitzelle doesn't stress this aspect of her history, was that not only had Martha been widowed at the age of 20, left with a 1-year-old child, Marianna Pelham, to raise alone (which she did only with the help of her own mother), but her father had died and died bankrupt when she was only 9. In both instances, It was her mother, Anna Folger Coffin, who found the way, running a shop and then a boarding house after the death of her husband, Thomas Coffin; and then joining a school run by a Quaker cousin, Susan Marriott in Aurora, New York, where both she and Martha found work to support themselves after the death of Martha's husband, Peter Pelham (Bacon, 1980).

Hoblitzelle notes how Martha's ironic sense of humor served to insulate her from the pain of the scorn and ridicule heaped on the courageous feminists of the 1840s and 1850s and indicates this may have been a "technique through which Martha coped with the myriad aspects of her life" (1974, p. 46). Perhaps her cool humor abandoned her when one of her daughters became potentially too intellectual, risking, in Martha's maternal mind, that safe haven only an appropriate mate could provide. Whatever the motivation, Martha's sharp response to Eliza regarding the Reading Society revealed a paradox at the heart of her motherhood, an idea developed so well by Hoblitzelle.

Some 5 years later, it was Eliza's sister Ellen's (age 15) turn to be scolded by Martha in conjunction with reading practices. The text at issue was the very popular *Ruth Hall* (1854),[5] an autobiographical story of a young widow who, against formidable odds (including a publisher-brother who wouldn't help her break into print), became a very successful writer. The book, written by Sara Payson Willis Parton under her penname, Fanny Fern, created a scandal at the time as it held up Nathaniel Parker Willis, editor of a popular New York weekly, *Home Journal* (Baym, 1984, p. 17) to both ridicule and criticism (Baym, 1978; Warren, 1986). *Ruth Hall*,[6] unlike much of the fiction that we have seen the young women read, tends toward irony and satire. And unlike many of the novels of the period, it can still amuse.

The series of exchanges about, to, and with her daughter Ellen regarding *Ruth Hall*, published in 1855, not only speaks specifically of the novel, but it also offers a view into Martha Coffin Wright's complex and ambivalent attitudes toward novel reading and the role of women (and women writers) in society. At the time of the first letter exchange, Ellen was undergoing water cure treatment (for an unspecified reason and about which, it is clear from the letters, Martha also had some reservations) at the same spa[7] where her sister, Eliza, was undergoing water cure baths in anticipation of an easier childbirth than she had experienced with the birth of her first child.

The first letter of this series came from Martha and was addressed to Eliza and the family as a whole. It began with concern over Ellen: "I hope Ellen will be very careful what acquaintance she makes, and not be anxious to be Ruth Hall, & be invited to walk." In a private sheet meant for Eliza, Martha ended this part of the letter with:

> How delightful your gymnastic exercises must be, this warm weather—I hope you will let the D[octo]r know, that part of Ellen's indisposition arose from over-exercise, and watch that in her ambition to excel she does not do more than her strength can bear. Lovingly—Ma (MCW to EWO: 7.28.55)

Nina Baym (1978) says of this very popular novel, which, as noted above, had more humor and irony than many other novels read by the young women of the family:

> The theme of *Ruth Hall* is the gifted, virtuous heroine mistreated by her family—hardly anything new. Nor is the anger expressed in it something new; the question of how to deal with anger gets a different answer in works like *The Lamplighter* or *The Wide, Wide World*, but the presence of anger is understood as a basic fact of the heroine's emotional makeup.... The unconventional aspect of *Ruth Hall* is that it generalizes from the heroine's unfortunate experiences, not to the formation of a superior family structure centered on the heroine, but to a repudiation of the kin and marriage structure entirely. At the end of the novel the autobiographical heroine, who has taken the pen name "Floy,"[8] is satisfied with an independent career and has no wish to enter any domestic situation. (p. 252)

No wonder Ellen's reading of the book worried her mother—Ellen had aspirations to be a Ruth Hall!

A writer? A heroine? Ellen's positive responses to *Aurora Leigh* (1856/57), Elizabeth Barrett Browning's "epic of the literary woman herself" (Moers, 1976, p. 40) only a year and a half later—"[It] is perfectly splendid (EWG to EWO: 1.20.57); and "It is perfectly magnifi[que]! I did enjoy it so much" (EWG to EWO)—suggest a creative hunger, a marked characteristic of both these mid-19th-century writer/heroines, Aurora Leigh and Ruth Hall.

In her introduction to the contemporary edition, Joyce Warren (1986) also reviews its publication and reception history: "When conservative critics reacted violently to *Ruth Hall*, they did so with reason: it was a revolutionary book" (p. xx). She lists several of the reasons why the book was attacked:

> the author's lack of femininity in seeking revenge (a woman was expected to be gentle and submissive); her self-portrayal in heroic terms (a woman was

supposed to be selfless and self-effacing); her failure to show filial piety because she criticized her father, brother, and in-laws (a woman must be respectful of and deferential toward her male relatives); her vulgarity (a woman should never be lacking in female delicacy); and her sacrilege in satirizing devout people (the crowning glory of any woman was her religious piety and respect for religion). (p. xx)

Warren notes that the attacks were against the author, not the book itself. And thus, Warren says, the critics "miss the book's revolutionary message..., its insistence that a woman should be independent" (1986, p. xx). If Hoblitzelle (1974) is right—that Martha's primary goal was to steer her daughter(s) into matrimony and away from vocational interests—her perception of this book as a threat cannot be surprising. Yet a few months earlier, on March 15th, she had written, probably to Lucretia, that she had not "found anything objectionable" in it (*SSC*; MCW to ?: 3.15.55). Martha had read the book on the recommendation of Elizabeth Cady Stanton, who had written a favorable review of it in the feminist journal *Una*. The complexity and ambivalence inherent in Martha Coffin Wright's makeup was once again in evidence.

Barbara Sicherman's (1979) observation that Victorian women fictionalized themselves—and Ronald J. Zboray's (1993) that it was a national pasttime for both women and men—appears to have been taken as a matter of fact by Mother Martha. The very next day after her letter to Eliza expressing concern about Ruth Hall, the character, Martha addressed a personal letter to Ellen (i.e., not one that would go to other members of the family). In it, with *Ruth Hall*, book title *and* character, clearly in mind, she warned Ellen that indeed books have power. Martha, confirming Hoblitzelle's thesis, seemed especially concerned by books that suggested women could succeed on their own—that even with children and widowhood, they could attain literary fame and even become stockholders (Ruth Hall, character, did all of these!).

Addressed to "Ellen Wright, Invalid," Martha wrote:

My dear Ellen—I was glad to receive your letter, and hope you will continue to write—Your aspirations for the benefit of the benighted individual on the sofa, were probably thrown away—I should be sorry for you to be on sufficiently intimate terms to be invited to walk, by any one of whose antecedents you know nothing. You must be very guarded in your conduct—enjoy all you can of your novel life, and describe to me all that you see—Avoid reading—such books are exciting—I w[oul]d much rather you w[oul]d write than read, at present—I was sorry not to have seen the letter to Anna that Aunt Lucretia speaks of—If you write from Clifton send your letter to me to mail, and that will save the writing the same thing twice.... You can probably have part of your washing done there, as cheap as to send it by express, so you had better do so[a]k availing y[ou]rself of every chance to send home—keep your acc[oun]ts straight, & be careful not to lose anything. I hope Eliza will hurry off the letters as soon as possible to the Flume.[9] Be a good girl & correct all your faults, and come home strengthened physically & morally to gladden the heart of,

Your affectionate Mother (MCW to EWG: 7.29.55)

A deeper, more psychological explanation for Martha Coffin Wright's harshness of tone regarding her daughter Ellen's novel reading—remembering both her similar response to Eliza's Reading Society and Hoblitzelle's analysis of Martha's domestic directives to Ellen—is set forth in Madeleine Grumet's *Bitter Milk: Women and Teaching* (1988). She discusses two women writers, Agnes Smedley and Zora Neale Hurston, both successful, but at great cost to themselves:

> [They] found secret wells within themselves where they could hide their worlds from the maternal legislation that declared them forbidden territories. These recalcitrant daughters and their worlds terrify the mother and grandmother who dare not cross their borders. And it is not only the confinement of culture, history, and poverty that we find in the maternal refusal to play in a daughter's magic garden. The refusal also signifies a defense against the lure those places hold for the mothers themselves. (p. 160)

These places might yet tempt!

Now, whether Martha Coffin Wright's stern directives to her daughter Ellen were the result of her "struggle to subdue her own rebellious voice that bursts forth now and again" or whether Hoblitzelle's more domesticated view was closer to Martha's intentions, we will probably never know. Perhaps it's a bit of both. In any case, we can see that to have given her daughters license to become Ruth Halls, she would have not been doing her maternal duty. After all, Ruth Hall (and the author of *Ruth Hall*) had hardly had an easy time of it, earning her own way as writer and mother, with no help from anyone, even from her own brother, the well-known editor!

Martha Coffin Wright, herself, of course, as noted above, had been left a widow very early in her marriage with a very young child to support. By this time in her life (the mid-1850s when she also was in her mid-50s), she was more actively engaged in the struggles of feminism, having been somewhat of a holdout before that according to Lucretia Coffin Mott's biographer, Margaret Hope Bacon (1980), and others. As an acute observer of her sister Lucretia's struggles earlier, and of the feminists in general, Martha perhaps could not, in good conscience, have wished the same for her daughters.

Another factor might have been working on her as well. Both Alexis de Tocqueville in 1835 and Ronald J. Zboray, more currently (1993), have made strong cases for the lack of economic stability within antebellum America. Perhaps Martha Coffin Wright remembered the fate of her own mother as well as her own early widowhood with its attendant problems of earning a living for her young daughter, Marianna, and herself through school teaching. In any case, she certainly can be seen, in these excerpts regarding texts and characters, to be hemming in her daughters' moves toward what she must have perceived "as a willful thrust toward an identity-seeking that could only in mid-nineteenth-century America have placed them at odds with mainstream understandings" (Grumet, 1988, p. 161). It simply would not have been a comfortable spot—as Martha appreciated all too well.

The Young Lady's Friend?

If the scandalous *Ruth Hall* was a text to discourage—"such books are exciting"!!—another text was given quite different treatment by Martha Coffin Wright, although the same impulse—to steer her daughters safely through the dangerous waters of late girlhood and early womanhood— most likely undergirded both directives. A book that was (and is) a true "discourse of control" in the Foucauldian sense, *The Young Lady's Friend* by British Quaker Eliza Rotch Farrar (and a distant cousin of Martha Wright), remains the quintessential manual of deportment.

Called by Ann Douglas "the best etiquette guide of the day" (1977, p. 267), the well-circulated book[10] was written for the daughters of the British upper classes "who could afford Paris fashions" (Strasser, 1982, p. 131). According to Douglas, in keeping with her thesis of the collusion of sentimentality between ministers and woman writers, Mrs. Farrar was "a woman ... who believed the 'great business' of feminine life was shopping, and [she] cautioned her readers to beware lest their voices be 'heard above the gentle hum around you, either in laughter or conversation'" (p. 267).

Obviously another variation upon Showalter's idea of "negative capability" (Fetterley, 1978), *The Young Lady's Friend* (1836) is written on a yes/but rhetorical pattern; Eliza Rotch Farrar never gave without also taking away: "It is the privilege of woman to be the ministering spirit at the couch of the sick. Of all her social duties none is of more importance, or more frequent recurrence, than this" (p. 40). While it is (and was) certainly possible to quarrel with the discourses of the day situating woman as ministering angel, in the light of the hold of the "cult of true womanhood," certainly taking care of the sick was a responsibility of genuine importance and its fulfillment could and did bestow upon woman a true measure of her value—to herself and to others. After several pages of instruction in the care of the sick—don't wear silk because of its "rustling noise" (p. 42); put pieces of coal on the hearth "with the fingers, protected by an old glove" (p. 43)—tongs [are] too noisy; "lose no time in changing" creaking shoes

(p. 43); "sweep . . . a sick room . . . on your knees" (p. 49)—Eliza Rotch Farrar made clear to her reader where true authority rested. This quiet ministering angel cannot even be trusted to judge what is or is not a spoonful of medicine:

> If you are directed to give a teaspoonful of anything, show the spoon to the doctor, and ask if it is to be heaping full, or only even full, as there is a material difference in the size of spoons, and in the manner of filling them. (p. 56)

Cathy N. Davidson (1986) asserts: "True literateness . . . ideally entails increased autonomy [whereby] the reader can choose among different authorities" (p. 69). One can wonder how truly literate Eliza Rotch Farrar wanted her reader to be, given her stream of messages that encouraged the kinds of self-sacrifice outlined above. But this, too, she clarified:

> The connexion, in many minds, is still very close between *blue stockings* and *dirty stockings*; let nothing be done to strengthen it; but let ladies of the present day who have highly cultivated minds, make a point of showing the world that their attainments are not incompatible with due attention to domestic affairs and personal neatness. (p. 96)

Clearly, the entire tome can be read as an extended criticism upon the reader, inspiring guilt on every page. Yet, reflecting the central argument of reader-response theory, that meaning is constructed by the reader, Jean L. Silver-Isenstadt (2002) finds a liberatory aspect to Mrs. Farrar's text. Not only did "the author encourage her readers to approach the male physician with less anxiety " (p. 90), she was "also a strong advocate of physiologic self-knowledge for women [and] spurred her readers to greater study" (p. 268). Silver-Isenstadt (p. 268) quotes directly from *The Young Lady's Friend*:

> Would you not like to hear how your lively feelings depend on your circulations. . . . Will you not be willing to learn how the stomach operates on the food . . . and why the pound cake gives you the headache? (pp. 144–145)

This book, which appears to have been a favorite of Martha Coffin Wright's, was the topic of two extended comments in the correspondence. The first, a retrospective reflection, was from an undated letter from Martha's oldest daughter, Marianna Pelham Mott, written sometime in the spring or summer of 1858.

> I have at last written to Uncle William's Isabella as I hinted above—but letter & book are not yet gone—I found an English reprint of Mrs. Farrar's book— less than half the size—there was an English Preface too—where with English Arrogance it was intimated that the writer of this preface thought it a pity a

book with so many good things in it should not be read on account of the "National peculiarities with which it is strongly marked"—so now she has left out these—I can't tell exactly what they were & [the editor] substituted a few English ones—I miss some of the parts I used to think a little prudish & old maidish—& to tell the truth the book is of a much more readable size than the one I painfully absorbed & vainly tried to mould myself upon some 15 or 20 years [ago]. (MPM to MCW: 3.31.[58; internal dating, Box 207])

In this letter, Marianna, now almost 33, revealed that sometime between the ages of 13 and 18, she had valiantly tried to absorb the lessons of Mrs. Farrar, most probably at the behest of her mother. In the correspondence as a whole, Marianna presented herself as just a tad flip[11] and she was suspicious of anything too intellectual. But as one of the matrons within Lucretia Coffin Mott's circle—Marianna was both her niece and her daughter-in-law—Marianna led the life of the proper 19th-century lady, but one with a sense of humor.

Just a few months after this letter from Marianna to her mother, *The Young Lady's Friend* again arose as a topic of "conversation." Once again, Ellen, now age 18, was at the Clifton Springs water cure spa. Now some 3 years after her encounter with *Ruth Hall*, Martha Coffin Wright wrote to her with the same cautions, and in the same tone, regarding the company she kept:

And so two bright stars have risen on your horizon—I am very glad for you to have so much to relieve the tedium of your stay—two bright intelligent friends are not to be found everywhere. I quite agree that "The Young Lady's Friend" written by your cousin Eliza Rotch Farrar is eminently practical, suppose you begin with that. When Marianna's young cousin Isabella Pelham wrote to her for some book that w[oul]d be some guide to her, on entering society, she sent her that, as containing information on almost every point, and she was much pleased with it. I don't believe you have looked at it, since you were old enough to appreciate. (MCW to EWG: 6.29.58)

Clearly, Martha Coffin Wright held this text in high esteem and clearly, too, during the approximate and critical ages of 12 to 18, *The Young Lady's Friend* was a book placed by Martha on her daughters' reading agenda.

Ann Douglas (1977) notes, critically of course, that Mrs. Farrar served, for a time, as a mentor and chaperone to Margaret Fuller—but only for a time:

A woman ... who believed the "great business" of feminine life was "shopping," and who cautioned her readers to beware lest their voices be "heard above the gentle hum around you, whether in laughter or conversation," had only limited usefulness as mentor to a girl whose wit was to make Emerson laugh more than he liked and whose compelling conversation was destined to silence professional talkers. (p. 267)

Joan N. Burstyn (1985) in her article, "Sources of Influence: Women as Teachers of Girls," stresses the importance of finding texts that over a span of time are influential in their effects. It is interesting to note that Mrs. Farrar's book has a copyright date of 1836, some 20 years before Martha suggested Ellen reread it. Thus the messages of constriction it set forth persisted as influences on young women over at least two generations. (Some might ask if they ever went away.)

No doubt Douglas's harsh reading of Farrar is colored by her own strong thesis that 19th-century writers indoctrinated their readers into "the shopping mentality." But what was this negative book, one from which Margaret Fuller fled, doing at the top of Martha Coffin Wright's reading list for her daughters? And, what then was the net effect of having to absorb the messages of *The Young Lady's Friend?*

We have Marianna Pelham Mott's reaction, which seemed to indicate a genuine ambivalence toward the text. On the one hand, she sent the book westward to indoctrinate a new generation, but "to tell the truth," she admitted, she was glad that the edition was shorter as well as less "prudish and old maidish" than the one that she had read as a girl. Amazingly, one can still hear the guilt Eliza Rotch Farrar was capable of inspiring even in one who tried "painfully" to absorb its messages. Twenty years later, Marianna remembered ruefully her failure to be the paragon the author demanded.

I would love someday to run across Ellen Wright Garrison's reaction to the book, either when she presumably read it that summer or as a retrospective. As a feisty young lady herself, I can imagine it would be rather rude. Of Eliza's reactions, I have yet no record. However, she was extremely conscientious, worked very hard, perhaps to a fault, was often hard on herself, and had perfect deportment. It is not a stretch to imagine that the textual yes/buts of Eliza Rotch Farrar became part of Eliza Wright Osborne's life-long subjectivity,[12] reinforced as the pattern was by so many similar messages of the times.

The Male Sentimentalists

While women authors held a central place in the reading of these young women, and the references to them yield a picture of a committed and, for the most part, enthusiastic readership, certainly there were also references to the male writers of the period. With the exception of Charles Dickens, these references did not appear to have had the everyday immediacy of the references to the women writers, but still they are revealing.

According to Ann Douglas (1977), "The best-known sentimental male writers in ante-bellum America were the magazine writers—Washington Irving, Nathaniel Parker Willis (editor and nonsupportive brother of Sara Payson Willis Parton, known as Fanny Fern, author of *Ruth Hall*), Donald Grant Mitchell (known as Ik Marvel), and George Curtis" (p. 236). They modeled themselves, according to Douglas, on Washington Irving and his *Sketches*. "Unlike Nathaniel Hawthorne, who complained bitterly about the low tastes of the feminine reading public, Willis and his sentimental brethren set themselves to please the ladies" (p. 236). Whether they succeeded in doing this or not, they did succeed in becoming financially successful and famous within their own times.

Praised by Emily Dickinson as a "great book" (Capps, 1966, p. 123), Ik Marvel's *Reveries of a Bachelor* was given high praise to Eliza by a Philadelphia friend, Joe Lord, on the eve of her wedding to "another man." In his August 1851 letter to her, Joe Lord expatiated on the book:

> I have been enchained today by that delightful book the Reveries of a Bachelor, and for a very matter of fact person I don't know anything that has ever gone to the spot more directly than those lame [?] reveries—and as I heard someone remark the other day it seems impossible to think of him as a Bachelor. (JL to EWO: 8.24.51)

Of this work, Ann Douglas writes:

> The world of *Reveries* ... is virtually depopulated: its creatures are those of the narrator's fancy. The characters are pale and derivative like members of some family in which generations of inbreeding have weakened the stock almost unbearably; they have listened only to each other for too long. Their models were from the start literary ones; they are faint with nostalgia for their predecessors in the pages of Addison, Steele, Sterne, and Goldsmith. (1977, p. 240)

Douglas quotes from the text in continuing her criticism:

> Mitchell's *Bachelor* inquires pointedly: "can any wife be prettier than an after dinner fancy, idle and yet vivid, can paint for you?" The sentimental narrator's ever-present consciousness that he is but dreaming, is a subtle reminder that he is the dictator as well as the servant of his feminine readers' imaginative needs. He never forgets that he has the author's power—which becomes all-important when literature is commercialized—of withholding; he can interfere with the reader's range and rate of consumption. (p. 240)

Moreover, continues Douglas:

> The relationship between the sentimental narrator and the... maiden about which he fantasizes is extremely complex and richly revelatory. He courts identification with her because her feminine resources are precisely the ones he needs. Her emotional susceptibility, her subjectivity are inspiration. He comes as near as he can to the suffering of the female while still savoring the titillation involved in identifying with the male who caused it. Her weakness and isolation are in a sense his own and thus he both exploits and rejects her. The sentimental author was dependent on female suffering for his material just as he was dependent on female readers for his livelihood, but he resented and subtly tried to reverse this subjugation. The women in his pages exist only to give the narrator ... something to do: they provide him with a vocation. (p. 239)

In arguing that ministers, women writers, and certain sentimental male writers were selling their impoverished vision to the American women reading public, Douglas thus calls attention to the negative messages regarding women that these writings encoded.[13] After each example of Marvel's high-minded reading selections, which he shared with his imagined bachelor audience, he noted a negative:

> Your copy of Tasso, a treasure print of 1680, is all bethumbed and dog's-eared, and spotted with baby gruel. Even your Seneca ... is all sweaty with handling. . . . . The nurse is getting dinner, you are holding the baby. Peggy is reading Bruyere. (p. 176)

And so it continued for many pages. Douglas observes how the Bachelor indulged in imaginative reveries of unfaithfulness to the very women he sentimentalized (p. 239). She does not speculate on what effect such reading would have on the female reader who had been swayed into thinking that these "authors who accommodated themselves to the feminine sentimental mode" (p. 376) had her best interests at heart.

Eliza commented on the text, *Doesticks*, by another of the sentimentalists, Mortimer Neal Thomson, "a professional humorist" (Hart, 1965, p. 841), whose pseudonym helps to make the point: Q. K. Philander Doeskins. During her 1855 stay at the Clifton Springs Water Cure, she wrote to her husband:

> Dearest husband, It is seven & a half. I have just finished breakfast & perhaps am not just in the right condition to write after eating. Elly is snorting over Doesticks which arrived all [safe?] with the hat box last evening. (EWO to DMO: Summer Series, 1855)

A few days later in another letter to her husband, Eliza expressed her own opinion of the book:

Doesticks you can take home with you, I haven't read any of consequence in it & think it dreadful flat—Elly has read it through & seemed to enjoy it. (EWO to DMO: Summer Series, 1855)

This book, *Doesticks*, which Eliza, unlike her sister Ellen, did not enjoy, was a collection of Thom[p]son's contributions to newspapers of the time (Hart, 1965, p. 841). Another of Thom[p]son's books is mentioned favorably by Ellen Wright. Called *Plu-ri-bus-tah* and subtitled, *A Song That's By No Author* (1856), this text is "a long parody of Hiawatha, [and] important for its satire on feminism, Barnum, the Kansas civil war, the Know-Nothing movement, spiritualism, free love, and the almighty dollar," according to James Hart in his *Oxford Companion to American Literature* (1965, p. 841). Perhaps the difference between Eliza and Ellen's reaction was one of age, as Eliza was older by 10 years. Presumably, *Doesticks* contained the same anti-feminist messages as his *Plu-ri-bus-tah*. Possibly age had inoculated Eliza against messages that would tend to work against her. Or perhaps, as suggested by Joan N. Burstyn,[14] Ellen could laugh at what Eliza took as serious attacks.

It was Judith Fetterley (1978) who first called attention to the pernicious possibilities inherent in the reading of texts by male writers whose belief systems are not in sympathy with the woman reader. While it is the novel that Fetterley uses to make her points, I extend her analysis to semi-novelistic texts like *Reveries* and *Doesticks*. It is Fetterley's argument that in American fiction from Washington Irving's *Rip Van Winkle* to Norman Mailer's *An American Dream* (and not excluding works of James, Faulkner, and Hemingway in her discussion) "the female reader is co-opted into participation in an experience from which she is explicitly excluded; she is asked to identify with a selfhood that defines itself in opposition to her; she is required to identify against herself" (p. xii).

In the fiction that Fetterley has chosen to analyze (not that she couldn't have chosen other works to make her point), "power is the issue" (1978, p. xiii)—just as it was in the 19th-century novels analyzed by Nina Baym (1978), Susan K. Harris (1990), and Jane P. Tompkins (1985). Fetterley sees a doubled effect of the issue on women readers when they read these male authors. First there is

the powerlessness which results from the endless division of self against self, the consequence of the invocation to identify as male ... [and second], each of the works chosen ... presents a version and an enactment of the drama of men's power over women.... [S]he is required to dissociate herself from the very experience the literature engenders. (p. xiii)

Fetterley's example of *Rip Van Winkle* will help make the point of how the male characters are supposed to be "everyperson":

The drama of power in our literature is often disguised. In "Rip Van Winkle," Rip poses as powerless, the hen-pecked husband cowering before his termagant Dame. Yet, when Rip returns from the mountains . . . to discover that his wife is dead and he is free to enjoy what he has always wanted, the "Shuck's M'am, I don't mean no harm" posture dissolves. (1978, p. xiv)

The effect of such encoded woman hatred can only be surmised, but Fetterley goes out on a limb. She invokes Lillian Robinson's important question of the calculus of the matter:

Though one of the most persistent of literary stereotypes is the castrating bitch, the cultural reality is not the emasculation of men by women but the *immasculation* of women by men. As readers and teachers and scholars, women are taught to think as men, to identify with a male point of view, and to accept as normal and legitimate a male system of values, one of whose central principles is misogyny. (p. xx)

The suspicion of women embodied in *Reveries of a Bachelor* and by extension, *Doesticks*, is clear. Selected by the principle of randomness (just open the book and copy what is there), let's hear again from the Bachelor. He was sitting before the fire musing on the man of sensibility. One of his antidotes was reading "old, placid Burton when your soul is weak" or "Cowper when your spirit runs into kindly, half-sad, religious musing" (1851, p. 67). But what of the times when life really turned against him? Never you mind, for

with a woman it is worse; with her, this delicate susceptibility is like a frail flower, that quivers at every rough blast of heaven; her own delicacy wounds her; her highest charm is perverted to a curse. She listens with fear; she reads with trembling; she looks with dread. . . . If she loves—(and may not a Bachelor reason this daintiest of topics)—her love is a gushing, wavy flame, lit up with hope, that has only a little kindling matter to light it; and this soon burns out. . . . She does not look deep enough to see that the passion is gone. . . . She needs disappointment to teach her truth. . . . But let her beware how she sinks under any fancied disappointments: she who sinks under real disappointment, lacks philosophy; but she who sinks under a fancied one, lacks purpose. (pp. 70–71)

Obsessed with her reading, his cure for her was for her to "abjure such poets as Cowper, or Byron, or even Wordsworth; and if she must poetize, let her lay her mind to such manly verse as Pope's" (p. 71). If one misogynist weren't enough for the task, perhaps another, Pope, would straighten her out! The edge here is unmistakable. Perhaps one could be on guard for the voice that criticized you when you know that was its goal, such as that of Farrar's in *The Young Lady's Friend*, but how did one feel, what were the defenses, against the voice that identified with you only to reject you (Douglas, 1977, p. 239)? Tania Modleski (1986), another commentator on the power of the male text, is not at all circumspect in answering these rhetorical questions: "Because of their economic and emotional dependence on men, women have historically been forced to find ways to enjoy or pretend to enjoy even the most virulently misogynistic texts" (p.123). One can speculate on the effects.

Father Knows Best

The remaining category of reading external to the choosing of the young Wright/Mott/Osborne women themselves was one whose intent was not at heart misogynist, but still bears on the issue of reading as an act and practice that can be double-edged. At a time when Eliza, a young married woman, was living in Buffalo and her mother was visiting in Philadelphia, she and her father corresponded. The letters from her father were tender and, in them, he appeared to recognize gender inequities. He gave her $10 as recompense to spend as she wished, and then he suggested several reading possibilities to her:

> You will see from Ma's letter that I called to see Mrs. Worden[15] last week and was presented with "The Japan Expedition" published by Forsythe [?], a large work in four books—two only of which are yet out—with outst[anding] plates, a most splendid thing. I will let you see it someday when you come home, and if Milly [Eliza's 4-year-old] will be good she may look at the pictures but mustn't touch them. Have you finished Kanes Exploration? If you have, I will lend you the life and works of John Adams in ten vol[ume]s a most interesting work of revolutionary doings [first] vol. of the Japanese[Expedition] is very engrossing—You may read that someday. (DW to EWO: 1.23.57)

The instructions for reading are curious and even a bit like Ik Marvel's: Don't soil the books. Take books only one at a time! Finish what you are reading before you start another. He will give permission for her to *see* both of the current splendid volumes of *The Japan Expedition* with their outstanding plates, and when she finishes Kane's *Explorations*, he will lend her the *Life and Works of John Adams*. He must be a believer in serial reading! Don't start one book until you finish the one you are reading now!

Now it is not my intent here, for many reasons, not the least of which is that we must be grateful for such a rich reading reference, one that is so reflective of the interests of the times, to make David Wright into some kind of villain (although it is clear that his wife often did not find him to be the unalloyed feminist that his brother-in-law James Mott was). What *is* interesting here is the contrast of reading material from the kinds the woman readers shared with one another, as they developed and extended their own community of readers and authors, as well as the contrast in reading styles. For the women readers, there was no evidence even to begin to suggest that books must be read one at a time or that borrowed books—and they were always swapping and borrowing books—had to be handled with care.

The difference in genre, too, is obvious—travel books and biographies as opposed to "romances." A little less obvious is that the books David Wright described *were* more expensive than the books the women typically shared. Kane's *Second Expedition* cost him $5 (DWAB: 11.8.56), whereas Eliza was able to purchase a copy of *Little Dorrit* for only 50 cents the next June. The inequality of address is also worth noting. This was not the sharing of texts by equals but, rather, an exchange propelled by a didactic motive. A reader of much nonfiction work himself, David Wright appears here to be providing his 26-year-old daughter with the same kind of informative texts he had purchased all his buying life.

Perhaps he had noticed that since her marriage, Eliza had herself become a reader of works of nonfiction, which can be seen to be in three categories: books of nonfiction by women, including the didactic *Domestic Treatises* and *Cookbooks* of Catharine Beecher and a literary autobiography, Miss Mitford's *Recollections*; books on the water cure treatment by the leading (male) authorities of the time;[16] and travel books: *Adventures on the Mosquito Shore* (11.55); Bayard Taylor's *Central Africa* (12.7.54); and the *Burning of Moscow* (8.22.54). This last category suggests that David Wright was alert to and encouraging of his daughter's reading interests, even if there were some fatherly strings attached!

TOWARD CONCLUDING

Throughout this chapter we have seen how in differing ways women were asked to read, if not against their own interest (though I believe this to be true), at the very least they were asked to read against the grain of their own selections. Warren Adams asked Eliza to read very conservative voices: Daniel Webster's dedicatory *Speeches*, Jeffery's *Essays*, North's [Wilson], *Noctes Ambrosianae*; he tried to persuade her that almost any male author was "better" than Maria Edgeworth, where the mark "better" no doubt signaled gender. When Eliza tried to begin her Reading Society, she suggested not *Charms and Countercharms* but *Sartor Resartus*, Carlyle's proclamation of his own professional writing status, and Lamb's *Essay's of Elia,* which placed "man" as the measure of almost all his musings.

When Eliza's father recommended reading titles, they were of the lives of famous men and the journeys and travels of yet other famous men. Such titles and such content send a message. Travel books by women did exist, of course, but were not as famous or of as high a status as was Commodore Perry's. In my own teens, my father said to me, on thanking me for getting us both some library books, as was our usual practice: "It's all right to get *some* books written by women, but we know, don't we, that the best books are written by men." It took me many years to overcome the sentiment. "How deep it is," as Martha Coffin Wright said, as we will see, of her 5-year-old nephew's comment that men are smarter! Of course, on one level both fathers were absolutely correct. Men, because they have had wider opportunities for more and livelier experiences, were often able to write about adventures most women could only dream of having (Tompkins, 1985).

The waters of the sentimentalists could have been even more treacherous for the woman reader. Under the guise of appreciating and flattering women, some of these authors, such as Thom[p]son, held overt, anti-feminist views, while others such as Ik Marvel were more covertly anti-woman, advocating male infidelity (at least in their reveries). Of the net effect of these readings, there can be no "proof." But it takes not much of a stretch to see that they could produce a negative resonance regarding one's expectations for oneself. I suspect the effect may not be unconnected to the wash-rag scolding that Eliza received from Elizabeth Cady Stanton, who admonished her for having nothing better to do than stitching on a dish cloth. Stanton expected more from the daughter of Martha Coffin Wright. It is unlikely that Elizabeth Cady Stanton foisted off Eliza Rotch Farrar on her own daughters!

Within the stifling confines of the mid-19th-century's literary corset, Eliza Wright Osborne probably stretched as far as she could, given the very real restrictions on these young woman, not the least of which was the relatively scanty, girl-centered education she received (Putala, 1988). But where she could stretch, she did.

LITERACY, LIKE LIFE, FINDS A WAY

Eliza Wright Osborne, from at least some months before the birth of her first child, if not earlier, was an advocate of water cure principles. In 1853 she purchased two books on the topic, one of which, for $1, may have been Doctor Thomas Low Nichols's *Esoteric Anthropology.* A feminist, Nichols, along with his wife, Mary Gove, was an advocate of water cure principles as well as an outspoken supporter of women's health and sexual emancipation. His book

> balked at nothing. Practical as well as scientific, it explained the processes of water cure; the gestation, delivery and management of infants; the methods

of contraception and the nature of many emotional disorders.... Intended to save the world, *Esoteric Anthropology* was an extremely thorough, broad-ranging, and sexually explicit work. (Silver-Isenstadt, 2002, p. 140)

The principles that Eliza learned in the water cure texts, which also included one by Dr. Russell Thatcher Trall, and in her numerous sojourns in water cure establishments, were important to her throughout her life. From them, she appeared to have learned about spacing of children (her family smaller than those of her mother and aunts) and possible means of birth control. In a letter of April 19, 1853, Eliza wrote to her husband, Munson:

> How dearly I do love you, darling & how much I miss you.... I forgot in that list to put down a Vagina Syringe—Ask Fowler [a general store] about the India Rubber Ones which are said to be nice & don't forget to get one & a filterer. (EWO to DMO: 4.19.53)

In addition to this intriguing hint, her knowledge of water cure principles were also the bases for the health practices she provided for her family, especially as these related to nutrition and exercise. In this area also, she was able to establish the knowledge and the sense of authority that is concomitant to genuine learning, that sense of autonomy spoken of by Cathy N. Davidson (1986) as a mark of "true literateness" (p. 69).

As part of a 19th-century reform movement, the water curists encouraged females to become doctors and, in fact, between one-fifth and one-third of the hydropathic practitioners were women" (Donegan, 1986, p. 194). It also encouraged females to overcome the sickliness fostered by their diet and dress (Burstyn, 1984). According to Donegan "pioneering efforts of women like Elizabeth Blackwell and Harriot K. Hunt to gain access to regular medical education coincided with hydropathy's emerging popularity" (1986, p. 194). Though not a water cure doctor, Harriot K. Hunt was a reformer and protested paying federal taxes because women did not have the vote. She made almost yearly appearances at the various Women's Rights Conventions and authored an autobiography, which Eliza Wright Osborne read while taking the waters at Clifton Springs in 1858. She wrote a note to her husband encouraging him to read the book:

> It's getting dark so I can't write longer to you now—I've just finished Harriot K. Hunt's book & like it so much you must read it sometime—It makes me feel more than ever the necessity of female physicians though there can be few like her & wouldn't I like to have her—the female D[octo]r here has fizzled out. She was very dressy & fond of beaux. [She] had lots of love letters to answer & wasn't very well liked on the whole. She hasn't been here since I have. (EWO to DMO: 6.27.58)

Here Eliza, through text, grasped onto potentially liberatory, reform thinking that extended the learning and capabilities she had already accomplished through her own reading of the water curists. Thus, in spite of forces that would (passively and actively) constrict, restrict, and control her—and by extension other young women (she was now headed toward age 30)—Eliza Wright Osborne managed to find that space in the margins where she was allowed some room: she wrote that she wished she had a doctor like Harriot K. Hunt, *not* that she wanted to be a doctor like Harriot K. Hunt!

The meaning of Cousin Pattie's words of September 21, 1849, to Eliza who was struggling with an eye problem, "Don't read novels just because the year is up" is lost in time. But the negative is crucial and its connection with novel reading is not accidental. Ruth Miller Elson (1964), prefiguring Elaine Showalter's concept of negative capabilites (Fetterley, 1978, p. xxi), outlines the 19th-century depiction of the ideal young woman: "The ideal female is most easily described in negative terms: 'Her voice is gentle; her pronunciation is delicate; her passions are never suffered to be boisterous; she never talks politics; she never foams with anger'" (p. 306). The wonder is not why many (if not most) young women of this time and place failed to use all their capabilities but, rather, how they often managed to maximize so many of them. Through their reading, they could learn important health principles and practices for themselves and their families. And in their writing, they made of the everyday an art in words, "publishing" themselves in letters that still resonate with their talent with the word.

NOTES

1. The title page of the 1844 edition reads, "By a Lady/ Edited by the Rev. M. Sewell."
2. The child Martha Coffin Wright was carrying at the Woman's Rights Convention of 1848.
3. The possibility does exist that it could also have been from Joseph Lord, a future brother-in-law of Pattie (MML), but that the letter is in the Osborne Family Papers suggests the writer is David Munson Osborne.
4. Drawn from the Garrison Family Papers in the Sophia Smith Collection of Smith College.
5. It "sold more than 50,000 copies in within eight months" (Kelley, 1984, p. 5).
6. It was republished as part of the American Women Writers Series of Rutgers University Press where Joanne Dobson, Judith Fetterley, and Elaine Showalter served as general editors, with the introduction and editing of the text itself by Joyce W. Warren (1986).
7. Eliza Wright Osborne was a frequent visitor at the spa in Clifton Springs, New York, her visits coinciding with various stages—prior, during, and after—of childbearing.

8. It is curious to note that one of the pet names for Florence Osborne (1856–1877), second daughter of Eliza Wright and David Munson Osborne, with whom Eliza was pregnant in August 1855, was "Floy."

9. A vacation spot in New Hampshire frequented by the family.

10. It also had a later American edition.

11. The only "naughty" joke I have read in the letters was attributed to her and centered on a pun about "busts" in Madame Tussaud's wax works museum and female anatomy.

12. I hope this text did not make her feel as guilty as it still makes me, but I fail to see how it could *not* have had such an effect. I did once share a few selections of the book over a lunch with my mother and we enjoyed a good and healing laugh.

13. This anti-woman bias is also evident in the selections Zboray (1993) quotes from *Reveries*, with its possible negative depiction of women's talk (p. 113) and Marvel's critique of the woman reader, his wife (p. 160).

14. A personal communication based on her own work on Ellen's education, Spring 1995.

15. Mrs. William H. Seward's sister, Lazette Maria, a frequent visitor to her sister's home and a friend of Martha Coffin Wright (Conrad, 1960).

16. Purchases noted in her account books, Boxes 285 and 291, Osborne Family Papers.

CHAPTER 6

WRITING WELL:
IN SEARCH OF
"THE PARTICULAR"

Write me where you were when she arrived—what you
said—what she said & what you said when she said that.
Adieu Votre cousine, Pattie

(MML to EWO: 9.8.48)

There are forty things, I know, that you will wish I had written & perhaps
I can think of them in the next letter.

(MCW to EWO: 10.3.56)

"Nothing in the epistolary line could give me more pleasure than communing with you," wrote Martha Mott (Lord) to Eliza Wright (Osborne) on May 9, 1848. In just this one characteristic sentence, over so many years between the young women, Pattie corroborates Carroll Smith-Rosenberg's vision of the deep connections among and between 19th-century women. Her immensely influential, celebratory essay of 1975, "The Female World of Love and Ritual,"[1] situated letter writing within women's lives in the mid-19th century as the glue that held together very close and supportive networks of women illuminates this study.

While Smith-Rosenberg described that world as rigidly gender segregated, which is not in accord with the Wright/Mott/Osborne family community or in line with the more recent scholarship, the women of this family did indeed develop and enjoy "supportive networks [that] were institutionalized in social conventions or rituals which accompanied virtually every important event in a woman's life, from birth to death" (1975/1985, p. 60).

Drawing on her evidence from "many thousands of letters" (p. 54) between and among women (as well as other personal writings such as diaries), Smith-Rosenberg found correspondence to play a crucial role in constructing these institutionalized networks:

> Especially when families became geographically mobile, women's long visits to each other and their frequent letters filled with discussions of marriages and births, illness and deaths, descriptions of growing children, and reminiscences of times and people past provided an important sense of continuity in a rapidly changing society. Central to this female world was an inner core of kin. The ties between sisters, first cousins, aunts and nieces provided the underlying structure upon which groups of friends and their network of female relatives clustered. (1975/1985, p. 62)

Those ties that provided "the underlying structure" of women's lives had much to do with the constant flow of letters that carried all the news of those lives. The "tell all" directive issued from the matriarchs, first from Anna Folger Coffin, wishing to keep her distanced family together, and then after her death in 1844, the directive came from her daughter Lucretia Coffin Mott (Bacon, 1980). Between Auburn, New York, and Philadelphia, the letters followed family members to Nantucket, Massachusetts, to the Flume[2] in New Hampshire, to the shore at Newport, to water cure spas in New York and Massachusetts, to Paris, to London, to Dresden. Year after year, letter after letter, the task was to relate the daily detail—"the particular" as they called it—to keep the closeness by recreating the material activities of the day for the one at a distance. Just as set forth by Smith-Rosenberg, the task was to keep together that inner core of kin no matter where or what the distance. Following upon her study, later researchers, of course, have continued to build on this landmark work.

FOLLOWING UPON SMITH-ROSENBERG: "THE PRIVATE WRITINGS OF MID-WESTERN WOMEN"

Elizabeth Hampsten (1982) is a wise, deep, and loving reader of the diaries and letters she uncovered in several Dakota archives. She declares in her preface to *Read This Only to Yourself: The Private Writing of Mid-Western Women*:

> If nothing else were to persuade me that reading private writings by ordinary women is not a whimsical exercise, it would be the seriousness with which these women took their own writings. Along with exchanging photographs and scraps of dress material, writing enabled women to keep in touch with one another. (p. viii)

Here Hampsten echoes Smith-Rosenberg's (1975/1985) readings of women's private writings. In her next sentence, she corroborates both Shirley Brice Heath's (1981) and Cathy N. Davidson's (1986) insights regarding the reason for women's fine letters: they supported and instructed one another in becoming better writers, thereby indicating the importance of correspondence in their lives. Hampsten continues: "It was important to write well in order to sustain one's audience, so it would continue to nourish such creative expressions" (1982, p. viii).

A key point Hampsten makes throughout her study is the very real difficulty in coming to enter into the actualities of these private writings. In contrast, the letters of men of the time period, because they are rooted in men's public experience that is most often related to their profession, are easier to come to understand. Hampsten's mode of reading the letters and diaries of the women of her study, rooted as the writings are in the experiences of the everyday, "asks of us ... a special inventive patience. We must interpret what is not written as well as what is" (1982, p. 4).

Resonating with my own readings of the Wright/Mott/Osborne letters over the years is Hampsten's lament: "I would like to know more ... " (1982, p. 13), a thought she often repeats while sharing her reading of the letter at hand. Wanting to know what is on the minds of the writers is part of what she calls her "quest": to find what the women are thinking and feeling (p. 17).

These pleas of Hampsten speak to this work as well, her insights providing avenues into the meanings of the very gendered content of the letters. Following the injunction of the matriarchs to "tell all", the Wright/Mott/Osborne women letter writers—novices and adepts alike—were faithful to the command and told the content of their days: what they did, with whom they did it, and also often the when and the where of their activities. And like many of the women of Hampsten's study, they are not as good in sharing the why. As Hampsten writes:

> [Their] language refers to objects, to work, and physical activity; it accounts for time..., it seldom generalizes and then wryly.... . If we read private chronicles such as [theirs] to find out what was on people's minds, we must allow that [the letter writer] does not tell us in so many words. Yet she affirms a

presence that is so rooted in the concrete and particular that that *is* the state of mind. (pp. 25–26)

It is Hampsten's argument regarding the women of her study that social class is the marker by which she is able to distinguish these mid-Western private writings of women. It is the working-class women whose language is unmetaphoric and that "refers to objects, to work, and physical activity" (p. 26). But what Hampsten sees in the writings of the more privileged women of her study is more of a distanced view of experience, one less rooted in the "concrete and particular" (p. 26) and with a more writerly conscious- ness. She quotes from an autobiographical essay as illustration:

> It has been my privilege to witness the passing of the saloon as the territory of Dakota became a state in 1889, to see roads laid out on section lines instead of taking a star by night in the heavens for a guide. (p. 26)

Hampsten sees here an imitation of the language of the sentimental novels of the time period. For Hampsten, too, the more privileged women's writ- ings often possess a "wider context" (p. 27). The content of the writings of the Wright/Mott/Osborne young women, who were decidedly *not* working class, was rooted in the very concrete particular, and often lacked an appre- ciation of the wider political world of their mothers. Thus their letters would appear to mirror more the features Hampsten notes as characteris- tic of the writings of working-class women of her study. However, the prose of the young Wright/Mott/Osborne women was frequently quite writerly, reflecting their wide reading and more cosmopolitan connections than the women of Hampsten's study.

Yet it was the concrete particular of the everyday that was the stuff of the letters of the young Wright/Mott/Osborne women, and that constituted the challenge and problematic of the writing task facing the correspon- dents. The relating of the everyday details constituted, as well, the same problematic presented to and by Hampsten: What are the meanings within those everyday particulars?

LETTERS OF JANE AUSTEN

Deborah Kaplan (1988), in her study of the letter writing of Jane Austen, also draws on Smith-Rosenberg to delineate "women's participation in a general, male-dominated culture and at the same time in a women's cul- ture" (p. 211). Kaplan's reading of Jane Austen's ambivalence regarding these differing worlds stands in contrast to the utmost seriousness noted by Hampsten of the women of her study. Their allegiance to the woman's culture and the importance of relating the daily, mostly gendered particulars is clear.

Kaplan writes that women's personal letters are a particularly revealing genre, "creat[ing] their intimacy by voicing cultural identifications shared by letter writer and reader" (1988, p. 212). Kaplan believes that Austen's letters "express multiple, indeed even opposing cultural values . . . because this private genre has no intrinsic censoring feature which would suppress or resolve cultural contradictions" (p. 212). She contrasts Austen's letters with her novels, which "as a public and ideological form resist expressions of cultural contradictions, and hence they [unlike her personal letters] do not fully convey the double nature of women's cultural lives" (p. 212).

Kaplan (1988) offers several categories (one of which, in particular, figures also in the Wright/Mott/Osborne letters) in which Austen's allegiance to either the subordinate woman culture or the male-dominated culture was conflicted or ambivalent: the actual subject matter of the letters, which included her interest regarding the subject matter; her attitudes toward female desires and female subordination; and the issue of what actually constituted "news." In only the latter category—the issue of what was to be reported as news—did Austen express genuinely contradictory positions. For Austen, the gentry world, where the male was dominant, and the domestic world of the woman were worlds that were incompatible, "offering opposing versions of what is newsworthy" (p. 221). Kaplan quotes Austen as saying that the difference "is enough to kill me," referring "to the domestic experience she records as 'important nothings' and 'little events'" (p. 221).

Sometimes in her letters, however, Austen was able, in a woman-culture mode/mood, which "values the experiences of daily domestic life," to "focus enthusiastically on what [she] refers to as 'particulars,' the details of family life" (1988, p. 221). According to Kaplan, Jane Austen, in her letters, had real difficulty with those particulars, realizing "everyday domestic occurrences are silly and trivial, *and* they are enormously interesting and significant" (p. 222). Kaplan also notes Austen's positioning regarding these details, revealing her ironic stance toward them in her use of "extreme diction," as well as her use of what Kaplan refers to as "revers[ing] the irony"—"asserting the triviality of her actions and discourse while implying their value" (p. 223). Exasperation with the relentless domestic chores (which included letter writing) certainly found expression in the Wright/Mott/Osborne correspondence; however, the contradictory allegiances are more muted than those expressed by Jane Austen in her letters. And for the most part, they do not think of their writing of these details as "trivial."

KITCH STUDIES THE SANCTIFICATIONISTS

In a study of letters written in the last quarter of the 19th century, *This Strange Society of Women: Reading the Letters and Lives of the Woman's Common-wealth*, Sally L. Kitch (1993), like Elizabeth Hampsten[3] and Deborah Kaplan, draws upon Carroll Smith-Rosenberg's key study (1975/1985), noting that "many historians have based important conclusions about women from their letters" (p. 19). Kitch makes use of the correspondence of the women to chart the narrative of the Sanctificationist's religiously inspired community of women from about 1879 to 1908. In drawing on Smith-Rosenberg's study, Kitch notes the significant role played by letters in both the women of her study and Smith-Rosenberg's:

> Letters helped to create bonds among women by giving them access to one another in the private realm which was often denied them in the public realm. [Further] letters contradicted separations [and] maintained long-distance neighborhoods and social groupings. (p. 22)

Kitch, in line both with the new cultural studies (Hunt, 1989) as well as some more recent gender studies that make larger claims regarding the role of literacy (Hansen, 1994; Kelley, 1996; Kelly, 1999; Motz, 1996; Zboray & Zboray, 1999) extends and expands on Smith-Rosenberg's claims:

> By keeping their hearts and minds rooted in relationships of their choice, as well as by providing input from distant friends and social norms, women's letters can be seen as a kind of counterfrontier of the female spirit. (1993, p. 22)

While expanding the ground of women's experience in being decision makers and business partners, Kitch found that the letters of the Sanctifica-tionists still had to be understood within Smith-Rosenberg's earlier under-standings of women's letters as crucial to matters of female "relationships and independence from male authority" (1993, p. 24). While the latter was not often overtly signaled in the Wright/Mott/Osborne correspondence, other aspects noted by Kitch are more clearly detectable: the importance of the letters to the women as signaled by "the numerous references to the writing, reading, sharing, and receiving of letters" (p. 247); "the focus on the immediate circumstances rather than larger contexts" (p. 242); the role of correspondence as a major source of entertainment (p. 249); and "its role as contributing to group solidarity" (p. 252).

More in line with the expansion of claims made by Kitch rather than in her linkages to Smith-Rosenberg's readings of women's letter writing, Catherine E. Kelly (1999), whose study is located within rural New England, states that the letters of her study "elaborated new meanings for old practices" (p. 176). Karen V. Hansen (1994), in her study also situated within rural New England, claims that letters held together a fraying society. Along these same lines of a society under pressure, Ronald J. Zboray (1993) makes an even stronger claim, averring that "the changeover from face to face oral communication to the written medium of the letter transformed the very nature of the self" (p. 118). He goes further, stating that "the world of print itself became a surrogate for community on a national scale, [thus] ultimately contribut[ing] to the destruction of that very way of life" (p. 121).

Thus, from a variety of perspectives and within a variety of disciplinary settings, many feminist researchers have found within women's letter writing, sources of strength and sources of evidence for seeking ways to understand aspects of the political, social, and cultural ramifications of this much-used genre, one once linked pejoratively to woman in her "private" sphere.

Letters are seen variously as a vehicle for maintaining gender segregation and strength (Smith-Rosenberg, 1975/1985); as documents whose content serves as markers of class (Hampsten, 1982); as expressions of dual cultures and, perhaps, contradictory allegiances (Kaplan, 1988); as a vehicle of cultural power related to literature (Hedrick, 1992); as a form of narrative (Kitch, 1993); and as vehicles for withstanding forces of historical fragmentation (Hansen, 1994; Kelly, 1999; Zboray, 1993).

These differences not withstanding, there is, for the most part, consensus on the importance of letters both as a gendered and gendering vehicle in the lives of 19th- (and 18th-) century women. There is, too, an understanding of the correspondence of women as resting on the "particulars" of daily experience even if, in the special case of Jane Austen, there is a degree of ambivalence regarding these details.

LETTERS, LITERATURE, AND WOMEN'S WRITING

As a genre, the domestic letters of women have been given relatively short shrift, often edited to root out the redundancies[1] to highlight the experiences of the famous men known to the women letter writers, and the *raison d'etre* of the collection in the first place. We have seen they were also criticized for being merely functional (Brown, 1989) and simplistic. Yet, several researchers have made linkages between letter writing and the literature of their times.[5] Sally L. Kitch (1993), in her study, for example, notes the rise of the novel, "which signifies the transcendence of plain and unpretentious language over the formal and stylized language typical of ... male dominated literary genres" (p. 22) and she notes, as well, how letter writing often served women as a bridge to professional authorship. Drawing from a literary perspective, Kitch states that few "studies have interpreted the letter as a genre of women's narrative" (p. 19). Moreover, toward the end of her study, she comes to feel that the set of correspondence of the Sanctificationists of her study becomes a text worthy of being analyzed in terms usually reserved for literature:

> The letter writers wrote with a sense of audience; they engaged in characterizations of themselves and others; and their reports, aspirations, and problems can be seen as plot and theme structures. (p. 262)

Joan D. Hedrick, in a 1992 article in *Signs*, "Parlor Literature: Harriet Beecher Stowe and the Question of 'Great Women Artists,'" connects letter writing of the 19th century to the American literature of the period. Like Smith-Rosenberg and Kitch, Hedrick privileges and celebrates women's letter writing, finding in women's domestic writings links to mid-19th-century literary realism. Unlike Smith-Rosenberg and in line with more current researchers, Hedrick, in analyzing the work of Harriet Beecher Stowe, modifies past feminist work by seeing less rigid gender separation than did Smith-Rosenberg.[6]

In not equating women and their activities as exclusively within the private realm, Hedrick (1992) thinks the parlor games and the letter writing of the 19th-century family "suggest a continuity in voice, content, and implied audience between these informal literary exercises and the published literature of the period" (p. 278). Thus, she takes a broader view of women's connections with society than Smith-Rosenberg, more in line with later researchers such as Hansen, Kelly, and the Zborays.

Nothing in the Wright/Mott/Osborne correspondence contradicts either Smith-Rosenberg's central argument that letter writing served very powerful and positive emotional functions for women, or Hedrick's, Kitch's, and Zboray's argument that 19th-century women's correspondence had relational connections to the literature of the time period that included a sense of literary genre. Suggested by Smith-Rosenberg (1975/1985)[7] is the matter of woman's writing: What is it? Does it exist and, if so, what is its essence? What is the connection between the gendered status of women and how does this affect the form and content of their writing? Can we, indeed, detect a mode of "woman's writing"?

A CRUCIAL QUESTION

As can be seen as a subtext for many of the above theorists, discussions of writing and women have revolved often around the question, "Is there such a thing as woman's writing?"[8] Carolyn Kay Steedman (1982), in her study of a short piece of working-class little girls' writing, *"The Tidy House": Little Girls*

Writing, argues that unmistakably the piece of writing could only have been written by female children. More theoretically, in *Rape and Writing in the* Heptaméron *of Marguerite de Navarre,* Patricia Francis Cholakian poses the question, "Is there a built-in feminine way of writing?" (1991, p. 1).

For her readers, Cholakian spells out the very real problematic inherent in this question by outlining the two poles of thought to choose from in a consideration of the woman writer: one, an "epistemology that defines the gendered self as a social construct; [and two] ... a politics that claims the uniqueness of women's experience" (1991, p. 2). The former stance stresses the role of the discourses in development, whereas the latter stance essentializes woman, seeing all females—and thus their writing—over time, place, and race as producing uniformly "different" texts and lives.

Cholakian draws on the work of Nancy K. Miller to move around and through this real bind:

> Nancy K. Miller has attempted to find a way out of this impasse by arguing that difference lies in the content and themes of women's texts. She finds untrue the assertion that feminine writing by women does not yet exist. Miller contends that those who have been looking for difference in "an insurgance of the body" [Cixous] or in the "level of the sentence"[9] have been looking in the wrong place. It is situated, she argues, "in the insistence of a certain thematic structuration, in the form of content." (1991, pp. 2–3)

Cholakian, connecting "feminine writing" to issues of power, asks:

> Miller's definition of feminine writing would seem to privilege content over form, but is it possible to separate the two?... As Miller elaborates on the repressed content of female fantasy, she hypothesizes that it is "not erotic impulses, but an impulse to power: a fantasy of power that would revise the social grammar in which women are never defined as subjects. ..." In Miller's analysis, ... male desire is erotic, whereas female desire is political. A woman desires the power that will elevate her to the status of subject. (p. 3)

Cholakian next joins issues of power to woman's subjectivity:

> Miller's use of the term "social grammar" in conjunction with the sentence elements "subject" and "object" implies a way to approach women's writing in terms of structure.... If... we look at how women's desire to be defined as "subjects"... affects the "grammar" of their narratives, we may be able to find evidence of feminine writing not only in the content but in the form of their works. (p. 3)

Miller theorized that the "difference of woman's writing" could be found not in form *per se* or content *per se* but rather in the "structuration of content." While not spelling out all the ins and outs or possible variations,

Miller offers a road map for coming to think about the writings of women in a nonpejorative manner. The problematic of the woman writer as subject is, of course, an aspect of this issue.

After a consideration of the passion involved in the actual writing of the Wright/Mott/Osborne letters, the rest of the journey of this chapter considers first the matter of the content of the letters. What indeed are the "rules" of letter writing that helped determine what was actually in the letters? Second, the challenge of organization—structure—of all the details of content by the young letter writers and the rules devised are identified. Third, the matter of their writing as influenced by their reading is addressed. Finally, the central issue regarding women's writing—evidence for its existence within the nexus of form and content, its "thematic structuration," to use Nancy K. Miller's telling term—is considered.

"PUT ON YOUR BONNETS AND LET'S GO": THE LETTERS AS A VITAL MATTER

A major point made by both Carroll Smith-Rosenberg's and Elizabeth Hampsten's studies is the "heartfelt seriousness" embedded within their correspondents' letter-writing projects. This observation is vital, too, in coming to understand the correspondence of the young Wright/Mott/ Osborne women. The centrality of the letters and the letter writing practices in their lives is always evident, part of both the letter's form and structuration and is revealed in the passionate intensity that derived from that importance:

> Your splendid letter this morning has made me leave all the bustle below stairs and seat myself for a quiet chat. It is a fact that I longed for one of your interesting productions but not that I was waiting for one before giving ends and sides. (MML to EWO: 5.28.53)

So wrote Martha Mott (soon to be Martha Mott Lord) to Eliza Wright Osborne on May 28, 1853. Throughout the entire correspondence (echoing Hampsten's and Smith-Rosenberg's recognition of the importance women accorded to letter writing), the receipt of a letter was marked by this special intensity of expression. Often, the intensity expressed was that of deep-felt pleasure. One month later, when Pattie was visiting in Buffalo, she wrote to Eliza: "What delightful letters of yours my dear cousin I have to answer—how can I express myself sufficiently grateful. You cannot imagine how much pleasure I derived from those original 8 pages" (MML to EWO: 6.30.50). And one more selection to illustrate the emotional power tapped by the receipt of a letter:

> My engaged Cousin, I made an attempt last Sunday to write to you but my mind was so occupied I could not proceed and gave up in despair. Your inimitable production received yesterday has encouraged me to make an effort and try to recover that entertaining style that in earlier periods characterized my epistles. (MML to EWO: 12.22.50)

Praise for an excellent letter, awareness of epistolary style, and the power of the letter to reach the bedrock of emotion can be seen to reside in this excerpt.

Sometimes the intensity combined pleasure and pain with a dash of irritation:

> I have been in a raging fury for a week and concluded our correspondence was about to close. My feelings at the termination of such a delight—as our communications have ever been to me—were of the more agonizing description. Imagine my intense happiness when Tom [her brother] this evening handed me your inimitable effusion. We had become really alarmed at your long silence—and feared serious consequences from the startling intelligence my letter contained. (MML to EWO: General Folder, 1848)

But most often, and very often, the reader, now turned writer, expressed heartfelt appreciation for letters received: "Great excitement! arrival of the mail—put on your bonnet & let's go," wrote Pattie, recalling for Eliza a shared activity from a recent visit: "It isn't half the fun to go alone" (MML to EWO: 7.8.55). This brief selection illustrates not only how much the arrival of the letter meant to the women (here even after they were married) but also the central role of the letter in the family's social existence.

This depth of response for letters received is a unifying mark of the entire correspondence between and among the young women—and their mothers and aunts and (later) their husbands (though it must be added, the same breathless intensity does not necessarily apply to brothers and uncles, at least in the letters as preserved in the Osborne Family Papers).

Although not as common, given the human reluctance to write, which they also sometimes expressed, the actual writing of a letter also could give rise to the same expression of pleasure as the receipt of letters. Pattie wrote to Eliza in 1847: "Being rather a forlorn Sunday, I concluded I would stay home & write to you—not that I have anything very particular to say, but for the extreme pleasure which it affords me" (MML to EWO: 3.23.47).

If the receipt and even the writing of the letters could produce genuine pleasure, the recipients, in their turn, were very generous in bestowing praise upon letters received. As we have seen above, Marianna labeled her sister's letter as "splendid." The highest praise was reserved for "inimitable effusions," but "acceptable" and "interesting" and even "sublime" were labels used to tell the letter writer she had performed well. In an 1850 letter, for example, Marianna wrote to Eliza: "I went up to Aunt E[liza's] to read her choice selections of that sublime letter." As it happened, Marianna had forgotten the letter, but, on a visit the next day, "they enjoyed it" (MPM to EWO: 11.21.50).

Throughout all the years of the correspondence, one can "hear" praise such as the above for the fine letters that had been, obviously, gratefully received. This show of appreciation appears to have been as much a part of the "rules," the conventions that guided the writing of these letters, as the two major ones that guided all the letter writing: first, provide a complete account of one's activities to the other via the "particulars"; and second, make the account as interesting a rendering as possible.

Content: Rule One: Tell All

"We Want to Know Everything"

The "tell-all" directive of the matriarchs[10] was the guiding premise of the correspondence, clear to all the writers and frequently explicit. Pattie wrote to Eliza on March 8, 1846: "Tom and Marianna have kept you informed of all our doings and sayings during the past winter." As if it were now her responsibility, she detailed the events of the past evening where, among other things, they "played charades and proverbs" (MML to EWO: 3.8.46). In a letter three years later, Pattie demanded of Eliza no less than this full recounting: "Write to me often—tell me everything about everyone" (MML to EWO: 5.31.49). A year later, of a male friend of Eliza's, Pattie demanded: "Do tell just what he said about Mother Goose" (MML to EWO: 5.8.50).

A content analysis of several of the letters of these women, covering the years 1846 to 1853 (see Appendix A; Putala, 1988), took them from ages 15 and 17 to about ages 21 and 23 and the beginnings of their married life. This analysis, when coded and analyzed, revealed how the content of their letters revolved almost exclusively around their gendered designation, the roles that would be expected of them as young wives and mothers:

The particulars of which these friends and cousins wrote were the stuff of their lives: a multitude of visits to friends and family; a round of evening activities that included dances, parties, and trips to concerts and operas; concerns about hairdos and yokes and silks; information about illness and deaths, births and engagements. Obviously of importance to the writers were references to mutual acquaintances, especially if they were males. Pattie keeps her cousin up to date: "Only three invitations this week—tomorrow at Theresa's—a Charade party at Ned Needles—I'm going with George [to be her husband in four years]—Tuesday at Martins'—Wednesday at Joseph's—I don't mean to be so dissipated another winter." (MML to EWO: 2.5.49; Putala, 1988, p. 2)

Mothers were very particular about having *all* the particulars: "I hope you will enter rather more minutely into your everyday experiences," Martha Coffin Wright wrote to her daughter, Eliza. In this same letter but in pages dated the next day, Martha repeated her demand: "Write more particularly about the children" (MCW to EWO: 1.21.51). Well trained, Eliza provided her husband with the same kind of recounting: "I will wash Millie[11] . . . before entering into particulars as to what I did & where I went yesterday" (EWO to DMO: 9.9.53). Nothing but everything was the goal and the hope: "Now," concluded Pattie in a letter to Eliza, "haven't I written a lot. You must write me everything in return" (MML & AB to EWO: 11.50: General Folder).

Clearly, what they wrote to each other—and to their mothers and aunts, and even their fathers and brothers (though with some differences)—regarding their concerns and activities was all marked by their engenderedness. For these young women, the particulars they exchanged regarding their reading, most of their outside activities, their home responsibilities, their socializing, their schooling—all fit into the framework of what was expected to be their fate: homemakers, serene and loving providers of the evening sanctuary for their husbands and, finally, mothers (Kaestle, 1983). Other than these gender-centered activities, the young women, in their correspondence with each other, made little note.

As these young women became older, got engaged, married, and had children, the content of the letters became a fully detailed record of their day—their domestic tasks and their other assorted activities. The letters of the women provide a record of all the accoutrements and peripherals of the domestic: purchases, "commissions" (a favorite family word for purchases made at the request of others), the preparing of food, the making of rugs (a favorite pursuit of Lucretia Coffin Mott), the caring for and growth of children, and the health and healing (or death) of family members. Yet, just as Hampsten (1982) writes of the working-class women of her study: "They give virtually no information regarding . . . politics . . . and they almost never express an opinion" (p. 68). For the young Wright/Mott/Osborne women, even as they became older, Hampsten's statement holds for the most part, though they (especially Eliza) definitely did offer opinions on some political matters.

"What Is Not There"

Just as Elizabeth Hampsten (1982) suggests of the letters of the women of her study, the reading of these letters also requires of the reader speculation on what is not mentioned, what is not a category of content within the letters. Of the larger world of which their mothers were a part, Lucretia Coffin Mott as abolitionist, feminist, Quaker minister, and Martha Coffin Wright as abolitionist, feminist, and sometime writer, as well, there is little sign in the cousin correspondence. Pattie wrote to Eliza in December 1848: "Father and Mother are Abolitionizing at Germantown. I'm going to Annie Needles to talk over the party." In this same letter, Pattie told Eliza not to expect letters "any *plus souvent que autre fois*" (any more often than formerly) because while "my fair excuse is indeed over ... now I have lots of sewing to do & French to study" (MML to EWO: 12.31.48).

The fairs were yearly events held by the Quakers to raise money for their abolitionist activities. Not once in all the times these fairs were mentioned over the years by the young women were its purposes ever discussed (although the amount raised was sometimes noted). The omission can be explained, of course: there was no need to mention its purpose because that was so well known to them. Nevertheless, their references to the fairs were always rendered in a social context, just one more activity in the visiting round robin.

Moving through the homes and lives of these young women, but only at the periphery, were many of the famous personages of the era. Pattie had the opportunity to hear William Henry Channing: "Sunday," she wrote to Eliza, "Everybody gone to meeting. I went to Church this morning to hear Mr. Channing—he was somewhat stupid" (MML to EWO: 5.9.48). Now her assessment was not off the mark, as it was generally considered that William Henry Channing (1810–1884) was not as fine a speaker as his more famous uncle, William Ellery Channing (1780–1842).[12] Instead of informing Eliza of any of the content that was perhaps "somewhat stupid," Pattie, age 20, went on to describe how she and two male companions managed to get through the sermon: "Harry and Emmor endeavored to console themselves with me by whispering" (MML to EWO: 5.9.48).

Some months later Eliza was visiting her cousin Pattie in Philadelphia. She wrote to her mother of a visit by William Lloyd Garrison, abolitionist and editor of the powerful *Liberator*. "Aunt L[ucretia]," wrote Eliza, "wanted us to go and hear Garrison speak but we preferred staying home thinking one sermon a dose" (EWO to MCW: 9.26.49). Neither Eliza nor her cousin Pattie could quite bestir themselves to hear this famous (infamous, to some) person speak on the most important topic of the day. (Interestingly, Eliza's sister Ellen was later to marry a son of Garrison and his namesake.)

What Is There: A Record of Culture

Importantly, where the content of the writings of Wright/Mott/Osborne young women—and older ones, too, differs from Kitch's and Hampsten's is that their content does provide a record (not of the politics of the time) of the culture and art of the period. Readers, art goers, song and opera listeners, the Wright/Mott/Osborne women left a record of their varied and strong participation in the culture of their era.

The letters also provide a record of 19th-century cultural affairs because family members—women and men—participated regularly and often in the cultural events of the day. They attended lectures, went to operas and museums, and read widely and knowledgeably the current books, newspapers, journals, and magazines of the era. In telling everything, they left a record of their time and their lives.

With the exception of this cultural participation, the similarity of the content of these comfortably situated women with the content of letters Hampsten (1982) shares of the working-class women of the Plains is striking: "Women's letters tend to be filled with information about other people—illnesses, letters received, occasional visits, gossip and news—but except for mentioning the weather, they say very little about physical [i.e., geographical] surroundings" (p. 39). The content of both the working women of Hampsten's study and the content of the letters of the Wright/Mott/Osborne women was very much tied to their gendered daily activities and their immediate domestic environment, although the letters of these women do provide a record of the many visits, visitors, trips, and journeys—foreign and domestic—of the family.

Stories, Cautionary and Interesting, Become the Content

The desire for contact and closeness through correspondence did not diminish as the young women became older. In the letters written as these young women mature and become wives and then mothers, the content of the letters remained focused on a recounting of the details of their daily lives. As any shift in a life stage would make appropriate, some changes in content categories can be noted. Some of them faded away, such as talk of boys and beaus, for example, while others were added. The content of the letters as the women became older revolved around their various, daily activities: the aesthetics of domesticity, gardening and decorating, for example, as well as visiting, shopping, the doing of "commissions, participation in cultural events, and dinner parties." Concerns regarding issues of health and illness (and death, of course) as well as issues related to the getting, keeping, and care of servants increasingly arose as topics in their correspondence.

In addition to these life-stage shifts in the content categories of the letters, significantly more and deeper attention was addressed to stories or events in people's lives, especially as these affected the women they knew, particularly as the events reflected misfortunes. No doubt these stories could now appear in the letters because the daughters of the families had come of marriageable age or were already married and thus no longer had to be protected from the "facts of life." Indeed, it may well have been thought important for them to become aware of the real possibilities related to those very "facts" of vital importance to them as females in mid-19th century America.

In a letter (Box 207: MCW to EWO: "Needn't send this away") full of stories, Martha Coffin Wright wrote to her daughter Eliza tales of three women. She first mentioned that recently married Caroline Stratton Wood, a second cousin close to Lucretia, is "not too happy" with her husband, Charles; next she mentioned a woman about to be married to a widower with several children "whom I presume feels competent" to take on this new household; and, lastly, she wrote of a servant who, after just 3 months of marriage, had just experienced a difficult delivery of a 10-pound baby: "I was sorry for her imprudence and her suffering." Marked by a generosity of spirit perhaps not always characteristic of the times, Martha delivered a cautionary message as well as one that reflected a broad humanity.

Most of these shared stories had a direct bearing on a woman's fate either through problems of health or those associated with economic decline (or both), as reflected in this story shared by Martha with Eliza, as she wrote here of a common acquaintance, Mrs E____, whose

> hollow eyes & attenuated & transparent fingers show that she is declining. [She] is saying as she moves to her father's—that her husb[and] w[oul]d take the two boys, & the youngest & M. . . . Think how it must rend a mother's heart to give up her children under such circumstances. Her room looked very neat & comfortable. (MCW to EWO: 3.17.57)

Martha Coffin Wright appeared here, both in an uncharacteristic sentimentality as well as in her approving notice of the orderliness of the sickroom, to reveal the hold "the cult of true womanhood" might have had upon her. More frequently in the letters as in her life, she appeared more at odds with this ideology of sentimentality.

A few days later Martha sent another letter that was likewise full of stories. One clearly reveals Martha as the feminist she most often was. She recounted the sad tale of a woman who had been beaten by her husband, as told to her by Mr. Kniffen.[13] He had said to Martha: "Well I don't believe in striking a woman but what do you suppose made him [the husband] strike her. There must a been so'thing made him do it." Martha Coffin Wright here used his ungrammatical language to show her contempt for his misogynist, ignorant beliefs (MCW to EWO: 3.25.57).

This education through life stories became an important aspect of the letters. For the most part, it appears that even when the stories were about moral missteps, the attitude of the Wright/Mott/Osborne women was not one of condemnation for such human slippage but rather reflected a deep understanding of human frailty. In this aspect of the letters, conflicting ideologies do seem to surface.

Telling the News: "You Didn't Say Nothing about Nobody"

Related to this moral story telling as an aspect of content was the oft-repeated request for "news" in the correspondence. Catherine E. Kelly also records of a young woman of her study the same pressing desire for information: "We have no such thing as News," lamented adolescent Harriet Goodell of rural 1854 Amherst, Massachusetts (1999, p. 2). Certainly for the young Wright/Mott/Osborne women "telling the news" was a part of "telling all" and, as such, a driving force of the content of all the correspondence. But as they became older, there appears to be a more insistent demand for news about people. For example, Eliza, at the start of her 2-year stay in Buffalo, took her mother to task for not sharing any news in her last letter:

> I want to write a word or two to send back with Aunt Lucretia's letter, which I have just been reading to Munson. Ellis [a cousin] going on to N.Y. indeed— Is she smit too? Did Marianna write & why didn't you send it of[f]—shld've & why didn't you hammer out a little mite longer note while you were about [it]. I shall look impatiently for something decent in the shape of an answer to my letters—you didn't say nothing about nobody—just write me a scrap all about Mr. Wood, not to be sent on.... I want to know what all's going on. (EWO to MCW: General Folder 1857)

Later in this same letter, after responding to the one piece of news her mother *did* include, Eliza provided her mother with a great deal of information about hometown acquaintances:

> & do you know Charley is paying attention to ... Anna & Sarah to Conrad, who is said to be lacking although so pretty—How do I know so much? Why Carry got back Wednesday night. (EWO to MCW: General Folder, 1857)

If knowledge is power, it may well depend upon what kind of knowledge is important and to whom it is important. In terms of the kind of power described by Richard D. Brown (1989) as useful for helping men get ahead, the kind of knowledge discussed here would not be particularly advantageous. But, for women whose fate and future depended very heavily on making a good marriage, as so many of the novels they read made care to spell out, this kind of knowledge about people and motivation could prove to be very useful information to possess.

While the telling of story and news was undertaken by the women, the men of the family, too, tried to address this need—sometimes downright insistence—to know. On May 26, 1854, Munson got himself "off the hook" for not answering the particulars of Eliza's last letter, written while she was taking the water cure:

> I thought you would be looking for a letter again so made up my mind better just say that we are all well—as for any news I can't write any—for I see no one to get news from or is the fact that [daughter] Milly and the rest of [us] are all well, good news to my dearest wife—I have been to the Eclipse today, have you been! wasn't it pretty![14] (DMO to EWO: 5.26.54)

On a later occasion when Eliza was once again taking the water cure at Clifton Springs, Munson did have a story to tell—a truly scandalous one— of a dentist who had put a young girl to sleep with drugs and then took advantage of her. The young woman fled the town. In her next letter, Eliza thanked Munson profusely for this news and asked for more details: Does he know the young woman's present whereabouts? How is she, etc.? (DMO to EWO and EWO to DMO: Water Cure Series, August 1855).

Woman's oral language has, of course, long been connected pejoratively to gossip and indeed until the last 30 years or so, public estimation of women has often been guided by this stereotype. Past responses to the diary of Martha Ballard focused negatively on its writing as merely talk writ- ten down, a less privileged form of written language than more literary writing. Kitch's discussion of the letters of the Sanctificationists likewise calls attention to the former characterization of women's letters as mere talk: "chatter, whining, or gossip" (1993, p. 24). She writes: "Indeed, gossip itself has recently been rescued from disrepute" (p. 24).

The whole issue of what is gossip has, of course, been a matter of intense concern with feminist researchers. From this work, there is a growing con- sensus regarding the importance of "gossip" in bonding women to one another (Spacks, 1986, p. 22); in establishing standards of community behavior (Kelly, p. 1999, p. 102); and may even, according to Kitch, "repre- sent a link between public and private realms" (1993, p. 24).

Content: Rule Two: Be Interesting

If the fundamental rule that determined the actual content of the Wright/Mott/Osborne correspondence was to "Tell all," there was an important corollary which was very clear to all the writers, and one, of course, not unconnected to the telling of stories. That commandment was: "Keep us interested." As we saw above, generous praise was given for "acceptable," "quite good," and especially the "inimitable" letter. How did the writer, relating the daily, repetitive domestic occurrences, keep the interest of her reader? Sometimes they were fortunate at the time of their writing to have news of something out of the everyday—an engagement, a wedding—to report. Most frequently, however, there were no such exciting happenings. "Nothing happens to report here at all" was young Rebecca Yarnall's complaint in 1845, and one that often found its way into the letters, year after year.

Often the writers, especially the younger ones, expressed inadequacy for the task of interesting her reader while having little that was tangible to write. In August 1845, a former classmate of Eliza's at the Auburn Female Seminary wrote to Eliza, who was then away at boarding school: "I'm afraid my letter will not be as interesting to you as yours was to me." Eliza's cousin, Elizabeth Mott (Cavender, known as Lib) wrote to Eliza some 6 months later and expressed the same kind of worry: "The above has been waiting to be finished for several weeks—as a gentleman called here today who is going to Auburn, I thought I would try and find enough that would interest you to pay for the trouble of reading it" (EMC to EWO: 2.6–8.46).

Even the older, more practiced of the writers felt the pressure. The enormous premium put on this "being interesting" was, clearly, on the mind of Eliza in a letter written over three days in the middle of November 1853. She began her letter to her mother with a note of discouragement:

> Dear Creatures, How do you find yourself now, seeing you didn't get my Letter of eight pages that was so funny & nice & all that? I think it is discouraging after doing the best you can. I directed it to you.... I'll try my new paper now & see what I can spin out interesting. (EWO to MCW: 11.16–18.53)

Even though discouraged at the loss of the eight-page letter, Eliza would make the effort to engage her reader by "spinning out" what could be of interest.

Excuses were often of no interest to the reader. In a letter written just after Eliza had become engaged, Marianna explicitly criticized her for failing in this crucial requirement of being interesting:

> Your letter, stunning as it was with the great revelation [Eliza's engagement] was not so fertile as usual in those interesting little details which make your sheets so irresistible but goodness me ... I am afraid you will call this criticism and I shall smart two weeks hence. (MPM to EWO: 12.24.50)

Marianna made her demand crystal clear: "We must have much fuller private particulars." Here Marianna was not even content with "big news." She insisted on a full accounting of *all* the "interesting little details" of the occasion.

Clearly, an important aspect of being interesting revolved around the "particular," the telling detail. The letters of Anna Folger Coffin were accorded high praise for, in the rereading of them, one could often find something that hadn't been noticed before—"just that nugget that pleased," according to Eliza. As also seen above, they often used the word "detail," as in, for example, "for now I've covered all the details" (MML to MPM & TM: 6.7.55). Clearly, the detail was the letter's *raison d'être*, a crucial part of the essence of these letters. They craved it, praised it, responded to it, and got cranky if there were not lots of it. They also felt a real responsibility to make certain they provided it, especially for ones at a far distance.

In a letter written on July 8, 1855, Pattie wrote to Eliza:

> I had a nice little note from Aunt E[liza] yesterday—enclosing Mother's first letter—which I shall send to Lib tomorrow. What a wonderful woman she is. We were very much entertained with all those incidents of travel—how delightful the *custard* pie & *sponge* cake seemed. (MML to EWO: 7.8.55)

While another reader might have desired to know more about those "incidents of travels" experienced by Pattie's mother, Lucretia Coffin Mott,[15] what is clear is how the details that had been selected for sharing were praised for their specificity and the pleasure they gave. Pattie had labeled this pleasure "entertainment"—often a coded pejorative for the taken-for-granted "shallow" (or "extensive") reading (and writing) practices engaged in by women.

Not always on the best of terms with her Aunt Lucretia, Eliza, when residing in Buffalo where she would not have received the family letters sent regularly to Auburn, expressed her appreciation for her aunt's writing to her there: "It has been very kind of her to write all she has to me, so many items I wanted to hear, & was glad to know, that no one else would remember to write" (EWO to MCW: 7.10.56). In an undated letter to her husband, Eliza wrote: "Father will tell [you] of Mother's [letter] which told just what I wanted to know" (Box 206: "Dear Husband"). Perhaps her husband was not keeping her as informed as she would have liked to have been, a thought she expressed in a letter in 1854: "You didn't say whether the cherry trees are in bloom." The anticipating reader could only hope that the letter writer would think of or remember "just what I wanted to know." Perhaps such frustration would be remembered when the next letter was written and the writer would then expend the effort to get into the mind of the reader to provide "just what [the reader at a distance] wanted to know."

In 1855, Martha Mott Lord wrote to her brother and sister-in-law/cousin, Thomas and Marianna Pelham Mott, who had just sailed for Europe. In her letter, she provided detail after detail of life back home including the activities of the couple's children, who had remained behind:

The roses are in their prime & making up for last year's blight—quantities of cherries just ripening—I discovered Bel[16] & Maria H.[17] twice at the top of the trees. . . . [Bel] was talking of writing to you today. I hope Maria will send in a long letter tomorrow. . . . There is so much farm detail to tell you—that hickory tree looks healthy yet—maybe Ed[18] is doctoring it with "juices." (MML to MPM: 6.7.55)

Perhaps tired and somewhat overwhelmed at the task of describing it all and having already written a fair amount, in an end note Pattie expressed the belief that, at least for now, she had covered all the details: "Now I'm done till something turns up—those steamer days come round so fast it don't give a body time to collect any news worth shipping" (MML to MPM: 6.7.55). The "news worth shipping" here was understood to be not "news" in the sense of something dramatic but was understood as the selected detail scoured from the everyday and presented so that it could hold the interest of the reader—as well as inform.

While Pattie felt she had so thoroughly covered the bases she could hardly think of any more to say, she also expressed doubt that she had either selected or elaborated on them in such a way as to make it worthwhile for the reader to take the time to read them. While "entertainment value" would be a present-day phrase to describe Pattie's probable hopes (and fears), expressed here somewhat negatively, of writing something worth reading, family praise for letters well written leaves no doubt that an essential of the task of letter writing was to be "entertaining." The object was to take the detail of everyday day life and transmute it into a text that gave pleasure to the person(s) distant.

FORM: STRUCTURING THE PARTICULARS

The overriding characteristic of these many letters over years, thus, was the particular, the detail that recounted the daily activities of the women through the selection and highlighting of daily phenomena. This was as true for the letters of the young girls and women as it was for those of their mothers and aunts. We have seen how important the letters were to them from a very "functional," practical viewpoint—conveying the news necessary for the family's safety and closeness; we have seen that the content was centered on their activities, most marked by their gender; and we have seen how the letters themselves, in their receipt and in their creation, generated very deep emotional responses.

The centrality of all these details, saturated with the deeply gendered content of their daily lives had, of course, to make itself felt in the form that the letters took. The inherent problematic of the writing task can be seen, thus, as one of ordering these many but often unconnected details into a coherent, reader-friendly piece of writing. Their solution(s) to this formative, sense-making aspect of the writing task took on varied guises. While some of these guises can be seen to vary according to the age of the writer as well as purpose, these variations were not solely determined by the age of the writer. This is not to say that the younger writers did not develop in their mastery of the form, but it is to suggest that feminine writing "is situated ... 'in the insistence of a certain thematic structuration, in the form of content'" (Cholakian, 1991, p. 3, citing N. K. Miller).

Taking into account both Miller's definition regarding women's writing and its interpenetration of form and content (Cholakian, 1991) as well as Hedrick, Kitch, and Zboray's observations regarding the connections of women's writing and the literature of the time period, we can begin to consider the approaches the Wright/Mott/Osborne letter writers took to the dual problematic of the presentation of all the above particulars in a manner that would simultaneously hold the interest of their readers and make organizational sense.

We have already seen that the women had developed a form that both fulfilled the requirements of delivering vital family information and to answer the deep emotional requirements as set out so well by Smith-Rosenberg. Moreover, a writerly impulse was apparent in the self-conscious desire to keep the reader always an interested reader. That the letters were occasions for family gatherings (where they were read aloud) certainly would have heightened the desire to write an acceptable letter. If the drive to keep the other engaged represented an authorial consciousness, so too did their approaches to the organization, the presentation of all the many particulars.

A Stream of Consciousness Mode

In the letters of the younger women, especially those in their early adolescence, there might appear to have been little orderliness or logic to the enterprise, especially if textbook or male models are the standard (Hampsten, 1982). Particularly for the writers as young women (but by no means exclusive to them), a major organizing principle for the presentation and ordering of the daily details is what a post-Joycean would label "stream of consciousness." The overriding organizational pattern of letters written to the young women by other young women followed this pattern. This mode can be illustrated in the December 4, 1848, letter of a young and unpracticed writer, Cousin Mary from Wilmington:

They seemed to enjoy walking up the Brandywine more than anything else. I am glad to hear my garters are doing so well tied to the bed poster. The front yard must present quite a different appearance. (MW to EWO: 12.4.48)

Four months earlier, Pattie, an older, more accomplished writer, had written a letter to Eliza in which the same moves from subject to subject can be seen:

Fanny Wilson was here last [T]hursday looking as lovely as ever—she feels lonesome without Harry—I have bought my winter dresses—a cashmere and dark silk—both beautiful—the store windows look beautifully—the fall goods are very gay—you have probably seen the style of trimming bonnets—mine came home on Saturday—it looked so forlorn that I took the ribbon off— and consequently shall be occupied this morning in trimming it—My bag like Caroline's is finished. It is so pretty I am going to keep it instead of giving to the fair which was my intention. . . . I shall commence my French lessons about the first of October. I'm going in the morning unless Mary Mott comes—she has not written to me for some time—Now my dear anything else you want to know I refer you to your sister. Write me where you were when she arrived—what you said—what she said & what you said when she said that.

Adieu Votre cousine, Pattie (MML to EWO: 9.8.48)

While moves from subject to subject are easily detectable in this passage, it is also the case that one topic can be seen to flow with an easily filled-in internal logic. To appreciate the ability of the young women to handle the inherent problematic of their chosen writing form is to see not only that their early usage of the stream of consciousness form produced a letter that their readers found acceptable, but also their writerly awareness of such usage. Two months later, on November 18, 1848, Pattie wrote Eliza another news-filled letter. It was full of talk of clothes and visiting, of family comings and goings, and had in it, as well, sprinkles of French, a recipe for *blanc mange*, and even a small sketch of a hairstyle. In an end note she wrote:

What more could I tell you? You must pardon the style of this letter, its sudden jumps from one subject to another but I have so many questions to ask & answer, and so many little nothings to tell you that a graceful slide is impossible. (MML to EWO: 11.18.48)

Encoded in this selection were several matters of significance. First, note Pattie's awareness that "jumping from one subject to another" is hardly the ideal, suggesting that she was aware, perhaps through her schooling or the reading of letter-writing manuals,[19] of stylistics or "proper" form (Hampsten, 1982; Zboray, 1993). Pattie here revealed knowledge regarding the product of the act of writing: that "style" was an important issue that included both the handling and ordering of content as well as those more subtle aspects of writing that go under the label of cohesion. Her "graceful slide" pointed to a real awareness of the subtleties of fine writing. Crucial to observe, as well, is that embedded in this selection was Pattie's deep knowledge of the gender system under which she wrote and lived. That very content about which she was so careful to order well—and to present with grace—was characterized by her as "so many little nothings." More about this in the next chapter, "'Fixed Very Nicely Indeed!': A Focus on Gender."

In addition to using a stream of consciousness mode that simulated conversation, the younger writers, especially as they entered their middle teen years, presented the flow of details in a manner that prefigured the presentations of the more mature writers. These younger writers would often alternate between a chronological presentation of the events of the day or week and then would turn to the more conversational stream of consciousness form. In an early letter from Pattie to Eliza, the reader was first given information regarding something of immediacy: "Mary left us this morning" and then a thorough internal chronology of Mary's last day of visiting with her was recounted (MML to EWO: 9.21.49). Much of the rest of the letter followed the more typical form above. Thus, giving a history was a form that they felt free to use or not to use.

A Chronological Mode

As the young women got older, they certainly did not abandon the use of stream of consciousness, but as they gained better control, perhaps, of the process and/or the task became clearer to them, "telling all" in a chronological sequence became an important ordering principle. Perhaps, too, especially when writing specifically to their husbands (as opposed to a letter that would go the family rounds), they wished (or were asked!) to send home a more exact accounting of their time. Eliza wrote to Munson, perhaps on the occasion of her first time away from him:

> I'll give you a history of my doings since you bid me farewell, & left a precious tear on my cheek, a parting gift, dearest, which was evidence of your love [for] your wife—& a proof of your being a little bit sorry to leave her.... But to return to the beginning ... (EWO to DMO: 4.19.53)

As with Pattie's recognition of her use of stream of consciousness, we can detect here in this excerpt of Eliza's a writerly awareness of the use of chronology as the ordering factor of her content, including its precise vocabulary, "history." To aid in this chronology of the everyday, to keep their record of memory, the writers developed certain techniques. One was to relate, in order, the sequence of events and activities to the one or ones not present, calling it a history. Memory, of course, was not infallible. To support it, the women frequently mentioned the use of journals in helping them remember their activities (EWO to DMO: 2.22.55; EWO to DMO: 1.19.59). On one of her trips away from home, Martha Coffin Wright directed Eliza to keep a journal so that she wouldn't forget anything important. During her married life, Eliza often kept a journal, as well, that was a record of her many activities.[20]

Both the younger and older woman writers tried in their letters to relate the daily occurrences of interest to their reader as fully as possible. Whether arranging chronologically or using a more conversational stream of consciousness mode, the writers felt real pressure to tell the news (before it was forgotten) as here in a letter to Eliza from her sister Marianna:

> Tell Floy[21] I'll try to get her a flat iron, & a little tea kettle too if she wants it. You never said anything about your eye salve that I raced after, nor whether Carry went to Buffalo—When Joe [Lord] was here I was at Sharon, unfortunately. He says I owe him a letter. . . . Baby was a year old day before yesterday. Thomas gave her a spoon & fork. She has been sick today. D[octo]r comes everyday to see Emmie.[22] (MPM to EWO: 3.4.59)

It appears as if Eliza were rushing to tell all she could remember before something important was forgotten—as happened to her some 3 years earlier when fate intervened. In a letter to her mother while she was in Buffalo, Eliza wrote: "I sent the letters off in a hurry the other day. To be sure, so I did—& what the rest of that paragraph was is lost to posterity. I was obliged to leave just then & alas the consequences" (EWO to MCW: 7.10.56). Just as in conversation, it was easy to become sidetracked!

Deborah Kaplan (1988) comments on the stylistic features of Jane Austen's letters as they related to news:

> News is indicated in her letters to Cassandra not by extended narratives, by stories, but by short, informative bursts of prose. News is also demarcated by sudden and rapid changes of direction, usually without preparatory transitions. Although not every letter employs them, the majority use dashes frequently to take the place of descriptions and transitions. They reinforce the bulletin-like quality of the discourse and enable sudden shifts that obey no principles of ordering, except, occasionally, chronological sequencing. (p. 216)

While this description also fits the Wright/Mott/Osborne letters, these gaps and leaps are for the most part equivalences of the "logic" of conversation. And, indeed, Kaplan continues in her next paragraph: "The letters evoke writer and reader especially vividly, asserting the primacy of a verbal communication, face-to-face gossip upon which these letters are modeled" (p. 216). To clinch her point, Kaplan quotes Austen herself in a letter to her sister Cassandra: "'I have now attained the true art of letter writing, which we are always told, is to express on paper exactly what one would say to the same person by word of mouth'" (p. 216).

RULES OF RESPONSE: YOUNG WRITERS

Yet another influence on both the organization of the letters was the requirement to respond to the previously sent letter or letters. As young letter writers, their letters to one another were not as regular and frequent and thus this convention did not guide the content. Relating everyday occurrences in such a way as to interest the other might have taken all the energy. As the young women became older, perhaps as their sense of the "other" grew stronger and/or they became closer friends with more shared activities and concerns, their letters became more regular. These shared concerns—upcoming or past visits, the fate of a particular beau—required a response.

In a letter of February 5, 1849, Pattie first positioned herself for her upcoming reader, Eliza, and then provided the news in chronological order: "It's snowing. . . . Let me answer all your questions." In the letter quoted above of September 21, 1849, from Pattie to Eliza, Pattie began with an event of the most immediate importance—"Mary[23] has left us this morning"; she then provided for Eliza an internal chronology of the last few days of Mary's visit; she wrote next of her most pressing concern—the hope that Eliza would soon come visit. Lastly, in the concluding part of the letter, the reader can "hear" Pattie responding to Eliza's last letter point by point in a pattern first of response and then of elaboration. In the letter of February 5, 1849, Pattie was explicit about this format: "Let me answer all your questions" (MML to EWO: 2.5.49). A year earlier, Eliza's mother revealed this same pattern: "Writing in haste I may have forgotten to reply to something—will try to remember in my next" (MCW to EWO: 5.?.48). A few years later, Martha described the same pattern: "I will look over your letter again & answer more at leisure. It was a real nice one & I will deliver the message" (MCW to EWO: 3.6.57).

Rules of Response: Later Demands

As the young women became older still and took on family responsibilities by virtue of their age or by marriage, this requirement to respond to particular "particulars" became even more of an expectation. Indeed, such expectations become especially stringent as the care of young children became involved. As we have seen above, Martha Coffin Wright's letters to her daughter Eliza could contain almost strident demands for information regarding the siblings left in Eliza's care. Yet she could also place herself in Eliza's shoes regarding needed and wanted information: Toward the end of a letter to Eliza, she wrote: "There are forty things, I know, that you will wish I had written & perhaps I can think of them in the next letter" (MCW to EWO: 10.3.56).

To fulfill these expectations of response—both the necessary as well as the desired ones—to what was often, of course, the vital need to know of the welfare and problems and needs of the young, different approaches were taken. Often the letters to be responded to were reread immediately prior to the writing of the letter being composed. With the letter in front of her (or him), the writer would respond point by point. For example, while visiting in Philadelphia, Eliza demanded of her husband information about the health of the children. After making several inquiries in a series of letters in 1854, Eliza provided her husband Munson with explicit directions for answering her letters: "Do collect all my letters & next Sunday instead of going to church sit down & answer all questions therein" (EWO to DMO: 5.20.54). He must have learned his lesson well, for a few years later he wrote to her: "I've just been looking over one [of] your letters to see if there is anything I've not answered" (DMO to EWO: 10.31.58).

With the complex nature of the "rounds" of the letters, sometimes the response to the items had to be done from memory. Given the nature of memory, as well as the level and amount of particulars that might have needed to be responded to, the writer sometimes missed an important item. A third variation was a rereading of the letter only immediately prior to finishing the one being composed, in which case the responses to questions or requests from the earlier letter or letters would be addressed at the conclusion of the letter in process. A fourth was to trust memory and hope for the best: "Oh, here is what you need (and want) to know." Often, the writer hoped for the best, crossing her fingers that she had covered the requests of the previous missive by dint of her thorough coverage of her own and the family activities up to that point.

These demands, and assents to demands, highlight the "functional" aspect of the letters. Often there was a real need and/or desire to know, for example, of the health of a child or parent left behind. Within this understanding, demands for news may not be unreasonable. Martha Coffin Wright expressed the possibilities of frustration that the communication system of the time imposed. The letter writers tried to do their best not only to be interesting but also to take care of the perceived needs of the other.

Complicating the rules of response (and not unconnected to the more literary issue of audience sensitivity) were other factors as well. These long letters were often composed over several days and frequently more than one member of the family would be contributors to any particular letter, if not actual coauthors. This was especially true of the letters from Philadelphia where two and three generations often shared the same dwelling—and correspondents.

Another aspect of this matter of shared authorship was stated by Pattie to Eliza in 1848: "All particulars [about her father buying a new house] I leave for Mother's letter which will be sent as soon as Aunt M[artha]'s is received" (MML to EWO: 11.18.48). At this time Eliza was only 18 and presumably would not feel too much frustration at having to wait for the details of this particular transaction. But as the young women became wives and mothers, they, as we have seen, needed to hear what they needed to hear. On a visit to Philadelphia, Eliza was required to wait several days for news from her husband, Munson. In a letter written over several days, Eliza's frustration and genuine worry increased with each day and finally turned into anger. At her wit's end, she sent her brother-in-law, Thomas, to the post office. Munson had gotten the address wrong and two letters were waiting. Eliza's relief was palpable. Her very long letter reveals roller-coaster emotions. Thus, in spite of everyone's best efforts to respond to the needs of the other, slippages occurred.

But they all tried hard not to disappoint (or worry) their awaiting reader either by not finding enough particulars to share or by not presenting them in an "interesting fashion," which meant writing with style, using "a graceful slide" to take the reader from subject to subject (MML to EWO: 11.18.48).

THEIR LITERATE PROSE

Their awareness of the matter of the actual writing within their letters is signaled by what we would consider their metacognitive awareness of style and its enactment through literary features such as a "graceful slide." Thus, in addition to the problematics of the form/content inseparability as posited by N. K. Miller as the sign of "woman's writing" (Cholakian, 1991, p. 3)[24] is another vital aspect of the letters as writing that also has within it an embedded duality. Long dogging discussions of the value of woman's writing has been the tension of their writing being considered, pejoratively, as talk written down alongside a consideration of woman's prose as having its own and literate worth (Kitch, 1993, p. 24)—as does the "fine" writing of the "best" (male) authors. Illustrated in the excerpts throughout this study—and inseparable from the form/content reciprocity—is the

Wright/Mott/Osborne women's use of writerly prose, thus contradicting the persistent pejorative that characterized letter writing for women of the 19th century as merely talk written down.

A Fine Literateness

A very self-conscious writerly quality can be detected throughout the correspondence, such qualities marking an important distinction between these letters and those of Hampsten's (1982) working-class women writers "whose language is unmetaphoric" (p. 20) and that "refers to objects, to work, and physical activity" (p. 26), and who wrote as if literature were not part of their lives.

Listen to some of Pattie's letter to Eliza some three weeks before Eliza's wedding. Pattie was writing from Buffalo, visiting a more distant branch of the family and perhaps feeling more lonely than usual:

> Most adorable relative, Why have I not been favored with a second communication from your inimitable pen? In vain have I hoped as each day's mail arrived to be gratified by a specimen of your chirography. My fond anticipations have sustained severe disappointments. My Philadelphia correspondent [presumably her intended, George Lord] is the only one who has not neglected me. His letters freighted with affection enable [me] to bear up under so many slights. (MML to EWO: 8.12.51)

Making herself into "the damsel in distress," Pattie at once mocked her own writing yet clearly enjoyed shouldering the most high-blown style of the times, both in vocabulary and self-dramatization. (Clearly, too, she had a keen ear for woman's "proper" place in the 19th-century order.)

With its relatively complex sentence structure, its writerly vocabulary choice, its consciously high-blown manner, and its rhythmic flow, this passage reads not at all like conversation, even the written conversation of published works. Rather, it reads more like the 19th-century prose these young women were reading every day. Furthermore, its hyperbolic use of the literate mode showed mastery of this aspect of language and was, as well, a vehicle for gender irony, revealing again their full awareness of society's evaluation of their gendered status.

Conscious practitioners of the art of writing,[25] these young 19th-century women writers were able to label and distinguish a plain style from a flowery one, as reflected in this self-consciously writerly sentence of Pattie as she closed the day's writing: "The minutes are creeping along so fast that 'Time's river, resistless in its course,' will soon sweep me to the Ocean of my chamber—What awful writing—past 11. Good night" (MML to EWO: 11.18.48).

In an earlier letter Pattie had written:

> While Mother was away last week, I felt more lonely than ever you did—two days were spent at Coulter's, but the evenings were mostly alone—I longed for you to be here. You have no idea how stupid it was—nobody in town—My last resort was novels. (MML to EWO: 9.8.48)

This passage selection was certainly very conversational, with the voices easy to detect. But the first sentence was more writerly than conversational, beginning as it does with an adverbial phrase and the stem of it containing the prose-like "than ever you did."

One of the novels Pattie resorted to that evening was *Sir Theodore Broughton* by G. P. R. James, the rather overwrought and long-winded novelist who is one of the sources of the first line of a present-day novel contest: "It was a dark and stormy night...." Perhaps she had internalized some of his flowery prose, which to her was in contrast to her own plain style.

Audience

In addition to complex sentences and precise word choice, the Wright/Mott/Osborne letters had another significant text-like feature. The public qualities of the letters dictated a certain necessary explicitness, and readers would sometimes express crankiness if there were a lack of clarity (although care was given to be as clear as possible). For example, the Mott family was blessed with a number of "Anna's." Almost always their last initial would be added in order not to put a strain on audience comprehension.

One of the marks of a writerly consciousness concerns an appreciation of audience, the intended recipient of one's writing. Both Hampsten and Kitch stress (as does this study) that one of the problems of the writing task for women letter writers concerned the intended recipient of the letter. Complicating the writing task of the Wright/Mott/Osborne women was that, often, letters would be read by more than one party. Many of the letters between Auburn and Philadelphia were not written to a particular individual, but were intended as "family sheets," to be read by the family as a whole, often "going the rounds" via travelers going from one city to the next. Moreover, even if a letter were intended for a particular individual, there were no real guarantees regarding privacy. Often, too, letters were written by more than one family member, with each adding a section of their own.

In her analysis of the letters of the Sanctificationists, Kitch (1993) notes how difficult it was for these women to write to the group as a whole:

Despite the wish of group members to be at some point the audience for every letter writer, and despite stated goals to diminish fleshly ties in the community, in practice a writer's blood relatives were most likely to constitute her primary audience. (p. 262)

The ties of kin were strong.

That such audience sensitivity might be reflective of the literate conventions above, and, thus, the product of aware writers would find support in the reading of almost any of the letters of the women—and even the girls. The writers tried hard to "hear" the needs of the other, to put that need of the reader to know in the forefront, and then they tried to truly engage the other through making the everyday interesting.

Frank Smith (1982) also lends his support: "Writers [with a sense of audience] are not skilled because they have this special sense; they may be said to have this sense because they are skilled writers" (p. 80). As we have already witnessed, the Wright/Mott/Osborne women were of this category—they were writers of genuine skill. With real sensitivity to the writing task relative to the aspect of audience, they made two complementary moves, imagining the future recipient and sharing with that recipient their own specific location.

Imagining of the Other and Positioning of the Self

When the girls and women wrote, they often made two complementary moves that indicated a great sensitivity to this "literate" aspect of writing. On the one hand, they kept in the forefront of their writerly consciousness an imagining of the other—what the intended recipients of the letter might be thinking or what they might be doing, thus placing the reader within her own environment. Not only did they do this imagining of the other, but the writers also often took care to give a positioning of themselves, allowing the reader to be able to place the writer, in turn, in her setting.

As we saw in a selection above, Pattie told Eliza in the opening of a letter that it was snowing outside. Letters quite often started with a reference to the weather. An undated letter of Martha Coffin Wright's began: "Oh bright and pleasant" (Box 207: 1857 or 1858), sharing with her reader the very sunshine of her day. More frequently, the writer described the interior, her actual position in the house when writing, as in Eliza's 1848 opening to her mother: "Here I am at last sitting at Pattie's desk" (EWO to MCW: 10.12.49). Somewhat later Pattie began a letter to Eliza both by positioning herself for the reader and imagining what the reader was about. First she imagined where Eliza would be: "You are about this time washing the 4 babies" and in the next sentence placed herself for her reader: "We have just finished breakfast" (MML to EWO: 11.18.48).

In a letter from Philadelphia to her home in Auburn, a young Eliza provided a context for her mother, first by letting her know exactly where she was seated and then by providing information about the happenings in the household of her Aunt Lucretia: "My dear Mamma, Here I am at last sitting at Pattie's desk—everything is in confusion as the carpets are just going down" (EWO to MCW: 10.12.49). It seems that William Lloyd Garrison was about to make an appearance an entire week earlier than planned. In a double positioning, Pattie wrote to her cousin Eliza, who had just returned to her home in Auburn after another visit: "I followed you in all the journey—the weather was delightful. . . . Imagine me now comfortably fixed at Marianna's with a prospect of remaining here several days" (MML to EWO: 5.8.50).

This aspect of the correspondence—the positioning that provided the deep contextualization of the face-to-face meeting—was echoed in their use of the terms of conversations, providing the sense that the writing was actually performing the act of conversation or even *was* conversation. Pattie, though deep into preparations for her wedding, eagerly dropped what she was doing to "talk" to Eliza (who couldn't attend the wedding because of the imminent birth of her first child): "Your splendid letter this morning has made me leave all the bustle below stairs & seat myself for a quiet chat" (MML to EWO: 5.28.53). In an earlier letter, Marianna had also used the word "talk": "It is a long time is it not since I had any talk with you" (MPM to MCW: 3.31.58, Box 207).

Often the letter writers used the word "commune"—"Nothing in the epistolary line would give me more pleasure than communing with you" (MML to EWO: 11.21.50) and "Let me commune with you" (9.21.49)—which also suggests the "writing as talk" aspect of the letter writing. Marianna's: "I was so full of your letter I could not wait" (MPM to EWO: 12.24.50) was reflective of this same facet of the writing. And one last quote to illustrate the embeddedness of "orality" within their writing: "I wish I was going with her [to Auburn]. You can hear from her so many things that is scarcely worthwhile to write, everything tells so much better" (MML to EWO: 9.8.48).

In addition to the vocabulary of talk is the actual mode of it as well. In a letter to her husband, Eliza was explicit in her use of the conversational mode: "Where have I been since I wrote & what have I been doing?", she imagines her husband asking her as she wrote to him on February 11, 1855, while on a trip to Philadelphia. "Let me tell you," was what she seemed to say next: "Friday morning I went round to Anna B. Practiced a little—found the piano considerably out of tune." In a letter 3 years later, Eliza answered an imagined query: "Who are the Bemans—Why their teacher's children" (EWO to DMO: 12.5.58). It is almost as if she were constructing the conversation they would have been having if they had actually been together.

Thus, it would appear that these reciprocal categories of audience awareness—locating oneself for the reader and imagining the other for the writing task—served more than one role. Such deep contextualizing certainly would ease the reading task by making explicit the writer's actual location, as well as the reader's imagined one. As importantly, in positioning themselves for the other and imagining the reader for themselves as they wrote, they were able to maintain the closeness of face-to-face conversation or at least its illusion.

This imagining of the other (as also evidenced by their responses to individual particulars through the language of conversation) suggests how important keeping the closeness was to them, despite their distance. Sounding throughout the correspondence and often expressed by the girls and the women but also by the men, was a very strong dislike of "lonesomeness"—of being alone. Expressed, too, is a corresponding sense of missing the other.

After Eliza had departed for home from one of her visits to Philadelphia, Pattie wrote to her: "Tis not half the fun to write in my book alone" (MML to EWO: 5.8.50). In a letter written after her mother had visited her in Buffalo, Eliza felt particularly lonely: "Now I will go back to the day you left & say how dull & lonesome it was" (EWO to MCW: 3.6.57). Even flowers could keep one from feeling lonesome. Bemoaning the death of her indoor plants because of a winter freeze, Martha wrote to Eliza: "They are a great deal of company" (MCW to EWO: 12.8.55).

Sometimes the letter writer, here Martha Coffin Wright, put the community's feelings regarding loneliness into words:

> All the rain came for me—We had a regular clean up shower last night and the streets were washed clean & frozen dry this morning & a more beautiful sunny day never dawned—This is all I can say now—let it bring so many moments companionship to my dear husband & daughter, for I do feel sorry to think of you so alone—Very Affectionately, Your M[artha]. (MCW to DW: 2.10.59)

Orality

While there is much in these letters that can be seen to be the product of conscious, writerly decision making or "literateness," there is also, as we have seen embedded in our discussion of audience, a great deal of textual evidence for what has been called, demeaningly, "orality." Hampsten (1982) says of the manner of writing of the working-class women of her study:

> The mode that ... does characterize the spare, plain style is conversation.... Few were worried about the letter form as such.... While the grammar books

urged virtually a separate language, away from speech, for what was to be committed to paper, women wrote in order to create substitutes for their own voices. (p. 95)

Clearly, too, both the language and the concept of conversation was driving the writing of these letters of the Wright/Mott/Osborne women. Their letters were full of the terminology of oral language and oral experience—the spoken word, as heard by them as well as that said or read aloud by them. The first part of an undated letter written to Eliza Wright Osborne by her mother Martha Coffin Wright is worth quoting as an illustration of the abundance of oral experience within the everyday:

Marianna & I went to Furness'[26] Ch[urch] yesterday & heard a good sermon—After dinner I wrote till 4 and then went to Anna Hopper's to see if Lue had any word to send to Ellen, and to find where Sister L was. [A]s they expected her to tea, I concluded to stay, but she did not come. Anna came home with me, and [cousin] Ellis came in & read to us in one of his English papers—He heard [Edward] Everett's[27] lecture, & seemed no better pleased with its "glittering generalities" than Mr. Mellen[28] was when he heard it, tho he had defended it so stoutly at Roadside on Thursday—Many young Quakers went because it was delivered in the Opera house & that was their first opp[ortunit]y to see that superb amphitheatre. (Box 207: "Oh! Bright & pleasant," 1857 or 1858)

In many of the letters, we can see the clues to the actual orality encoded in these letters as well as the writer's awareness of this mode, as in the following multiple command: "Write me where you were when she arrived—what you said—what she said & what you said when she said that—Adieu Votre cousine Pattie" (MML to EWO: 11.18.48). In many of the letters, too, was the actual vocabulary of conversation—"Let us commune and chat"; the discomfort with being alone—"Mother is gone so my last resort was novels"; the awareness that the mode of writing was from subject to subject, almost as a dialogic—"I have so many questions to ask & answer." All this evidence suggests that the conversational mode was not simply one of default—because they were "closer to the oral"—but rather this mode reflected the deep motivational springs of their correspondence.

These moves for keeping the family concerns an open, continuing, and vital process maintained the flow of felt conversation and connection. Overall, thus, it is striking how often, for how many writers of both sexes, and of all the varying ages the language of conversation was used to describe their intentions. Orality has, of course, always been seen as an inferior mode of communication contrasted pejoratively with the mode of literateness (Goody, 1987; Ong, 1982; Street, 1995).

Blended Oppositionals: A Sign of "Woman's Writing"?

This wending of the writing of the letters between the oral and the literate was not the only seemingly dichotomous mode integral to the writing of the letters. As we have seen, the writers blended form and content, as denoted by Miller as a mark of woman's writing. Needing to share their everyday particulars in a manner both clear and interesting, they developed, not from the more formal examples to be found in the letter-writing manuals of the time, a form that would enable them to share from the distance their lives and needs.

Third, they also manifested the modes both of the working-class women of Hampsten's study as well as that of the more privileged ones. At once self-consciously writerly in their language and concerned with cultural events including wide reading, the focus of their writings was on the everyday particular. With a passion for news and having the pressure of multiple and "public" readings of their productions, they often wrote with a "literate" vocabulary and a complex sentence structure. Yet, while the play of language might have been absent from the writings of the women of Hampsten's study (though found in both the Kelly [1999] and Zboray & Zboray [1999] documents), what is striking is the similarity in content, the detailed information regarding the condition of the everyday: illness, news, visiting, and chores, as well as their deep commitment to the detailed particular.

Out of these three seeming oppositionals, they developed a recognizable, much appreciated written link and vehicle for their extended family, as outlined by Smith-Rosenberg (1975/1985). In our search for "woman's writing," it is interesting to note that the men of the Wright/Mott/Osborne family sometimes took it upon themselves to write this form that the women had constructed over years for their own needs. These efforts, though praised by the women, tended to fall short, focused on their own feelings rather than the "news" of others. For example, Thomas Cavender, husband of Eliza's cousin Elizabeth Mott Cavender (Lib), wrote to Eliza on November 23, 1845:

> And now you see I have taken a large sheet: but how do you suppose I am to fill it? I am no hand to write Mott letters, as we call the kind which pass so frequently between Auburn and Philadelphia. I never hear anything of the little matters of interest which daily occur among your cousins here, and if I did, I could not repeat them. . . . But suppose I try my hand at a Mott epistle. (TC to EWO: 11.23.45)

While providing some specifics regarding an upcoming family gathering, he expressed very strong opinions regarding a cousin taking a pew in a church: "I think it is a foolish move, considering Mrs. Mott's position in her

Society." Seldom were such value judgments made by the women—at least in their letters. Although the letter of the Wright/Mott/Osborne women was recognizable as a form by Tom Cavender, his content did not follow its pattern of the telling of the everyday, which Hampsten saw as "the women keeping the pattern intact day after day [as their understanding of] the mark of well regulated and successful life" (p. 68). In this contrast we can begin to see an outline of the answer to the question: "What is the difference of woman's writing" (Cholakian, 1991) and what does it tell us about gender, about power, about writing, about artistry?

THE CRUCIAL QUESTION, ONCE MORE

This chapter has as its central question the issues of woman's writing. Does it exist, and if it does, what is its difference? From the evidence above, we can agree with Cholakian (1991) that woman's writing does indeed already exist, not just as a hope. If its key resides in "a certain thematic structuration, in the form of content" (citing N. K. Miller, p. 3), clearly, letter after letter, year after year, detail after detail, the content of the Wright/Mott/Osborne women's letters was inextricable from the heavily gendered nature of their daily existence. Unlike Jane Austen (Kaplan, 1988), the women of this study had little conflict regarding the value of their "women's particulars"—not that they were not sometimes weary of it or that they always graciously accepted the gender inequalities of their times without thought or complaint. But their letters celebrated those very particular details that often gave Jane Austen, letter writer, trouble.

For each other, the Wright/Mott/Osborne women made the everyday interesting. They sought out exactly that detail that they knew their reader would appreciate, even relish. They ordered the details using the logic of the face-to-face conversation that they wished they could be sharing. They also used the chronology of their domestic day to make their experience come alive for the other at a distance. In imagining the other at a distance, they helped to break down the distances between Auburn and Philadelphia and, in placing themselves for the other, they provided a live image for their reader. To keep the interest of that reader, they didn't hesitate to use the most high-blown language drawn from their wide reading, with its often Latinate vocabulary and complex syntax. They tied it all up with the registers and vocabulary of conversation. Distinctions were not the order of the day; sharing and making the everyday interesting for the other was the essence of their letter writing.

Like Patricia Francis Cholakian (1991), Susan J. Hekman (1990), in *Gender and Knowledge: Elements of a Postmodern Feminism,* draws upon the writings and beliefs of Hélène Cixous (1980, 1986 [with Clément]) that woman's writing does not yet exist, and she sets out some of the difference that, according to Cixous, is the mark of feminine writing:

> Feminine texts are different from masculine texts. They do not rush into meaning. They remain at the threshold of feeling; they are tactile. Writing the feminine is writing that has been cut off by the (masculine symbolic). The point of feminine writing is not the creation of a new theory but a displacement of the old oppositions, particularly that of the masculine/feminine. It will thus have a formlessness that is antithetical to dualistic thought. (p. 45)

Defending Cixous (if she needs it!) against charges of essentialism, Hekman notes Cixous's belief: "Feminine writing is a style, not a signature; it can be written by a man or a woman" (p. 45).

These distinguishing marks that Cixous sets forth are also inherent, vital characteristics of the letters of the Wright/Mott/Osborne women. They match up with what this French feminist, Cixous, denotes as the marks of female writing, aptly describing many of the significant features of the Wright/Mott/Osborne women's letters. Their letters did not rush into meaning, but rather were an offering that could bring meaning to the everyday; the content was the content of their very gendered dailiness; the particulars were ones of their own and not of their husbands'. The content was the content of the activities of their own lives. Central to the letters was what they are doing, "where they were going, and who was going with them" (to quote an old Irish folk song). Their stream of consciousness and their embedded chronology reflected their command over the thousands of details to which they brought their own form; and finally, they did not speak the language of opposition, creating an "us against them." Rather, they sought to minimize difference, to make all in their circle an essential constituent of their family community. As Shirley Brice Heath (1991) notes: "For those cut off by gender, race, or class from frequent face-to-face interactions with established and elite contemporary communities, writing has provided a channel of communication for building communal links on paper" (p. 4). What literate links!

NOTES

1. And subtitled "Relations Between Women in Nineteenth-Century America."
2. A vacation spot and hotel in New Hampshire frequented by the family.
3. Kitch also draws on Hampsten's study, citing the women's "independence from male authority" (p. 24) as well as issues regarding language usage (pp. 242–243).

4.　Alan G. Hill, the editor of *The Letters of Dorothy Wordsworth* (1981/1991), writes in his introduction that many of her letters "are too full of the minutiae of daily life to appeal to a modern reader, though they have their value for the specialist" p. xvii), not appreciating the bedrock of the "minutiae."

5.　The line of research of epistolarity that focuses on the mutually influential and reciprocal relationship between 18th- and 19th-century letter writing and the novel is fascinating and could also yield productive insights.

6.　Nancy Grey Osterud's (1992) study of 19th-century farm families of upstate New York similarly finds less separation between the genders.

7.　In her introduction to the series of essays that included "The Female World of Love and Ritual" (1975) and focused on French feminists.

8.　Just as we saw in Chapter 3 that feminist researchers have and are theorizing modes of reading women's writing.

9.　In *A Room of One's Own*, Virginia Woolf called attention to the problem of the "male" sentence as an unsuitable vehicle for woman's writing, although "Jane Austen looked at it and devised a perfectly natural, shapely sentence proper for her own use and never departed from it" (1929/1989, pp. 76–77).

10.　First given by Anna Folger Coffin (1771–1844), the directive was taken up by her daughter, Lucretia Coffin Mott, upon the death of her mother (Bacon, 1980, p. 156).

11.　Millie (Emily) was the first child of Eliza Wright and David Munson Osborne.

12.　Bacon (1980) and Palmer (2002).

13.　A relative of David Wright's.

14.　Note Munson's use of the predicate adjective "pretty," which is usually considered female language usage!

15.　A knowledge of the family members makes clear that the referent here is Lucretia, not her more stay-at-home sister, Eliza Yarnall.

16.　This was Isabel Mott, daughter of Thomas and Marianna Pelham Mott.

17.　This was Maria Hopper, a cousin.

18.　Probably Edward Davis, a brother-in-law.

19.　I have no evidence of their use of letter-writing manuals, such use also suggested by Davidson (1986).

20.　There are only a few of these in the Osborne Family Papers.

21.　This was Florence Osborne, second daughter of Eliza and David Munson Osborne.

22.　This was Emma, second daughter of Marianna Pelham and Thomas Mott.

23.　This was Mary Woodall, a cousin from Wilmington.

24.　Whereby woman's writing "is situated 'in the insistence of a certain thematic structuration, in the form of content'" (Cholakian [1991, p. 3], quoting Miller).

25.　See Hobbs, 1995; Kelly, 1999; Kitch, 1993; and Zboray & Zboray, 1999.

26.　William Furness was "a Philadelphia Unitarian minister and abolitionist" and a friend of Lucretia and James Mott (Bacon, 1980, p. 64).

27.　He was the "other" speaker at the Gettysburg dedication.

28.　He was a minister from Auburn and an acquaintance of Martha Coffin Wright.

CHAPTER 7

"FIXED VERY NICELY INDEED!" A FOCUS ON GENDER

How many thousand things, unimportant in the abstract, but by no means trifling in the concrete a housekeeper has to think of.

(MCW to DW: 2.10.59)

You are yourselves the problem.

Sigmund Freud

"Yesterday morning I went down to Lib's to call & she made me stay to dinner. She is fixed very nicely indeed. It is a beautiful house & everything is nice there." (RY to EWO: 8.14.45). With utter rock-bottom pragmatism, 15-year-old Rebecca Yarnall, cousin to both Eliza Wright (Osborne) and Elizabeth (Lib) Mott Cavender, expressed, in describing her visit to their recently married cousin, what really counted in the lives of most white, middle-class, mid-19th century young women—a house with "everything nice." Unfortunately, Rebecca's word "fixed" was both apt and prophetic. Lib Mott Cavender was indeed *fixed*—for life, with a husband who was to leave her sick and miserable and bankrupt.

Reading and Writing Ourselves into Being, pages 181–211

For most young woman of the mid-19th century, as for the young woman of many a time and place, gender was the central determinant of her life (Cott, 1977; Hansen, 1994; Lerner, 1993; Personal Narratives Group, 1989). To be born a white female in mid-19th-century America was to be handed a road map with an already prescribed itinerary. (To be born black and female had, of course, gravely harsher prescriptions.) While this itinerary certainly varied from class to class, in at least some significant ways, it contained less variation than that between the sexes. This holds especially in the three grooved avenues highlighted by Sidonie Smith (1992) and drawn from the work of Teresa de Lauretis (1987)—their fates, their desires, and their discourses. These avenues as forms of what de Lauretis (following Foucault) sees as the regulating "technologies of gender" form the structure for looking at gender construction operating "as spaces in the margins of hegemonic discourses—social spaces carved in the interstices of institutions and in the chinks and cracks of the power-knowledge apparati" (p. 25). For de Lauretis, the construction of gender "takes hold ... in the micropolitical practices of daily life and daily resistances that afford both agency and sources of power or empowering investments" (p. 25). Literacy practices themselves, of course, are crucial as vehicle and site for the "micropolitical."

Before pushing on some of these practices, in the spaces and boundaries of the lives of the Wright/Mott/Osborne women, as made (inadvertently) visible in their letter writing, a brief review of relevant work—both that which views women's literacy practices as sites for agency and resistance and that which tends toward a cautionary stance for making claims regarding literacy as necessarily liberatory—follows.

RE-ENVISIONING THE SEPARATE SPHERES

Centered on the domestic—otherwise at their own peril—most mid-19th-century women were dominated by the cultural messages inherent in the powerful "cult of true womanhood" (Welter, 1966). The cult ordained women as keepers and the kept of the domestic and morality and the Victorian idea of "separate spheres" (Smith-Rosenberg, 1975/1985) where the social world was divided into the public and the private, women relegated to the latter, allowed a narrow swatch of culture and morality. Young girls, according to the critical Ann Douglas (1977), were a group "whose potentialities are largely suppressed" (p. 79) and who were made well aware of their limited options. Indeed, as we have seen in Chapter 5, the mothers and aunts—two of the originators of the Woman's Rights Convention of 1848—actively instilled in their daughters and nieces those very messages against which they fought throughout their own lives with such fierce passion and intelligence.

More recent scholarship has tended to view the lives of women and men as less rigidly gender-segregated than that described by Smith-Rosenberg (1975/1985) in the earlier cited, immensely influential article, "The Female World of Love and Ritual: Relations Between Women in Nineteenth-Century America." Nancy Grey Osterud (1992), for example, in her fine text on 19th-century rural life, saw family life on farms as much less sex-segregated than that presented by Smith-Rosenberg and others. Other researchers, as well, have been rethinking the concept of separate spheres itself, believing that it does not do justice to the complexity of the public/private interface or to women's creativity in pushing against those constraining binaries. Ronald J. Zboray (1993), connecting literacy with the construction of the idea of the separate spheres, wonders if under what he sees as the pressures resulting from "the inundation" of information of the antebellum period,

> women themselves did[n't] create the women's sphere as a prescriptive ideal, an attempt to give women mastery over their own self-construction? Were the bonds of womanhood a response to the boundlessness of the culture? (p. 157)

The authors[1] in *Gendered Domains: Rethinking Public and Private in Women's History*, a collection of essays edited by Dorothy O. Helly and Susan M. Reverby (1992), problematized the entire notion of separate spheres, especially as it tended to universalize women's oppression. In their introduction, Reverby and Helly suggested that it was no longer possible to maintain that there are

> two spheres of social reality: the private, domestic sphere of the family, sexuality, and affectivity, and the public sphere of work and productivity.... Instead, we can envision several inter-connected sets of social relations—relations of work, of class, of race, and of sex/gender. (p. 8)

They quote Linda Kerber's caveat from her much-cited review article of 1988 that began the current reshaping of the concept: "The language of separate spheres was vulnerable to sloppy use ... [and] historians referred, often interchangeably, to an ideology imposed on women, a culture created by women, a set of boundaries expected to be observed by women" (p. 12, citing Kerber, 1988, p. 17).

Two more recent texts, *A Very Social Time: Crafting Community in Antebellum New England* (1994) by Karen V. Hansen and *In the New England Fashion: Reshaping Women's Lives in the Nineteenth Century* (1999) by Catherine E. Kelly, both placed within 19th-century rural New England communities, have focused on the realm of the social—reading circles, visiting, gossip, courtship—as the mediating ground between the public and private realms. Both authors use these social activities to ground their observations in broadening ideas of women's societal influence beyond the domestic.

Like Helly and Reverby, Hansen critiques the notion of separate spheres, and like Kelly challenges and expands our ideas regarding women's role in creating their communities. In her critique of the entire notion of separate spheres, Hansen concurs with the utility of the concept over the past (now) 30 years, but states that "a widespread diversity of assumptions and definitions has clouded these debates." Moreover, she finds:

> As omnipresent as the categories are in contemporary academic discourse and the popular imagination, and as powerful as they appear to be, by themselves, they prove highly inadequate for conceptualizing human behavior in antebellum New England. (1994, p. 5)

For Hansen the "dichotomy [of separate spheres] insufficiently addresses the complexity of working people's behavior and cultural practices" (p. 25). The social dimension that she and others have highlighted

> builds a framework for representing that sphere of interactive relations which built and transformed 19th-century communities.... . [Thus] ... the common corollary to public and private—the idea of separate spheres—must be replaced by an acknowledgement of the extensive mingling of the sexes in daily life. (pp. 25–26)

With this acknowledgment that men and women did not live strictly separate lives, Hansen concedes the power of the ideational gender roles that tended to dominate most women's lives via the (unequally structured) realm of the political:

> Underneath the mingling of the sexes lay a deeply gendered division of labor, in the household and in the world of work. Women continued to retain major responsibility for household work and child rearing. The culture continued to expect men to be the primary breadwinners. Because of this, while the concept of separate spheres should be rejected, the awareness of a *gendered* social and economic division of labor must be retained. (1994, p. 26)

Similarly, Catherine E. Kelly (1999), stressing the importance of the role of the social, notes of the inhabitants of the New England countryside that "throughout the antebellum period, provincial sociability persistently defied the rigid separation of spheres" (p. 189). It is her argument that the transformation of the rural countryside from a home to a market economy involved the cultural work of women. Previous studies, she notes, have not "address[ed] the cultural work performed by changes in consumption and sociability, in gender roles and identity" (p. 16). Kelly argues that changing courtship patterns "refashioned the middle class" (p. 18); "defied the divisions between public and private" (p. 125); that women's work was more highly valued whether it was going to visit to nurse distant relatives or to make better and larger dinner parties as sociability beyond the home became more common. Yet, as Kelly claims larger cultural roles for women as agents and engines of change, she likewise has to concede that not all the transformations served to benefit women. While their work may have gained some of them some status, in some sense more work may have actually been generated. The dinner parties given by rural women, for example, required that they learn the more complex entertainment patterns of their city sisters. Even more compellingly, while women might have more say over suitors, the changing economy gave men wider choices outside the home and yet more authority within it.

Both Kelly and Hansen make strong cases for an increased intermingling between the sexes in a wide variety of social arenas, more than Smith-Rosenberg had projected in her study. But Hansen also calls attention to Mary P. Ryan who, while demonstrating that the boundaries had changed, stated that the direction the change took was not necessarily liberating for women:

> By the mid-nineteenth century, however, the ideological boundaries grew rigid and altered white middle-class women's behavior. Thus we witness a shift in the prescriptive limits of the private sphere and a contraction of women's access to activities outside the household. (Hansen, 1994, p. 11, citing Ryan, 1981)

Kelly, while conceding Ryan's point, suggests toward the end of her text that, while women living in cities might have experienced the pull back into the home, the rural women of her study had permanently transformed their rural environment. For Hansen, too, the mediating middle ground of the social world provided a wider forum for women. Yet both Hansen and Kelly concede the hovering presence of systems of inequality. They concede, too, that Ryan's observations of women's mid-19th-century retreat into the home, cannot be ignored.

MORE CAUTIONARY VIEWS

While these more current views serve to enlarge our understandings regarding women's expanding role via the social realm and a breaking down of the strict boundaries of the public/private spheres, some earlier but still deeply revisionist scholarship has tended to look at limitations and restrictions imposed on the 19th-century woman. These revisions have followed upon feminism's first and second waves that, most appropriately, had celebrated woman's lives and accomplishments (those, to reiterate, lives white and privileged). These rather darker views of revisioning are reflected in Christine Stansell's (1987) critique of Smith-Rosenberg's influential "Female World of Love and Ritual" (1975/1985).

Stansell (1987) sees a darker side to the close and nurturing "inner core of kin" uncovered by Smith-Rosenberg, which women generated and maintained through letter writing and visiting:

> The inevitability of life in a "closed and intimate female world" smothered young women of ambition and spirit, sent others to their sickbeds, and fueled the hatred of the first 19th-century feminists for a society that (... to paraphrase [Lucy] Stone) drove forth young men to work while it kept the women at home, eternal dependents, fashioning knickknacks. (p. 471)

Felicity A. Nussbaum (1988), too, shares this less celebratory view of the possibilities inherent in women's domestic writings. She speculates about Hester Thrale (1951), famed for her *Thraliana* (1951), or domestic chronicles, in which she detailed not only the conversations of Samuel Johnson in his visits to her estate but also her own complex domestic life:

> In *Thraliana*, Hester Thrale includes personal revelations (especially about Samuel Johnson), reports of social gatherings and visits, a series of stories on an arbitrary topic, translations and imitations and original compositions, tidbits of information—whatever occurs or is told to her that she thinks is worth remarking and remembering. (1989, p. 217)

In her diaries and "Family Book," Thrale chronicled the daily development, education, illnesses, and births of her children (as well as the deaths of several of them). It is Nussbaum's contention that Hester Thrale, in *all* of her writings, "offers us a paradigmatic instance of a woman who resisted hegemonic formulations of gendered subjectivity even as she reproduced them" (1989, p. 166). Unwittingly, Hester Thrale may have reproduced in text the very inequalites that hemmed in her actual life.

GENDER THROUGH PRIVATE WRITINGS: "FATE, DESIRE, AND DISCOURSE"

In the reading of women's private documents, it is, to use Nussbaum's felicitous and insightful words, within the "spaces of the commonplaces"—"the places [within private writings] where meanings about gender meet and struggle for dominance" (p. 149)—that we need to look to garner an understanding of women's positions and positioning. According to Nussbaum, it is

> in these spaces between the cultural constructions of the female and the articulation of individual selves and their lived experience, between cultural assignments of gender and the individual's translation of them into text, that a discussion of women's . . . writing can be helpful. (p. 149)

If it is in "the spaces in the commonplaces where the meanings meet," then within these spaces, what is the range of meanings and behavior that is revealed when women wrote so long and so frequently to each other (and to men, as well) over time, over lifetimes?

We have noted the relative absence of revealing personal information on the part of the Wright/Mott/Osborne letter writers, their reticence toward revealing deeper emotional motivations, the heart and soul of so much contemporary writing. We have seen, too, that Elizabeth Hampsten (1982) ponders this issue as well, lamenting how little we know of so many women, even those who have left writings behind. This issue regarding the autobiographical writings of women has been of keen interest, as well as a problematic, to a range of feminist scholars (Benstock, 1988; Buss, 1996; Cholakian, 1991; Motz, 1996; S. Smith, 1992; Spacks, 1988).

The Gendered Self

Sidonie Smith in her essay, "Resisting the Gaze of Embodiment: Women's Autobiography in the Nineteenth-Century," traces the rise of the development of self in Western thought, in which there were claimed to be "stable boundaries around a singular, unified, and irreducible core. . . . Independent of the outer world, [this] 'self' is neither constituted by nor coextensive with its social roles and private attachments" (1992, p. 76). Needless to say, Smith suggests that this self, the "I" of Western history, reason, and autobiography "is gendered and it is male" (p. 79).

In this essay, Smith notes her indebtedness to Nussbaum (1988), for the use of the word "commonplaces" (1992, p. 86) in showing how Elizabeth Cady Stanton provided herself with what Marilyn Ferris Motz (1996) labels the private alibi, a cover for her more radical stances of agency and autonomy. Second, she notes her appreciation for Nussbaum's recognition of the fissures, the contradictions that could contest, destabilize, and contradict the ideology inherent in the separate spheres.

Smith also reflects on woman's problematic use of the word "I." She asks, after reviewing the 18th-century origins of the 19th-century male sense of self as expressed in autobiography, "who is this 'woman' interpellated in the discursive economies of patriarchy? And what does she know of 'selfhood' or 'selfhood' know of her?" (1992, p. 80).

To begin to frame her answer in distinguishing the difference of women's autobiography from men's, Smith draws heavily on film theorist Teresa de Lauretis's (1987) concept of "technologies of gender" that "hypostasized an ideology of sexually marked 'selfhood' in the nineteenth century that rigidly construed and partitioned masculine and feminine spheres of desire, fate, and discourse" (1992, p. 80). The phrase "technology of gender" issued from Foucault and defined by de Lauretis, as a

> starting point ... to think about gender ... propos[ing] that gender ... , both as representation and as self-representation, is the product of various social technologies, such as cinema [her site of inquiry], and of institutionalized discourses, epistemologies, and critical practices, as well as practices of daily life. (1987, p. 2)

De Lauretis notes Foucault's (1976) definition of gender as "'the set of effects produced in bodies, behaviors, and social relations' ... by the deployment of 'a complex political technology'" (p. 3, citing *The History of Sexuality*, Vol. 1, p. 127). Her theorizing from Foucault's understandings is immensely useful for understanding how writing and reading as personal and social practices might reflect and then reflect back on literacy as a fundamental "technology of gender": "The sex/gender system ... is both a sociocultural construct and a semiotic apparatus, a system of representation which assigns meaning (identity, value, prestige, location in kinship, status in the social hierarchy, etc.)" (p. 5). If the construction of gender is located in the semiotic, reading and writing practices are crucial sites of observation.

De Lauretis sums up her major point: "The construction of gender is both the product and the process of its representation" (1987, p. 5). A few pages later, she outlines two important questions: "not only how the representation of gender is constructed by the given technology, but also how it becomes absorbed subjectively by each individual whom that technology addresses" (p. 13). In a later text, *Alice Doesn't* (1984), de Lauretis asks these same two questions, in reference to Virginia Woolf's *A Room of One's Own* (1929/1981): "How does 'I' come to know herself as 'a woman,' [and] how is the speaking/writing self en-gendered as a female subject" (p. 182). Unanswerable questions all, we can at least begin "to locate the sign of the feminine in a woman's work" and "to fill in the blank pages" (Cholakian, 1991, p. 220).

A Catalogue of Gender Categories

The correspondence of the Wright/Mott/Osborne women, as we have seen, can be viewed as one long gender reference. The subject of the letters was their lives in all their diurnal detail. Both Martha Coffin Wright and Lucretia Coffin Mott, in their correspondence to each other and their political allies, would write of activities and issues relating to their shared social movements. But even in many of these letters, domestic matters are not ignored. With this exception, the bulk of the correspondence in the Osborne Family Papers that was to and/or from women reads as a catalogue of gendered categories. Living lives so deeply marked by gender, so too were the letters they wrote. Is this how the gendered self is constructed? As Teresa De Lauretis (1984) asks: "How does 'I' come to know herself as 'a woman,' how is the speaker/writing self en-gendered as a female subject?" (p. 182).

To ask these vital questions another way using de Lauretis's categories as noted by Sidonie Smith (1992): How do these markers of gender differentiation—of fate, desire, and discourse—denote real differences between the lives of men and women? How do these categories of difference (in which gender construction as both product and process is or has occurred) reveal themselves in the correspondence of the Wright/Mott/Osborne women?

Certainly, as we have seen in the reading and writing chapters, these technologies of gender—the reading and writing processes and practices of the young Wright/Mott/Osborne women and the directives issued regarding these practices (from both mothers and society)—were saturated with "what it means to be of one gender and not the other." Gender placement and gender differences, thus, were the very air they breathed, the premises and strictures so "natural," so much a part of them, that both their reading and writing practices were profoundly marked by such assumptions.

This engenderization, as is so often true of the everyday, the "taken for granted" that provides one's very ground of being (that experience that de Lauretis uses to "designate an ongoing process by which subjectivity is constructed semiotically and historically" [1984, p. 18]), was seldom explicit in the writings of the Wright/Mott/Osborne women. Because gender was such a powerful given, their understandings and beliefs about gender were only sometimes explicitly mentioned. It is important, of course, to try to get at these beliefs, whether explicit or more subtly expressed. For the most part, these beliefs must be teased out from the welter of details that make up the content of the letters.

For example, remarks and actions between mother and daughter, in this opening statement by Martha Coffin Wright in a letter written on February 22, 1855, reveal these taken-for-granted assumptions: "My dear Eliza, It seems hardly necessary to send a bulletin as Munson [Eliza's husband]

intends writing, but perhaps he will only send the downtown incidents"
(MCW to EWO: 2.22.55). The bulk of the letter, the at-home "incidents,"
focused on problems with the servants and "talking" about people's stories—their upcoming business ventures to far-off places—as well as talk
about their health and the "history" of their daily activities. In contrast to
what the men would write, it was the task of these letters by the women to
write the everyday. Implicit in the content of their letters, as illustrated by
just this small excerpt, was the gendered reality of their lives. Implicit, too,
was their understanding that men wrote of one world and women another.
And the "only" suggests they did not always devalue their own experience.

De Lauretis (1984) claims "that each person goes to the movies with a
semiotic history, personal and social, a series of previous identifications by
which she or he has been somehow en-gendered" (p. 145). So, too, did the
Wright/Mott/Osborne women come to their writing (and their reading,
too) with a "semiotic history." But in their writing (and their reading, too),
they were helping to make that history that both reveals their engenderization and continued in the creation of it. Their fate and their desire, teased
out from their discourse, inscribed the profound engenderization of their
lives and the discourse, in turn, worked to reinscribe that destiny: "The
construction of gender is both the product and the process of its representation" (de Lauretis, 1987, p. 5). We need to see how these modes of fate,
desire, and discourse interact in the construction of their destiny.

Their Fate

Of the three gender markers drawn from the work of de Lauretis (1987)
via Sidonie Smith (1992), the hand of 19th-century gendered fate is the
most easily discernible in the letters of the young women. The central
determinant of their gendered lives was their having been born with the
female body. For them, "anatomy was destiny." Little argument was possible. Most women of the time seemed to comply with the rigid gender
expectations, even such famous women as Harriet Beecher Stowe and
Lucretia Coffin Mott. The price for not complying is suggested by Emily
Dickinson's enclosure (Gilbert & Gubar, 1979; Wolff, 1986). Although in
line with a more celebratory envisioning, Dickinson's enclosure in the
house of the patriarch is taken to be a conscious, indeed revolutionary
choice of a woman in full recognition of her artistic power (Dobson, 1989;
Messmer, 2001; Petrino, 1998; M. N. Smith, 1992).

Only One Real Choice to Make

For most mid-Victorian young women, marriage was "it"—the central
(and perhaps only real) decision of her life. Even in the lives of those

women whose chroniclers see larger expectations (see, e.g., Motz, 1996), marriage was still the option most young women selected. For females, truly anatomy was destiny. Her fate was sealed through the proscriptions and prescriptions of the times. Her education was a limited one. Her possibilities few. Indeed, according to Sidonie Smith (1992), one of the recurring themes in women's auto- and biographical accounts is their realization of their inadequate education. Cathy N. Davidson (1986) provides examples of the woman's fiction of the early Republic that encouraged self-education for its readers. And Nina Baym (1978) has noted that one of the roles of woman's fiction was to help educate women into making that one important choice of marriage, a good choice.

Employment opportunities, of course, were narrow, and over and over in the correspondence of the Wright/Mott/Osborne family, it can be noted that almost any reference to female employment or employability came in connection with a crisis that necessitated the woman earn money. For the males of the family, it was a different story. Eliza Wright Osborne's brother, Matthew Tallman Wright (1834–1854), took off for California (where unfortunately he met with a fatal accident in San Francisco Bay and drowned,[2] but at least he fulfilled his dream to go West). The other two of her brothers, Willie and Frank (as well as at least two cousins), went to Harvard, and were always described in terms of becoming and being citizens and coming to have interesting careers. All the young women of this generation get married, had dinner parties and babies, read novels, and wrote letters.

These young women were inscribed by discourses of control such as Eliza Rotch Farrar's *The Young Lady's Friend* (1836), which hammered at the importance of being a lady, a role designed to limit options and negate any behavior that was not put into the service of others. It should not be surprising, then, that comments regarding "being a lady" can be detected in the Wright/Mott/Osborne correspondence. In fact, they roll off the pen of several writers with ease.

Thomas Mott, married to his cousin Marianna, who was also Eliza's half-sister, wrote to Eliza in 1846 and told her of the current activities of Marianna and his sister, Pattie (MML): "Marianna & Pat are upstairs & judging from the sounds you might suppose they were anything but young ladies— one pretty well advanced in her years and the other pretty well past them" (TM & MPM & MML to EWO: 3.8–9.46). At this time, his wife Marianna was 21 and his sister Pattie was only 17—the hold of the cult of true womanhood was being placed on them through his observations of their behavior. Yes, of course it was good humored. Nevertheless, a criticism and a judgment regarding women's short blooming period can be inferred by us and absorbed by them.

The indoctrination started early and was taken up by other members of the family. Eliza's uncle, Thomas Mayhew Coffin, brother of Lucretia and Martha, unmarried, with old-fashioned penmanship and turn of phrase, took up his part of the task of indoctrination during Eliza's first month at boarding school at Mansion Square in Poughkeepsie, New York. In what, most probably, must have been intended to be good and loving advice to his young and lonely niece away at boarding school, he delivered (and thus helped to impart) one of the crippling messages of the times: "Believe me my dear niece I would much prefer to hear that you were the general favorite of the school, than of your having made proficiency in your studies—much as this is to be desired" (TMC to EWO: 9.2 [or 21].45).

His sister, Lucretia Coffin Mott, in a letter to Eliza on October 4, took her to task for what might have been an attempt at a refusal to be so constructed: "Thy uncle has taken such an interest in thy being away at that school, and in thy expected visit here, that if thou could answer his letter prettily, we should be much gratified" (LCM to EWO: 10.4.45).

Always a prompt responder to letters, why had Eliza not answered this one? The reasons for her tardiness in responding may, of course, have had nothing to do with his negative views regarding her possible desires to excel in her studies, but on the other hand, how does one respond "prettily" to such constraining advice? As her Aunt Lucretia knew and expected, any reader (or the sister of any reader) of Farrar's *The Young Lady's Friend* would know exactly how to respond in this manner. Furthermore, her Aunt Lucretia's tone and request seemed to be in line with the same kind of constriction Eliza's mother Martha sometimes placed on her as well.

Seemingly undaunted in his quest to help his niece negotiate a successful future through wise use of present actions, her Uncle Thomas praised Eliza at the end of her first term when she had done well: "You have only to cultivate the talents that nature has bestowed upon you to ensure that your path through life will be strewn with flowers" (TMC to EWO: 12.22.45). And in the spring of that same school year, he wrote to her that she might want to return to school in the fall. He wanted for Eliza "to avail yourself of the advantage that is offered you as the facility of interesting others will depend in a degree, upon the information that you possess" (TMC to EWO: 4.5.46). Proficiency in school learning, it would appear, should take a back seat to learning how to attract a future husband, although *some* learning might prove its utility in this endeavor. Despite her uncle's real encouragement on the one hand and his constricting admonitions on the other, Eliza did not return to her boarding school but, back home in Auburn, she did take both dancing and French lessons! As dancing would have been a way to meet beaux and as French could be seen as enriching the potential evening sanctuary that would be part of her future responsibilities, it would appear that Eliza must have learned the pitfalls of too much education, as well spelled out for us in Susan Phinney Conrad's *Perish the Thought* (1976) and hinted at by her uncle in her formative year at boarding school.

It would thus appear that family members took care to inculcate the beliefs of the cult—not necessarily out of harshness or desire to be punitive but because such beliefs were so deeply ground into them and because they felt it was their duty to pass them on—perhaps to make life easier by helping young women get accustomed to the yoke gradually.

The Dinner Party

Given its importance in the correspondence, the first dinner party of the newly married young woman must have been a significant gender marker of fate. In a letter written to Eliza just a few months after her marriage, her sister Marianna gave Eliza a scolding:

> I will begin by criticizing your letter which while it gave account of the most alarming stage of dissipation of your quiet townspeople—did not dwell enough upon your own feelings, impressions, and sentiments—your home life and its doings and your own oyster supper—your maiden effort—when of course we expected you to be very minute—you passed over with the exciting information that it passed off well a week ago—when we were dying for a peep behind the curtain—to see if the coffee held out and was not too thick—whether the biscuits were not heavy. (MPM to EWO: 2.11.52)

In this same letter, Eliza's sister commented on some of the information Eliza did relay in her last letter, much of it apparently about the young men of Auburn—while young women gave dinner parties, young men were on their way to full citizenship.

In an undated letter but probably of 1857 or 1858, Martha Coffin Wright described the "first" hostessing of a dinner party of another newly wed couple:

> Augusta and John and Anne [Needles] called but they could not stay long as they were going to Mt. Holly—I liked John's looks and Augusta looked very pretty and happy—she likes housekeeping—had a family party of twelve and was dreadfully afraid her muffins and fried oysters etc, wldn't hold out, but they did—it reminded me of some of Marianna's earlier experiences. (Box 207: MCW to EWO: "Oh bright & pleasant")

Catherine E. Kelly (1999), reading her data differently, makes a country/city dichotomy on the dinner parties of rural New England, noting in her examples that rural women often could not quite "pull it off" (pp. 173–175) with the panache of city women. But that such parties were recorded still suggests that, just as it was for the young Wright/Mott/

Osborne women, the first dinner party was a significant gender marker in the life of the recently married 19th-century young lady.

Desire(s)

In coming to understand the role of desire, the second of these three markers of gender in women's lives, feminist theoreticians (Cholakian, 1991; de Lauretis, 1984, 1987) often make use of Freud's (in)famous and influential question: "What does a woman want?" De Lauretis (1984), in a chapter called "Desire in Narrative," quotes Shoshana Felman quoting Freud himself to show how his question:

> paradoxically excludes women from the question, bars them from asking it themselves.... Throughout history people have knocked their heads against the riddle of the nature of femininity.... Nor will *you* have escaped worrying over this problem—those of you who are men; to those of you who are women this will not apply—you are yourselves the problem. (p. 111)

After providing commentary from Felman, de Lauretis states: "What Freud's question really asks, therefore, is 'What is femininity—for men?' In this sense it is a question of desire: it is prompted by men's desire for woman, and by men's desire to know" (p. 111).

But what is desire for woman? The authors of *Fashioning the Feminine* (1991), Pam Gilbert and Sandra Taylor, who, among others, show how cultural texts work to structure desire, suggest that woman's desire doubles back on herself because it is so enmeshed in images of her desirability to the other. They continue: "This focus on appearance and sexuality has particular relevance for the construction of femininity in young women and girls and helps to explain why the body tends to be taken on as a project" (p. 13).

Indeed in the Wright/Mott/Osborne correspondence, seldom are women or girls mentioned without some remark as to their appearance. Even a baby girl did not escape comment on her appearance. Martha Coffin Wright wrote of Eliza's baby in 1856: "The baby [FO] is very good & sleeps well, but is not very pretty—Eliza is improving" (*SSC*; MCW to EWG: 4.11.56). The importance of appearance within the family is also suggested in an earlier letter from Martha to Eliza in which she said that while Eliza's sister, Marianna, was pretty, Eliza was attractive. Such conversations suggest the pervasiveness of the idea that appearance for woman was indeed a crucial matter—a strongly held belief even for women such as Martha Coffin Wright, who, after all, was "enlightened."

To enact wishes and desires of one's own, to have a sense that as a subject, a person, one can activate desire into action, requires agency (de Lauretis,

1984, p. 104), more agency, certainly, than simply cultivating appearance or holding it to be important. If women in Gilbert and Gubar's (1979) telling phrase had "fallen into gender" and if, as we have just seen, their gendered place was continually in the process of being defined as one of maintaining "ladylikeness" and one of being careful not to learn too much lest one couldn't attract anyone—meaning, of course, a husband (but of course learn a little so you *will* attract someone)—just, then, how much room to name desires differently from these could they act upon? What sense of vision of themselves beyond these constricting expectations of appearance and pleasing the other (at the expense of the cultivation of mind) could they hold? How much sense of agency did they believe was theirs? What marked their expressed desires—only what they were "permitted" to desire? Or could they speak outside of the system that had such a stranglehold on them in envisioning possibilities for themselves?

In her school days, Eliza Wright *could* express strong wishes quite contrary to the obedience and constrictions that made up not only the tenets of the cult but some of the daily air she breathed (and read, as we have seen). Again, Uncle Thomas Mayhew Coffin is involved. It had now been a year since Eliza had been at boarding school and this letter to her showed that she and her uncle continued to have what we would now tend to label "interpersonal difficulties."

In May 1848, Martha Coffin Wright, visiting her sister Lucretia Mott (and her brother Thomas M. Coffin) in Philadelphia, wrote to her daughter Eliza who was taking care of the home scene during her mother's visit:

> Uncle Thomas s[ai]d the other evening he believed he sh[ou]ld travel in Europe after he retired from business—I told him it was your intention to do the same & he would have to take you. He said you were too loquacious. You ought to have "made an effort" as Mrs. Chick[3] says to be more agreeable on your journey and you forgot in leaving him to thank him for his care—you must be more thoughtful next time. (MCW to EWO: 5.2.48)

Strong-minded, articulate (it is to be guessed from her fluency with the pen), eager to be a world traveler, not always as thoughtful as the advice books (to say nothing of her mother and aunt) would encourage her to be, Eliza had not "dreams" of European travel but "intentions." An intention such as this was rather more than the suffocating cult of true womanhood might have considered proper and possible—let alone her aunt and mother! While still at school in Poughkeepsie, Eliza, keeping her eye on the state of the river as an indicator for when she could travel home, wrote prophetically to her mother that she would make a first-rate traveler (*SSC; EWO to MCW: 3.20.46*). And, indeed, she did, visiting the American West, going to Europe several times, and in 1904, at the age of 75, Eliza Wright Osborne even managing to travel to Egypt (Underwood, 1911)!

In this letter of March 20, 1846 (*SSC*), Eliza distanced herself from her classmates by relating how she was not afraid of thunderstorms and didn't hide under the bed, but rather went out on the piazza and picked up the hail stones the storm had delivered. Five years later, while on her honeymoon, Eliza described this same kind of physical bravery in a letter written back to her parents and siblings:

> We have also been to the "Cave of the Winds," & clear under the American Falls as far as we could get. The guide was quite carried away with my stock of nerve. Two gentlemen went with us & after we came out, said if it had not been for me they would have backed out—I wasn't at all frightened but had a glorious shower bath & got so delightfully cool, that it was really refreshing. (EWO to Creatures: 9.7.51)

Her stance, as reflected here, was, of course, at odds with the standard picture of Victorian womanhood—as she seemed to be well aware! This sense of independence did not begin on her honeymoon.

While still at school in Poughkeepsie, Eliza and her Aunt Lucretia had a bit of a tussle over Eliza's desire for a measure of autonomy:

> In thy acceptable letter rec'd 10 days since, thou ask if thou cannot come down the river [the Hudson] with the girls and not wait for thy teachers. If there should be any one with them, who would take charge of thee, & have thy trunk conveyed to the Phila[delphia] boat ... the risk would be great.... Suppose we leave it for thy teachers. (LCM to EWO: 10.4.45)

In a later letter, this one to her sister Martha, Lucretia added yet another brushstroke to this picture of incipient independence that Martha quoted in her letter to Eliza: "Aunt L[ucretia] said," wrote her mother Martha, "that you were one who could get along without a special caretaker better than some. She said, 'Yes, Eliza's dignity of manner would be a protection for her'" (MCW to EWO: 1.10.46).

It was not only to her mother and her Aunt Lucretia that Eliza expressed a desire for independence and self-determination. Writing to her brother (Matthew) Tallman on April 3, 1846 (*SSC*), she stated: "Catherine[4] says I shall not go home alone [from Poughkeepsie to Auburn] and I say I <u>will</u> unless one of the girls that is going west goes as soon as school is out for 'I'll be switched' if I wait a day" (*SSC*; EWO to MTW: 4.3.46). Eliza believed in a measure of independence for her friends, too: "Caroline was ... hopping mad cause her mother wouldn't let her go alone to a dance which I think is pretty silly, don't you" (EWO to MML: 11.16.46). Eliza assumed her friend and cousin Pattie was in agreement with her.

As we saw in the last chapter, Anne L. Hoblitzelle, in her 1974 study that centered on Eliza's sister, Ellen Wright (Garrison), contended that Martha

Coffin Wright never encouraged Ellen to think of the possibility of a profession for herself. And as we have seen, Martha Coffin Wright appeared to discourage and even criticize Eliza regarding the Reading Society started by her, an activity that could nurture her intelligence.

However, on at least one occasion, Martha Coffin Wright did seem to support an interest outside of the domestic. In a letter on February 10, 1851, to Eliza, Martha described a courtroom scene in Philadelphia, a kind in which Eliza, now age 20, had once apparently expressed an interest in witnessing:

> You will see by the papers a notice of the arrest of a black woman as a slave, the mother of six children, one an infant. Miller McKim[5] sent us word when the trial w[oul]d come on & considered it important that as many as could should be present to show an interest in the case.—accordingly everyone went and were much interested in the progress of the trial. I wished you would have been there—as you wished an opp[ortuni]ty might again occur of listening to the eloquence of opposing counsels & the ingenious questioning of witnesses. (MCW to EWO: 2.10.51)

Just as Mary Kelley (1996) claims for the women of her study, this letter showed that Eliza *did* have intellectual desires, ones that were important enough to her to have been expressed to her no-slouch-in-this department mother. Indeed, the vocabulary of law was one that Martha Coffin Wright fully expected her daughter to appreciate. Perhaps now that her daughter Eliza was safely engaged to be married, Martha felt freer to express interests outside of the domestic.

However, in this same letter Martha delivered a lecture to Eliza regarding card playing and asked her about her piano practice: "How many hours a day do your housekeeping duties allow you to practice" (MCW to EWO: 2.10.51). The remainder of this letter by Martha Coffin Wright focused on the domestic issues of the moment—Eliza's need to purchase underwear for brother Willie, for example. Why didn't she guide Eliza to her father's law books?

In contrast to Eliza's clear sense of independence as a school girl and honeymooner, once she was married she expressed more ambivalence. On the one hand, she could explode to her husband for his failure to let her have at least the appearance of independence. In August 1855 Eliza spent a few weeks at the Clifton Springs Water Cure Spa. Apparently at the train depot in Auburn, her husband Munson spoke to an Auburn doctor regarding Eliza's traveling by herself. Eliza wrote to Munson on her arrival in Clifton Springs:

> Dr. Thompson ... made himself very agreeable—as far as Cayuga but don't for pity's sake introduce [me] in just this style again—My wife—she is <u>without</u>

company—just as if she wasn't able to take care of herself. (EWO to DMO: 8.28.55)

Just as when a schoolgirl she could decide when to leave for the semester so, as a married woman, she was capable of getting herself where she needed to be—and on her own. But a year earlier, she had herself expressed some doubt about travel on her own: "I tried to get John to go on to New York with me but he can't & I am going to be alone. I guess I am capable of taking care of myself" (EWO to DMO: 6.1.54). Such doubt could only undermine the sense of agency that helps enact desires in service of growth.

Discourse

The correspondence of the Wright/Mott/Osborne women was clearly a labor of love, worthy of the writer's very best efforts, and directed at making the everyday interesting through a recounting of the activities of the everyday and providing just that special detail that would please the reader. The difference of woman's discourse—her speaking, her reading, her writing—has been the subject of intense and varied feminist research over the past 20 years, as we have seen in previous chapters.

Theorists seeking that "difference" of woman's writing (e.g., Cholakian, 1991) suggest that that difference rests in content. From that perspective, the entire Wright/Mott/Osborne correspondence of the women can be viewed as saturated with gendered content. The correspondence of the women is one large gender reference: the content of their deeply gendered lives *is* the content of their writing. That was the mission of the letters: to tell their very much marked-by-gender lives to each other.

And, thus, almost all their discourse was marked by and filled with evidence of their gender—and their engenderization. As we have seen, the dominant tone in the letters, as reflected in the deep happiness that letters received brought to the recipients and the praise these letters so often earned, was if not an expression of joy at least of genuine satisfaction in the telling of their lives. However, darker notes can be detected, ones that tell of bleaker gender tunes than we have so far heard.

First, sometimes it is possible to detect a weariness with the task of letter writing itself, a weariness that may point to their evaluation of the letter's inevitable domestic content. Subtle negativities emerged in passing phrases as they describe their offerings as "so many little nothings"; or apologize for a "plain style." For the younger women, this darker aspect was also reflected, paradoxically, in their complaint that they had very little about which to write. As befitted young women whose fate would almost certainly revolve around the domestic, they often, especially in their early teens, bemoaned this fact: "Nothing happens to tell here at all," wrote Rebecca Yarnall to Eliza on May 12, 1845.

Kate Shotwell, a Poughkeepsie school friend of Eliza, expressed the same frustration in a letter written to Eliza during the next summer of 1846: "Nothing of any importance has occurred within the last week or two—Time drags on" (KS to EWO: 7.7.46). Three weeks later, cousin Rebecca repeated her complaint of the year before: "You tell me to write long letters. What am I to write about—nothing happens here at all but Weddings" (RY to EWO: 7.27.46). A real sense of *ennui* sometimes seemed to overtake them in those early years. Waiting for the prince to come could be so tiresome (Gilbert & Gubar, 1979, p. 113)!

Even after their prince had arrived, this same sense of weariness can sometimes be detected—for their mothers as well. Sometimes they inquired, especially after they had already recounted a goodly number of their gendered items—is it worth doing all this? Eliza, as a young married woman, told her husband Munson "If you don't think it worth writing [that is, all the little details] let me know & I won't offend again" (EWO to DMO: 5.12.54).

Even among themselves,[6] the women sometimes wondered about the value of their detailed accounts: "Are you tired of hearing all these plans [regarding an upcoming move]?" wrote Marianna to Eliza (MPM to EWO: 9.19.57). And even Martha Coffin Wright, inveterate letter writer, was not immune from this self-doubt. In an 1857 letter to her daughter Eliza she wrote: "Tell me if it pays to wade thro[ugh] so many pages that you knew before.... I forgot to ask you to enclose the note telling how I got home, tho' perhaps it was not worth it." And in an end note to this letter she repeated the theme: "I cannot inflict any more on you now" (MCW to EWO: 3.6.57).

When they used the phrase "so many little nothings" to refer to their own content, which was, after all, the very stuff of their daily existence, it suggests how deeply they had internalized society's evaluation of what they spent their lives not only doing, but detailing! Even such a noted minister, speaker, and writer as Lucretia Coffin Mott could fall prey to this unease:

> I don't like to blot any part of Marianna's fair pages with my commonplace— but as she has no time this morning to go on & complete the unfinished sentence ... there was no way but for me to fill up the blank, put my nothing ... with it & let it go promising a better [one] next time. (MPM & LCM to EWO: 2.9–11.52)

Second, if they could sometimes doubt the value of their own accounts of their own content, they could also, as we have just seen in Lucretia's offering, sometimes mock themselves using the vocabulary of the moral discourses that surrounded them. On December 8/9, 1848, Pattie used the vocabulary of the moral discourses to pretend to scold Eliza regarding her use of her time: "How dissipated you are—to play whist four nights in the week." Often they refer to their trips outside the home as "gadding" (MML to EWO: 3.23.47) or "traipsing" (EWO to DMO: 5.12.54), the pejoratives reflecting their awareness of society's evaluation of women. Their mocking hyperboles seem to echo their novel reading. Pattie wrote to Eliza in 1850 and told her when she had last seen the young man, George W. Lord, she was to wed in 1853: "It is now two days since I beheld his radiant visage" (MML TO EWO: 12.22.50).

Even Martha Coffin Wright, a woman of rectitude, could put the label of dissipation on her own activities. After a night at the opera, Martha wrote to her daughter Eliza: "I felt rather tired this morning, not having rested sufficiently yet for dissipation" (MCW to EWO: 2.11.59). It is to be doubted that Martha Coffin Wright was in serious search for the pleasures of dissipation that previous evening. When Pattie, now Martha Mott Lord, on her honeymoon wrote to Eliza (MML to EWO: 8.1.53): "I amuse myself eating maple sugar and immediately after dinner ... I shall indulge in a cardinal—it is very cooling when properly taken," it is doubtful that she was any more truly "indulgent" than her Aunt Martha was particularly "dissipated."

Third, while thus skewered upon and fixed within the dominant ideology in terms of fate and desire, running as a subterranean rivulet that only occasionally rose to the surface was a countervoice. It was not heard often and came more from the younger women. It was a voice most often expressed in terms of some variety of humor. This countervoice commented on their gendered position and the activities that devolved from that. In a letter on May 12, 1854, Eliza gave her mother, who was visiting in Philadelphia, a long list of "commissions," or desired purchases. She ended her list with a commentary on stockings and then wrote: "I don't know what I shall do if I live 20 years longer—and my understanding increases as it has in the last 20" (SSC; EWO to MCW: 4.18.59).

As in Deborah Kaplan's (1988) account of the letters of Jane Austen, hyperbole and irony are put into service as commentary. What cannot be said out loud can be said through forms of humor. And it can start relatively young, as in this letter from Rebecca Yarnall, age 16:

> Don't you tell Mr. Lennard that I send my respects to him, for don't you know that it is very naughty for "Little Girls" like you to tell stories, I am shocked completely. Don't you dare so polut [pollute?] your letters by letting him add any. I only wish you to ask Mr. Allen whether he remembered the "Little One" but not from me. But enough of this stuff. (RY to EWO: 7.26.46)

Like Jane Austen, they used the stylistic feature of irony to make their points (Kaplan, 1988). In writing to Eliza on May 9, 1848, Martha Mott (Lord) made use of "extreme diction" to comment on their mutual friendship and gender, as well as to close her letter:

> With no little pleasurable emotion will I leave this charming domicile to rest myself for a long time in your mansion of happiness where will be heard <u>pendant le jour</u> the merry laugh of youth & the infantile shouts of joy—I feel myself now completely exhausted. Adieu. (MML to EWO: 5.9.48)

The hyperbolic humor and the exaggerated, high-blown Victorian language seem to reflect Pattie's understandings of the relative position of women—and her sense of humor. This same rhetoric of exaggeration was used in another letter to Eliza from Pattie that referred to Marianna: "Moving has so unsettled her she cannot compose herself to the proper degree to answer such an important communication" (MML to EWO: 1.26.51). Eliza, a few years later, positioned herself toward the content of her current letter in much the same way. After providing examples of children's talk, she wrote "Ain't it interesting to outsiders" (EWO to MCW [?]: 7.10.56). Not only could they use hyperbole as consolation, they could also play with the language of their constraints. After she had become engaged, Pattie wrote to Eliza how homebound she had become: "Etiquette closets a maiden after her cards are out" (MML to EWO: 5.28.53). It is clear they had no doubt about the relative position of their gender—and the enclosure it often entailed—but what is also clear is that they were able to use the language of irony and humor in their own defense, for their own purposes.

FATE, DESIRE, AND DISCOURSE COME TOGETHER

In an interlocking nexus of desire and fate within their own discourse came what Nina Baym (1978) points to as the one genuine choice open to the young woman of the 19th century—and thus the organizing principle around which many of the novels of the period revolved—her choice of mate. Marriage was the central event of novel and of life (Baym, 1978). "Waiting for the prince to come" (Gilbert & Gubar, 1979, p. 113) was the key to the young woman's existence. Nowhere in the Wright/Mott/Osborne correspondence was the excitement as palpable as when one of the young women became engaged. Such events produced "a tumult of anticipation."

"I have been expecting that seal for some time and yet when it really came I was all knocked in a heap. To think that it is a fixed thing," expounded Pattie Mott on December 22, 1850, in her reply to the news of

Eliza's engagement. In her next sentences, Pattie evoked communion in the past, the present, and the future:

> We had a beautiful sermon this morning but I would find myself continually with you planning the future, reviewing the past—the many talks we have had about Warren,[7] [and] Munson.[8] Marriage, brides-maids etc. etc.— Believe me, dear Eliza, your engagement pleases me very much. (MML to EWO: 12.22.50)

Striking about this passage was its strong, nonironic language, alive with the power of joy and deep connection. To be so surprised as to be "knocked in a heap" was not the usual language of this correspondence because, of course, events of this magnitude seldom entered their lives. But when they did, these singular events were rendered—and felt—as high drama. Indeed, Pattie compared the news of the exciting event to story:

> Soon after breakfast Tom [her brother, Thomas Mott] came up bringing your letter with the enclosed note—which unfolds such a tale—that I immediately forgave you [for not writing] and have seated myself with the intention of filling a sheet & sending instanter. (MML to EWO: 12.22.50)

Eliza's half-sister and Pattie's sister-in-law, Marianna, was likewise taken aback by the news, so much so that she risked genuine trouble with Eliza: "Your letter, stunning as it was with the great revelation was not so fertile as usual in those interesting little details which make your sheets so irresistible" (MPM to EWO: 12.25.50).

Marianna fully expected to be taken to task roundly for this criticism of her sister, but she very much wanted to hear all "those interesting little details" about this "stunning revelation" with which Eliza was usually so generous regarding events of so much less import. And in fact, Eliza was taken to task a week later by her mother for not letting *her* share some of the "interesting little details" of this unusually dramatic event. Martha's peers, her sisters and friends, got into the act, too. Over tea, they pounded on the table demanding that Martha share what she knew with them of her daughter's engagement. Martha, in turn, wrote to Eliza how difficult it had been for her not to be able to share this exciting news because of the vow of secrecy to which Eliza was holding her.

Once these two critical events of a young woman's life were determined—the choice of mate and the first dinner party—what became of her "strong intentions" for travel and her determination to be independent? Where did her desire turn?

GENDER BELIEFS MADE EXPLICIT

We have now seen how gender—a semiotic history of fate and desire via the discourses—acts implicitly, structuring the day and structuring both the content and the language of the letters. Sometimes bemoaning their fate and its sometimes boring dailiness; often taking their lives with deep seriousness as they recorded the multitude of bits and pieces and made high drama of the events of their engagements and weddings; putting themselves down through self-deprecating humor and irony; relating the fates of others through story; and sometimes expressing desire for adventure and professional work—they left traces of their own consciousness of their gendered status.

Carl F. Kaestle (1983) and Mary P. Ryan (1981), as sound historians, both make the point that simply because people are surrounded by a strict system that prescribes roles, such does not mean that people actually follow them or believe in them. What were Eliza's own beliefs about gender? What were the beliefs about gender held by the women of the family?

It is important to try to find and listen to the threads of beliefs that made up the more explicit network of understandings regarding gender held by the Wright/Mott/Osborne women. Hard to come by because such understandings were so taken for granted, yet sometimes these women did reveal fairly directly their own beliefs about gender (not our reading of them). Just every once in a while through the welter of the detail was the revelatory remark, the "what hasn't been expressed," the "what can't be hidden or kept silent one more minute." These explicit statements, though few, do give us some tracings of their understandings of where they were situated.

An Explosion of Gender Frustration

Martha Coffin Wright began a letter on February 10, 1859 to her husband with a rare (at least in the letters!) explosion of gender frustration. In Philadelphia for an extended stay, she wrote in her first letter after arrival:

My dear David,

My very first business, as well as pleasure, is to commence this letter to you (the pleasure would be greatly enhanced, if I had my own Arnold's ink, instead of this thick stuff, and Ellen has run up stairs to get it for me) luckily my pen & ink & glasses and keys etc were not forgotten. I marvel how I got off without leaving half. You go so often, and only for a day or two, how <u>can</u> you be expected to understand how many thousand things, unimportant in the abstract but by no means trifling in the concrete, a housekeeper has to think of in leaving for two or three months—a woman too, with the thousand little needles & threads & scissors & various kinds of knitting & work to be accomplished in the future—I had planned just <u>so</u> much to do before start-ing—then coming a day earlier, the work of three days was crowded into two,—and that last morning seems like a nightmare—but for Eliza's ready assistance, I really believe <u>the handle</u> [bundle?] would have been left—What a composed, efficient "one of a thousand" she is. Now to begin from our parting.... (MCW to DW: 2.10.59)

In this sometimes pained address to her husband of 30 years, Martha Coffin Wright revealed some of the truths and tensions of her—and by extension, the other women of the family's—daily existence. Obviously expressing very strong feelings, upon which the lid was usually kept, at least in her letters, she, in effect, was telling her husband (to use current vernac-ular): "You just don't get it." Even with servants (mostly Irish "girls"), even with multiple helping hands of sisters and aunts, the reality of mid-19th-century life, even for women of their relatively high status, rested in impor-tant (though not sole) measure "on many thousand things, unimportant in the abstract but by no means trifling in the concrete."

Martha Coffin Wright showed here her excellent command over the lan-guage: the language construction itself, in its effective and repetitive use of the word "and"—"needles and threads and scissors and various kinds of knitting and work"—aided her in making her point. The letter proceeded to continue into the characteristic smoothly flowing, grammatically com-plex sentence of so many of these talented letter writers as she recounted her travels and arrival.

"Men are Smarter Than Women"—As Everyone Knows

What did—and does—it mean, importantly, that they encoded "all these thousand little things"? For that was the very task of the letters: to relay for sharing all "those many thousand things, unimportant in the abstract but by no means trifling in the concrete." As we have seen, the role of the let-ters was precisely to encode these "thousand details" of their everyday exist-ence. In a letter to her daughter Eliza written the day after this unusual expression of strong feeling was, interestingly, another very revealing and rare expression of rock-bottom gender understandings. The topic once again was related to sewing, this time to the sewing machine, a recent invention and family purchase:

They were telling something of the children's Sayings [a Grace Greenwood column[9]] yesterday—Little Isaac [Hopper, age 6] wanted to sew on the machine—make shirts for his doll—His mother said it was out of order—well, he could fix it, he said—no he couldn't, Anna [Mott Hopper, his mother] said. He insisted he could. Anna said Lue [his older sister, age 21] can't fix it—Isaac said he could, 'cause said he, "*men* are smarter than women." (MCW to EWO: 2.11.59)

Martha Coffin Wright allowed herself only: "Think how inborn the sentiment is" (MCW to EWO: 2.11.59). It would appear that for her, Little Isaac's statement was a belief, not an eternal verity, and a belief not shared by all. It would appear that she expected that her reader, her daughter Eliza, would share her point of view, not that of 6-year-old Isaac. It is likely she did not need to say more!

It was not that the women of these families, as more current scholarship suggests, did not have the respect of their husbands or fathers. They did. David Wright, husband of Martha Coffin Wright and father to Eliza, wrote a letter to an official or head teacher at his oldest son's (Matthew Tallman Wright) prospective school on October 3, 1846. He took himself to task for not having been of more help to his wife and provided the school official with praise of her as well. He confessed that he was "too much buried in my business to be able to assist her in the least, but I do not doubt she has more than well attended to her part." He hopes Dr. Lee "will take good care of our boy and train him for a useful man & good citizen," the last word not often used in the letters in reference to those of the opposite sex, perhaps because indeed they weren't real citizens, not having the right to vote (DW to Dr. Lee: 10.3.46).

Clearly, too, David Wright held his daughter Eliza in high regard. In a series of letters written to his daughter in 1857, now living in Buffalo, while his own wife (and the usual family letter writer) was out of town, he suggested that Eliza read the books which he, a lawyer, author, and sometime political candidate, was currently finding interesting. One was the biography of John Adams, whose son, [John Quincy Adams] had made a trip to Auburn in 1843, and another book was on Commodore Perry's recent, well-publicized expedition to Japan.

In this series of letters to her when she was in Buffalo, he was very solicitous regarding the difficulties of caring for small children when her husband was away on business matters. David Wright understood, too, the strains that could beset the young and conscientious mother. In recognition of her devotion and hard work, he gave her $10. Her father, too addressed her as someone who understood the financial nuances and trials of her husband's business concerns and tribulations. He shared with her his worries about potential difficulties facing the new reaper business of her husband Munson because of possible undercapitalization. While his wife certainly did not characterize him as a feminist (though they were quite close), toward his daughter Eliza, David Wright showed real respect for her as well as for her intelligence and knowledge.

Pulling in the Gender Reins

By all accounts, Eliza Wright and David Munson Osborne had a truly sat-isfactory marriage. He appeared genuinely to esteem her intelligence and to depend on her business sense, sometimes telling her how much he liked to talk over his business matters with her. Furthermore, he entrusted some business matters to her when he was on the road. But[10] David Munson Osborne could also pull in the gender reins, fast and effectively, as revealed in the following inter-change regarding the infamous Bloomer costume.

The brainchild of Elizabeth Smith Miller, cousin of Elizabeth Cady Stan-ton, and popularized by Amelia Bloomer of Seneca Falls, the outfit of knee-length dress over ankle length pantaloons was created to help make everyday life a much easier proposition. The outfit was taken up by Eliza-beth Cady Stanton and other feminists. Cartoons and commentary of the day ridiculed it and its wearers savagely. According to one of Lucretia Cof-fin Mott's biographers (Bacon, 1980), her children, who would include Pattie, refused to have anything to do with it. The Bloomer costume was finally dropped even by Stanton who decided she could endure no more ridicule because of it. She felt that the commotion it caused was getting in the way of political reform, drawing too much attention and energy away from the main contest. (Indeed, she wrote in her autobiography, *Eighty Years & More. Reminiscences, 1815–1897* [1898/1971], that if she had known how much ridicule, in general, she would have had to endure over the years, she might not have forged ahead.)

Eliza first mentioned Bloomers in a letter to her brother, Matthew Tall-man Wright, who was traveling in California: "How are Bloomer dresses out West—some two or three frights have put them on here & look horridly" (*SSC*; EWO to MTW: 1851). It does not take much interpretation to have a fair understanding of Eliza's position regarding the Bloomer costume!

However, a few years later, in one of the few instances I have read where she commented favorably on women's rights advocates in her early and middle years, she wrote that she saw it as a step back for Lucy Stone to stop wearing them. In the spring of 1854, Eliza decided to wear a pair herself, but only with her friend and cousin Pattie and then only for walking in the woods (good Romantic that she was). For this, for her a quite daring move reflecting some of her early independence, she received a rare correction from her husband who quite clearly did not want her to be seen in them. Eliza wrote to him on May 12, 1854:

Pat[tie] & I have got bloomers all fixed for walking in the woods & we are going to astonish the natives as soon as possible. I trimmed my flat [a hat] today. (EWO to DMO: 5.12.54)

Munson responded on May 16:

> Yes I keep strict accounts of expenses—the umbrella & [tooth]-brush are down—I am sorry you are going to make yourself look ridiculous by wearing bloomers though just to do so in the woods will do, but not to go through the streets with them. It only makes you the subject for laughter and the effect is anything but pleasant. Goodbye now, dear Lizzie. (DMO to EWO: 5.16.54)

Eliza wrote back on May 20:

> I don't think the bloomers will look ridiculous at all. They are the only proper things to wear in the country—but we haven't had them on yet—now for all the particulars since I wrote.... (EWO to DMO: 5.20.54)

In her next letter to him, on May 23, she told him, yes, she and Pattie had worn them, but then she reassured him that she would not flout convention:

> Pattie & I put on bloomers & took a walk off in the woods. The birds were singing & everything looking so lovely we sat under a tree in full view of the beautiful plain which lay below us, consequently we were on one of the numerous hills around & walked & talked. [Saw a] bright red bird with black wings, the first one I think I ever saw.... After sitting a while ... we came back, dressed ourselves becomingly & went to the post office. (EWO to DMO: 5.23.54)

It would appear that becoming appearances and pleasing one's husband could out-weigh convenience of dress and even conviction!

"No Hard Studying, Please"

From their own words, we are able to discern one more plank of the gender system within which they conducted their lives. The reference comes from the early 1870s, which, while somewhat beyond the time frame of this study, points back to beliefs regarding gender held by members of the family. A major tenet of mid- and late-19th-century ideology was the belief that women's reproductive organs required a great deal of blood to fulfill their biological function. Women, thus, could do themselves and their future productivity damage if they overdid, physically or mentally (Burstyn, 1984; Ehrenreich & English, 1979; Smith-Rosenberg, 1975/ 1985). This strongly and widely held tenet was used to keep women in their place and undereducated. The argument had it that if women were to overuse (perhaps even use!) their mental powers, the brain would steal the blood supply required for reproduction. An overly educated woman, thus, would be unable to perform her major function of childbearing.

This belief appears to have been held by female members of this enlightened family. Lucretia Coffin Mott, shockingly for someone of her radical stances and one who believed so much in the possibilities of women, appeared here, at least, to have voiced this belief about the dangers of "overdoing" (in this case physical overdoing). On May 2, 1848, Martha Coffin Wright, herself 4 months pregnant, was in Philadelphia and wrote to Eliza who was home in Auburn:

> Aunt L[ucretia] expressed much uneasiness lest you should exert yourself too much to have everything in order before I come home—as you did when I was away before—& she begged me to caution you against doing too much. I hope you will be careful & not do more than is proper—for I shall not mind "turning in" when I come home & getting things in order. (MCW to EWO: 5.2.48)

That this overdoing could be directly connected to the belief in the centrality of the uterus in women's lives—as opposed to the brain—was revealed by Eliza some 22 years later. In 1872, Eliza was in Europe and had met a daughter, Emma, of a friend of her mother. Eliza worried that too much studying had debilitated the young woman and suggested that she be told in no uncertain terms that she must regain her strength and never study as hard again. The holding of such a belief would certainly tend to discourage any strenuous mental activity. (Eliza's son went to Harvard and her daughters attended finishing schools in Massachusetts and Germany.) Eliza wrote to her mother from Paris:

> Tell Mrs W____ I [would] love to have her [Emma].... She ought not to study too hard—such a nervous organization requires great care to keep the right equilibrium. I shall caution whoever has charge of her not to let her overdo matters by studying <u>too</u> hard—To return to purchases.... (EWO to MCW: 8.11.72)

One doesn't have to take as hard a line as Ann Douglas (1977)—who felt that woman's reading in the 19th century amounted to a crash course in consumerism—to wonder if more study might have led to less focus on purchases! Curious, too, was Eliza's use of language: she appeared to have absorbed not only the beliefs but the actual medical terminology of the day.

THE INTERLOCKING OF FATE, DESIRE, AND DISCOURSE

From these instances of explicit references specific to their gender beliefs, it can be inferred that the appearance of conventional "ladylike" deportment was important to husbands and conceded by wives, that women experienced gender frustration, and that these women had a very clear grasp of their options within the system. They may have protested when their husbands—who were, after all relatively enlightened—enacted society's inequities; but they bowed to the inevitable. Martha continued to deal with grace with all "the thousand little things" and focused a great deal of her energy (for she was, after all, also a political activist) on the care of her children, often putting their interests ahead of that of her cause. Visiting Eagleswood, where her children were in school, she was asked by Sarah Grimké to read a newly written piece. Martha did but only briefly. Her focus was, by her choice, on her children. And Eliza made a point to reassure her husband that she had conformed and wouldn't look "ridiculous" in public (although in private she wore men's shoes and was proud of it!). Finally, we have seen that Eliza subscribed to at least one of the more crippling of 19th-century beliefs: that women were physically at risk if they "overdid" in using their intellect. After all, as every good 19th-century reader—and, it would appear, every 6-year-old male—knew, women's brains *were* smaller than men's. Men were smarter than women.

How was Eliza—and by extension, the women of her time—schooled into this intense focus on the details of domestic life? Why were her strongest expressions of desire saved for the marital decision?[11] How did she learn that too much study was a dangerous thing for a woman? How did she know it was best to reassure Munson she had put on a nice outfit—"We dressed ourselves becomingly"—to go into town and would not be seen if she dared to wear the Bloomer costume?

From the beliefs held within the family as outlined above, we can see the profound hold of the 19th-century gender system on these women and their lives. From their own explicit words and actions, we can see their acceptance of the system. How could 13-year-old Rebecca *not* have assumed her Cousin Lib was "nicely fixed"? Everything she heard, wrote, and read pointed to this inevitability—and its inexorable desirability.

We have seen, too, though, that some resonances of resistance can be detected. It was held as an option through high hopes for travel and independence. As a young housewife, Eliza Wright Osborne was the kind of self-reliant housekeeper Elizabeth Cady Stanton (1898) could have admired (and perhaps did!): "The mouse hasn't been caught yet but I mean to get a trap & some cheese tonight & dispose of him before breakfast" (EWO to DMO: 5.21.55). But we also see how quickly resistance could be squashed with a few well-chosen husbandly words. Eliza reassured her husband she had dressed "becomingly"—this woman who sometimes wore men's shoes because they were more comfortable!—with this one word marking her own capitulation to the appearance code of the "cult of true womanhood" as well as her rejection of a feminist stance, at least one so visibly marked.

Finally, we have seen and can see how aware they were of the whole damaging superstructure made possible through the technologies of gender. Having imbibed the tenets against them—women must not overuse their intellects, women were gadders, men were smarter—they often turned, through irony and humor, these negative imputations into art.

"Nicely fixed," in Rebecca Yarnall's telling phrase, and more so each year with the growing success of her husband's farm machinery business, Eliza Wright Osborne's life, as inscribed in the letters, was centered (perhaps, as hints in the correspondence suggest, with a vengeance) on her household and its tasks. An "efficient, one-of-a-thousand," her domestic activities were crucial to her, and she clearly often "overdid" in the matter of domestic chores, ignoring her Aunt Lucretia's advice. On what appeared to have been her first visit away from her husband, she wrote: "There is so much I want to do." And over the course of all her years she did, inscribing her doings in page after page of family letters. And to the end of her days, the content of her letters is filled with the tasks of her days. To use Margaret Himley's (1991) vocabulary of worth, Eliza Wright Osborne's work became "her works."[12]

NOTES

1. Barbara Sicherman's essay "Sense and Sensibility: A Case Study of Women's Reading in Late Victorian America," which, "analyzes the subversive and daring role reading played for the women of the Hamilton family" (Helly & Reverby, p. 18), figures in Chapter 4.

2. Bacon, 1980, p. 155.

3. A *Dombey and Son* reference (Dickens, 1848).

4. Presumably a teacher at Eliza's school in Poughkeepsie, Mansion Square. Possibly Catherine Ireland?

5. An abolitionist and close friend of Lucretia Coffin Mott. "The two discussed, debated and argued endlessly...for almost forty years" (Bacon, 1980, p. 58).

6. Although not with the frequency or insistency of Jane Austen (Kaplan, 1988).

7. Warren Adams, a former suitor of Eliza's.

8. David Munson Osborne, the favored suitor.

9. A "journalist and feminist activist" (Blain, Grundy, & Clements, 1990), Grace Greenwood, a pseudonym for Sara Jane Lippincott, was an occasional visitor to the home of Lucretia Coffin Mott. A writer of a successful book in 1850, *Greenwood Leaves* (Baym, 1978), she also wrote stories for children and newspaper columns.

10. I thank Joan N. Burstyn for helping me consider this possibility (personal communication, Spring 1992).

11. Her later years tell a somewhat different story and were based on her under-standings of the importance of cultural activities, reflected in her serious book collecting and in her providing for the leaders of the women's move-ment a comfortable gathering place to meet and plan and rest.

12. The value of her "works" are noted, too, on her gravestone.

CHAPTER 8

ENDINGS

Don't read novels just because the year is up.

(MML to EWO: 9.21.49)

A woman desires the power that will elevate her to the status of subject.

P. F. Cholakian (1991)

To come to the end of a study of young 19th-century women's "domestic" writings is to appreciate deeply their desire to be subjects in their own existence, in their own narrative (Cholakian, 1991, p. 85). It is also to wish to frame that yearning in as celebratory a manner as possible. Struggling against this potent desire are both the learned biases against women's writings of the everyday—"only," "mere," "just" (along with all the concomitants of such biases relative to content, structure, and language)—as well as the found patterns of evidence that suggest limits of expectations both from within and without. Put up against both the deeply learned lessons that privilege traditional authorial writings and suggestions of limits are the uncovered "works" and *their* found value. These productions, which still provide delight as well as stores of knowledge, must be celebrated, as so well suggested by the work of Mary Kelley (1996), Catherine E. Kelly (1999), Marilyn Ferris Motz (1996), and Ronald J. and Mary Saracino Zboray (1999). How best to underscore the value of the young Wright/Mott/

Reading and Writing Ourselves into Being, pages 213–240
Copyright © 2004 by Information Age Publishing

Osborne women's writings yet still do justice to the real restraints under which the young women and their works lived?

In celebrating the worth of the correspondence of these young 19th-century women and in claiming more ground and more space relative to their literacy practices by reviewing the wealth of information they have provided regarding these practices is to go against a lifetime of lessons learned all too well regarding what is "great" writing. Moreover, this close examination of the writings of the young Wright/Mott/Osborne women (as well as that of their mothers and aunts) raises other questions, which stem from past experience in living as a girl and woman raised under an ideology not significantly different from theirs.

It is both possible and necessary to wonder about some might-have-beens—lack of agency (Kelley, 1984) and lack of the freedom of vocation (Baym, 1978) as just two matters of importance. Were the gifts and talents of this otherwise privileged group of young women stifled or at least stalled? Why didn't (or couldn't) Eliza Wright Osborne (as just one talented woman among many) take her authorial talent to heart? Why didn't she play the "real" writer—that is, an author who tried for the sake of her talent to do "serious" writing—that her abilities for writing could have made possible for her? To place this kind of onus on a woman of the past with all the constraints on her is, of course, not fair. Yet not to acknowledge and then celebrate and then wonder about that talent that was hers (as well as that of the other women in the family) is to be a worse kind of unfair.

This new-found gift of the correspondence of the young Wright/Mott/Osborne women will continue to give if only these nagging queries are addressed, along with creative ways of seeing that can suggest the kind of possibilities sensed by Kelley, Kelly, Motz, and the Zborays: woman grappling with her clearly perceived understandings of her own inferiority relative to standards she hasn't set but with an equally clear understanding that what she has achieved has been gained against formidable barriers.

A question posed by Patricia Francis Cholakian (author of the 1991 feminist study *Rape and Writing in the* Heptaméron *of Marguerite de Navarre*)— "What if we were to think of these 'personal' writings by and for women as a form of publication?"—is one avenue of healing. From their own words, I have no evidence that these young women might have thought of their writing in this manner. But in the care they took, the concern with penmanship, the learning from one another, the artful search for what would be interesting, the use of literary language and forms, the time invested in the task, the place of letters as the centerpiece of many family occasions that included the men of the family—it does make sense to think of the letters sent the rounds to all branches of the family as a form of publication.

Valuable ideas have their own timetable. In her 1992 text, *Rowing in Eden: Rereading Emily Dickinson*, Martha Nell Smith has developed this same question and, in so doing, has enabled the bringing together of this new question with the four questions above to help to value appropriately the everyday works of the young Wright/Mott/Osborne women. Nell Smith, in her reconceptualization of Emily Dickinson's work through many avenues, all focused on the question "What is publication?", provides ways of thinking about the "private" writings of women that places such writings in a more privileged position.

Nell Smith encourages thinking about authorship as a continuum. In this, she draws on a 1991 article by Cheryl Walker: "We need to develop 'a new concept of authorship that does not naively assert that the writer is an originating genius' creating closed artifacts, but is a textual producer whose enterprise is generative, turning every reader into a coproducer or coauthor" (p. 76). For Nell Smith, "The idea of authorial continuum proves a valuable tool for beginning to understand the very complicated symbioses among author, text, and reader" (p. 76).

Unlike Emily Dickinson, who put the totality of her existence at the disposal of her authorial mission, the young Wright/Mott/Osborne women put their letter writing into the service of the work of community. They gave themselves the pleasure of text creation—the play of language, the search for the interesting particular, the fashioning of domestic detail that, while fulfilling functional literacy needs, also became eminently readable and satisfactory to produce—and to read.[1]

Before following the conclusionary avenues to which these observations lead, a return to the origins of this study is necessary.

THE PROBLEMATIC(S) OF LITERACY

The central problem of this study arose from critical theorist Harvey J. Graff's (1987) understanding of the history of literacy as replete with contradictions and paradoxes, with literacy rates and achievement not obviously and always correlated with the expected categories. He opened the door for questioning the inherent promises embedded within most understandings of literacy. What is it that literacy would or wouldn't do for people, in the present case, the young mid-19th-century Wright/Mott/Osborne women? Would proficient literacy capabilities confer agency, confer a desire for a vocation? These are crucial questions, and ones not yet sufficiently developed by all the male historians of literacy. As a key point, Graff (1987) confirms that, for women of the mid-19th century, literacy didn't even confer "fair and commensurate rewards" for the same work nor did it confer status on the employment opportunities they were allowed (p. 356).

Such contradictions illustrate Graff's methodological point that such questions can only be addressed by attention to specific historical contexts.

Thus follows the need to contextualize the works of the young Wright/ Mott/Osborne women within the range of feminist research regarding reading and writing. This contextualization, while not really changing the questions that arise from the literacy myth *per se*, shows that, yet again, the ingredients of a field of scholarship can be altered when sufficient attention is provided to and directed at the endeavors of women.[2]

Having placed Graff's central question within the keen and large opus of feminist research on literacy in general and reading and writing in particular, the time has come for a reckoning that takes into account literacy's dual faces: the celebratory views (Kelley, Kelly, Motz, and the Zborays) and the more cautious ones (Douglas, Hobbs, Kaplan, Kitch, Nussbaum, and Tompkins). Several interlocking themes revealed in and through the data provided by the young Wright/Mott/Osborne women writers need to be explicated.

Three major themes relative to the central question regarding literacy and its benefits and liabilities emerged throughout all the chapters—the abundance and complexity of the literacy undertakings of the Wright/Mott/ Osborne women; the benefits and nurturance they provided for themselves through their own discourse practices—their own writing and their reading of formally published writers; and the dual faces of literacy, the both/and of liberation and constraint, the question underlying this study.

These three themes are reviewed and discussed in this final chapter. Interwoven into this discussion is the metaphor of spaces as well as Teresa de Lauretis's (1987) concept of "technologies of gender." Taken together, these themes and concepts make clear that any study of women's literacy practices can alter past understandings that have given attention only to the literacy practices and experiences of males (white and western). Perhaps, too, we can find the means to heal the split subject through the concept of the development of a feminist consciousness (Gordon, 1994; Lerner, 1993).

TWO UNDERLYING CONCEPTS

"Technologies of Gender": T. de Lauretis

Before embarking on a recitation of the emerging themes, it is necessary to call attention to two concepts without which the following cannot be written. The first calls attention to Teresa de Lauretis's (1987) understandings of the "technologies" that regulate women. As embedded in ideology as literacy itself, the field of the history of literacy has tended toward undervaluing the role of literacy in women's lives and for failing, as well, to appreciate the complexity of their literacy processes and productions. To draw upon the insights of de Lauretis, literacy can be seen as a "technology of gender," a vehicle for "'the set of effects produced in bodies, behaviors, and social relations'" (p. 3, citing Foucault, 1976, p. 127), which both construct and demark gendered subjectivity.

Neither constructed solely by the discourses (such as cinema, de Lauretis's field of inquiry) nor yet surely a product of her own individual consciousness (The Personal Narratives Group, 1989), woman, placed in specific historical contexts, can be seen as certainly under constraints formulated by those ubiquitous political technologies of control that still surround us. Yet, also woman can be seen as being able sometimes to select and transform these technologies of gender for her own purposes and effects, as highlighted so well by Mary Kelley (1996), by exercising their agency via their literacy practices. So it was with Eliza Wright Osborne and her cousins, sisters, mother, and aunts.

"The Spaces in the Commonplaces": F. Nussbaum

Over time, feminist writers and researchers have consistently found the metaphor of spaces indispensable for thinking about women's lives, beginning with, as Teresa de Lauretis notes in *Alice Doesn't* (1984), Virginia Woolf's *A Room of One's Own* (1929/1981). Felicity A. Nussbaum (1988), in a discussion of autobiographical works by 18th-century women writers, also calls on the metaphor of space to make her insightful points:

It is within the "spaces of these commonplaces"—between the cultural constructions of the female and the articulation of individual selves and their lived experience, between cultural assignments of gender and the individual's translation of them into text, that a discussion of women's ... writing can be helpful. (p. 149)

If it is in "the spaces in the commonplaces where the meanings meet," then within these spaces what is the range of meanings and behavior that is revealed when women wrote so long and so frequently to each other (and to men, as well) over time, over lifetimes?

Nussbaum (1988) thus directs our attention to women's spaces—always within their own "history, language, and culture" (p. 149)—as the unit of analysis, the place on which to push in a consideration of the intersection of gender and writing. In this concluding discussion of the literacy of the young Wright/Mott/Osborne women, issues of actual space figure prominently, and the metaphor provides, thanks to all the work accomplished by feminist researchers and writers from Virginia Woolf on, useful and important insights. Now we can embark on our conclusionary journey.

TO THE THREE MAJOR THEMES

The three major themes that have emerged from this study—literacy's complex and abundant status in the lives of the young women, the gifts they provided to themselves through their literacy practices, and the double-edged nature of literacy's role in their lives—illustrate both the rich complexities and the contradictions that, according to Graff (1987), have been literacy's concomitants throughout history. These themes illustrate, as well, the importance of addressing close attention to women's literacy productions and practices, understood within a specific historical context.

Complexity and Abundance

Very striking regarding all the foregoing is the centrality of literacy in the lives of these young Wright/Mott/Osborne women. Even taking into consideration the built-in bias of taking as central what is one's own topic and viewing the data from that lens only, it is apparent that, in the lives of these relatively privileged white women (especially that generation of cousins and friends who came of age in the 1850s), the culture of the word— both reading and writing—played a strikingly significant role. This immersion in literacy practices had been in place long before they had been born and continued to be vital in the lives of their descendants long after their departure from life (and indeed continues so to this day). Clearly, the Wright/Mott/Osborne women's relationship to the symbolic—from their wide reading to their valued letter writing—bespeaks a rich complexity that has largely gone unremarked by the male historians of literacy but "recovered" by Kelley, Kelly, Motz, and the Zborays.

Two Refutations

Before looking at the specifics of complexity and abundance within the correspondence, two important refutations relative to standard understandings regarding female literacy of the 19th century must be noted. Relative to these standards, that is, male understandings (Brown, 1989; Gilmore, 1989; Lockridge, 1974; etc.) of women's literacy (including Graff, 1987; Kaestle, 1991; Zboray, 1993), two salient and contradictory points emerge.

More than "Mere" Entertainment. First, women's reading has been presented by the male historians of literacy as based on an understanding that its primary source has been the novel and its primary *raison d'être* has been "entertainment"—understood, of course, as in "mere entertainment." The data related to reading within the Wright/Mott/Osborne women's correspondence gives the lie to this dismissive view of what women did when they read. Moreover, our close look at their reading practices leads to several important corroborations and extensions of the feminist research on reading practices of the past 20 years that has likewise shown the complex moves embedded in women's reading practices—once these practices are taken seriously.

Just as in reading, so in writing. The male historians of literacy have seen the writing practices of women, if indeed the women *could* write, as consisting of "functional" letter writing only, with perhaps the addition of the keeping of a diary. Until Laurel Thatcher Ulrich (1991) made sing the journal of Maine mid-wife Martha Ballard (that diary from which Ulrich built a social history of late 18th-century medical practices), only Ballard's misspellings and awkward syntax were worthy of note (Brown, 1989).

Their Literate Orality. Second, as part of their "putdowns" of women's literacy productions, the standard view of many of the male researchers/historians has persisted in viewing women's literacy in general and their writing in particular as closer to the "oral" mode of literacy rather than akin to the "literate," that is, what the well-educated male is capable of producing relative to content, vocabulary choice, and complexity of sentence. Again, this study, embedded as it is within the actual writing of the Wright/Mott/Osborne women, provides a rebuttal to this frequently made, broad pejorative. Yes, often they used the terminology of talk in presenting their writing, but their writing is, by any reasonable standard, use of writerly conventions, sentence length and complexity, vocabulary choice, and so on, quite "literate."

Three Key Points

Three general points relative to this complexity are particularly salient—their language-rich daily environment, their keen knowledge of the mid-19th-century literary scene, and their strong drive to improve and extend their own literacy as well as that of those around them. Lastly, attention is directed to some issues regarding the specifics of their reading and writing practices.

Drenched in Language. From their earliest writing attempts, the Wright/Mott/Osborne women accorded to language in all its manifestations—listening, speaking, writing, and reading—enormous respect. In fact, they lived a large part of their domestic days immersed in the enjoyment and production of the written word. Their letter writing took not only a large space in their psyches and social life, it also took much actual time as well as took up actual space. Their wide reading (that often privileged that "d____ mob of scribbling women," but that was by no means limited to the novels by women), as well as the reading of the continuous flow of fine and long and richly anticipated "effusions" between Auburn and Philadelphia also ensured that the day was laced through with both literacy events and literary practices.

Often, the evening entertainment was centered on reading—either reading out loud for the entertainment of those present, or their own private reading. The reading material could be the letters themselves or a novel (with Harriet Beecher Stowe a favorite: "She's so good on dark parlors," wrote Lucretia to her sister Martha). The evening entertainment often included language games (charades and sayings). And sometimes of an evening Martha Coffin Wright could be persuaded to write and share a poem of her own.[3]

These women should not be thought of as comfortable only with the less privileged language of the literary domestics or even "just" their own writings of the everyday, for they were as comfortable (at home, as it were) with the canonized authors (Dickens, Carlyle) and the Male Sentimentalists, ambidextrous, drawing on all their reading to make the literary allusions and connections that were their aids for the understanding of daily life. Shored up by this wealth of literacy practices, they can be seen to have enriched their environment, using their own literacy and that of others for the enhancement of their own world.

An Amplitude of Literate Knowledge. The young Wright/Mott/Osborne women had a great deal of knowledge regarding both their own and their society's practices of literacy. They possessed knowledge of varied reading practices: how to read for "pleasure," for developing codes of communication, for learning what they wanted to learn. They had knowledge even in their "teen" years of the 19th-century literary scene—its conventions, who its successful authors and editors were, knowledge of publication practices and of serialization, its benefits and drawbacks. They knew their society's vocabulary of critique and were able to use it to make recommendations from their own reading. Their written "conversation" was rich in literate terms—"editor," "bindings,"—and in the names of those considered the literati of their times—Dickens, Martineau, Willis.

Just as their reading revealed an understanding of the printed word's variety and pleasures, so the letters these young women wrote to one another revealed a genuine writerly consciousness. From early on, these young women "mastered" the conventions of their communicative form. They then successfully managed those rules in creating what can still be recognized as their own unique form, suited to their own needs and interests. Not only did they understand the more formal aspects of writing—acute awareness of audience, an appreciation of reader–author interaction, organization of narrative, the desirability of cohesion ("a graceful slide")—they also kept central the premiere rule of writing: Keep the interest of your reader. To that end, they used their wit, their anger, and their ability to be ironic to create language that in its semantics and syntax and content would delight their reader. That the content was their own every-day dailiness may be seen as the ultimate revenge.

Their Drive to be Literate. Those who have studied women's 18th- and 19th-century literacy (Davidson, 1986; Heath, 1981; Hobbs, 1995; Kelley, 1996; Kerber, 1980) have noted how women first worked to acquire literacy through their own efforts, and then worked toward perfecting that literacy. A real drive to make and keep themselves "literate" has been noted in both reading and writing. From Shirley Brice Heath (1981), we know that writing well was so important to young women that they helped perfect their abilities through practice and mutual instruction. From Cathy N. Davidson (1986), we know that women of the early Republic read novels that encouraged women to improve their writing. Moreover, the women of her study copied poems, selections, and their own letters into their diaries.

In the young women's letters in the Osborne Family Papers, there is ample evidence to make these claims that women supported their own literacy learning as well as worked to improve their own literacy practices. There is the direct evidence from their own words that they were their own instructors in writing and believed in the efficacy of practice: "I wish you were here to help me" (RY to EWO: 1.13.45); and "I hope to overcome [my dislike of writing] by practice" (MML to EWO: 11.1.46).

Copying the words of others was another form of practice. The Wright/Mott/Osborne young women copied out poems and adages over the years. They also attempted writing in a variety of genres: Pattie (Martha Mott Lord) wrote Valentines and an Epithalamium on the marriage of her brother; Eliza Wright Osborne wrote a verse describing her baby's nursery; Carrie Dennis, a school friend of Eliza's, wrote a parody of Poe; in midlife, Eliza Wright Osborne wrote some short travelogues as well as a memoir of her summer home and then, sadly, a memoir of her mother as well.

To conclude this outline of complexity, yes, just as Brown (1989) and Gilmore (1989) and Graff (1987)—and I am not being quite fair to the latter two literacy historians—have said, women of this time read novels and wrote letters. And yes, just as Kaestle (1991) would have it, they read (sometimes) for mere "entertainment." And yes, these Wright/Mott/Osborne women were often darn close to "orality," in the sense that has been a strong pejorative (though for more recent scholarship, being "literate" in its former elitest, *belles-lettres* sense does not preclude "talk," "dialogue," "conversation"). For this 19th-century family, it appears to have been a concomitant. Clearly, too, "mere" and "just" do not come close to doing any justice to their literacy products and practices.

Provisionings to One Another through the Gift(s) of Literacy

The lives of most mid-19th-century young women, even those who had dreamt of travel, as did Eliza Wright Osborne in her youth, were marked by domestic enclosure and real educational and political disadvantage. Yet, it is possible to see[1] that the practices and processes of literacy provided spaces within and through which the young Wright/Mott/Osborne women could extend their horizons. In addition to this expansion of mind, their own literacy practices also conferred emotional and psychological nourishment—benefits of making their lives interesting, providing pleasure, assuaging loneliness, and providing stimulation and space for the exercise of the mind.

Finding the spaces into which they could seep without censure, they can be seen to have used the crucial "functional" need that had to be fulfilled—writing the letters that were the communicative glue of 19th-century life (and which then came to be understood and, thus, of course, devalued as woman's work) to make their writing and reading sites for their own pleasure and "entertainment" and, to borrow Shirley Brice Heath's felicitous insight, their gift to themselves.

Four-cornered, this gift was built on their literacy practices. It can be seen, first, to have helped make and keep them less lonely, provided the solace that human life requires, and third, helped to make their relentlessly domestic, everyday existence more interesting. Finally, and so interesting itself because of the pejoratives heaped upon women and their 19th-century literacy practices, keeping the mind alive can be detected as a vital aspect of their correspondence.

Assuaging Loneliness

Thomas Alva Edison's biographer, Neil Baldwin (1995), among many other students of the 19th century, notes that Victorians tended to be very social. A driving force in the Wright/Mott/Osborne correspondence was a strongly felt need to maintain the closeness of face-to-face, person-to-person communication. Being alone or feeling lonely appeared to weigh very heavily on these young (and not so young) women—and the men of the family, as well. This general state of lonesomeness was often part of their letter's opening greeting and ran as a thread throughout the correspondence, often describing how uncomfortable loneliness was for them. Many a letter was written because the writer was alone and many a letter was gratefully accepted because it displaced the loneliness. Reading, too, was often written of as a companion in the place of those at a distance or those not at home.

Providing Comfort

Besides assuaging loneliness, their letters to one another provided additional levels of comfort. This comfort provided to themselves has been noted and/or surmised by feminist researchers. In providing her model of the female reader in which reading helps to serve as a psychic bulwark, Janice A. Radway (1984) observes that the contemporary romance readers of her study have no one to nourish them. She writes that in the reading of romances, the women of her study were able to provide for themselves a space of nurturance in which their own concerns and dreams were the subjects of the text. With no one in the contemporary family to nourish them, according to Radway, the women did it for themselves, over and over "restoring a woman's depleted sense of self" (p. 212). The novels themselves, according to Radway, "help to create a kind of female community" (p. 212).

Deborah Jones (1990) writes that many aspects of women's talk—"the exchange of information and resources connected with the female role as an occupation [that] centres around concrete tasks: recipes, household hints, and dress patterns"; scandal, or gossip, "marked by a considered judging of others, women in particular . . . are means by which women can nourish each other" (p. 246). Quoting Phyllis Chesler, Jones highlights the role of "woman's much maligned 'chatting': it affords women a measure of emotional reality and a kind of comfort they cannot find in men" (p. 248). In the Wright/Mott/Osborne letters—the supportive conversations that ran between Auburn and Philadelphia—the women created for themselves, out of their own daily activities, the bulwark of sustenance surmised by both Radway and Jones.

Making the Every Day Interesting

Deborah Jones (1990) surmises also that various aspects of women's everyday talk are not devoid of what she labels as "entertainment value" (p. 247). The young Wright/Mott/Osborne women lived relatively "fixed," closeted existences. Their day-to-day lives, even though greatly helped by the work of their servants, or "girls," revolved almost exclusively around their domestic responsibilities. A major portion of their days and thoughts were given over to the chores related to food, housekeeping, and children. The domestic rounds, the samenesses of the days, were often noted in their writing (see also Hampsten, 1982, *passim*).

The importance of the correspondence to the young (and not so young) women can be detected by listening to how they wrote about what is at the core of the letters, the "particular." The key to the letters was just that right detail that pleased—or better yet, delighted—the reader. The highest accolade the letter writers could receive was to be told that they had held the interest of their reader.

Clearly, the detail, the loving detail, is the crux. They crave it, praise it, respond to it, and get cranky if there is not lots of it ("You've said nothin' about nobody!"). While certainly the very real practical task—especially for the women as they incurred family responsibilities—was to cover all the important happenings and activities, the key rule, or at least the ideal, was be interesting. Yet all they had for fodder was the domestic detail. Women's writing, of course, has often been critiqued because of its domestic content. The Wright/Mott/Osborne women did not go whale hunting. They could not go off to the wilderness to build a cabin. Their education did not let them write powerful essays on self-reliance (Tompkins, 1985). To make their own daily existence more "interesting," they had only their own experience, their own dailiness to share with one another. Out of that they made the everyday interesting, even an art form.

A Hunger for Ideas: "Smarts" and Mind

More subtle, and rooted in that which we have been trained not to privilege, was another or perhaps deeper aspect of the word "interesting"—something that represented a genuine hunger for ideas that both Mary Kelley (1996) and Marilyn Ferris Motz (1996) highlight. The demand, the hope, that a letter would contain just that right item of interest and that all the news would be told or that a book would hold the interest can be seen as a need to make their everyday more vital. The repetitious domestic could be boring! But more was at stake. There seems to have been a deeper dimension of the meaning of "interesting."

When Eliza Wright Osborne asked of the ministers she went to hear that they be "interesting" or when she praised them for keeping her interest—it seems to have indicated a desire for ideas of importance. As we have seen, the readers, young and not so young, often used the word "interesting" to denote their approbation of a book they had just read. As the highest accolade they could provide, the epitome of the reading experience, this quality of "interesting" may be seen to be a means by which they could satisfy their need to feed their intellect. Their use of the vocabulary of transport to describe what their reading had done for them—it "dazzled," "bewitched," "charmed"—and their disappointment when a particular book did not have these effects indicated a need for the exercise of intellect not satisfied by their milieu.

Could it be that these young women—reading many of the novels of the day, which were often not weighty; having had an education that centered on what would make a young lady a young lady and a successful wife, homemaker, and mother; having not, for whatever reason, engaged in a profession—were hungry for intellectual stimulation? Not a question that can be answered, I think it is intriguing that Eliza Wright Osborne made use of Catharine Beecher's texts that would make of the domestic a science; that Eliza made herself a lifetime expert on (and participator of) the water cure and its associated principles of good health; and, finally, that Eliza Wright Osborne made herself into a sophisticated book collector, systematically reclaiming many of the texts of and by women that made up so much of the reading of her youth and young womanhood.

Their letter writing, too, can be seen to have been a stimulating challenge for their intelligence, their wit and humor, their memory, their organizational powers. They came to have informed knowledge regarding writing practices: knowledge of the mechanics of writing, the purposes of writing, the aesthetics of writing; they learned how to be entertaining, and how to be informational. With their letter writing, as well as their reading, they both intellectually and emotionally gave themselves what society so often withheld from them.

Literacy as Liberatory or Constraining?: The Central Problematic

These literacy practices of the young Wright/Mott/Osborne women, in showing the deep benefits that literacy practices can confer, illustrate the power of the literacy myth. Literacy—the ability to read and write well enough to put into effect positive results—can make a difference. Yet, Harvey J. Graff (1987) has made a life work out of correcting facile assumptions that literacy is always an unalloyed good, a mechanism of liberation, a means for a "chicken in every pot." Rather, it is replete with contradictions and paradoxes that call into question liberatory assumptions regarding its benefits. In his chapter, "The Nineteenth-Century Origins of Our Times," Graff disagrees with the standard liberal notion of literacy as unequivocally liberatory. He writes that according to Lawrence Cremin: "Literacy and education led to increasing diversity and choice, and the interaction of the individual with literacy and an expanding environment made possible a change in the quality, usefulness, and quantity of literacy" (p. 340). Graff cautions against this liberal stance:

> This transformative influence has not been proven. Literacy had other non-liberating uses. Its potential for liberation was at best one use among many, and perhaps not the dominant one. Literacy was also used for order, cultural hegemony, work preparation, assimilation and adaptation, and installation of a pan-Protestant morality; in addition, it contributed to work and wealth. America was not really unique or exceptional. High rates of literacy did not preclude contradictions or inequalities, regardless of rhetoric. (p. 340)

By examining both the reading and writing practices of these young women, it is possible to see how the literacy myth would work for them. In both their reading and writing, literacy can be seen to have been a force for advantage, providing for them both a space to say "no" and a centering of self-worth consonant with the development of a positive gendered subjectivity. After a consideration of these mechanisms of advantage, a discussion follows regarding ways in which literacy, both as a practice of the individual and as a force from without, can be seen as a decidedly conservatizing mechanism or, to use de Lauretis's (1987) phrase, a "technology of gender."

As the Myth Would Have It: Reading as Liberatory

Through Reading, A Space to Say "No." The role of gender has not been foregrounded in many discussions of the presumed transformative aspects of literacy or in discussions of its potential as a vehicle for constraints. It was Cathy N. Davidson's (1986) *Revolution and the Word: The Rise of the Novel in America* that brought the literacy experiences of women into this important conversation. Her book, deeply informed by postmodern understandings, highlights the ways in which the literacy practices of the nonelite members of the early Republic could be the vehicle for shifting the relationship of citizens (and woman) toward authority (an idea echoed by Motz, 1996). Davidson found, through her close study of reader responses to the novels of the early Republic, that the reading of both men and women could be seen to be a refusal to be constructed by the cultural authorities of the time. The very success of the novel—a form much argued against by prominent educators and churchman of the early Republic—bore witness to this refusal, according to Davidson.

We are fortunate to have the letters of the Wright/Mott/Osborne women, for in their correspondence we have the same kind of corroborative material from them as readers as Cathy N. Davidson (1986) found in the flyleaves of the novels of the young women of the early Republic. The young Wright/Mott/Osborne women left behind that same kind of evidence of their own refusal to be totally constructed by the discourses of the time. In their letters to one another, we have seen their suspicion of writings that would tend to constrain them, how they could stand up to the discourses (and these were powerful and plentiful) that would construct them. They were on record as not preferring pious novels, and Pattie made it clear that even the moralizing of Dickens was something to view with suspicion. Their own mocking irony, as well, regarding their own place in the gendered system of the times is likewise evidence they tried to stay out of the way of the discourses of control, attempting to be their own women.

The role of reading as a force for providing an avenue of resistance has been highlighted by several feminist researchers. In her study, Janice A. Radway (1984) sees the reading of romance novels as a kind of protest:

The reading of the novels, when looked at from the belief system of the readers ... that accepts as given the institution of heterosexuality and monogamous marriage, can be conceived as an activity of mild protest and longing for reform necessitated by those institutions' failures to satisfy the emotional needs of women. (p. 213)

Furthermore, reading the romances may have helped them assert themselves as they "compare their own behavior with that of passive, "namby-pamby" heroines" (p. 218). Radway celebrates the "unmistakable and creative ways in which people resist the deleterious effects of their social situations" (p. 218).

Patricia Francis Cholakian (1991), as well, writes of the importance of the ability to say "no." The tales of the *Heptaméron* of Marguerite de Navarre, as well as other novellas of the time,

were not able to destroy the ideology of their historical moment. [However they were able] to shift meaning away from masculine systems and problematize the meanings of "love," "honor," "desire," "joy." By writing about these from a female perspective, they have opened up a space where, all signs to the contrary, women can choose to say no. (p. 206)

We have seen examples of how, in their reading, the young women were able, at least at times, to offer a kind of resistance to that which would mold them, consistent with Davidson's and Cholakian's understandings. As Radway surmises, "people do appropriate mass culture for their own purposes" (1984, p. 221), which is not, however, to discount its power. Radway continues: "Interstices still exist within the social fabric where opposition is carried on by people who are not satisfied by their place within it or by the restricted material and emotional rewards that accompany it" (p. 222). What did the young Wright/Mott/Osborne women do with the space(s) they may have made for themselves?

Through Reading: The Space to Become "Subject." Agreeing with both Patricia Francis Cholakian (1991) and Nancy K. Miller (1986)—as well as much other feminist research on the topic of the role of discourse in the creation of subjectivity—Susan J. Hekman (1990) writes: "Discourse creates subjects as well as objects" (p. 64). Through both their reading and writing practices, the young Wright/Mott/Osborne women can be seen to have activated and privileged their own way of being in the world. As we will see in more detail (after our discussion of the ways reading acted as a positive force), these young women wrote themselves as the heroines of their own daily history. Just as they made themselves the subject of their correspondence, and thereby can be seen to have helped themselves shore up and develop their own sense of themselves, so in their reading they can be seen as having been able to develop their own sense of themselves as worthies.

In three ways, their reading of the texts of their times can be seen to privilege them and their lives: one, they *were* the subject of much of their novel reading; second, many of these novels provided powerful models; and third, the novels gave permission for them to think of "becoming" (Gordon, 1994).

First, in much of the reading that they did and then shared with one another, they *were* the subject. Their favored books were about, by, and for women. The theme of many of the novels that they loved centered on the two significant issues that faced the 19th-century young woman, their choice of mate, critical in that era of rare divorces, and the importance of developing a sense of independence in the face of life's difficulties (Baym, 1978; Harris, 1990). As developed so well by Jane P. Tompkins (1985), the form and content of many of the novels was the "particular," the loving detail of the everyday lives of the books' heroines.

Second, with their selection of woman authors they provided themselves with models of character, possible self-identity (Sicherman, 1989), and modes of self-fashioning (Kelley, 1996; Zboray & Zboray, 1999). These characters gave them a currency for the exchange of ideas and lessons. Dreams of resistance may also have been generated by their reading of novels in which women were the leads. With their minds peopled with these female characters of substance, characters solving problems and confronting challenges, these young women could expand their ideas of what they could become, even if only in their hopes.

Third, Lyndall Gordon (1994), in her biography of Charlotte Brontë, extends the concept of what characters can mean to the woman reader. Of Lucy Snowe, the heroine of *Villette*, Gordon writes: "What Lucy is to be—a woman in command of work and language—seems improbable at the outset" (p. 258). But what Lucy can suggest to the female reader is a "woman [who] must create herself" (p. 257). Gordon continues her discussion and in it adds a dimension for thinking about the 19th-century woman character and woman reader and writer: "To rise is an imaginative act" (p. 257). The goal is what Gordon calls "interior becoming," the rising above

the disabling conditions which blocked women's rise. For "interior becoming," the only precedents are women like the Brontës and, following them, Emily Dickinson, George Eliot, Olive Schreiner, Virginia Woolf, Sylvia Plath, and vast numbers of obscure women who left no record of their desires and discoveries. They are waiting to be found in the unlit tracts of the past. (pp. 257–258)

To suggest that the Wright/Mott/Osborne women could have taken from their reading of the sentimental novel the means for "interior becoming"—of "rising from the shadows [and] looking to the future" (p. 274), "demonstrating a capacity to overpass old limits ... [and] offer[ing] the incentive to look for further possibilities in human nature" (p. 258) is not to make too great a leap. Susan K. Harris (1990) would go much further as she speculates on more radical possibilities inherent in the 19th-century novels about women and suggests they might have "broached heretical ground" (p. 21). Comparing the women's novels to the message of self-reliance embedded in *Moby Dick*, she writes, "The radical aspect of women's texts consists of their suggestion that a woman can be an Ishmael—that she can stand alone" (p. 21).

I would make a more modest suggestion regarding the role of the novels—as well as the other books by and about women that they read, more in line with Lyndall Gordon (1994). While I find little evidence that these texts precipitated any dramatic feminist action in their readers,[5] I would make an educated guess as to their possible "radical" effects, based on my own history as a woman/reader and my knowledge of Eliza's later writings and experience. These texts may have offered a space both literal and figurative for Gordon's idea of "interior becoming."[6]

We have seen the space their reading offered from the cares of the day, as suggested by Radway's work on the reader. But it is also possible that the novels gave them permission in their heads to think of becoming—taking the works of Charlotte Brontë as examples—a headmistress of a school (*Villette*) or mistress to a Rochester (*Jane Eyre*), and these benefits may also have been long range. A constant reading fare that "emphasiz[ed] female self-reliance" (Harris, 1990, p. 9) could have helped the Wright/Mott/Osborne women become the self-reliant housewives so praised by Elizabeth Cady Stanton (1898/1971). Furthermore, it could have helped Eliza Wright Osborne and Martha Mott Lord to become the self-reliant, capable widows into which they evolved. Harris (1990) points out that the novels have hidden within them "the voice that celebrates female genius" (p. 23). As suggested by Kaestle (1985), literacy's benefits may be more long range than short term.

To her end, Eliza Wright Osborne was reading and rereading the books of her youth and young womanhood, and moreover, collecting them for her library (which she had built). It is not too much of a leap to think that the books that provided "transport" and relief from loneliness and *ennui* in youth would have provided companions for later years. Generally speaking, the young Wright/Mott/Osborne women's very reading practices, as well as the development of their reading history as a group (that is, knowing themselves to be long-time, active, capable readers), could have helped to provide them with an overall sense of themselves as worthy from an "intellectual" perspective (Radway, 1984). Literacy, as Graff (1987) has noted, is in and of itself a phenomenon of privileged status.

Through Reading: Control of their Bodily Destiny. If their reading helped to establish a privileged sense of themselves, providing them with a gendered subjectivity that enhanced their being in the world, it was also a direct force for giving them control over their bodies, particularly regarding pregnancy. In the history of literacy, the connection between advancement in literacy levels and birth control has been the subject of much discussion and speculation. The literacy myth would have it that, as literacy levels and rates improve, birth rates tend to decline. The birth rates of the young women herein certainly were lower (with an average of four children as opposed to six) than those of their mothers and aunts. Yet, too, the literacy levels of the two generations were on a par. Perhaps in this case, the difference had to do with a greater ease in procuring reading material with the relevant information. There is disagreement in the literature as to whether this generational difference rested in access to information, access to actual devices of birth control, or differences based on motivational factors (Brodie, 1994).

Eliza Wright Osborne bought those 19th-century water cure texts that advocated women's control over their own bodies (Cayleff, 1987). It would appear from the spacing of her own children (and her request of her husband for his purchasing a possible birth control device, the vaginal device) that, through her reading, she was able to confer some control over the fate of her body through control of her reproduction. Her knowledge of the reproductive processes and/or birth control methods allowed her some means with which to have a say over her own body through the spacing of her children. Her life-long commitment to and use of water cure and homeopathic principles is evident throughout her letters. Her life-long reading of the texts of the prominent water curists of the day (Doctor Trall and the Nichols, Mary Gove and Dr. Thomas), as well as her frequent stays at water cure spas, provided her with information for establishing a measure of control over her own body.

Women of Eliza Wright Osborne's generation (those, of course, who were privileged to have access to print materials) could, thus, read and use information from their reading for their own ends. It is possible to interpret her reading to learn about the beneficial effects of water cure procedures and rest cures as "a refusal to be constructed by the discourses," as posited by Cathy N. Davidson (1986). The wide and varied reading of the Wright/Mott/Osborne women can be seen as a way to have constructed a more efficacious self than the discourses of the time would have it, a self to put up against what Lyndall Gordon (1994) calls "the disabling conditions which blocked women's rise" (p. 257). In their lives there was yet another powerful mechanism of literacy, their ongoing practice of correspondence, that offered yet another site and space for the construction of a positive gendered subjectivity.

As the Myth Would Have it: Writing as Liberatory

Through Writing: Making Themselves "Subject." Enormous claims relative to the literacy myth regarding what writing can do for people abound in the literacy literature. To want to be cautious regarding these claims, especially regarding those otherwise without ample autonomy, doesn't mean speculation regarding its positive role is impossible. Smith-Rosenberg (1975/1985), in her introduction to her collected essays, which includes the "The Female World of Love and Ritual," directs attention to

> the ways women manipulated men and events to create new fields of power or to assert female autonomy... [If] we reject the view of women as passive victims, we face the need to identify the sources of power women used to act within a world determined to limit their power, to ignore their talents, to belittle or condemn their actions. (p. 17)

In fact, writing theorists suggest that writing itself represents an act from which issues of power cannot be excluded. The very act of writing—taking pen to paper to produce meaningful text—itself requires a stance of authority (Gilbert & Gubar, 1979; Gilbert & Taylor, 1991). Other theorists of writing suggest that the act of writing represents the desire to be an active subject that expresses a will to power, not eroticism as many male literary theorists would have it (Cholakian, 1991; Miller, 1986). If this is the case, then the Wright/Mott/Osborne women can be seen to have daily enacted that drive, that in their 19th-century milieu, if less cloaked, would have been as suspect as infidelity (Cholakian, 1991).

Through Writing: The Carving Out of Space and Time. The letter writing of the Wright/Mott/Osborne women operated as a powerful force in terms of time (both in their writing but also in the reading of them) as well as space. The actual writing of the letters—a major daily task—was often accomplished within the "public rooms" of the houses, and thus was a very visible activity. The products of these writing activities, once at their destination, also possessed a metaphoric place at the center of family activity. The readings exclusive to the women included times when letters were read aloud in kitchen areas or in the parlors, depending on the time of the visits. In the evenings during the "family descendants" meetings, men became participants in the reading of and listening to the letters of the women. Thus, as an activity understood as both work and pleasure, it carved out large arenas of actual time and space.

If the letter writing and its later reading can be seen to have taken up actual space, it also can be surmised to have created metaphoric room, genuine psychic and emotional expanses for the women themselves—for their language, for their activities, for their talk, for their needs, interests, hopes, and possible expectations. They had created a genre of their own,

232 Reading and Writing Ourselves into Being

one that fit their needs, that privileged their own activities, that allowed them a place to play with language, to try out different "languages," a genre the men of the family found worthy of hearing and imitating.

Through Writing: Their Own Publishing House. In line with the insights of Martha Nell Smith (1992) regarding the poetry of Emily Dickinson, these young women can be seen to have taken the care with the proffered artifact that a "real" writer would have. On the verge of publication, as the letters were sent on their way, these young writers had the same hopes and pride of an offering that the more formally published writer is said to experience. Moreover, their "gift to the world" has endured, and still has the capacity of continuing to give on giving! The letters are still a joy to read— with the reader hoping for just that detail that pleases and tells more than may appear on the surface. Like the efforts and works of Emily Dickinson, the productions of these young Wright/Mott/Osborne women can be seen to have parallels in the world of formal publication.

Profoundly focused on their own concrete, inescapable daily female "particularities," these letters at once represented their best efforts with language (their own version of the Arnoldian "best that was thought and written"), as well as their best efforts toward supporting and nourishing their own female existence. Under the cloak of the domestic, which was also their reality, they carried on what may be seen as their own publishing house!

In and through their correspondence with one another, the Wright/ Mott/Osborne women truly made themselves subject. It was their comings and goings ("Put on your bonnets!"), their domestic activities, their documentation of the children's cute sayings and doings, their observations of the social scene that were recorded and read aloud and celebrated and reread and shared in the evening with all members of the family community. As much as the money earned by the men, the writing can be seen to have provided the ligaments and tendons that formed and held together the social fabric of their lives.

An examination of issues of literacy, when linked to feminist research, provides evidence that the power of literacy practices to benefit lives is not negligible. What women "do" with their self-selected reading is (simplistically put) self-enhancing, providing space, time, knowledge, references, and characters to give them much with which to people and deepen their sphere of living. With relatively advanced levels of writing, the young women of this study made many moves that were decidedly advantageous to the development of a self worthy of commendation. Unfortunately, again corroborating feminist research, discursive practices of literacy can also be seen to be an avenue of constriction of that same sphere.

As the Literacy Myth Wouldn't Have It: Literacy as Constraining

In both their reading and writing practices these young women appeared to have been able to resist at least some of the forces that would regulate them. Consistent with the insights of Cathy N. Davidson (1986) and Janice A. Radway (1984), as less powerful members of society, these young women seemed to have been able, at times, to read the texts that would control them in such a way as to refuse to take up the encoded subject positions. They voiced skepticism regarding pious novels; they made fun of moralizing, the dominant reading practice of the time. Davidson and Radway have made it easier to see how such refusals within literacy practices could open important spaces for the privileging of ideas and autonomy. By taking such stances against the molding discourses of the day, a young woman could construct herself not as a "namby pamby" dependent, but rather as a person capable of independent thought. In their voluminous and daily writing practices, they likewise literally made themselves subject, earning and bestowing upon themselves the linguistically privileged center of the family's attention.

Defining the purpose of feminine writing as not that of erotic fantasy but rather as a "fantasy of power that would revise the social grammar in which women are never defined as subjects," Patricia Francis Cholakian (1991, p. 3) illuminates the enormous potential residing in writing (and by extension, reading) practices for the creation and reinforcement of a valued gendered subjectivity whose power we can imagine. Unfortunately, if discourses can create subjects, according to Hekman (1990), building on the work of Foucault, it can also create objects. There is a darker, less liberatory side to literacy practices that countered this privileging of their own sense of being subjects, actors in their own lives.

Through Reading: Regulated by the Discourses. The discourses of the day—the textbooks, the pious novels, the sermons, the male sentimentalists, the mother-discourse, the advice books, and the household manuals—were all heavily weighted with moral strictures and guidelines that prescribed the characteristics of "proper" behavior and proscribed anything but that "proper" behavior as well. While we have seen that the young Wright/Mott/Osborne women could take a stance on their own behalf, we can also guess at the potential of these discourses of control to infiltrate the mind.

Fortunate to have this evidence of their ability to withstand these powerful cultural discourses, we can only surmise the long-range, subtle and not-so-subtle effects. We can ponder how much room they had within these discourses that sought to construct them consonant with the prevailing, self-sacrificing ideology of gender. And we can make inferences.

In much of their reading, these young women both learned their place and were constantly reminded of it (as if they needed to be!). The male sentimentalists; the pervasive climate of satire and ridicule; the discourses of control liberally provided by school textbooks, journals, and books, as well as by their mothers, aunts, and uncles—all provided clear and frequent reminders of the limits. Certainly the young women would have "learned their place" through their reading—the school books that constantly preached at them and showed them their future roles; the constant criticism of the Eliza Rotch Farrars; the male sentimentalists who covertly used their own dislike of women to make overt humor at their expense; the satire that surrounded them such as the monthly cartoon reprinted from *Punch* in their beloved *Harper's* that so frequently showed deep hostility toward women. It went so deep that even such a stalwart as Elizabeth Cady Stanton (1899/1971) wished, at times, she had not embarked upon her life work.

The extent of the effects of these discourses of control we can only imagine. Indeed, what are the effects of reading that which seeks to mold one, that which is written from a dim and negative view of one's present behavior or outlook? What effect does it have when the mother and the husband act as agents of control? When Martha Coffin Wright strongly scolded her daughter for returning late from a Reading Society meeting, which Eliza had instituted with intelligence, knowledge, and excitement, what was the message she sent? When Eliza's husband, Munson, wrote it would take a man to feed their daughter, what effect did that have on Eliza? What were the effects of the warning from this same husband for Eliza to be careful at least in public of showing liberationist views through dress, lest she make a fool of herself (and him)? Such effects of the discourses operate subtly but effectively. The consequences are the subject of Gerda Lerner's (1993) lament for women's lost creative contributions, *The Creation of a Feminist Consciousness:* "Over and over in history we find thinking women internalizing self-denial" (p. 34) and afflicted by "thwarted ambitions, aborted talents, and long despairing silences" (p. 32). Countered perhaps by the more recent trend to see women's development through literacy in a more powerful, celebratory light, still, women did and do operate under constraints of gender.

Through Writing: Implicating the Beloved "Particular." Received notions of what constitutes "advanced" literacy writing behaviors focus on the "higher" levels of thought—logic, synthesis, analysis (Finkelstein, 1979; S. Smith, 1992). Women's everyday writings, focused upon a detailed recounting of their daily lives for and to one another, have been seen as deficient in these higher-order cognitive modes. The content of women's writing—its everydayness, its domestic setting—has likewise stood in the way of making it a privileged form. Not able to do adventurous things and not well-educated enough to write about much else, most women have written about what they have been allowed to know.

In her 1992 article discussing 19th-century women's autobiography, "Resisting the Gaze of Embodiment," echoing moralist Hannah More, Sidonie Smith summarizes the critique:

> Woman remains "naturally" less rational than man. Rather than working logically, her mind works from the margins of logic: her way of knowing and interpreting is less abstract, less integrative, less transcendent, less impartial, and less self-conscious than the interpretive mode of "metaphysical man." (p. 81)

Smith continues: "Inhabiting domestic space..., she exhibits a less authoritative 'feminine' mode of engagement with the world, one characterized as intuitive, irrational, particularistic, and practical. Consequently 'woman' cannot theorize, cannot universalize" (1992, p. 82). Smith next calls on Hannah More, who though on record, as we have seen, as praising the writing abilities of women despite their lack of formal instruction, can also damn them for that same lack, clearly not one of their own making. Women, Hannah More declares:

> seem not to possess in equal measure the faculty of comparing, combining, analysing, and separating ... ideas; that deep and patient thinking which goes to the bottom of a subject ... nor that power of arrangement which knows how to link a thousand connected ideas in one dependent train, without losing sight of the original idea out of which the rest grow, and on which they all hang. (p. 82)

Smith explicates More's critique:

> the nineteenth-century woman's relationship with the word [was a problematic one]. With only limited access to education and to public activity, they could not take advantage of the full play of words with their powers to name, control, authorize. Without the power of words and public discourse, without the power to theorize on and from her own, "woman" and women remain silenced, unrepresented, subject always to the theorizing and fictionalizing of man. (p. 82)

Other researchers, as well, have stressed the importance of this differential in relation to the word. Graddol and Swann (1989), in a discussion of contemporary language issues, draw on language theorist Deborah Cameron, who argues: "In the western and more urban world it is not basic literacy which women are denied, but the necessary experience to develop the diverse communication skills and appropriate language needed to deal with large institutions" (p. 144). Kept from high-status literacy and language, women are then "constructed ... as poor communicators" (p. 144), or in Hannah More's description, weak in abilities of "comparing, combining, analyzing, and separating ... ideas" (quoted in S. Smith, 1992, p. 82).

At the core of the Wright/Mott/Osborne correspondence was the detail—just that right "particular" from the everyday that would delight and inform. The defining task was not just to find the pleasing nugget, however. It was to tell all: "We want to know everything," the matriarchs ordered. The arrangement of the particulars that told all often depended on a recounting—relating first "this" and then "that." While sometimes certainly shaped in artistic fashion to highlight that which was "interesting," an orderly sequencing was the primary mode. They acknowledged this in their use of the terms "history" and "recounting." They took the "tell-all" mission to heart, filling page after page, year after year with the details that were content and substance of their correspondence. As a reviewer criticized 19th-century novelist and biographer Mrs. Gaskell (whose 1857 *Life of Charlotte Brontë* was a purchase of Eliza's father), they "made the minute momentous" (Spacks, 1985).

At the heart of the 19th-century sentimental novel was the same kind of domestic detail that was similarly the heart and core of the Wright/Mott/Osborne correspondence. Jane P. Tompkins (1985) viewed the reading of the sentimental novel as a "strategy of survival." Focused on the sacramentalization of the detail similar to the Wright/Mott/Osborne letters, the novel, like the household activity it celebrated, "redeemed the particularities of daily existence and conferred on them a larger meaning" (p. 168).

Tompkins quotes at length from a scene from Susan Warner's *The Wide, Wide World* (1851) and then comments:

> The making of tea as it is described here is not a household task, but a religious ceremony. It is also a strategy for survival. The dignity and potency of Ellen's [the heroine] life depend upon the sacrality she confers on small duties, and that is why the passage ... focuses so obsessively and so reverentially on minute details. (1985, p. 169)

For Tompkins, the ideology of sentimentality had a great deal to offer the young women of the mid-19th century, namely "a combination of sensual pleasures, emotional fulfillment, spiritual aspirations, and satisfaction in work accomplished" (1985, p. 167). Thus, "the domestic ideal ... gave them a way of thinking about their work that redeemed the particularities of daily existence and conferred on them a larger meaning" (p. 168) and "offering consummation in the present moment" (p. 170).

Tompkins does not ignore the possible price paid for this almost spiritual focus on the detail, the goal of which was "to conquer her own passions" (p. 172). Providing "a design for living under drastically restricted conditions... , [the sentimental novel] deals with the problem of powerlessness by showing how one copes with it hour by hour and minute by minute" (p. 173). As Tompkins says: "Learning to renounce her own desire is the sentimental heroine's vocation, and it requires ... a staggering amount of work" (p. 176).

In her critique of the same culture of abnegation that Tompkins is able to render with such historically imaginative understanding, Ann Douglas, in *The Feminization of Culture* (1977/1988), takes the same domestic detail of story and sermon and has it serve as the subject for her criticism of 19th-century sentimentality:

> The special realm for ministers as for women was that of the little, the over-looked but indispensable detail; by an obvious compensatory process, they were believers in the adage "a stitch in time saves nine," tellers of the tale about the finger in the dike. They were pledged, professionally, to the insignificant and its crucial effect on the unconscious. (p. 130)

The net effect, according to Douglas, was the anti-intellectual nature of much of 19th-century writing, especially that directed at women.

For Tompkins (1985), "the crucial effect on the unconscious" on the 19th-century woman reader could have been a positive one. Noting that Charles Kingsley "in an unfriendly review of Warner's book ... quipped that it should have been called 'The Narrow, Narrow World ' because its compass was so small" (p. 184), she says that the wideness needs to "be measured ... by the fullness with which the novel manages to account for the experience of its readers" (p. 185). She concludes: "The sentimental writers had millennial aims in mind. For them the world could be contracted to the dimensions of a closet because it was in the closet that one received the power to save the world" (p. 185).

Yet, even if the detail provided the means for the sanctification of the everyday, it is still important to ask about what could have been the effect upon mind of this intense focus on the descriptive detail—page after page, day after day, week after week, month after month, year after year—of writing that took as its subject matter the smallest happening of the everyday. It certainly developed fine and fluent letter-writing ability. And it must have sharpened the eye and pen to notice just the right and telling detail that would entertain the reader even upon multiple readings (and "hearings"). And it provided, as well, a firm matrix of support, as Smith-Rosenberg (1975/1985) noted so many years ago. She had it precisely right. Yet did the writing of the detail, the beloved particular, provide "their author's quest for status as subjects" (Cholakian, 1991, p. 220)?

TOWARD CONCLUDING: HEALING THE SPLIT SUBJECT

The Young Wright/Mott/Osborne Women as Models

Thus, we close with the need to heal the split subject—woman who knows herself to have her own drive to power and still woman who knows all too well where "real" power is located (Cholakian, 1991). Thinking of the young women's writing as a form of publication—thinking of them as providing for themselves their own house of publishing with themselves as heroines of their own text—is to begin to claim some of the needed healing.

The meaning of Pattie's command to her friend and cousin Eliza— "Don't read novels just because the year is up"—may be lost to us. After all, as Mary Jacobus (1989) notes: "The feminine takes its place with the absence, silence, or incoherence that discourse represses" (p. 51). What is not lost is the power of the young Wright/Mott/Osborne women as models of literateness: their knowing use of literate modes of language, their use of everyday particulars as the vehicle for their emotional nurturance, and stimulation of their intellects.

While resistance *per se* was not a serious option, Eliza Wright Osborne seemed to have found, at least in her early married years, much satisfaction in organizing the domestic and fulfilling its myriad obligations—"all those thousand little details"—with grace, intelligence, and panache. Interestingly, when Eliza came to use the literate knowledge in which she had been immersed all her life, she used it not to write but to collect those very books that had been the likely source of her fine and complex sentences; the source of her vocabulary, the source of her moral beliefs, and the source of her devotion to the word.

Ceilings/Sealings

Over the many years this study has taken and down the many avenues the writer of this study has wandered, only one conclusion—not in the sense of ending but in the matter of coming to believe—has come to mind, over and over. And not from anything as tangible as a "particular" or pieces of data but from trying to breathe the air they breathed in which gender constriction was the *lingua franca*, the very atmosphere within which they existed. Somewhere, somehow there was a lid, a ceiling, a limit they bumped up against; a closed gate, a shut door beyond which they were not able to go. The possibility, the opportunity for using the gifts of language, the gift of expression—it didn't quite happen. They had the time, the equipment, the room—and yet and yet.

Unlike the working-class women of Elizabeth Hampsten's (1982) study, the young Wright/Mott/Osborne women had the metaphoric, figurative language to draw on and they had their wide reading from in which they could see examples of woman as writer and woman as problem solver. They had ready access to the "highest" cultural vehicles of the time, *Harper's* and *The Atlantic Monthly.* They had the well-practiced language of their letters, they had the language from their wide reading, they had language about language. Language, particularly for Eliza, was the creative medium of choice. Yet, they seemed not to have been able to break through or out of the form. They hardly ever went beyond the descriptive detail, which gave so much but which perhaps also kept them contained. They, like Hester Thrale, perhaps "resisted hegemonic formulations of gendered subjectivity even as [they] reproduced them" (Nussbaum, 1988, p. 166).

Both/And: Literacy as Liberatory and Constraining

Was literacy liberating or conservatizing for the young Wright/Mott/Osborne women? We can see it either way because it was both. Through both their reading and writing, they did not allow themselves to be totally controlled. Through their reading of women's novels and through their information-seeking of what was liberatory to them, they were able to exert some measure of a counterforce against that which would constrain them, able to make an earned intellectual space for alternative ways of thinking. While their challenge was more muted than that of their mothers and less directly political, they had more powerfully organized discourses lined up against them.

Perhaps they were able through their writing to resist consciously the potentially constraining discourses in which they were immersed—the text-books, the ubiquitous Eliza Rotch Farrar (and all the other moralizers), the *Punch* cartoons in their favored *Harper's.* By sometimes articulating through writing their stance of opposition to that which would construct them, they were at least sometimes able to provide the labels and warnings for each other against that which might work against them, that which was not desirable, such as pious novels. And, using forms of irony, they were able to telegraph their own understandings of their attitudes regarding their secondary status.

Clearly, they detected dissonances within their times, or we would not be able to detect their occasional ironic stance regarding their own situation. Carving out large chunks of space and time; literally creating a recognizable text genre of their own to tell their own lives; making an art of the same "particulars" about which they could also be ironic; creating an antidote to boredom for which they could be praised by both sexes of the family; being "manfully" imitated though not surpassed in their own genre—while all the time "subject to the discourses" —they constituted themselves as subject, as writer, as artist. Not bad. Not bad at all!

AND FINALLY

Carolyn G. Heilbrun (1988) mourns that we don't have a text; Elizabeth Hampsten (1982) grieves for all the women lost to us in history; and Gerda Lerner (1993) laments that women over and over have to relearn, and then reclaim their own history because it is always being forgotten, displaced, lost. In her call for the creation of a feminist consciousness, echoed by Lyndall Gordon (1994) in her study of Charlotte Brontë, Lerner aims to heal the split subject through her own sadness and anger at all that has been lost; at all the wasted intelligence and talent. But we *do* have a text; we have found so many women and their lost texts; we see in them those palimpsests of female consciousness that can heal the split subject (Cholakian, 1991). This creation of a new social subject, according to Nancy K. Miller (1986), must contain all the ambiguities of Lucy Snowe, and by extension the ambiguities we have found throughout this study. Talented creators of genuine "works" (Himley, 1991), the Wright/Mott/Osborne women knew their worth—created that worth—and somehow lived with the full knowledge of their ambiguous status. Of course we have a text—they created it. Our role is to keep it in memory.

NOTES

1. Yet, it is also important to mark a real difference between a woman who chose to devote herself to making art in her poetry and letters (Messmer, 2001) and women who could write artfully but had not made the choice to center their lives on writing.
2. With the focus herein on women white and privileged by class and family history.
3. See Eliza Wright Osborne's many-paged memorial to her mother, Box 236.
4. And highlighted even more strongly by the "celebrationists": Kelley, Kelly, Motz, and the Zborays.
5. It must be noted that like their mothers, Eliza and Pattie made fortunate marriages.
6. Mary Kelley's development of the idea of the "learned woman" as one who "constructed an alternative possibility" through her own reading and based on her belief in her intellect (1996, p. 403) clearly provides corroboration of Gordon's idea.

APPENDIX A

DOCUMENTATION OF PRIMARY SOURCES: OSBORNE FAMILY PAPERS

Note One: The following listing of primary sources serves a dual purpose. It documents the letters and other materials that are the source of this literacy study of the Wright/Mott/Osborne women (and men) roughly between the years 1835 to 1862. These listings also serve the goal of expanding the Osborne Family Papers' finding aid by John Janitz. Written in 1971, it focused on the male members of the family and their correspondence and activities. With this study, the focus is on the letters of women. And there are many of them.

For this study, over 300 letters have been analyzed and coded. They are listed here (although several hundred more through 1890 serve as background knowledge and material for the finding aid). Copied from the originals in the Osborne Family Papers in Syracuse University's Special Collections Research Center, the writer, the date, and the location of the letter (the latter not always given) make up the listing. This is still a work in progress. There are still many letters of Eliza Wright Osborne's and other family members to be reclaimed from the archives.

Note Two: Double-asterisked letters are from the Garrison Family Papers, Sophia Smith Collection, Smith College, Northampton, Massachusetts. Permission to quote from these letters has been generously granted by Smith College and James D. Livingston, great grandson of Martha Coffin

Reading and Writing Ourselves into Being, pages 241–251
Copyright © 2004 by Information Age Publishing

and holder of the literary rights of her and her descendants' papers, the Wright Family Papers.

BOX 1

* Among other documentation in this box are "love letters" of Peter Pelham and Martha Coffin Wright.

BOX 2

** LCM to AC (typed; original in *SSC*): August 3, 1835

BOX 3

** EWO to MPM: January 19, 1838, Aurora, *SSC*
  * Deborah Woodall to DW: August 13, 1838, Wilmington, Delaware
  * William Pelham to MCW: March 25, 1841, Washington City
  * Helen Morgan to EWO: April 19, 1841 or 1848? Aurora?
** MCW to LCM: May 19, 1841, *SSC*
  * William Pelham to MCW: June 19, 1841, Little Rock, Arkansas
  * EWO to MCW: September 8, 1841
  * MCW to William Pelham: November 2, 1841 (a copy)
  * MPM to EWO: May 2, 1842, Philadelphia

BOX 5

  * Frederick P.Wright to DW: February 27, 1844, Tulls[?]Township, Pennsylvania
  * EMC to EWO: April 7, 1844
  * RY to EWO: January 13, 1845, Philadelphia
  * RY to EWO: May 12, 1845, Philadelphia
  * RY to EWO: May 17, 1845 (and January 31, 1845; "copied in"), Philadelphia
  * RY to EWO: August 14, 1845, Philadelphia
  * RY to EWO: August 30, 1845, Philadelphia
  * TM & MPM to EWO: August 31, 1845, Philadelphia
  * TMC & LCM to EWO: September 21, 1845, Philadelphia
  * MML & LM to EWO: October 4, 1845, Philadelphia

* Ad & Anna to EWO: October or August 15, 1845, Auburn Female Seminary
* MPM, MML, & TM to EWO: November 10, 1845, Philadelphia
* TC to EWO: November 23, 1845, Philadelphia
* RY to EWO: November 26, 1845[?], Philadelphia
* TMC to EWO: December 22, 1845, Philadelphia
* EMC to EWO: January-February 1846[?], General Folder, Philadelphia
* TC to EWO: January 11, 1846, Philadelphia
* Frederick P. Wright to DW: February 23, 1846, Tullytown, Pennsylvania
* TM & MPM & MML to EWO: March 8–9, 1846, Philadelphia
** EWO to MCW: March 20, 1846, Poughkeepsie, *SSC*
* EWO to MTW: April 3, 1846, Poughkeepsie
* TMC to EWO: April 5, 1846, Philadelphia
* Rebecca Thomas to DW: May 3, 1846, Monroe County
* Kate Shotwell to EWO: June 9, 1846, Mansion Square
* RY to EWO: June 29, 1846, Philadelphia
* KS to EWO: July 7–16, 1846, Mansion Square
* RY to EWO: July 27, 1846, Philadelphia
* DW to Isaac Hopper: September 8, 1846, Auburn
* RY to EWO: September 11, 1846[or 44?], Philadelphia
* DW to Dr. D. Lee: October 3, 1846, Auburn
* MML to EWO: November 1, 1846, Philadelphia
* EWO to MML: November 16, 1846, Auburn
* MML to EWO: March[?] 23, 1847, Philadelphia

BOX 6

* MCW to EWO: May 2, 1848, Philadelphia
* MML to EWO: May 9, 1848, Philadelphia
* MML to EWO: September 8, 1848, Philadelphia
** MCW to LCM: September, 21, 1848, *SSC*
* MML to EWO: November, 18, 1848, Philadelphia
* Mary to EWO: December 4, 1848, Wilmington
* MML to EWO: December 8, 1848 [?]
* MML & to EWO & LCM to "Dear Ones": December 31, 1848, Philadelphia
* MML to EWO: February 5 [or 8], 1849, Philadelphia
* MML to EWO: April 17, 1849, Philadelphia
* MML to EWO: May 31, 1849, Philadelphia
* WA to EWO: August 1, 1849, King(s) Ferry, New York
* WA to EWO: August 21, 1849, King(s) Ferry

BOX 7

* Nellie Adams to EWO: September 14, 1849
* MML to EWO September 21, 1849, Back Parlor
* ECS to LCM: September 26, 1849, Grassmere
* EWO to MCW: October 12, 1849, Philadelphia
* LP to EWO: May 5, 1850
* MML to EWO: May 8, 1850, Front Parlor Sofa
* Lottie Pearl to EWO: May 19, 1850
* MML to EWO: May 25, 1850
* Carrie Dennis to EWO: May 31, 1850, Canandaigua
* Nellie Adams to EWO: June 8, 1850, Homer
* MML to EWO: June 30, 1850, Buffalo
* DMO? to EWO: July 5, 1850
* Carrie Dennis to EWO: August 19?, 1850
* MML to EWO: August 23, 1850, Philadelphia
* CD to EWO: September 9, 1850, Canandaigua
* EWO to DMO?: October 25, 1850
* MML & AB to EWO: November 1850 [?] [not 1848]
* MML to EWO: November 21, 1850
* JL to EWO: December 8, 1850
* MML to EWO: December 8, 1850[?] [in wrong box]
* MML to EWO: December 22, 1850, Philadelphia
* MPM to EWO: December 24, 1850
* EWO to MML: Between December-January [?], 1851
* MCW & MPM to EWO: January 9, 1851[?], Philadelphia
* MCW to EWO: January 22, 1851, Philadelphia
* MML to EWO: January 26, 1851, Philadelphia
* MCW to EWO: February 10, 1851, Philadelphia
* MML to EWO: March 21, 1851, Philadelphia
* MML to EWO: May 28, 1851 [?]
* MML to EWO: July-August, 1851 [not 1850]
* MML to EWO: August 12, 1851, Buffalo
* Joseph Lord to EWO: August 24, 1851
* EWO & DMO, note to Dear Creatures: Sept. 7, 1851, Cataract House, Niagara Falls
* MPM to EWO & LCM to MCW: February 9 &11, 1852 [not 1855]

BOX 8

* EWO & DMO and DMO to EWO: Scraps to and from Clifton Springs (some 1853 or all 1855?), General Folder

* MPM to EWO: February 14, 1853, Philadelphia
* DMO to EWO: April 19, 1853
* EWO to DMO: April 19, 1853
* EWO to DMO: April 21, 1853
* MML to EWO: May 28, 185[3?]; & June 15.
* LCM to MML: July 28, 1853, Sunbury Farm ["long planned bridal trip over"]
* MML to EWO: August 1, 1853, Succasunna
* EWO to DMO: August 7, 1853 [or 1855; EOH took off socks; for dating]
* DMO to EWO: August 8, 1853 [?]
* EWO to DMO: September 9, 1853, Auburn
* DMO to EWO: September 9, 1853, Rochester
* DMO to EWO: September 13, 1853, New York
* EWO to MCW: November 16, 17, & 18, 1853 [not 1833]
* Rebecca Thomas to DW: November 27, 1853, Buckingham
** EWO to MCW: December 1853, SSC
* CD to EWO: February 15, 1854 [or 1857?]
* Rebecca Thomas to DW: April 13, 1854, Buckingham
* EWO to DMO: May 12, 1854, Succasunna
* EWO to DMO: May 16, 1854
* DMO to EWO: May 16, 1854
* DMO to EWO: May 17, 1854
* EWO to DMO: May 20, 1854, Sucky
* DMO to EWO: May 21, 1854, "Office"
* EWO to DMO: May 23, 1854
* EWO to DMO: May 26, 1854, Philadelphia
* DMO to EWO: May 26, 1854
* EWO to DMO: May 27, 1854, Philadelphia
* DMO to EWO: May 29, 1854 [in Box 9]
* EWO to DMO: June 1, 1854, Philadelphia
* MML to EWO: June 7, 1854, Succasunna
* DW to Rich Harris: August 25, 1854, Auburn
* Wm Richardson to DW: September 1, 1854, Albany
* FP Wright to DW: September 5, 1854, Tullytown
* T. Weld to DW: November 20, 1854, Raritan Bay Union, Perth Amboy, New Jersey
* MCW to EWO: November 29, 1854, Auburn
* EWO to MPM & TM: Misc. Folder of 1855 [in Europe]
* DMO to EWO: ND; "Good morning my dear wife"
* MCW & DMO to EWO: February 5, 1855, Auburn
* DMO to EWO: February 5, 1855
* EWO to DMO: February 9, 1855

* EWO to DMO: February 11, 1855, Philadelphia
* MPM to EWO & LCM to MCW: February 9 & 11, 1855 [or 1852]
* EWO to DMO: February 13, 1856 or 1855
* EWG to EWO: February 14, 1855, Eagleswood
* EWO to DMO: February 16, 1855, Raritan
* EWO to DMO: February 18, 1855, Raritan, Still
* EWO to DMO: February 22, 1855, Philadelphia
* EWG to EWO: February 25, 1855, Eagleswood
* MML to MPM & TM: June 7, 1855, My room
* ? to ?: June 18, 1855, check scrap [George Lord?]
* ? MD & LCM ?: June 18, 1855, Auburn
* MPM ?? or MD? to DMO & EWO: June 24, 1855, Oak Farm
* MML to EWO: July 8, 1855 [?], Sucky
* EWO to DMO: July 27, 1855
* EWO to DMO: July 28, 1855
* MCW to "Blamed if I know who I am addressing this to . . ." & EWO: July 28, 1855 ["a letter beginning in Clifton and ending at Paris"]
* MCW to EWG: July 29, 1855, Auburn [to Clifton]
* EWO to DMO: July 31, 1855, Clifton
* DMO to EWO: August 1855, Wednesday
* EWO to DMO: August 2, 1855, Clifton [not 1853]
* DMO to EWO: August 10, 1855
* DMO to EWO: August 15, 1855, Palmyra
* EWO to DMO: August 21, 1855, Clifton Water Cure
* DMO to EWO: August 23, 1855, Auburn
* EWO to DMO: August 28, 1855
* EWO to DMO: September 4, 1855
* EWO to DMO: September 6, 1855
* MCW to EWO: September 7, 1855, Auburn
* EWO to DMO: September 10, 1855
* MCW to Miss Hizer [?]; LCM to MCW [?]: November 12, 1855
* Deborah Woodall to DW: November 27, 1855, Wilmington
* EWO to DMO or MCW?: 1856, General Folder
* EWO to DMO: February 13, 1856 or 1855
* EWO to DMO: March 19, 1856
* MCW to EWO: March 23, 1856[or 1857?], Auburn, letter and poem
* MCW to CP [copy to EWO]: Summer 1856? [Comment on attack on C. Sumner]
* EWG to MCW: May 20, 1856, Sharon
* WW to EWO: June 16, 1856 [?], Eagleswood [more likely 1858]
* EWG to EWO: July 4, 1856, Auburn
* EWO to MCW(?): July 10, 1856, Buffalo [was in Box 206]
* MCW to EWO: October 3, 1856, Roadside

* EWG to EWO: October 5, 1856, Eagleswood
* EWG to EWO: October 12, 1856, Eagleswood
* MCW to EWO: October 31, 1856
* EWG to EWO: November 1, 1856, Eagleswood [to Buffalo]
* EWG to EWO: November 10, 1856, Eagleswood
* MCW to EWO: December 6 [?], 1856 [?] [to Buffalo]

BOX 9

* MCW? to ?: Scraps relating to engagement of Augusta Stratton, General Folder
* MCW to EWO: January 3, 1857, 35 South Twelfth St., Philadelphia
* DW to MCW: January 6, 1857, Auburn
* DW to EWO: January 7, 1857, Auburn
* EWG to EWO: January 20, 1857, Eagleswood
* DW to EWO: January 23, 1857
* DW to EWO: January 30, 1857, Auburn
* MCW to DW: February 2, 1857, 35 S 12th St., Philadelphia
* DW to EWO: February 5, 1857, Auburn
* MCW to EWO: February 7, 1857, Philadelphia [Drawings by Maria Mott?]
* MCW to DW: February 8, 1857, Philadelphia
* MCW to EWO: February 9, 1857, Philadelphia
* DMO to DW: February 15, 1857, Buffalo
* CD to EWO: February 15, 1857, Sandusky
* MCW to EWO: March 1, 1857, Auburn
* EWO to MCW: March 6, 1857, Buffalo
* MCW to EWO: March 6, 1857, Auburn
* FW & EWO to MCW: March 15, 1857, Buffalo
* MCW to Mr. Mellen: March 15, 1857, Auburn
* DL Halsey to DW: March 16, 1857, Victory
* MCW to EWO: March 17, 1857, Auburn
* EWO to MCW: March ?, 1857
* MCW to EWO: March 23, 1857 [or 1856], Letter and poem
* MCW [& CW] to EWO: March 25, 1857, Auburn
* MCW to EWO; April 6, 1857, Auburn
* WPW & FW to MCW: April 25, 1857, Eagleswood
* MCW to EWO: April 27, 1857
* MPM [not EWG] to EWO: September 19, 1857, The Oaks [in wrong box]
* FW to MCW: February 14, 1858?, Eagleswood [in wrong box]
* MCW to EWO: April 5, 1858, Philadelphia [childbirth letter]

* DMO to EWO: May 2, 1858, Cleveland [New York?]
* DMO to EWO: May 24, 1858, Utica
* EWO to DMO: May [or March] 30, 1858
* EWO to DMO: June 10, 1858
* EWG to A [or Lue?] H: June 19, 1858, Clifton
* DMO to EOH: June 20, 1858, Baltimore
* DMO to EWO: June 20, 1858, Baltimore
* DMO to EOH: June 20, 1858, Baltimore [her 5th birthday]
* DW to EWO: June 23, 1858, Auburn
* EWO to DMO: June 24, 1858, Clifton Springs
* DMO to EWO: June 26, 1858, Philadelphia
* EWO to DMO: June 27, 1858, Clifton Springs
* MCW to EWG: June 29, 1858, Auburn
* MCW to EWG: July 7, 1858, Auburn
* MCW to EWO: July 10, 1858, Auburn
* EWG to EWO: July 17, 1858, Auburn
* DMO to EWO: July 18, 1858, Delaware House
* MCW to EWO: July 19, 1858
* EWG to EWO: July 23, 1858, Auburn
* JL to EWO: August 14, 1858, Buffalo
* MC Sayre to EWO: August 15, 1858
* MC Sayre to EWO: September 8, 1858, Clifton Springs
* EWO to DMO: September 10, 1858
* DMO to EWO: September 12, 1858, St. Louis
* EWO to DMO: September 16, 1858, Auburn
* EWO to DMO: October 15, 1858, Eagleswood
* DMO to EWO: October 17, 1858, Home
* EWO to DMO: October 19, 1858
* DMO to EWO: October 22, 1858, Auburn
* EWO to DMO: October 25, 1858
* EWG to EWO: October 27th or 28, 1858, Auburn
* EWO to DMO: October 28, 1858 [20-page letter; data saturation point!]
* DMO to EWO: October 31, 1858

BOX 10

* EWO to DMO: December 5, 1858, Roadside
* DMO to EWO: December 5, 1858
* WW to EWO: December 8, 1858, Eagleswood
* EWO to DMO: December 10, 1858, Philadelphia
* DMO to EWO: December 12, 1858, Auburn
* EWO to DMO: December 12, 1858

* FW to MCW: December 12, 1858, Eagleswood
* DMO to EWO: December 15, 1858
* FW to MCW: December 18, 1858, Eagleswood
* FO to EWO: 1859? [date through servants; TMO, an infant]. General Folder
* JL to EWO: January 6, 1859, Brooklyn
* EWO to DMO: January 19, 1859, Genesee St.
* DMO to EWO: January 21, 1859, St. Louis
* DMO to EWO: January 23, 1859, Chicago
* EWO to DMO: January 28, 1859, Auburn
* EWG [not MPM] to EWO: February 4, 1859, Philadelphia
* EWG & LCM to MCW: February 7, 1859, Philadelphia
* MCW to DW: February 10, 1959, Philadelphia [for 2 or 3 mos.]
* MCW to EWO: February 11, 1859
** EWO to MCW [& MPM &/or EWG]: February 12, 1859, Auburn, SSC
* DMO to EWO: February 15, 1859, Willard's [Hotel], Washington, D.C.
* MCW to EWO: March 8, 1859, Philadelphia
* EWG to EWO: March 8, 1859, Philadelphia
* DMO to EWO: March 13, 1859, St. Louis
* WPW to DW: March 20, 1859, Eagleswood
* FW to MCW: March 28, 1859, Eagleswood
** EWO to Ladies: March 30, 1859, Auburn, South St, No. 69, SSC
* EWG to EWO: March/April 1859 ["baby a year, day before yesterday" [so April 8]
* Emily Mott to DMO: April 8, 1859
* MCW to EWO: April 9, 1859, Philadelphia
* EWO to DMO: April 13, 1859, Auburn
* MCW to EWO: April 14, 1859, 127 S. Twelfth St., Philadelphia
* MCW to EWO: April 15, 1859, Philadelphia
** EWO to MCW: April 18, 1859, Auburn, SSC
* DW to Nephew [Edw. Kniffen]: August 13, 1859, Auburn
* FW to MCW: December 18, 1859, Eagleswood
* EWO to DMO: March 8, 1861, Auburn
* EWO to FO: February 2, 1862, Roadside
* EWO to EOH: February 2, 1862, Roadside
* EOH to EWO: February 2, 1862, Auburn
* DMO to EWO: February 3, 1862, Auburn
* DMO to EWO: February 5, 1862, Auburn
* EOH to EWO: June 1862?
* DMO to Dear Friends: July 6, 1862, London
* EWO to EWG [?]: July 14, 1862, London
* EWG to EWO & DMO: July 15, 1862, Auburn
* MCW to EWO: July 15, 1862, Auburn

* DMO to Dear Friends: July 20, 1862 York, England
* MCW to EWO: July 27, 1862, Auburn

BOX 11

* EOH to EWO: August 18, 1862 [EWO in Europe?]
* DMO & EOH to EWO: 1863, General Folder
* LCM to Precious Ones: March 11, 1864, Philadelphia
* EWO to EOH: March 19, 1864, with FO [water cure, 3–4 weeks]
* Laura Brown to EWO: October 28, 1864 [birth of HOS], Mt. Holly
* FO to DMO: 1865?, General Folder
* TMO to EWO: 1865?, General Folder
* EOH to FO: March 15, 1865[?]
* LCM to MML [My Precious Pattie]: April 14, 1865, Philadelphia
* EOH to Dear Mother & Baby: April 23, 1865, Auburn
* WW to MCW & DW ["My Dear Father & Mother"]: August 15, 1865 [engagement]
* EOH to EWO & FO: November 22, 1865, Auburn

BOX 206
UNDATED OR UNIDENTIFIED LETTERS; GENERAL FOLDER

* EWO to "Dear Friend" [MTW has just been declared missing]
* EWO to MCW?: Buffalo, July 10, 1856? "I ain't a doing nothing else"
* FO to EWO: "I have not much to say...", 1859ish
* EOH to EWO: June 1862 (?) [listed in Box 9 or 10?]
* EOH to EWO: August 19, 1862 [listed in Box 9?]

BOX 207
UNDATED LETTERS THOUGHT TO BE BY MCW

* MCW to EWO: c. 1846, January 10; to Poughkeepsie: "Dear E.... Of course the H..."
* MCW or EWO?: Copy of an old love letter?: "As to all that Greek..."
* MCW to EWO: 1852 or 53, "Dear Eliza, You are coming to carve the Turkey...", dated by *Bleak House* (1852-53).
* MCW to EWO: "Dear E.... Pa is very much opposed to Frank adding..."
* MCW to EWO: "Dear E, Why in the world..."
* MCW to EWO: "Dear E, Don't think I will stir out today..."

* MCW to EWO: "Dear E . . . I will set out the asters."
* MCW to EWO: "Oh! Bright & pleasant"—1857 or 1858
* MCW to EWO: "Dear E . . . Here is the letter just recd—"
* MCW to ?: ". . . so beautifully as Eliza does.."
* MCW to EWO: "Dear E . . .The last conclusion . . ."
* EWO to MCW: "My dear Mama. . . ."
* MCW to EWO: "Dear E, I have been looking for you all the afternoon . . .
* MCW to EWO: "Dear E, Sorry to disappoint you. . . ."
* MCW to EWO: "Roadside, 21st Monday, I have a few moments . . ."
* MCW to EWO[?]: "Morris Davis has bot out . . ."
* MCW to EWO: "Needn't send this away . . ."
* MCW to EWO: "Dear Betsey Jane, Despairing of ever getting any more sand
* MCW to EWO: "Dear Eliza the frontispiece is not quite done." —ca. 1862
* MCW to EWO: "Mr. & Mrs. Wright's happiness . . ." short note and invitation
to dinner
* MCW to EWO: "Dear E, Have you been out this lovely day?" (1853 or 55)
* MCW to EWO: "I send down for Mary & Carrie to spend the last days . . ."
* MCW to EWO: "Dear E, I don't know how I can possibly come . . ."
* MCW to EWO: "Dear E, It looks so much like rain . . ."
* MCW & DW & EOH (or FO or TMO or HOS) to EWO or MPM [in Europe?]
* MPM to MCW: "Philadelphia, March 31st; "Dearest Mamma. It is a long time . . .," date by "King John" play at Eagleswood
* MCW to EWG[?]: Afternoon 21st—A letter from Patty . . ."
* "Carrie Dennis writes. . . ": Dresden, April 11, 1872, 73, or 74??
* ? to EWO: "Dear Eliza, "I found Mrs. Dennis in the Library last evening . . ." [talk re someone sick]
* MCW to EWO: "Dear E, You say you can't spend Sundays"
* DMO to MCW: "Dear Mother, Eliza feels kind a doleful with her cold"
* Card: Homeopathic Medical College of Pennsylvania, Commencement 3.3.51. On front of card: Dear Eliza, I sewed til 10.
* Scrap from MCW to EWO: "Shan't you be up this afternoon"
* Verse starting, "Dear Miss Florence [FO] . . ." with note: "Unfinished at the time of her death." 1872?

APPENDIX B

PART I

Non-correspondence Documentation— Osborne Family Papers

1827–1828

* Box 284: Financial Ledger, Volume 129, 52 pages (about half). Business accounts of school run by Anna Coffin & Martha Coffin Pelham (Wright)

1838–1873 [WITH GAPS]

* Boxes 236 and 344: Account books 1–16 and 17 by David Wright (some inaccurately attributed to David Munson Osborne); these account books include years 1838 to 1859 with no gaps; one other account book covers January 1867–January 1873. They provide an invaluable literacy resource. Referenced as DWAB: David Wright's Account Books.

1841

* Box 4: Preprinted invitation addressed "Dear Sir" and sent (presumably) to DW from The Auburn Literary Association dated November 23, 1841, asking "you to favor them with a Public Lecture or Disserta-

Reading and Writing Ourselves into Being, pages 253–257
Copyright © 2004 by Information Age Publishing
253

tion upon such Historical, Literary or Scientific subject as you may choose to select."

1852

* Box 285: "Expenses commencing January 1852"—account book of EWO.
* Advertisement of "Ladies' School" in Auburn with listing of course of instruction, dated July 16, 1852, and on the reverse side a note from MCW to EWO.

1853–1859

* Box 291, Volume 165: Account books of EWO, January 1853–March 1859; 15 pages copied. Fine literacy resource.

1854

* Printed letter from Anti-Slavery Office, Boston, October 23, 1854, asking for contributions; note nonsexist salutation: "Dear Friend."

1857

* Subscription expiration notice for *Evening Post* sent to David Wright; DW sent "for two copies, one for Willie & one for self"; "Respectfully Yours, Wm. C. Bryant & Co."

1865

* Box 291, v. 166: Financial Ledger, December 1865, 9 pages (1 page, January 1866)

1875

* Box 236: Memoir of Martha Coffin Wright by Eliza Wright Osborne; Version 'C', 1–16; Version A, 1, 12, & 13; from Box 240, 5 typed pages (by TMO?)

1879

* Box 285, Volume 139: EWO. Inventory Ledger, 4 pages

1877

* Box 253: "The War of the Roses," July 5, 1877, parody by TMO

1885

* Box 285 [?], Volume 140: EWO. Inventory Ledger, pages 2–6; "Contents of Closets; D.M. Osborne House, August 1885"

1892

* December 1, 1892: "In account with T. M. Osborne Trustee and Exec. Dr." list with large expenditures for books, e.g., Sotheran, November 17, 1892, for $890.44, covering September 1–November 30.

1895

* Box 285: "Statement of E.W. Osborne's % fin. [?] 1895"; 1 page. Note expenditures for books and book duties
* Box 240: Club notes by EWO [attributed to TMO] including retrospective of Elizabeth Cady Stanton's 80th birthday celebration.

1907

*Box 285: "EWO's possessions, 1907." Listing of stocks and properties.

BOX 206

* Poem: DMO to EWO?
* Letter and poem from EWO to acquaintance who had lost a baby [listed twice]

BOX 233

* Folder 1832–1926: Anonymous and Miscellaneous
  * Verse: EWO: "Be Kind to Each Other," September 14, 1847
  * Verse: EWO: "Our Nursery" [Baby 'a year and a day'—c. 1854]
  * Verse: "Epithalamium"—by MML for TCM & MPM, August 15, 1845

BOX 236

* Folder 1861, Volume 45: Day journal of EWO [have March & April]
* Memoir by Elizabeth Cady Stanton on MCW

BOX 240

* "The History of Dingy the Kitten" by TMO [lit acq]
* Inventory: "Old Furniture" by EWO but typed (one notation in her hand?)
* "Letter Writing and Old Letters" by TMO, 5 pages, typed.
* *American Ideals,* by TMO

BOX 253

* HOS: "My brother, Thomas Mott..." 27 pages
* Typed biography of TMO by Thorsten Sellin

BOX 291 [OR 8]

* A memoir, "The Records of Willow Point," in EWO's hand.

BOX 315

* "Woman's Rights": February 14, 1855—school exercise by EWG

BOX 316

* Scrapbook of obituary notices of DMO
* Obituary notice of EWO; full newspaper page

PART II

Non-Osborne Family Papers Documentation

1882

* Copied selections from first Minute[s] book of Women's Education & Industrial Union, pp. 17–25, 40, 96–97, 161–162. From YMCA, Auburn, New York.

1907 (?)

* History of WE&IU, "Read at the Twenty-fifth Anniversary," submitted by Mary Y. Hart, Recording Secretary, presented by Mary C. Steel. From YMCA, Auburn, New York.

1910

* From Minutes of WE&IU, pp. 30-31. From YMCA, Auburn, New York.

1911

* "A tribute to the memory of Eliza Wright Osborne" by Grace Underwood, 9 pages. From files at Case Museum, Auburn, New York.

1915

* Compilation of Annual Reports of WE&IU, by Mrs. H.B. Stevenson, June 1915. From YMCA, Auburn, New York.

1922

* *The Union News, Fortieth Anniversary: 1882–1922*, April 25, 1922, Vol. 7, No. 6. From YMCA, Auburn, New York.

APPENDIX C

CODING CATEGORIES FOR CONTENT ANALYSIS OF 1988 PAPER, "NO GREAT EXPECTATIONS"

Abol Act—abolitionist activities
acq—acquaintance mentioned
app—appearance
b & c—babies and children
car—carpets
cl—clothes
comm—commissions
c. e.—cultural events: lectures, museum visiting, opera, art
d & j—diaries and journals
D—death
d—discipline; may add a "G" for guilt when detected
da—dances
dw—dwellings (talk about houses or house building)
E—Expectations; includes boredom and anything else suspicious
ed—education
    ed non a—nonacademic
    ed sch—schooling
ex—excursions; short trips for getting ice cream, etc.
f—food; will add "rec" when recipe included
F C—family community

Reading and Writing Ourselves into Being, pages 259–261
Copyright © 2004 by Information Age Publishing

fa—fairs
Fa—Father(s)
Fam Per—famous person
Fel Pr—felicitous prose
fl—flowers
Fre or F—French
fl—flowers
fr & fr—friends and friendship
furn—furniture
G—guilt (See discipline)
g. ref—gender reference
ga—games
gar—gardening
gi—gifts
hair—hairdos
hea—health
hors rid—horseback riding
h. c.—household chores
I—illness
LW—letter writing
lit ref—literary reference (See reading reference)
lo—loneliness
M—Mother(s)
m you—missing you
mon or $—money
mus—music
out ac—outdoor activity
P—particulars (actual use of the word)
par—parties
rec—recipe (See food)
r. ref—reading reference
Rel—religion
rela—relatives
ro—romps
ser—servants
sew—sewing
sh—shopping
sib—siblings
Sp Ev, G or B—special event, good or bad (e.g., a robbery)
T—time
tr—transportation
tr & tr—traveling and transportation
Ving—visiting

Vors—visitors
W—weather
w & d—wants and desires
wed—weddings

Note: Where an attitude or perspective is noted (as opposed to a mention only), such will be noted with an "A" or "P"

CARL KAESTLE'S (1983) CATEGORIES

Creator of evening sanctuary
   —could look for under education, French, reading, etc.
Manager of frugal and healthy household
   —could look for under carpets, household chores, sewing, etc.
Nurturer and instructor of children
   —could look for under babies and children, siblings

APPENDIX D

A BIBLIOGRAPHY OF READING CITATIONS IN THE WRIGHT/MOTT/OSBORNE CORRESPONDENCE: 1835–1862

The reading shared by the young Wright/Mott/Osborne women and their families, along with account-book documentation of their book purchases, offers us a glimpse into 19th-century literacy practices. It also offers us a sense of what we may consider metaphorically to be their "library," an idea I owe to Peter B. Mosenthal. It is a library of the mind that provided family members a matrix of referential understandings for communicating and for deepening their knowledge of and engagement with the world.

This bibliography highlights many of the actual texts in the correspondence and/or listed in the account books of David Wright (DWAB) and his daughter, Eliza Wright Osborne (EWOAB) between 1835 and 1862, located within the Osborne Family Papers. A work in progress, the entries include bibliographic data, the date of its mention or listing, the letter or listing where cited, and, in many cases, a reference from the letter writer/reader.

In the future these citations will include contemporary references, indicating some of the text's reception history. Sources of information have included the National Union Catalogue, and WorldCat (through First Search, OCLC), Penfield Library, and SUNY Oswego, as well as the texts,

Reading and Writing Ourselves into Being, pages 263–272
Copyright © 2004 by Information Age Publishing
All rights of reproduction in any form reserved.

particularly Altick's *English Common Reader* (1957), as cited in the References.

CITATIONS

[A]esop's Fables (1857). Possibly *The Little Esop.* Philadelphia: H. C. Peck & Theo Bliss. MCW to EWO: 1.3.57. "A new edition with better engravings than Esop made two or three thousand years ago." EWOAB: 3.28.57.

Adams, John [1735–1826]. (1850). *The works of John Adams . . . with a Life of the Author, Notes, and Illustrations.* Boston: Little, Brown and Company. DW to EWO: 1.23.57. "I will lend you the life and works of John Adams, a most interesting work of revolutionary doings and memories."

Arabian Nights. LCM to AC: 8.23.35; *SSC?*, "I hope Martha won't let Mary Anna pore over [it]."

Austen, Jane [1775–1817]. (1814). *Mansfield Park.* "Mansfield Park: A Novel. In Three Volumes. By the Author of 'Sense and Sensibility,' and 'Pride and Prejudice.' London: Printed for T. Egerton, Military Library, Whitehall, 1814" (Facsimile of title page of first edition, Penguin Classics. London: Penguin Books, 1985). EWO to MCW & MPM & EWG [?]: 2.12.59; *SSC* . "To console me I stopped into Hewson's book store & borrowed Mansfield Park one of Miss Austen's works. . . . I wasn't quite carried away, though it was very well written indeed."

Beecher, Catharine [1800–1878]. (1846/1852) *Domestic Receipt Book. Designed as a Supplement to her Treatise on Domestic Economy.* Boston: Harper & Brothers. "Miss Beecher's Cook Book" EWOAB: 7.9.52; 88 cents.

— (1841). *Treatise on Domestic Economy for the Use of Young Ladies at Home and at School.* Boston: Harper & Brothers. "Miss Beecher's Domestic Economy." EWOAB: 7.10.52; $.88

— (1855). Possibly *Letters to the American People on Health and Happiness.* New York: Harper. "Miss Beecher's Book." EWOAB: 11.7.55; 50 cents.

— (1856). Possibly *Physiology and Calisthenics for Schools and Families.* New York: Harper & Brothers. "Miss Beecher's Book." DWAB: 5.23.56; 50 cents.

— (1857). Possibly *Common Sense Applied to Religion; or the Bible and the People.* New York: Harper & Brothers. "Miss Beecher book." DWAB: 12.2.57; $1.00.

Beecher, Henry Ward [1813–1887]. *Sayings [re free trade].* DWAB: 5.5.58; 87-1/2 cents.

The Bible, passim. WA to EWO: 8.1.49. "I do not expect you to read these volumes [later *Noctes,* see Wilson, below], as I once did the New Testament . . . (with the promise of a present from my Mother)—that is without skipping a page, line, or word. . . ." EWO to DMO?: 10.25.50. "[Elly] reads [your note] regularly every evening before retiring on the same plan as a chapter in the Bible, I suppose." MML to EWO: 5. 28. 53 [not '50]. "Had a number of presents—[from] Maria—family Bible. (Possibly Elizabeth F. Ellet's [1812? –1877] *Family Pictures from the Bible* [1849]. New York: G. P. Putnam?)

Books of Etiquette. MCW & MPM to EWO: 1.9.51. "After consulting a whole library
  of Books of Etiquette and after sleepless nights . . ., I have come to the decision
  . . . that our Munson should write the first letter to me [MPM]."
Brontë, Charlotte [1816–1855]. (1847). *Jane Eyre*, "An Autobiography. Edited by
  Currer Bell. In Three Volumes. London: Smith, Elder, and Co., Cornhill."
  (From facsimile of title page of first edition, Penguin Classics. London: Penguin Books, 1985). EWOAB: 1.24.52; $1.00. MCW to EWO: 3.8.59. "Our knowl-
  edge of Charlotte Brontë made [Jane Eyre] real to us."
— (1849). *Shirley*. "A Tale by Currer Bell, Author of 'Jane Eyre.' In Three Volumes. London: Smith, Elder and Co., 65, Cornhill. 1849." (From facsimile of
  title page of first edition, Penguin Classics. London: Penguin Books, 1974).
  EWO to MCW: 2.12.59; SSC. "I read Shirley to pass away the time. I found it
  quite as entertaining as at the first reading."
— (1853). *Villette.* "By Currer Bell, Author of 'Jane Eyre,' 'Shirley,' Etc.; In Three
  Volumes; London: Smith, Elder & Co., 65, Cornhill; Smith Taylor & Co., Bom-
  bay; 1853. The Author of this work reserves the right of translating it" (From
  facsimile of title page of first edition in Penguin Classics. London: Penguin
  Books, 1983). EWOAB: 3.11.53. EWG to MCW: 5.20.56. "I rested awhile and
  read Villette and then sallied forth in search of boots."
Browning, Elizabeth Barrett [1806–1861]. (1857). *Aurora Leigh* (1857/56). EWG to
  EWO: 1.20.57; "Aurora Leigh is perfectly splendid"; EWG to EWO: 2.3.57. "Do
  read Aurora. It is perfectly magnific! I did enjoy it so much."
Bulwer, Edward, Lord Lytton [1803–1870]. (1843). *The Last of the Barons.* New York:
  Harper. DWAB: 3.25. 43; 25 cents.
Byron, George Noel Lord [1788-1824]. "[Spent] . . . the evening in reading Byron."
  WA to EWO: 8.21.49.
Carlyle, Thomas [1795–1881]. (1833-4 [Fraser Magazine]. (1848). New York:
  Harper & Brothers. *Sartor Resartus.* EWO to DMO?: 10.25.50.
Chesebro' [Chesebrough], Caroline [1825 (1828?)–1873]. 'Drummer's Daughter."
  Possibly periodical story. EWG to EWO: 10.27.58. "Aren't you glad [it] is not by
  Mr. Higginson?" EWO to DMO: 10.28.58. "Don't you think [it] fizzled out
  entirely?"
Child, Lydia Maria [1802–1880]. (1855?). Possibly *The Progress of Religious Ideas,
  Through Successive Ages* (1855?) 3 vols. New York: C. S. Francis. Or, *Isaac T. Hop-
  per: A True Life* (1853). Boston: John P. Jewett. "Mrs. Child's Book." DWAB:
  8.13.56: $4.00.
— (1831). Probably *The [Little?] Girl's Own Book.* New York: Carter, Hendee and
  Babcock. EWO to DMO: Box 206, May, June 1858. " Mrs. Child's Book or Miss
  Leslie's." See listing below.
— (1855). Possibly *Rural [Hours]* [?]. New York: George P. Putnam. (Published in
  1855 as *Journal of a Naturalist in the United States.* London: Richard Reprinted
  1968 from 1887 edition. Syracuse, NY: Syracuse University Press. EWOAB:
  1856.
Craik, Dinah Maria Mulock [See Mulock].
De Quincey, Thomas [1786–1859]. *Collected Editions, The Confessions* [?]; or possibly
  a periodical article? MPM to [EWO?]: 6.7.54: "A delight."

Dickens, Charles [1812–1870]. (1852/1995). "Battle of Life." In *The Christmas books* (pp. 209–276). Ware: Wordsworth Classics. MML to EWO: 3.23.47. "Have you read [it]? We saw it played at the Museum the other night and were delighted with it."

— (1853). "*Bleak House* by Charles Dickens. London: Chapman & Hall, 193 Piccadilly." (From facsimile of title page of first edition in Penguin Classics. London: Penguin Books, 1985.) Serialized 1852–53 by Harper & Brothers. MML to EWO: 2.14.53. "Bleak House don't interest me as much as Copperfield or Dombey."

— (1850). "*David Copperfield, The Personal History of.* by Charles Dickens. London: Bradbury & Evans, Bouverie Street." (From facsimile of title page of first edition in Penguin Classics. London: Penguin Books, 1987). Serialized 1849–50. DWAB: 1.2.51; 50 cents.

— (1848). "*Dombey & Son, Dealings With The Firm Of: Wholesale, Retail and for Exportation.* London: Bradbury & Evans, Bouverie Street 1848." (From facsimile of title page of first edition in Penguin Classics. London: Penguin Books, 1985.) Serialized 1846–48 in New York by Wiley & Putnam; in Boston by Bradbury & Guild. MML to EWO: 3.23.47. "Poor little Paul's death was so sorrowful," MCW to EWO: 4.2.48, *re* character[s].

— (1854). "*Hard Times for These Times.* London: Bradbury & Evans, 11, Bouverie Street." (From facsimile of the title page of the first edition in Penguin Classics. London: Penguin Books, 1969). EWOAB: 8.14.54.

— (1852/1995). "The Haunted Man." In *The Christmas Books* (pp. 277–353). Ware: Wordsworth Classics. MML to EWO: 2.5.49. "I don't like it near as well as the other Christmas stories."

— (1838–39/1842). *The Life and Adventures of Nicholas Nickleby.* Philadelphia: Lea & Blanshard. MPM to EWO: 2.9-11.55[or 53]. "We thought Mother [MCW] to be very brilliant today. Of course it is more comfortable to be a Mrs. Nickeleby than a Minerva—and much more agreeable to most of humanity."

— (1855). *Little Dorrit.* MCW to EWO: 4.25.57. "I have been reading [it]. There are a great many good things in it."

— (1837). *Pickwick Papers,* Serialized in Philadelphia, 1836–37 by Carey, Lea & Blanshard; in New York 1837–38 by James Turney. (Note: Serialization information from Vann, J. Don (1985). *Victorian Novels in Serial.* New York: Modern Language Association.) EWO to DMO: 1.19.59. "Elly's reading [it] out loud."

Douglass, Frederick [1817? –1895]. (1845). *Narrative of the Life of Frederick Douglass, An American Slave. Written by Himself.* Boston: Published at the Anti-Slavery Office, No. 25 Cornhill. (From facsimile in Henry Louis Gates Jr., Ed. [1987]. *The Classic Slave Narratives.* New York: Mentor [Penguin Books]). Life of Frederick Douglass: DWAB: 6.20.45; 50 cents. EWO to DMO: 8.28.53. "I have most finished Douglass's Life & am not dreadfully interested." See Stowe, below.

Dumas, [Alexandre, Pére et Fils]. MML to EWO: 11.21.50. "[That] dress does not require short skirts. Get the book and read it. It is by Dumas and a first rate novel."

Edgeworth, Maria [1768? –1849]. (1825). *Works of Maria Edgeworth.* Boston: S. H. Parker. WA to EWO: 8.1.49; WA to EWO: 12.22.49.

Ellis, Sarah [1810–1872]. (1848–49). *Hearts and Homes (Social Distinction or Hearts and Homes)*. 3 vols. London: Tallis. LP to EWO: 5.5.50. "Have just finished Mrs. Ellis's 'Hearts and Homes' and liked it very much. Have you ever read it? I think it would interest you."

Farrar, Eliza Ware (Rotch) [1791–1870]. (1836). *The Young Lady's Friend: A Manual of Practical Advice and Instruction to Young Females on Their Entering Upon the duties of Life After Quitting School. By a Lady* (1836, 1st ed; 1840, 3rd ed.). London: John W. Parker, West Strand. MCW to EWG: 55. "[It] is so eminently practical. Why don't you start with that?"

Fern, Fanny (pseud.). See Willis, Sarah Payson.

Fitzball, Edward [1792–1873]. *Crock of Gold* [or *The Murder at the Hall* by Edward Fitzball, melodrama in two acts; adapted from the novel by MF Tupper]." MML to EWO: 5.11.47. "Have you read [it]. [I] saw it at the museum last week."

Gaskell, Elizabeth [1810–1865]. (1857). "*The Life of Charlotte Brontë*. Author of 'Jane Eyre,' 'Shirley,' 'Villette,' &c. by E.C. Gaskell, Author of 'Mary Barton,' 'Ruth,' &c.... In Two Volumes. London: Smith, Elder & Co., 65, Cornhill. 1857." (From facsimile of title page of first edition; Penguin Classics, 1975). DWAB: 7.8.57; $1.50.

Greenwood, Grace (Sara Jane Clarke Lippincott [1823–1904] [an acquaintance of MCW]. "Sayings" (A newspaper column): MCW to EWO: 3.8.59.

Griffith, Mattie [Browne, Martha Griffiths] [d. 1906]. (1857). *Autobiography of a Female Slave*. New York: Redfield Press. (Reprint, Detroit: Negro History Press). MCW to EWO: 1.3.57. "If you have not read it, get it. It has been over-praised, but it is a very readable book, & remarkable for strong Anti-slavery argument."

Griffiths, Julia (1853). *Autographs for Freedom*; Cambridge. EWO to MCW: 12.53, SSC. "Pa gave me a very pretty book, Autographs of Freedom."

Higginson, Thomas Wentworth [1823–1911]. "Physical Courage." Possibly an *Atlantic Monthly* article. EWG to EWO: 10.27.58. See Chesebrough, above.

Howitt, Mary [1799–1888]. (1843). *Alice Franklin: A Tale. Another Part of Sowing and Reaping*. London. RY to EWO: 5.17.45. See *Sowing and Reaping*, below.

— A Book. Possibly *Stories of Domestic and Foreign Life*. London. (1853?) or Burritt, Elihu (1810–1879); or *Thoughts & Things at Home & Abroad* by Elizabeth Barrett with a memoir by Mary (Botham) Howitt. (1854, 364 pages). EWOAB: 5.2.54: Book, Miss Howitt's.

— (1840). *Sowing and Reaping or What Will Come of It*. London: 1841. [Tales for the People and their Children]. RY to EWO: 5.17.45. "Because you write me a good long letter by Tom Mott, I will send you Sowing and Reaping and Alice Franklin which is a continuation of the first. I think you will like them & they are the only ones that I have that you have not read I believe. I mean all the interesting ones."

Hunt, Harriot Kesia [1805–1875]. (1856) *Glances and Glimpses or Fifty Years Social including Twenty Year Professional Life*. Boston: John P. Jewett and Company. EWO to DMO: 6.27.58. "You must read it sometime. . . . It makes me feel more than ever the necessity of female physicians."

James, G. P. R. [1801? –1860]. (1848). *Sir Theodore Broughton or Laurel Water*. Leipzig: B. Tauchnitz. MML to EWO: 9.8.48. "My last resort was novels." EWO to

DMO?: 10.25.50. "There are [not] many persons here that care about reading anything but James' forlorn novels."

Jeffrey, Francis [1773–1850]. (1848?). Possibly *The Modern British Essayists*. Philadelphia: Carey & Hart. "Essay's." WA to EWO: 8.21.49. "[His] Essays have been a great treat to me for the last few days. . . . I am persuaded you will be delighted with this volume."

Kane, Elisha Kent [1820–1857]. (1853). *Arctic Explorations: The Second Grinnell Expedition in Search of John Franklin* or *History of the Grinnell Expedition.* DWAB: 4.17.54; Kane's History of the Expedition, $3.50. "Kanes 2nd Expedition": DWAB: 11.8.56; $5.00. DW to EWO: 1.23. "Have you finished [it]?"

Kavanagh, Julia [1823[4] –1877]. (1853) *Daisy Burns*. MML to EWO: 2.14; 3.3.53. "I was quite interested last evening looking over Daisy Burns."

— (1851). *Nathalie: A Tale* by Julia Kavanagh. Copyright Edition. In Two Volumes. Leipzig: Bernhard Tachnitz. EWOAB: 2.14.52; 75 cents; MPM to EWO: 2.9.53 [or 55]. "A bewitching novel . . . resembling Jane Eyre was the means of paving a large area in that warm place."

Kingsley, Charles [1819–1875]. (1850). *Alton Locke*. London: Chapman and Hall. MML & MPM to EWO: 12.8.48. "[I]t is very good. N. P. Willis thinks it is by the author of Jane Eyer—but it seems to me very different & I should think was written by one of the sterner sex. " MML to EWO: 12.22.50. "Why don't you like it? . . .[The] plot is nothing but the sentiments therein expressed are of the right kind."

Lamb, Charles [1775–1834]. (1845/1820–1823). *Essays of Elia.* New York: Wiley & Putnam. "Essays of Elia." EWO to DMO?: 10.25.50.

Leslie, Eliza. (1831). *The Girl's Book of Diversions; or, Occupation for Play Hours*. Monroe and Francis. EWO to DMO: Box 206, 5/6.58.

Lewis, Matthew ("Monk"). (1796). *The Monk: A Romance. In Three Volumes.* London: Printed for J. Bell, Oxford Street. MML to EWO: 2.5.49. "Stephen's [?] Monk I have not read. I should like to very much."

Lingard, John [1771–1851]. Possibly *History and Antiquities of the Anglo-Saxon Church?* (1845) or *History of England . . . .* (6th ed., 1854–55). MML to EWO: 6.7.54. "Causes severe pain in the eyelids."

Livingston, David [1813–1873]. (1856). *Travels and Researches in South Africa?* (1856) or *Missionary Travels and Researches in South Africa.* Livingston's Africa. DWAB: 12.28.57; $2.25.

McIntosh, Maria [1803–1878]. (1848). *Charms and Counter-Charms.* New York: Appleton & Co. MML to EWO: 9.8.48. "My last resort was novels. Sir Theodore Broughton and Charms and Countercharms were all I read. The 1st is pretty good, but don't read it though—the other is much better than To Seem and To Be. It is very interesting."

— (1846). *Two Lives or, To Seem and To Be.* New York: D. Appleton & Co. MML to EWO: 5.11.47. "Have read To Seem and To Be." MML to EWO: 9.8.48. See *Charms and Counter-Charms*, above.

Macaulay, Thomas Babington [1800–1859]. Possibly *The Lays of Ancient Rome* (1842) or *History of England* or *Essays* [both appeared in 1848]. MML to EWO: 5.31.49. "I have put my Macaulay away for a while to acknowledge the receipt of your letter."

Martineau, Harriet [1802–1876]. (1848). *Eastern Life: Present and Past*. Philadelphia: Lea & Blanchard. "Eastern Travels." MML to EWO: 2.5.49. "Have you seen [it]? It is highly spoken of."

— (1845). *Letters on Mesmerism*. New York: Harper & Bros. Letters. DWAB: 2.19.45.

Marvel, Ik. See Mitchell, Donald Grant.

Mitchell, George Grant (1822–1908). Ik Marvel (pseud.). (1850). *Reveries of a Bachelor: A Book of the Heart*. New York: Baker & Scribner. JL to EWO: 8.24.

— (1850–54). *The Lorgnette or Studies of the Town by an Opera Goer*. 24 nos. published in 24 semi-monthly parts (January 20–April 24, 1850; 1854 last date in *NUC*). [The Lorgnette. Apr. 14, 1859. United States Steam Power Printing Office. Issued by Arch Street Theatre (Philadelphia)]. "The Longette." MML to EWO: 12.8.48: "Have you read [it]? If not procure it."

Mitford, Mary Russell [1787–1855]. (1852). *Recollections [of a Literary Life; or Book, Places, and People* by Mary Russell Mitford, Author of 'Our Village,' Belford Regis,' etc. New York: Harper & Brothers, No. 82 Cliff Street.' EWOAB: 4.24.52; $1.00.

Mulock, Dinah Maria (Craik) [1826–1887]. (1853). *Agatha's Husband*. MML to EWO: 6.7.54. "[It] is not at all to my fancy. It makes woman such a poor little dependent fool—not a bit like Jane [Eyre]."

— (1857). *John Halifax, Gentleman*. EWG to EWO: 1.20.57. "[It] is all the rage here."

Nichols, Dr. Thomas Low [1815–1901?]. (1853). Possibly *Esoteric Anthropology or Marriag: Its history, character, & results; its sanctities & its profanities; its science & its facts*. Port Chester, NY: Privately published. EWOAB: 2.26.53; "Dr. Nichols Book."

North, Christopher (pseud.). See Wilson, John.

Parton, Sara Payson Willis. See Fern, Fanny.

Peck, George Washington (Cantell A Pigly, pseud.) (1849). *Aurofodina or Adventures in the Gold Region*. New York: Baker & Scribner. WA to EWO: 8.1.49.

Perdicaris, G. A. (1845). *The Greece of the Greeks*. New York: Paine & Burgess. EWO to MML: 11.16.46. "What are you reading nowadays? I am reading Greece of the Greeks. It is quite interesting."

Perry, Commodore Matthew Calbraith [1794–1858]. (1857). *The Japan Expedition*. DW to EWO: 1.23.57.

Pike, Mary Hayden Green [1824–1908]. (1854). *Ida May: A Story of Things Actual and Possible*. By Mary Langdon [pseud]. Boston: Phillips, Sampson and Company. EWG to EWO: 2.14.55. "Fitz Birney (you see I choose the best ones) lent me 'Ida Mays' and I like it ever so much. That isn't a novel is it? Have you read it? Next I want to read Ruth Hall."

Reade, Charles [1814–1884]. (1856). *It is Never Too Late to Mend: A Matter of Fact Romance*. London: R. Bentley. EWO to MCW: 3.6.57. "What a queer thing it is… Reads as if written by a shoemaker."

Scott, Walter [1771–1832]. (1847/1834). Edinburgh: R. Cadell. *The Poetical Works of Sir Walter Scott*. " Scott's Poetical Works." DWAB: 8.4.47; $1.25. MML to EWO: 12.31.48. "A present from Anna [Mott]." MML to EWO: 1.26.51. "Dickens's Works, indeed! No you don't. Just send me an order for Scott's Works. I don't owe you a page of Dickens."

Sedgwick, Catharine Maria [1789–1867]. (1837). *Live and Let Live.* New York: Harper. MCW to LCM: 5.19.41; *SSC?* "I was going to give her [a servant?] "Live & Let Live" and "*some novels.*"

Sewell, Elizabeth Missing [1815–1906]. (1844). *Amy Herbert.* By a Lady. Edited by the Rev. W. Sewell. New York: Harper & Brothers. MML to EWO: 3.23.47. "I don't like pious novels."

Shakespeare, William [1564–1616], *passim.* EWO to MCW: 10.12.49. "Sarah [Yarnall] and Beck [Rebecca Yarnall] stopped in to see us . . . on their way home from one of Fanny Butler's readings—Antony & Cleopatra. The folks talk some of going Monday night."

Squier, Ephraim (George Samual Bard, pseud.) [1821–1888]. (1855). *Adventures on the Mosquito Shore* [First edition, 1855, under title *Waikna*] or *An Adventure on the Mosquito Shore.* EWOAB: 11.55; "On the Mosquito Shore."

Stephen's [not Lewis, M. G.? (1775–1818)]. *The Monk: A Romance.* MML to EWO: 2.5.49. "I should like to read [it] very much."

Stephens, (John?) [1805–1852]. (1838) *Incidents of Travel in Greece, Turkey, Russian, and Poland*[?]. New York: Harper & Bros. Travels in Europe EWO to DMO?: 10.25. 50.

Stevenson, John [1761–1833)]. (1813). *The Burning of Moscow.* or *The Russian Sacrifice,* "an historical & musical drama in 3 acts" (WorldCat). Dublin: Printed for author by Graisberry & Campbell. EWOAB: 8.22.54; 25 cents. [Book or performance?]

Stowe, Harriet Beecher [1811–1896]. (1856). *Dred: A Tale of the Dismal Swamp.* DWAB: 9.11.56; $1.75. MCW to EWO: 10.3.56.

— (1859). *The Minister's Wooing.* SSC; EWO to MCW: 4,18.59. "Don't the little dressmaker remind you somewhat of Miss Soule? [the Wright's seamstress]"

— (1854). *Sunny Memories of Foreign Lands.* 2 vols. Introduction by C. E. Stowe. Boston: Phillips, Sampson, and Company. LCM to MCW: Box 206, 1862? "So good on dark parlors."

— (1852). *Uncle Tom's Cabin:* or *Life Among the Lowly.* Boston: Jewett & Son. DWAB: 8.14.52; $1.50; EWOAB: 4.24.52. EWO to DMO: 8.28.53. "I have most finished Douglass's Life and am not dreadfully interested—don't think it should be named in the same year with Uncle Tom's Cabin." DWAB: 10.27.56; for Phebe, 37-1/2 cents.

Strickland, Agnes [1796–1874] & Eliizabeth [1794–1875]. (1841–1848). *The Lives of the Queens of England from the Norman conquest with anecdotes of their courts, and first published from official records and other authentic documents, private as well as public.* 2nd ed. London: H. Colburn. 12 vols. Philadelphia: Lea & Blanshard. "The Queens of England." MML to EWO: 9.8.48. "I want father to give [it] to me but we are so 'darned' poor."

Sue, Eugene [1804–1857]. (1844) *The Mysteries of Paris: A Romance of the Rich and Poor.* New York: J. Winchester. MML to EWO: 11.21.50. "Planned a quiet evening to read the Mysteries of Paris."

Taylor, Bayard [1825–1878]. (1856) *Journey to Central Africa,* 10th edition. "Central Africa." EWOAB: 12.7.53; $1.50.

Thiers, M. [Louis Adolphe, President of the French Republic; 1797–1877]. (1838). *The History of the French Republic.* London: Whittaker [?] & ?. London, 1845.

EMC to EWO: 2.8.45. "Rod [?] gave me Mr. Thier's French Revolution. I think you will be interested with it."

Thomson, Mortimer [1831–1875]. (1855). *Doesticks: What He Says*, by Q.K. Philander Doesticks (pseud). New York: E. Livermore. EWO to DMO: Summer series 1855. "Ellie is snorting over Doesticks."

— (1856). *Plu-ri-bus-tah. A song that's-by-no-author* . . . Perpetrated by Q.K. Philander Doesticks. Livermore & Rudd .

Thumb, Tom, Book about. MML to EWO: 3.23.47

Trall, Dr. [Russell Thatcher [1812–1877]. EWOAB: 3.8.53. Dr. [R. T.] Trall's Book; $2.50.

Webster, Daniel [1782–1852]. (1848). Possibly *Speeches and forensic arguments*. Boston: Perkins, Marrin & Co. "Speeches." WA to EWO: 8.21.49. "In the index . . . you will find my favorite articles [of this gifted orator] marked."

Whittier, John Greenleaf [1807–1892]. (1850). *Poems*. Boston: B. B. Mussey & Co. "Poems." DWAB: 3.3.54; $2.50.

Willis, Nathaniel Parker [1806–1867]. (1846 [c. 1845]). *The Complete Works of N. P. Willis*. New York: J. P. Redfield. "Complete Works": MML to EWO: 5.9.48. "Somebody sent Mary the complete works of N. P. Willis very handsomely bound."

Willis, Sarah Payson (Fern, Fanny, pseud.) (1855). *Ruth Hall: A Domestic Tale of the Present Time*. New York: Mason Brothers. MCW to EWO: 2.14.55; "I hope Ellen will not be anxious to be Ruth Hall." MCW to LCM or MPM[?]: 3.15.55; *SSC.* "Mrs. Stanton showed me the notice she had written of Ruth Hall in *Una* & you who have read the work must be sure and read the notice. I liked it. The harsh remarks of the press had deterred me from reading the work, but I began it at once and have not found anything objectionable." MCW to EWG: 7.28.55. See Pike, above.

Wilson, John [1785–1854]. (1843). (North, Christopher, pseud.). *The Noctes Ambrosianae of Blackwoods*. Philadelphia: Carey & Hart. WA to EWO: 8.1.49. "It contains 'full many a gem of purest ray serene' [but] there is much . . . in the Noctes which is worthless now."

PERIODICALS CITED: A SAMPLING

The Atlantic Monthly. A periodical "formed in 1857 by a group of New England brahmins who intended it to be a beacon of culture to the masses,... a New England Blackwood's ... which ... began to define the terms in which literature would be read and to select which books were worthy to be read" (Hedrick, pp. 288–29). DWAB: 12.28.57; 25 cents; regular purchase thereafter.

Blackwood's. "One of the major reviews of the nineteenth century. It was founded in 1817, as a miscellany of stories, verse and literary and political articles, under the editorship of 'Christopher North,' the pseudonym of its founder, John Wilson.... James Hogg [a Scottish pastoral poet of considerable vogue... together with Wilson ... contributed a column to Blackwood's entitled *Noctes Ambrosianae*" (p. 573, Notes to Mrs. Gaskell's *Life of Charlotte Brontë*, Penguin

Classics, 1975). WA to EWO. 1849; EWOAB: 8.28.55. "Give my love to Ma & Pa if he has returned & if he comes . . . he must bring Blackwood to me." MCW to EWO: 9.7.55. "I got Blackwood yesterday—a very tantalizing chapter leaving off where you wish it had begun."

Cultivator. DWAB: 12.6.50; $1.00; 12.10.56.

Evening Post. DWAB: 4.27.48; $4.00; 3.21.56; $3.00; 1.7.57; $5.00.

Godey's Lady's Book?? A periodical "which first appeared as a monthly miscellany in 1830" (Kelley, 1984, p. 19).

Harper's. Periodical begun in 1850. Among "feminism's most 'violent' and uncompromising foe . . . which molded public opinion" [S. Conrad (1976), *Perish the Thought,*" pp. 170–171].

Household Words [Charles Dickens journal]. EWO to DMO: 5.26.54. "Had time to run out & git Putman and Household Words before the train started."

Northern Independent. DWAB: 7.25.57: $1.00.

New England Review. DWAB: 1.8.48: $3.00.

Putnam's Monthly Magazine. EWO to DMO: 5.26.54. See *Household Words,* above.

NEWSPAPERS CITED: A SAMPLING

Cayuga New Era. 1847–1857. DWAB: 4.24.48; $2.00.

Cayuga Patriot. DWAB: 6.30.47.

Cayuga Tocsin. DWAB: 9.29.47; $14.22.

[Auburn] Daily Advertiser. Began as a daily in 1846 and "a strong paper since its foundation, an earnest exponent of the Republican party and its principles." (Monroe, J.H. [1913]. *Historical records of Auburn, NY).* DWAB: 12.3.55; $7.50 to 1.1.55.

Liberator. William Lloyd Garrison's "outspoken" weekly abolitionist newspaper began publication on January 1, 1831. DWAB: yearly subscription references.

Philadelphia Ledger

APPENDIX E

TWO LETTERS FROM THE OSBORNE FAMILY PAPERS

Martha Mott (Lord) to Eliza Wright (Osborne): 1.23.47 and Eliza Wright (Osborne) to DMO?: 10.25.50

Letter One: A "typical" letter full of visiting and news and reading and writing

Philada. F[irs]t Mo. 23rd - 1847

My dear Cousin

Being rather a forlorn Sunday, I concluded I would stay home & write to you; not that I have anything very particular to communicate, but for the extreme pleasure which it affords me—Marianna has written all about the fancy party at C. Stratton's, we have ^had^ another since that, but it did not compare with the first one - it was at Anna Hand's and her father made her promise not to have any music - so that it was rather stupid—we tried to get up a dance with singing but were unsuccessful—I was a Swiss girl—Sally Pelmer [?] was to have been a Cracovian maid but she was sick with a cold—Anna Brown had a small company last friday for Thomas Yarnell & wife—but they declined - all the descendants were there and we had a pleasant time—George Earle has his violin & played & sang - Maria too had company last week—Mary was playing most all the evening for them to dance—you don't know how pleasant it is for her to play so much—she has

Reading and Writing Ourselves into Being, pages 273–278
Copyright © 2004 by Information Age Publishing
All rights of reproduction in any form reserved.

done taking lessons & is now going to teach me. I fear I shall be a dull scholar; it seems so hard to play with both hands—I suppose you knew that Bessie was learning—Mary is going to teach Walter Brown. You were more fortunate than your cousin in having New Years calls I had not one - it is not the fashion here to call at that time, but if it were ever so I should not have any - "<u>Thanks be praised</u>"—

Have you read the Battle of Life? I do not like it

2)

as well as his other Christmas stories - it is rather un_____adal [?] but it is very interesting & I think [xed out] Clemency's character is excellent—we saw it played at the Museum the other night and were delighted with it—Clemency & Britain's were acted admirably and were very amusing—Edward & Maria—Tom & Marianna – Mary. Theresa Hallowell & myself went—I have been reading Amy Herbert - & don't like it, did you ever read it? It is edited by a Reverend Somebody. I don't like pious novels

Sunday—This is the only day that I can find time to write. I'm such a gadder out every day and almost every evening—there have been so many little parties this winter & very few large ones—We are invited to Mary S[?]overing's next wednesday 125 invitations—Marianna's party last Wednesday was delightful—George's [Lord or Earle] violin was a great addition—Mary & I were at a violin party the next evening at Sue Jones'— we staid till nearly one o'clock much to the discomfort of our venerable parents—

I was so sorry I did not copy my Valentine in this letter and not have filled up mother's with it. I will however copy one that I sent to Nathan Clapp—he received one which he took with him wherever he went trying in vain to find who sent it - he strongly suspected me—Anna wrote the lines for me —

Dear Nathan if thee want to hear
Who sent that Valentine - give ear
One evening as we sat at tea
As full of fun as we could be
Cornelia Martin said let's try
If we can write some poetry
And send around to every beau
I'm writing that they shall not know
Then Emma Corbit said she'd show
What she could do for Charlie O,
Rebecca Rowland added gaily
That she would write to Samuel

And Martha Mott said in a trice
That she fixed on Richard Price
Then black eyed Fannie Wilson spoke
She said he's mine it would provoke?
If anyone she called a friend/Such
foolish rhymes to her should send
But still said she it very true is
I've some prepared for Henry Leavis
Miss Price then put away her hylons?
And took her pen for Marshall Lyons
And Nathan dear to thee in fine
I volunteered—thine Caroline
Caley

3)

Uncle Tom's is too long to copy - but it is very good -

...Mr. Vaughn (the editor of the true American after Clay left it) took tea here last evening he is trying to raise a sufficient sum of money, to enable him to go on with the paper; he thinks it did a great deal of good in the southern states—Marianna is making a perfect little hood for Bell, she is going to braid a cloak for her - the little beauty has nothing to wear now and has to be in the house all the time—she is a lovely baby growing prettier every day - she shows a decided affection for her Aunt Pattie -

This poor miserable letter seems hardly worth sending I have had it about so long - but as there seems no chance of my hearing from you without giving you some evidence of my existance I'll venture—Such delightful weather as we have now makes winter clothes feel and look so forlorn that I don't like to go out

...Mary and I were up at Marianna's to tea last evening. Tom was so busy with his books that he was not up from the store till 9 o'clock - we were invited to a little party at Theresa Hallowell's but having been up for two nights before, till one o'clock we did not incline to go—the first evening at Eliza Needles a little party for her brother Edward from Baltimore—the second at Robert Massey's—we had dancing at both places - Did you know that Henry L[?]andis was married about a month ago—Fannie Palmer was bridesmaid - he married Miss Pearce—very intelligent & considerable wealth but not at all pretty—The Palmers expect to move to the country the last of this month—they expect now to live there always - but I guess they will be tired in a year or so & come back—Tallman's school seemed to pine [?] away.

4)

rather suddenly the scholars were not so taxed as Dr. Blimbers were - & their enjoyment appeared to be of a different nature—I suppose you saw the pictures of his boys enjoying themselves—Poor little Paul's death was so sorrowful—Mr. Dombey, I think, will take Walter into the firm & he will marry Florence—Mary has an invitation to spend next winter with J. Hallowell—I think she had better accept she seems to be a general favorite - I'm used up now—don't you think it is time—Good bye.

   Write soon to   Your blessed cousin Pattie

Letter Two: "The Reading Society" Letter: Eliza Wright (Osborne) to David Munson Osborne? It is full of local and family information and has a flirtatious tone.

Auburn, Friday morning Oct 25th 1850

My dear friend: I do not like the idea of not having a regular commencement it seems too formal and distant to suit me. I have just received the beautiful book you sent for which I return many thanks-What kind fairy led you to send the very one I have been wishing to see. Elly, too, will be delighted especially with the note, as you hold a permanent place in her affections. And you are really going to start next Monday, and leave us nice people for an indefinite length of time now the date of your departure is fixed, your destination seems farther off "Do I pity you?"—Most assuredly I do—however, now I think of it, I believe I was only to pity you, because those nice plans for this week could not be realized

You have only answered half my question, as to what you have been saying and doing—and that is the latter half That letter reached you just in time did it! It was dated Saturday I know, but it was written Friday morning and I received your letter Thursday night—I was writing to Pattie this morning, when the package came and after reading your note, I concluded as I felt like it to commence this. As a general thing my letters will be of many dates, and many minds—And you think Pattie nice and "admire her excessively"—but for all that, I don't believe you know how very lovely she is, nor how smart, she is a particular favorite of mine, and I love her dearly - and (as young ladies must have confidantes) tell her everything.

How much did you see of that nonsense I wrote Pattie—for which you think it necessary to apologize—Mother put it into my head, or I shouldn't have thought of it, twas merely a speech you made, which I did not notice at the time—perhaps she put that construction on it, that I might be more industrious, whether it had the desired effect, I shall leave her to judge— for the present Adieu—

2)

Monday morning—My thoughts are with you this morning, & I might as well add a line or two—What beautiful weather you have to commence your journey, though I suppose you are feeling somewhat dispirited, at the thought of leaving so many dear friends, however—"There's a good time coming boys" & those cards & cigars will help to pass way the time - & don't get sick, or fall overboard, or do anything unpleasant during your sojourn in Savagedom.—It is funny for me to commence a letter before receiving one from you. I am a privileged person in that respect and do a great many queer things, people give up in despair sometimes trying to fathom me, (the difficulty is they look beyond) and console themselves with saying, "She is a strange girl "

Last week was rather gay. I went to a lovely dance given by the gentlemen and there is nothing equal to dancing after all—the next evening to a bridal party at Gov. Sewards—for Fanny Worden of course she looked interesting & pretty, brides always do, you know she is a beautiful dancer & I had quite a pleasant time—a gentleman inquired after you asked if you were not a genius—"Yes I thought you were & very smart & very nice—I will repeat what you wrote me, "don't think I mean to flatter you in the least"-oh no nothing of the sort I assure you—he wished to know when you were going to sail but I was ignorant of the day, at that time and could not enlighten him—Now I must leave you and add to Pattie's letter -she hasn't written to me yet, the witch   Au revoir

The few moments that yet remain of daylight, shall be improved—Tall-man was busy in the back part of the store a day or two ago, when one of the clerks came to him, and said "The gentleman from California who was visiting you is in the store"—of course he presented himself with a smiling countenance and "the perfect image of yourself" was before him—unfortunately it was

3)

not really yourself or I should have seen you—the weather continues beautiful & another young lady & myself are trying to get up a reading society—it would give us great pleasure if you would join us—I think you would find it rather more interesting than sitting up half the night earning dust [?]—What shall we read first? Sartor Resartus, Essays of Elia. anything in fact you recommend, we shall no doubt find interesting—We think of commencing with Stephen's Travels in Europe. I have read them but there are a good many who have not and I do not think there are many persons here that care about reading anything but James' forlorn novels, in fact they have hardly three ideas to boast of. However, they can dance and "carry-on"—so I've no doubt we shall have quite a nice time, if we can really get it up, which I somewhat despair of—we ought to be out drumming up recruits, this splendid weather, but I have hurt my foot in some way. and consequently have to limp about the house in the most graceful manner imaginable. It is really well you are not here to chase me round the house in search of letters, which are all the time reposing quietly in your portfolio. I have to sit still & <u>look on</u> while Mother does the sweeping—I am thankful there are no dances in view at present. I am going to try and have a fancy party this winter, there has never been one here, and as long as I have to be here winters—I will endeavor to put some life into the stupidest set I ever came across. Charades, too, shall take their chance, and I mean to have some fun. I intend taking music lessons this winter—so do you not think I shall get along—what would I not give for a nice race on Fort Hill, or anywhere. I did not know it was such a bother not to be able to walk. I can eat the chestnuts to be sure, but that will not give me so much pleasure as for you to eat them for me. Much obliged for the love you sent instead of Kates'. I'll use it. Now if I had a fine Arabian like Di Vernon, I would be off til dinner time, and have a glorious ride, minus any companion but my own thoughts which would keep me busy enough and in riding 'tis generally a bother to be obliged to talk to anyone, the exercise has generally a quieting

4)

...effect upon me. Elly was reading over for the hundreth time your note to her, the other evening, (she reads it regularly every evening before retiring on the same plan as a chapter in the Bible, I suppose) when Willy said, "I shouldn't be so <u>darned</u> proud of a letter"—her only objection to it, is that 'tis not so long as mine...

REFERENCES

Acker, Joan, Barry, Kate, & Esseveld, Johanna. (1991). Objectivity and truth: Problems in doing feminist research. In Mary Margaret Fonow & Judith Cook (Eds.), *Beyond methodology: Feminist scholarship as lived research* (pp. 133–153). Bloomington: Indiana University Press. (Original work published 1983)

Altick, Richard D. (1957). *The English common reader: A social history of the mass reading public, 1800–1900*. Chicago: University of Chicago Press.

Avery, Kevin J. (1999). *Movies for manifest destiny: The moving panorama phenomenon in America* [Online]. Catalogue essay, Montclair Art Museum. Available at www.tfaoi.com/aa/3aa/3aa66.htm

Bacon, Margret Hope. (1980). *Valiant friend: The life of Lucretia Mott*. New York: Walker & Company.

Baldwin, Neil. (1995). *Edison: A Biography*. New York: Hyperion.

Bambara, Toni Cade. (Ed.). (1970). *The black woman: An anthology*. New York: Signet Books.

Barker, Wendy. (1987). *Lunacy of light: Emily Dickinson and the experience of metaphor*. Carbondale: Southern Illinois University Press

Baym, Nina. (1978). *Woman's fiction: A guide to novels by and about women in America, 1820–1870*. Ithaca, NY: Cornell University Press.

Baym, Nina. (1984). *Novels, readers, and reviewers: Responses to fiction in antebellum America*. Ithaca, NY: Cornell University Press.

Belsey, Catherine. (1980). *Critical practice*. London: Methuen.

Benstock, Shari (Ed.). (1988). *The private self: Theory and practice of women's autobiographical writings*. Chapel Hill: University of North Carolina Press.

Berger, Peter L., & Luckmann, Thomas. (1966). *The social construction of reality*. New York: Doubleday.

Blain, Virginia, Grundy, Isobel, & Clements, Patricia. (1990). *The feminist companion to literature in English: Women writers from the Middle Ages to the present*. New Haven, CT: Yale University Press.

Reading and Writing Ourselves into Being, pages 279–288
Copyright © 2004 by Information Age Publishing

Blake, Brett Elizabeth. (1997). *She say, he say: Urban girls write their lives*. Albany: State University of New York Press.

Bogdan, Robert C. (1982). *Illiterate or learning disabled?: A symbolic interactionist approach to the social dimensions of reading and writing*. Paper presented at the International Reading Association's Special Seminar, The Social Dimensions of Literacy, Syracuse University.

Bogdan, Robert C., & Biklen, Sari Knopp. (1982). *Qualitative research for education: An introduction to theory and methods*. Boston: Allyn & Bacon.

Brandt, Deborah. (1995). Accumulating literacy: Writing and learning to write in the twentieth century. *College English, 57*(6), 649–669.

Brodie, Janet Farrell. (1994). *Contraception and abortion in nineteenth–century America*. Ithaca, NY: Cornell University Press.

Brodkey, Linda. (1996). *Writing permitted in designated areas only*. Minneapolis: University of Minnesota Press.

Brown, Richard D. (1989). *Knowledge is power: The diffusion of information in early America, 1700–1865*. New York: Oxford University Press.

Bunkers, Suzanne L., & Huff, Cynthia A. (1996). *Inscribing the daily: Critical essays on women's diaries*. Amherst: University of Massachusetts Press.

Burstyn, Joan N. (1984). *Victorian education and the ideal of womanhood*. New Brunswick, NJ: Rutgers University Press.

Burstyn, Joan N. (1985). Sources of influence: Women as teachers of girls. In June Purvis (Ed.), *Proceedings of the 1984 Conference of the History of Education. History of Education Society*.

Buss, Helen M. (1996). A feminist revision of New Historicism to give fuller readings of women's private writings. In Suzanne L. Bunkers & Cynthia A. Huff (Eds.), *Inscribing the daily: Critical essays on women's diaries* (pp. 86–103). Amherst: University of Massachusetts Press.

Capps, Jack L. (1966). *Emily Dickinson's reading, 1836–1886*. Cambridge, MA: Harvard University Press.

Cayleff, Susan E. (1987). *Wash and be healed: The water-cure movement and women's health*. Philadelphia: Temple University Press.

Chartier, Roger. (1994). *The order of books: Readers, authors, and libraries in Europe between the fourteenth and eighteenth centuries* (Lydia G. Cochrane, Trans.). Stanford, CA: Stanford University Press.

Cholakian, Patricia Francis. (1991). *Rape and writing in the* Heptaméron *of Marguerite de Navarre*. Carbondale: Southern Illinois University Press.

Cholakian, Patricia Francis. (2000). *Women and the politics of self–representation in seventeenth-century France*. Newark: University of Delaware Press.

Cixous, Hélene, & Clément, Catherine. (1986). *The newly born woman* (Betsy Wing, Trans.). Minneapolis: University of Minnesota Press. (Original work published 1975)

Cochran-Smith, Marilyn. (1984). *The making of a reader*. Norwood, NJ: Ablex.

Conrad, Earl. (1960). *The governor and his lady: The story of William Henry Seward and his wife Frances*. New York: G. P. Putnam's Sons.

Conrad, Susan Phinney. (1976). *Perish the thought: Intellectual women in romantic America, 1830–1860*. New York: Oxford University Press.

Conway, Jill Ker. (1982). *The female experience in eighteenth- and nineteenth-century America*. New York: Garland.

Coontz, Stephanie. (1988). *The social origins of private life: A history of American families, 1600–1900*. London: Verso.

Corbett, Mary Jean. (1992). *Representing femininity: Middle-class subjectivity in Victorian and Edwardian women's autobiography*. Oxford, UK: Oxford University Press.

Cott, Nancy F. (Ed.). (1972). *Roots of bitterness: Documents of the social history of American women*. New York: E. P. Dutton.

Cott, Nancy F. (1977). *The bonds of womanhood: "Women's sphere" in New England, 1780–1835*. New Haven, CT: Yale University Press.

Cromwell, Otelia. (1958). *Lucretia Mott*. Cambridge, MA: Harvard University Press.

Coultrap-McQuin, Susan. (1990). *Doing literary business: American women writers in the nineteenth century*. Chapel Hill: University of North Carolina Press.

Daniell, Beth. (1999). Narratives of literacy: Connecting composition to culture. *College Composition and Communication, 50*(3), 393–410.

Darnton, Robert. (1985). *The great cat massacre: And other episodes in French cultural history*. New York: Vintage Books.

Davidson, Cathy N. (1986). *Revolution and the word: The rise of the novel in America*. New York: Oxford University Press.

Davis, Natalie Zemon. (1975). *Society and culture in early modern France*. Stanford, CA: Stanford University Press.

Derrida, Jacques. (1976). *Of grammatology*. (Gayatri C. Spivak, Trans.). Baltimore: John Hopkins University Press.

Dobson, Joanne. (1989). Dickinson and the strategies of reticence. Bloomington: Indiana University Press.

Donegan, Jane B. (1986). *"Hydropathic highway to health": Women and water-cure in antebellum America*. New York: Greenwood Press.

Douglas, Ann. (1977). *The feminization of American culture*. New York: Viking.

Ehrenreich, Barbara, & English. Deirdre. (1978). *For her own good: 150 years of the experts' advice to women*. New York: Anchor Books.

Elson, Ruth Miller. (1964). *Guardians of tradition: American schoolbooks of the nineteenth century*. Lincoln: University of Nebraska Press.

Farrar, Eliza Ware Rotch. (1836). *The young lady's friend: A manual of practical advice and instruction to young ladies on their entering upon the duties of life after quitting school* (3rd ed.). London: John W. Parker.

Felman, Shoshanna. (1993). *What does a woman want?: Reading and sexual difference*. Baltimore: John Hopkins Press.

Fetterley, Judith. (1978). *The resisting reader: A feminist approach to American fiction*. Bloomington: Indiana University Press.

Finders, Margaret J. (1997). *Just girls: Hidden literacies and life in junior high*. New York: Teachers College Press.

Fingeret, Arlene (Hannah). (1983). Social network: A new perspective on independence and illiterate adults. *Adult Education Quarterly, 33*, 133–146.

Finkelstein, Barbara. (1979). *Regulated children / Liberated children: Education in psychohistorical perspective*. New York: Psycho-history Press.

Fish, Stanley. (1980). *Is there a text in this class? The authority of interpretive texts*. Cambridge, MA: Harvard University Press.

Flint, Kate. (1993), *The woman reader: 1837–1914*. Oxford, UK: Oxford University Press.

Flower, Linda. (1989). Cognition, context, and theory building. *College Composition and Communication, 40,* 282–311.

Foucault, Michel. (1976). *The history of sexuality: Volume I. An introduction.* New York: Vintage Books.

Gilbert, Pam, & Taylor, Sandra. (1991). *Fashioning the feminine: Girls, popular culture and schooling.* London: Allen & Unwin.

Gilbert, Sandra M., & Gubar, Susan. (1979). *The madwoman in the attic: The woman writer and the nineteenth-century literary imagination.* New Haven, CT: Yale University Press.

Gilmore, William J. (1989). *Reading becomes a necessity of life: Material and cultural life in rural New England, 1780–1835.* Knoxville: University of Tennessee Press.

Glaser, Barney G., & Strauss, Anselm L. (1967). *The discovery of grounded theory: Strategies for qualitative research.* New York: Aldine De Gruyter.

Goody, Jack. (1987). *The interface between the written and the oral.* Oxford, UK: Oxford University Press.

Gordon, Linda. (1986). What's new in women's history? In Teresa de Lauretis (Ed.), *Feminist studies/Critical studies* (pp. 20–30). Bloomington: Indiana University Press.

Gordon, Lyndall. (1994). *Charlotte Brontë: A passionate life.* New York: W.W. Norton.

Graddol, David, & Swann, Joan. (1989). *Gender voices.* Oxford, UK: Basil Blackwell.

Graff, Harvey J. (1987). *The legacies of literacy: Continuities and contradictions in Western culture and society.* Bloomington: Indiana University Press.

Greenblatt, Stephen. (1980). *Renaissance self-fashioning: From More to Shakespeare.* Chicago: University of Chicago Press.

Grever, Maria. (1989). On the origins of Dutch women's historiography: Three portraits (1840–1970). In Arina Angerman, Geerte Binnema, Annemieke Keunen, Vefie Poels, & Jacqueline Zirkzee (Eds.), *Current issues in women's history* (pp. 249–270). London: Routledge.

Grumet, Madeleine R. (1988). *Bitter milk: Women and teaching.* Amherst: University of Massachusetts Press.

Gurko, Mariam. (1974). *The ladies of Seneca Falls: The birth of the Woman's Rights Movement.* New York: Schocken Books.

Halliday, M. A. K., & Hasan, Ruqaiya. (1985). *Language, context, and text: Aspects of language in a social-semiotic perspective.* London: Oxford University Press.

Hampsten, Elizabeth. (1982). *Read this only to yourself: The private writings of Mid-Western women: 1880–1910.* Bloomington: Indiana University Press.

Hansen, Karen V. (1994). *A very social time: Crafting community in antebellum New England.* Berkeley: University of California Press.

Harding, Sandra. (1993). Rethinking standpoint epistemology: "What is strong objectivity?" In Linda Alcoff & Elizabeth Potter (Eds.), *Feminist epistemologies* (pp. 49–82). New York: Routledge.

Harris, Susan K. (1990). *19th-century American women's novels: Interpretive strategies.* Cambridge, UK: Cambridge University Press.

Hart, James D. (1965). *The Oxford companion to American literature* (4th ed.). New York: Oxford University Press.

Heath, Shirley Brice. (1978). Social history and sociolinquistics. *The American Sociologist, 13*, 84–92.

Heath, Shirley Brice. (1981). Toward an ethnohistory of writing in American education. In Marcia Farr Whiteman (Ed.), *Writing: The nature, development, and teaching of written communication* (2 vols., pp. 25–43). Hillsdale, NJ: Erlbaum.

Heath, Shirley Brice. (1991). The sense of being literate: Historical and cross–cultural features. In Rebecca Barr, Michael Kamil, Peter Mosenthal, & P.D. Pearson (Eds.), *Handbook of reading research* (Vol. 2). White Plains, NY: Longman.

Hedrick, Joan D. (1992). Parlor literature: Harriet Beecher Stowe and the question of "Great women artists." *Signs, 17*, 275–303.

Hedrick, Joan D. (1994). *Harriet Beecher Stowe: A life.* New York: Oxford University Press.

Heilbrun, Carolyn G. (1988). *Writing a woman's life.* New York: W.W. Norton.

Heineman, Helen. (1983). *Restless angels: The friendship of six Victorian women.* Athens: Ohio University Press.

Hekman, Susan J. (1990). *Gender and knowledge: Elements of a postmodern feminism.* Boston: Northeastern University Press.

Helly, Dorothy O., & Reverby, Susan M. (Eds.). (1992). *Gendered domains: Rethinking public and private in women's history.* Ithaca, NY: Cornell University Press.

Helsinger, Elizabeth, Sheets, Robin, & Veeder, William. (Eds.). (1983). *The woman question* (3 vols.). Chicago: University of Chicago Press.

Hill, Alan G. (Ed.). (1981). *Letters of Dorothy Wordsworth.* Oxford, UK: Oxford University Press.

Himley, Margaret. (1991). *Shared territory: Understanding children's writings as works.* New York: Oxford University Press.

Hinding, Andrea. (Ed.). (1979). *Women's history sources: A guide to archives and manuscript collections in the United States* (2 vols.). New York: R. R. Bowker.

Hobbs, Catherine. (1995). *Nineteenth-century women learn to write.* Charlottesville: University Press of Virginia.

Hoblitzelle, Anne L. (1974). *The ambivalent message: Sex-role training in mid-19th century United States as reflected in the correspondence of Martha Coffin Wright to Ellen Wright Garrison.* Unpublished master's thesis, Sarah Lawrence College, Bronxville, NY.

Howe, Susan. (1985). *My Emily Dickinson.* Berkeley, CA: North Atlantic Books.

Hunt, Lynn. (1989). *The new cultural history.* Berkeley: University of California Press.

Jacobus, Mary. (1989). The difference of view. In Catherine Belsey & Jane Moore (Eds.), *The feminist reader: Essays in gender and the politics of literary criticism* (pp. 49–62). New York: Blackwell.

Janitz, John. (1971). *The Osborne family: An inventory of papers in Syracuse University Libraries.* Unpublished copy in Special Collections Research Center, Syracuse University.

Jehlen, Myra. (1981). Archimedes and the paradox of feminist criticism. *Signs, 6*(4), 575–601.

Jones, Deborah. (1990). Gossip: Notes on women's oral culture. In Deborah Cameron (Ed.), *The feminist critique of language: A reader* (pp. 242–250). London: Routledge.

Kabelac, Karl Sanford. (1969). *Book publishing in Auburn, New York, 1851–1876: An introduction and an imprints bibliography.* Unpublished master's thesis, Cooperstown Graduate Programs of the State University College of Oneonta and the New York State Historical Association at Cooperstown.

Kaestle, Carl F. (1983). *Pillars of the Republic: Common schools and American society, 1780–1860.* New York: Hill and Wang.

Kaestle, Carl F. (1985). The history of literacy and the history of readers. In Edmond W. Gordon (Ed.), *Review of research in education, 12.* Washington, DC: American Educational Research Association.

Kaestle, Carl F. (1991). *Literacy in the United States: Readers and reading since 1880.* New Haven, CT: Yale University Press.

Kaplan, Deborah. (1988). Representing two cultures: Jane Austen's letters. In Shari Benstock (Ed.), *The private self: Theory and practice of women's autobiographical writings* (pp. 211–229). Chapel Hill: University of North Carolina Press.

Karcher, Carolyn L. (1994). *The first woman in the Republic: A cultural biography of Lydia Maria Child.* Durham, NC: Duke University Press.

Kelley, Mary. (1984). *Private woman, public stage: Literary domesticity in nineteenth-century America.* New York: Oxford University Press.

Kelley, Mary. (1996). Reading women /Women reading: The making of learned women in antebellum America. *Journal of American History, 83*(2), 401–424.

Kelly, Catherine E. (1999). *In the New England fashion: Reshaping women's lives in the nineteenth century.* Ithaca, NY: Cornell University Press.

Kerber, Linda K. (1980). *Women of the Republic: Intellect and ideology in revolutionary America.* New York: W.W. Norton.

Kitch, Sally L. (1993). *This strange society of women: Reading the letters and lives of the Woman's Commonwealth.* Columbus: Ohio State University Press.

Kuhn, Anne L. (1947). *The mother's role in childhood education: New England concepts, 1830–1860.* New Haven, CT: Yale University Press.

Lacan, Jacques. (1977). *The four fundamental concepts of psycho–analysis* (Alan Sheridan, Trans.). New York: W. W. Norton.

Landes, Joan B. (1988). *Women in the public sphere in the age of the French Revolution.* Ithaca, NY: Cornell University Press.

Lauretis, Teresa de. (1984). *Alice doesn't: Feminism, semiotics, cinema.* Bloomington: Indiana University Press.

Lauretis, Teresa de. (Ed.). (1986). *Feminist studies/Critical studies.* Bloomington: Indiana University Press.

Lauretis, Teresa de. (1987). *Technologies of gender: Essays on theory, film, and fiction.* Bloomington: Indiana University Press.

Leichter, Hope (1984). In Hillel Goelman, Antoinette Oberg, & Frank Smith (Eds.), *Awakening to literacy.* Portsmouth, NH: Heinemann Educational Books.

Lerner, Gerda. (Ed.). (1972). *Black women in white America: A documentary history.* New York: Vintage Books.

Lerner, Gerda. (Ed.). (1977/1985). *The female experience: An American documentary.* New York: Macmillan.

Lerner, Gerda. (1993). *The creation of feminist consciousness: From the Middle Ages to eighteen-seventy.* New York: Oxford University Press.

Levine, Lawrence W. (1988). *Highbrow/lowbrow: The emergence of cultural hierarchy in America.* Cambridge, MA: Harvard University Press.

Lockridge, Kenneth. (1974). *Literacy in Colonial New England.* New York: W.W. Norton.

Lyotard, Jean-François. (1984). *The postmodern condition: A report on knowledge.* Minneapolis: University of Minnesota Press.

McCarthy, Kathleen D. (1991). *Women's culture: American philanthropy and art, 1830–1930.* Chicago: University of Chicago Press.

McMurtrie, Douglas C. (1936). *A short-title list of books, pamphlets, and broadsides printed in Auburn, New York, 1810–1850.* Chicago: Chicago Historical Society.

Messmer, Marietta. (2001). *A vice for voices: Reading Emily Dickinson's correspondence.* Amherst: University of Massachusetts Press.

Michel, Pamela. (1994). *A child's view of reading.* Boston: Allyn & Bacon.

Miller, Nancy K. (1986). Changing the subject: Authorship, writing, and the reader. In Teresa de Lauretis (Ed.), *Feminist studies/critical studies* (pp. 102–120). Bloomington: Indiana University Press.

Miller, Susan. (1998). *Assuming the positions: Cultural pedagogy and the politics of commonplace writing.* Pittsburgh, PA: University of Pittsburgh Press.

Mills, Sara, Pearce, Lynn, Spaull, Susan, & Millard, Elaine (1989). *Feminist readings/ Feminists reading.* Charlottesville: University of Virginia Press.

Minter, Deborah Williams, Ruggles Gere, Anne, & Keller-Cohen, Deborah. (1995). Learning literacies. *College English, 57*(6), 669–687.

Modleski, Tania. (1986). Feminism and the power of interpretation: Some critical readings. In Teresa de Lauretis (Ed.), *Feminist studies/Critical studies* (pp. 121–138). Bloomington: Indiana University Press.

Moers, Ellen. (1976). *Literary women.* Garden City, NY: Doubleday.

Monroe, Joel Henry. (1913). *Historical records of a hundred & twenty years: Auburn, NY.* Geneva, NY: W. F. Humphrey.

Moore, Henrietta. (1988). *Feminism and anthropology.* Minneapolis: University of Minnesota Press.

Mosenthal, Peter B. (1984). Defining reading program effectiveness: An ideological approach. *Poetics, 13,* 195–216.

Motz, Marilyn Ferris. (1996). The private alibi: Literacy and community in the diaries of two nineteenth-century American women. In Suzanne L. Bunkers & Cynthia A. Huff (Eds.), *Inscribing the daily: Critical essays on women's. diaries* (pp. 189–206). Amherst: University of Massachusetts Press.

Nussbaum, Felicity A. (1988). Eighteenth-century women's autobiographical commonplaces. In Shari Benstock (Ed.), *The private self: Theory and practice of women's autobiographical writings* (pp. 147–171). Chapel Hill: University of North Carolina Press.

Nussbaum, Felicity A. (1989). *The autobiographical subject: Gender and ideology in eighteenth-century England.* Baltimore: John Hopkins University Press.

Ong, Walter J. (1982). *Orality and literacy: The technologizing of the word.* New York: Metheun.

Osterud, Nancy Grey. (1992). *Bonds of community: The lives of farm women in nineteenth-century New York.* Ithaca, NY: Cornell University Press.

Palmer, Beverly Wilson. (Ed.). (2002). *Selected letters of Lucretia Coffin Mott.* Urbana: University of Illinois Press.

Papashvily, Helen Waite. (1956). *All the happy endings: A study of the domestic novel in America, the women who wrote it, the women who read it, in the nineteenth century.* New York: Harper & Brothers.

Penney, Sherry H., & Livingston, James D. (forthcoming). *A Very Dangerous Woman: Martha Wright and Women's Rights.* Amherst: University of Massachusetts Press.

The Personal Narratives Group. (Eds.). (1989). *Interpreting women's lives: Feminist theory and personal narratives.* Bloomington: Indiana University Press.

Petrino, Elizabeth A. (1998). *Emily Dickinson and her contemporaries: Women's verse in America, 1820–1855.* Hanover, NH: University Press of New England.

Putala, Claire White. (1987). *Women writing letters to women: Is learning to write involved?* Unpublished manuscript.

Putala, Claire White. (1988). *No "Great Expectations."* Unpublished manuscript.

Radway, Janice A. (1984). *Reading the romance: Women, patriarchy, and popular literature.* Chapel Hill: University of North Carolina Press.

Rossi, Alice S. (Ed.). (1973). *The feminist papers: From Adams to de Beauvoir.* New York: Bantam.

Royster, Jacqueline Jones. (1990). Perspectives on the intellectual traditions of Black women. In Andrea Lunsford, Helene Moglen, & James Slevin (Eds.), *The right to literacy* (pp. 103–112). New York: Modern Language Association.

Ryan, Mary P. (1981). *Cradle of the middle class.* Cambridge, UK: Cambridge University Press.

Ryan, Mary P. (1982). *The empire of the mother: American writing about domesticity, 1830–1860.* New York: Harrington Park Press.

Scott, Joan A. (1986). Gender: A useful category of historical analysis. *The American Historical Review, 91,* 1053–1075.

Scribner, Sylvia, & Cole, Michael. (1981). *The psychology of literacy.* Cambridge, MA: Harvard University Press.

Shosa, Martha. (1992). Auburn schools. In Auburn Bicentennial Committee (Eds.), *Auburn: Two hundred years of history: 1793–1993* (pp. 47–53). Auburn, NY: Lakeside Printing.

Showalter, Elaine. (1977). *A literature of their own: British women's novelists from Brontë to Lessing.* Princeton, NJ: Princeton University Press.

Showalter, Elaine. (1979). Toward a feminist poetics. In Elaine Showalter (Ed.), *The new feminist criticism: Essays on women, literature, and theory* (pp. 125–143). New York: Pantheon Books.

Sicherman, Barbara. (1989). Sense and sensibility: A case study of women's reading in late Victorian America. In Dorothy O. Helly & Susan M. Reverby (Eds.), *Gendered domains: Rethinking public and private in women's history* (pp. 71–89). Ithaca, NY: Cornell University Press.

Silver–Isenstadt, Jean L. (2002). *Shameless: The visionary life of Mary Gove Nichols.* Baltimore: John Hopkins University Press.

Sklar, Kathryn Kish. (1976). *Catharine Beecher: A study in American domesticity.* New York: W.W. Norton.

Smith, Frank. (1982). *Writing and the writer.* New York: Holt, Rinehart and Winston.

Smith, Martha Nell. (1992). *Rowing in Eden: Rereading Emily Dickinson.* Austin: University of Texas Press.

Smith, Sidonie. (1992). Resisting the gaze of embodiment: Women's autobiography in the nineteenth century. In Margo Culley (Ed.), *American women's autobiography* (pp. 75–100). Madison: University of Wisconsin Press.

Smith-Rosenberg, Carroll. (1985). The female world of love and ritual: Relations between women in nineteenth-century America. In Carroll Smith-Rosenberg, *Disorderly conduct: Visions of gender in Victorian America* (pp. 53–76). New York: Oxford University Press. (Original work published 1975)

Soltow, Lee, & Stevens, Edward. (1981). *The rise of literacy and the common school.* Chicago: University of Chicago Press.

Spacks, Patricia Meyer. (1985). *Gossip.* Chicago: University of Chicago Press.

Spacks, Patricia Meyer. (1988). Female rhetorics. In Shari Benstock (Ed.), *The private self: Theory and practice of women's autobiographical writings* (pp. 177–191). Chapel Hill: University of North Carolina Press.

Spiller, Robert, et al. (Eds.). (1963). *Literary history of the United States: History* (3rd ed.). London: Macmillan.

Stansell, Christine. (1987). Revisiting the angel in the house: Revisions of Victorian America [Review of the book *Disorderly Conduct*]. *New England Quarterly Review, 60,* 466–483.

Stanton, Elizabeth Cady. (1971). *Eighty years & more: Reminiscences, 1815–1897.* New York: Schocken Books. (Original work published 1898)

Steedman, Carolyn Kay. (1977). *"The Tidy House": Little girls writing.* London: Virago.

Storke, Elliot G. (with Jas. H. Smith). (1879). *History of Cayuga County, New York with illustrations and biographical sketches of some of its prominent men and pioneers.* Syracuse, NY: D. Mason.

Strasser, Susan. (1982). *Never done: A history of American housework.* New York: Pantheon Books.

Street, Brian V. (1984). *Literacy in theory and practice.* Cambridge, UK: Cambridge University Press.

Street, Brian V. (1995). *Social literacies: Critical approaches to literacy in development, ethnography, and education.* New York: Longman.

Stuckey, J. Elsbeth. (1991). *The violence of literacy.* Portsmouth, NH: Boynton.

Taylor, Stephen, & Bogdan, Robert. (1984). *Introduction to qualitative research methods: The search for meanings* (2nd ed.). New York: Wiley.

Thrale, Hester. (1951). *Thraliana: The diary of Mrs. Hester Lynch Thrale (later Mrs. Piozzi, 1776–1809)* (Katherine C. Balderston, Ed.) (2nd ed., 2 vols.). Oxford, UK: Clarendon.

Ticknor, Caroline. (1913). *Hawthorne and his publishers.* Boston: Houghton Mifflin.

Tocqueville, Alexis de. (1956). *Democracy in America.* New York: Signet. (Original work published 1835)

Tompkins, Jane P. (1985). *Sensational designs: The cultural work of American fiction, 1790–1860.* New York: Oxford University Press.

Ulrich, Laurel Thatcher. (1991). *A midwife's tale: The life of Martha Ballard, based on her diary, 1785–1812.* New York: Vintage Books.

Vann, J. Don. (1985). *Victorian novels in serial.* New York: Modern Language Association.

Veeser, H. Aram. (Ed.). (1989). *The new historicism.* London: Routledge.

Walters, Keith. (1990). Language, logic, and literacy. In Andrea Lunsford, Helene Moglen, & James Slevin (Eds.), *The right to literacy* (pp. 173–188). New York: Modern Language Association.

Warren, Carol. (1988). *Gender issues in field research.* San Francisco: Sage.

Warren, Joyce W. (Ed.). (1986). *Ruth Hall and other writings.* American Women Writers Series. New Brunswick, NJ: Rutgers University Press.

Welter, Barbara. (1966). The cult of true womanhood, 1820–1860. *American Quarterly, 18,* 151–174.

Wolff, Cynthia Griffin. (1986). *Emily Dickinson.* New York: Alfred A. Knopf.

Woods, George B., Watt, Homer A., & Anderson, George K. (Eds.). (1941). *The literature of England: An anthology and a history* (2 vols.). Chicago: Scott, Foresman.

Woolf, Virginia. (1981). *A room of one's own.* New York: Harcourt Brace Jovanovich. (Original work published 1929)

Wright, Lyle. (1965). *American fiction, 1851–1875.* San Marino, CA: Huntington Library.

Wright, Lyle. (1969). *American fiction, 1774–1850.* San Marino, CA: Huntington Library.

Zboray, Ronald J. (1988). Antebellum reading and the ironies of technological innovation. In Cathy N. Davidson (Ed.), *Reading in America: Literature and social history.* Baltimore: John Hopkins University Press.

Zboray, Ronald J. (1993). *A fictive people: Antebellum economic development and the American reading public.* New York: Oxford University Press.

Zboray, Ronald J., & Mary Saracino Zboray (1999). *"Months of Mondays": Women's reading diaries and the everyday transcendental.* Paper presented at the 11th Berkshire Conference, Rochester, NY.

INDEX

A

Acker, Joan et al., 60
Adams, John, Life and Works of, 136, 205, 264
Adams, Nellie, xvi, 244
Adams, Warren, xvi, 2
    courtship letters, 119–120, 137, 202, 210, 265, 266, 268, 269, 271
Adventures on the Mosquito Shore, 137, 270
    see Squier, Ephraim
Agatha's Husband, 103, 109, 112, 269
    see Mulock, Dinah Marie (Craik)
Albany Argus, 9
Albany Evening Journal, 9
Alice Franklin, 95, 267
    see Howitt, Mary
Altick, Richard D., 264
Alton Locke, 18, 19, 100, 268
    see Kingsley, Charles
Amy Herbert, 117, 270
    see Sewell, Elizabeth Missing
Anthony, Susan B., xvi, 1
Arabian Nights, 21, 264
Atlantic Monthly, The, 10, 17, 94, 239, 271
Auburn, bookstores, 10–12, 17, 109, 264
    center of publishing, as, 11–13
    local histories, 11–13
Auburn Citizen, 3
Auburn Daily Advertiser, 10–11, 272
Auburn Female Seminary, 15, 161
Auburn Journal, 10

Aurifodina or Adventures in the Gold Region, 119, 269
    see Peck, George Washington
Aurora Leigh, 125, 265
    see Browning, Elizabeth Barrett
Austen, Jane
    letters of, 146–147, 149, 167–168, 178, 180, 200–201, 210, 264
    Mansfield Park, 109, 264
Avery, Kevin J., 81
    see Panorama of the Mississippi

B

Bacon, Margaret Hope, 9, 21, 51, 53, 124, 127, 144, 180, 206, 210
Baldwin, Neil, 222
Ballard, Martha, diary of, 30–31, 81, 160, 219
    see Ulrich, Laurel Thatcher
Bambara, Toni Cade, 55
Banvard, John, 81
    see Panorama of the Mississippi
Barker, Wendy, 24
"Battle of Life, The," 83, 99–100, 266, 274
    see Dickens, Charles
Baym, Nina, 4, 14, 17, 18, 29, 40, 84, 85, 86, 119, 210, 214
    novels, role of, 44, 87–88, 89–90, 95, 96–98, 99, 102, 106–107, 108, 114, 116, 118, 124–125, 134, 191, 201, 228
    as reference source, 17, 77

Reade, Charles, 17

Reading, character(s) in, 93, 100,
102–107, 111, 115–16, 126–127,
228

  discourses of control, 18, 21, 46, 49,
53, 62–63, 64–65, 67, 72,
116–117, 128–131, 151, 182,
191–192, 200, 203, 207–208,
216–217, 226–227, 230,
233–234, 239

  education, inspiring, 14–16, 26–27,
41, 44, 85, 117, 221, 224, 229

  effects upon, 17, 20–21, 26–27, 38,
45–46, 49, 50, 52, 54, 65, 83,
84–93, 96–99, 102–112,
115–116, 125–127, 129–140,
191–192, 226–227, 236–237
   see also Davidson

  functions of, 87, 107–110, 111–113,
115, 124, 150, 165, 218–225

  model of (Radway's), 110–112,
117–119, 223, 226–227, 229,
233

  novels/romances, 14, 22, 25, 26, 37,
44–45, 53, 55, 83, 84–93,
95–97, 99, 101–103, 106,
107–110, 111–113, 116, 117,
124–128, 134, 140, 146, 147,
149–150, 159, 172, 176, 180,
191, 200, 201, 213, 218–220,
221, 223, 224, 226–229, 233,
236–237, 238, 239, 240

  patterns of, 9–11, 14, 17–18, 22–23,
34, 45–46, 64, 84–93, 93–103,
105, 119–122, 122–131,
131–136, 136–137, 137–140,
192, 218–220, 225, 226–227,
228–229, 233–234, 236–237

  practices/ strategies of, 5, 13,
18–19, 20–21, 22–23, 29, 30,
35–37, 41–46, 52, 53, 83, 84,
85–86, 88, 89, 90–93, 95–97,
104–105, 107, 109, 111–112,
113, 119–22, 126, 136–137,
219, 226–227

Quaker influence, 20–22, 95–96,
107, 113, 116, 120, 123–124,
128

reader-response, as topic, 20, 23, 41,
56, 70, 81, 84–88, 90–94, 97,
105, 109, 110, 113, 129, 226

reader-responses, 18–19, 83, 91,
95–113, 115, 117–121, 125,
129–131, 132, 133–34,
136–137, 139,140, 220
  see also The Canon, Male Sentimentalists, Power Relations

Reading Society. see Osborne, Eliza
Wright

Reverby, Susan M. & Helly, Dorothy
O., 183–184
  see also Helly & Reverby

Recollections (of a Literary Life), 3, 137,
269
  see Mitford, Mary Russell

Reveries of a Bachelor, 132–133, 134, 135,
136, 138, 141, 269
  see Mitchell, Donald Grant (Marvel,
Ik)

Robinson, Lillian, 135

Rossi, Alice S., 13, 55

Royster, Jacqueline Jones, 46–47, 50

Ryan, Mary P., 7–8, 40, 185, 203

S

Sartor Resartus, 121, 137, 220, 265
  see Carlyle, Thomas

Scott, Joan A., 63–64, 70

Scott, Walter, 21, 100, 120, 269
  Poetical Works, 100, 269
  Quarterly Review, 120

Scribner, Sylvia & Cole, Michael, 36, 45

Sedgwick, Catharine Maria, 16
  Live and Let Live (SSC?), 270

"Self-fashioning," 24, 41, 90, 91, 92,
105, 117, 228
  see also Literacy Myth, Kelley, the
Zborays

Seneca County Courier, 10

Seneca Falls Woman's Rights Convention of 1848, 9, 13, 140, 182

Printed in the United States
24385LVS00001B/141-168